SELLING THEMSELVES
The Emergence of Canadian Advertising

Selling Themselves

The Emergence of Canadian Advertising

Russell Johnston

UNIVERSITY OF TORONTO PRESS
Toronto Buffalo London

© University of Toronto Press Incorporated 2001
Toronto Buffalo London

Printed in Canada

ISBN 0-8020-4495-6 (cloth)

∞

Printed on acid-free paper

Canadian Cataloguing in Publication Data

Johnston, Russell T. (Russell Todd), 1967–
Selling themselves : the emergence of Canadian advertising

Includes bibliographical references and index.
ISBN 0-8020-4495-6

1. Advertising – Canada – History.   I. Title.

HF5813.C2J63 2001   659.1'0971   C00-931067-3

Every effort has been made to identify the current copyright holders for the illustrations and quoted passages that appear in this volume. The author gratefully acknowledges the following companies for their kind permission to reproduce their works: Passages from *The Clockmaker*, by Thomas C. Haliburton, taken from the 1958 edition published by McClelland & Stewart Limited; passages from restricted files in the Timothy Eaton Company records, Public Archives of Ontario, courtesy of Sears Canada Inc.; 'Canada's National Advertisers' courtesy of the *Toronto Star*; 'The Old Home Paper' courtesy of the *London Free Press*; 'Saturday Night' courtesy of *Saturday Night* magazine; 'St Thomas Times-Journal' courtesy of the *St Thomas Times-Journal*; 'No Mortgages Published Now' courtesy of the *Guardian*, Charlottetown; map of the city of Ottawa courtesy of the *Ottawa Citizen*; 'The New Alignment of Marketing Zones' courtesy of Harrod & Mirlin/FCB Canada; 'Advertising in the Prairie Zone' courtesy of the *Winnipeg Free Press*; 'The Home Magazine of Motor Car Owners' courtesy of *Maclean's* magazine.

University of Toronto Press acknowledges the financial assistance to its publishing program of the Canada Council for the Arts and the Ontario Arts Council.

This book has been published with the help of a grant from the Humanities and Social Sciences Federation of Canada, using funds provided by the Social Sciences and Humanities Research Council of Canada.

University of Toronto Press acknowledges the financial support for its publishing activities of the Government of Canada through the Book Publishing Industry Development Program (BPIDP).

Contents

Acknowledgments

Many people helped in the preparation of this study. Among them, Ian McKay stands foremost. A more patient and trusting mentor could not have been had. He has provided support, both scholarly and material, which I cannot hope to repay.

A number of other scholars have also lent their time and wisdom to this process. Gerald Tulchinsky, Richard Ohmann, and Shirley Tillotson provided valuable commentary on early drafts of the manuscript. Paul McKenzie deserves a special thanks in this regard; he not only savaged all of my first ideas concerning this project, but also helped to salvage what remained. Klaus Hansen fostered my interest in the American historiography, while the late Donald Swainson supplied invaluable contacts in the pursuit of archival sources. In the later stages of writing, Robert Bergquist and Daniel Robinson provided valued support.

The core research was conducted at the Thomas Fisher Rare Book Library, at the University of Toronto. The staff there was endlessly patient with my requests to view fragile and irreplaceable materials from the Maclean-Hunter Publishing Archives. In particular, Albert Masters was a constant aid. Equally helpful were archivists Paul Banfield and George Henderson at Queen's University, Michael Moosberger at the University of Manitoba, Donna MacKinnon at the City of Vancouver, and Bob Sparrow at Sun Life Assurance Company of Canada.

At the University of Toronto Press, Gerald Hallowell took an interest in the manuscript, while Jill McConkey, Frances Mundy, and Wayne Herrington ensured that it got to press. Also crucial to this process were the anonymous readers who reviewed the manuscript; their reports were remarkable for their depth and generosity.

Research funding was provided by the Max Bell Foundation in the guise of a Donald S. Rickerd Fellowship in Canadian–American Relations. Without this assistance, much of my research would not have been possible. Further funding was provided by the School of Graduate Studies at Queen's University, and a T.G. Hamilton Research Grant courtesy of the University of Manitoba Archives. I would also like to acknowledge in this regard the timely research contracts provided by Ian McKay, Paul Banfield, and Shirley Tillotson. In the preparation of the book itself, the Aid to Scholarly Publications Program, of the Humanities and Social Sciences Federation of Canada, was crucial.

Several people with absolutely no interest in advertising suffered through the research and writing of this study. I hereby issue one free beer to Jeff Grischow, Mike Dawson, John Cosmopoulos, Martina Hardwick, and Ross Fair. My family too suffered through this process, though my parents did so in ways peculiar only to parents. For their endless faith and encouragement, I must thank Florence and Russell Johnston, and Rebecca and Derrick Thornborrow. Ann and Gary Posen, and Lucy Posen, have also welcomed me into their family, and provided me with a safe haven in Toronto during countless research trips.

To Sara Posen, I owe a great deal more than a beer and a thank you for my endless stories about 'advertising guys.' Her patience, wisdom, and sense of balance can be felt throughout this book, thanks to the many hours we have spent debating the finer points of marketing historiography. She has kept my eyes on the more important things in life. This book is for her.

SELLING THEMSELVES
The Emergence of Canadian Advertising

Introduction

Sam Slick pulled his cart up before the shop where Zeb Allen waited, leaning in the doorway. Slick was a pedlar from Connecticut, a specialist in clocks. Allen was a Bluenose, a Nova Scotian shopkeeper in the dry-goods line. In Slick's eyes, he was also a 'rael genuine skinflint.' They got to talking.

Slick ventured that after a year's travels throughout the province he would soon be done and out of the clock line. Zeb laughed: 'Most time ... for by all accounts the clocks warn't worth havin', and most infarnal dear too; folks begin to get their eyes open.' Slick responded in a 'confidential tone' that the goods he had been selling this trip out were indeed half-rate, poor stuff – he was ashamed of them. They were nothing like the goods he had carried years before. Trouble was, you couldn't get their like anymore. Had Zeb ever seen them?

> 'No,' said Mr Allen, 'I can't say I did.'
>
> 'Well,' continued he, 'they *were* a prime article, I tell you – no mistake there – fit for any market; it's generally allowed there ain't the beat of them to be found anywhere. If you want a clock, and can lay hands on one of them, I advise you not to let go the chance; you'll know 'em by the "Lowell" mark, for they were all made at Judge Beler's factory. Squire Shepody, down to Five Islands, axed me to get him one, and a special job I had of it, near about more sarch arter it than it was worth; but I did get him one, and a particular handsum one it is, copal'd and gilt superior. I guess it's worth ary half-dozen in these parts, let t'others be where they may ...'[1]

Did the pedlar have it with him, the shopkeeper asked? Sure enough he did, right bundled to save it from the hazards of the trip. Slick might unwrap it to afford the curious man a gander, but it was unavailable at any price. Zeb pressed on, and the clock was brought out. Just as the other described it, it was varnished and gilt and stamped prominently with the 'Lowell' name. Zeb was hooked.

> [He] offered to take it at the price the Squire was to have it, at seven pounds ten shillings. But Mr Slick vowed he couldn't part with it at no rate, he didn't know where he could get the like again ... and the Squire would be confounded disappointed; he couldn't think of it. In proportion to the difficulties, rose the ardour of Mr Allen; his offer advanced to £8, to £8 10s., to £9.
>
> 'I vow,' said Mr Slick, 'I wish I hadn't let on that I had it at all.'[2]

Nonetheless, he consented to part with it, under protest, and would deal with as he could the crestfallen squire of Five Islands.

As Slick pulled away from the store, he turned to his travelling companion: 'That 'ere fellow is properly sarved; he got the most inferior article I had, and I just doubled the price on him.'[3] Caveat emptor.

The travelling companion was the author himself, Thomas C. Haliburton, thinly veiled.[4] Haliburton's stories of Slick were written as a satirical commentary on Nova Scotian life in the 1830s, but they contained insights into 'human natur' that captivated readers for generations. And who better to be the vehicle of these tales of 'human natur' than a pedlar? The pedlar, dependent on sales for his livelihood, had to know when to push and when to pull his clientele, when to agree and when to argue, when to open and when to close the deal. At these skills, Haliburton's Slick was a master.

Commercial transactions gave Haliburton a fine setting to explore the foibles of humanity. In his dealings with Zeb, Slick exploited at least two of the seven deadly sins: pride and avarice. He did so in a way that allowed Zeb to believe that he was in control of the proceedings. He flattered his intelligence, agreed with him in his assessments, and feigned to take him into his confidence on this account. Zeb's own pride gave him the opening. From there, Slick drew out his avarice by stating that a neighbour was getting a good deal, and by establishing the scarcity of the product, its unlikelihood of being found again. There was a bargain afoot, just beyond Zeb's reach. This entire show was given a degree of verisimilitude by the reference to the trade mark – 'When an article han't the maker's name and factory on it, it shows it's a cheat, and he's ashamed to own it,' Slick asserts on the very first page of the book.[5] The trade mark becomes the sign of the maker's credibility and the clock's merit, a sign that anyone 'in the know' would recognize immediately. Through his confidence, Slick let Zeb into a charmed circle. He offered a tip of friendly advice – offered without the taint of commercial gain because Slick had nothing to gain by doing so. In short, Slick managed Zeb's decision-making process by supplying the 'consumer' with information that he knew would prompt the right action – that is, a decision to purchase the clock. Slick created desire.

By 1890 those who worked in the advertising trade thirsted for precisely this kind of knowledge and power. They wanted the same degree of control over consumers as the old-time pedlar had supposedly enjoyed. Then as now, the trade was composed of three basic sectors: media outlets, advertisers, and advertising agencies. Traditionally, media outlets meant newspapers, periodicals, and prime spaces such as billboards, public transit cards, and the like. Since 1920 this list has grown to include radio and television broadcasters and web sites on the Internet. By advertisers, we can understand any individual, company, or organization that pays media owners for space or time to publicize their products, services, or cause. The vast majority of advertisers are commercial businesses. The third sector, advertising agencies, operate as intermediaries between media outlets and advertisers. Agencies serve advertisers by recommending and designing campaigns. Such service may include anything from copywriting to package design to market surveys. However, agencies got their start by contracting space or time from media outlets on behalf of their clients, and this remains the core function of most agencies. Beyond these three groups, advertising has also employed people in numerous other occupations, but these have never assumed a permanent, fixed position within the trade. Artists, writers, photographers, typesetters, contract printers, and others may work for any of the main three groups, but advertising is neither the only nor necessarily the primary source of their income.

For the sake of simplicity, it seems appropriate to use the word 'adworker' in reference to everyone engaged in the advertising trade. While agency executives and publishers might have resented this description, it will serve a purpose here. On an immediate level, it offers a means to refer to the employees of publishing houses, agencies, and corporate advertising departments with one short term; it also avoids the pitfalls of the gender-specific 'adman' and 'adwoman.'

But on another level, it should remind us that the people engaged in the advertising trade were labouring at their daily jobs. They were not star characters of novels and movies or other works of fiction, such as Frederic Wakeman's *The Hucksters* (1946), which painted them in romantic – if frequently garish – strokes. Rather, they were salesmen and clerks, statisticians and typesetters, freelance writers and secretaries, whose weekly pay cheques all came from the same source: the manipulation of white space into meaningful, persuasive, commercial intelligence.

It was the advertising agents who emerged as the trade's key intellectuals. Agents sought out retailers and manufacturers who were not advertising and attempted to bring them into the fold. Many such businessmen believed that advertising was money poorly invested. The returns were difficult to trace. Agents eager to turn reluctant prospects into satisfied clients were compelled to justify the expense, and in so doing they began to theorize the *practice* of advertising itself. One of these agents was Albert Lasker, who in 1900 was a young and newly hired employee at the Lord and Thomas Advertising Agency of Chicago, Illinois. According to legend, Lasker made it his goal to uncover the secret of advertising, the essence of the successful ad that made it memorable and effective. His first belief was that advertising was news, no different from any other kind of information found in the papers. Effective advertising had to report the news about the product for sale.[6] Certainly, this had been the traditional role of advertising. As late as 1900 ads still appeared which merely reported that a certain retailer had new goods in stock, or that a manufacturer had created a new product which the reader might find useful.

Lasker's opinion was changed by a freelance copywriter, John E. Kennedy. Kennedy arrived in Chicago in 1904 after a very successful ten years selling men's clothing in Montreal. Hearing of Lasker's quest, Kennedy arranged to meet the younger man and share his secret. Lasker was not disappointed. Advertising, Kennedy confided, was 'salesmanship in print.' A copywriter had to do more than simply describe the goods for sale or make claims about their value. The copywriter had to re-create in cold type the sense of friendly persuasion that a salesmen might use in a personal encounter. Twenty years later, Lasker – by then president of Lord and Thomas – told his staff that this revelation had changed 'the whole complexion of advertising for all America.'[7]

Perhaps. Conceptions of advertising did change after 1900, but it would be more accurate to suggest that Kennedy's idea was only one of many attempts to define the nature of the business. Certainly, there were newspapers, magazines, and industry trade papers that had tried to educate their readers in the advantages of advertising. In the same year that Lasker met Kennedy, two books were written on this very topic: one by an agency team and another by a psychologist keenly interested in advertising.

Ernest Elmo Calkins and Ralph Holden ran a noted agency in New York City. In 1905 they published a tract called *Modern Advertising* to publicize their approach. Like Kennedy, Calkins in particular believed that advertising had to offer more than simply news about a product. He claimed that 'advertising is that subtle, indefinable, but powerful force whereby the advertiser creates a demand for a given article in the minds of a great many people or arouses the demand that is already in latent form.'[8] This indefinable force seemed to describe something beyond mere salesmanship, beyond mere persuasion. It implied some power latent in the written word that overcame sales resistance by appealing to the inner drives or desires of readers. This power could be tapped most effectively by artists, who were imbued with the vision and ability to harness that power.[9]

Walter Dill Scott took issue with this thesis. Scott, an academic psychologist, had given this 'indefinable force' a name – the power of suggestion. His thesis was rooted in the findings of empirical psychology, particularly those concerned with the association of ideas in the human mind and the ability to guide these associations through suggestion. It would not be a matter of art, but of science to determine the best associations that would indelibly link the product to the consumer's own needs and desires.[10]

Information, persuasion, suggestion, a force acting according to scientific laws: by 1905 the advertising trade had begun to accept these views of its work, and itself as a special elite with the power to shape public opinion. Henry Foster Adams, a business professor at New York University, tied these strands together in 1920 when he wrote that advertising was 'the endeavour of an individual or a group to persuade others, without personal solicitation and by means of a paid medium, to perform some specific act which will result in pecuniary advantage to the individual or group which is making the endeavour.'[11] This definition has remained at the core of advertising theory ever since. A recent Canadian textbook could have had Kennedy, Calkins, and Scott in mind when it described advertising as 'a persuasive form of marketing communications designed to stimulate positive response (usually purchase) by a defined target market.'[12]

Although many different types of media carried advertising, only newspapers and magazines provided something more than a mere delivery system. Advertising had always been a part of the press, but it had been peripheral to the primary function of newspapers and magazines: the provision of news and opinion. The audience for hoardings and handbills did not have to pay for the privilege of reading the commercial messages they contained. Newspapers made their living by collecting news relevant to their audience, and they charged that audience for the service. Advertising, when it was carried, was a source of bonus revenue throughout the early 1800s. Only after the introduction of faster technology in the printing trades – technology that demanded access to greater capital – did publishers cultivate advertisers as a steady source of income. As cultural studies scholar Richard Ohmann has argued, the technology in itself did not cause the change in publishing, although it provided the material condition that made it possible. Over time, publishers realized that their returns from advertising were limited only by the number of pages at their disposal. By 1900 Canadian publishers of mass market periodicals began to realize that their primary market was no longer readers seeking information. Rather, it was advertisers seeking media sympathetic to their corporate goals.[13]

This shift was a rational development within the publishing industry. Publishers too were businessmen, and there was no necessary contradiction between running a paper and pleasing one's advertisers. To them, the opposite was true. The massive circulation figures achieved by the most popular papers and magazines were built upon editorial content that readers enjoyed and found useful. Presumably, readers would not have bought them if they did not find them so.

This change was not monolithic. Although it did not become *impossible* to publish periodicals that did not enjoy mass appeal or the approval of advertisers, it did become more difficult. By definition, publications without mass appeal had fewer readers to support them. With smaller circulations, they also commanded less advertising revenue. As a result, publications catering to niche markets had a difficult time competing on the same terms. Higher-grade papers and inks, topnotch editors, well-known writers, artists, and photographers – all of these were the tools of the mass magazines. Traditional magazine genres and periodicals that served particular interests suffered by comparison as they became less and less able to afford these tools. As new media have become available to advertisers, this pattern has been repeated.

The development of advertising in the print media, then, is crucial to the story of advertising. Many of the persuasive techniques developed for print advertising after 1900 had been used in trade cards, posters, and billboards before 1900. However, these forms of display advertising did not inspire the same theoretical musings from a competitive trade press. Nor were they enmeshed in media offering ostensibly objective news-reporting and trusted editorial opinions. For these reasons, Raymond Williams has dubbed advertising 'the magic system,' a term that invokes both sides of advertising's social role. Advertising is 'magic' in so far as it endows material objects with identifications and associations that they otherwise would not have. On this point, Williams says no more than Kennedy, Calkins, and Scott. However, advertising is also a system, in that it provides financial support to cultural producers in the public sphere. It provides a structuring influence to publishing, broadcasting, and now new media. Hence, advertising's role in society is both cultural and structural.[14]

Scholars have examined these roles individually and in combination. The earliest critiques of advertising tended to draw upon both. As modern copywriting and illustration techniques became widespread after the First World War, they were met by a wave of popular and academic criticism. Some of this came from economists such as Stuart Chase and F.J. Schlink, who published one of the best-known commentaries in 1927, *Your Money's Worth*.[15] Very simply, they argued that advertising added unnecessarily to the cost of consumer goods: if demand for a product were genuine, consumers would seek out the product whether it was advertised or not. This meant two things. First, advertising represented an irrational business practice since it forced the public to bear an unjustified cost on top of the authentic costs of production. Second, when advertising drew attention to non-staple items, it distorted the natural (and hence 'proper') demands of the marketplace. Chase and Schlink did not challenge the industry's self-image; they too believed that advertising had the power to influence consumer behaviour. But working from this supposition, they argued that advertising was an ethically dubious practice. Similar conclusions were later drawn by A.S.J. Baster in England and John Kenneth Galbraith in the United States.[16] Still, these critics did recognize that new products were well served by advertising's ability to inform quickly and efficiently. Rather than eliminate advertising altogether, they sought to reform it. In Jackson Lears's terms, they wanted the industry to adhere to an ideal form of communication, which he dubs 'plain speech' – advertising that described the product, the price, and the nearest retailer without bombast. In essence, they wanted Lasker's information without Williams's magic.[17]

More critical were the second wave of economists and sociologists who questioned the connection between advertising and the role of media as modes of public communication. While these writers did not ignore the importance of specific advertising messages, their prime concern was for the financial structure of modern media outlets. Inspired by the propaganda efforts of various Depression-era governments and corporations, scholars such as Harold Innis in Canada, Paul Lazarsfeld in the United States, and the Frankfurt School in Germany made explicit the growing tension between corporate power and the free flow of information in the Western democracies. Jürgen Habermas's study of the public sphere draws upon all of these, and his approach is unusual only for its theoretical rather than empirical orientation. That said, Habermas and the Frankfurt School take a decidedly different tack in their conclusions. Although Innis and the Americans admitted that advertising posed a great danger to the free flow of information, they accepted this as the price of a society that guaranteed personal liberties. Habermas saw the domination of the public sphere by advertising-dependent media as a failing of the capitalist system.[18]

Where these scholars examined the structuring influence of advertising, other cultural commentators have dissected advertisements for their ideological content, to reveal the significance of particular advertisements and ad campaigns. The classic text in this regard is Judith Williamson's *Decoding Advertisements* (1978). In Canada, scholars have studied campaigns as diverse as the Canadian Pacific Railway's early tourist advertising and the images of women in consumer magazines. However, as communications scholars William Leiss, Stephen Kline, and Sut Jhally have pointed out, the pitfalls of content analysis are many. Whether or not any one method provides a legitimate or politically useful reading is outside the interests of this study. The reading of any one advertisement, campaign, or group of campaigns reveals more about the specific advertisers, agencies, and media involved than it does about advertising in general, let alone about the intended audience. Treating advertising as text cannot reveal the structure and workings of the industry itself since it only examines the role of specific signifiers to specific groups of authors and readers. Each campaign can be no more than a microstudy of the industry as a whole.[19]

A number of American historians have tried to get behind the ads, to explore the social and intellectual world of their creators. This approach has focused attention upon advertising agencies and related organizations, and it has been extremely illuminating. Daniel Pope, Stephen Fox, Roland Marchand, Jennifer Scanlon, and Ellen Garvey, among others, have drawn upon a wealth of primary sources to understand the people who made the ads.[20] More than any other group, it was the men and women who worked in the agencies who proselytized on behalf of advertising. The primary interest of the advertisers lay with their products and their factories; the primary interest of the publishers lay with their papers and their presses. It was the agents' job alone to think about advertising, day in and day out. There is a danger with this approach, however, and that is to credit agents with more power than they possessed. While they may have been 'heralds of modernity' – insofar as they introduced the world to the astonishing products created by modern science – they were not themselves responsible for these products. Nor were they the only spokesmen for modernity. The mores of the time were far more consciously probed in the sermons, fiction, and editorials of traditional cultural producers.

Furthermore, advertising is not created by *auteurs*. Advertising is created by committees. From the first idea for a campaign to the final printed page, an advertisement passes through many hands. Each brings a different perspective to the campaign and has a different goal in mind. This point was made abundantly clear by contemporary workers in the fine arts. Cultural producers who upheld romantic values and jealously guarded their independence of vision scorned their commercial counterparts and consistently argued that commercial art represented something lower in the hierarchy of creative expression. Agents were fashioning intellectual goods with a very practical purpose and at the request of specific clients. Even when armed with the latest statistics on their client's target market, agents found that their idea of an effective campaign could be rapidly shot down.[21]

Canadian historians have not examined the development of the advertising trade in great detail, whether from the standpoint of publishers, agents, or advertisers. The standard reference is H.E. Stephenson and Carlton McNaught's *The Story of Advertising in Canada*, published in 1940. This book remains a fascinating study. It was written to mark the fiftieth anniversary of Canada's largest agency, McKim

The uneasy relation between commerce and art was suggested in this ad for Stewart and Browne. *Economic Advertising* 8:9 (September 1915), 10.

Limited, where both men worked. Their discussion of changing consumer trends offers some valuable insights from their own long experience in the trade, but their analysis is limited by this same perspective. References to personalities and events tend to document their own firm, and advertising agencies are given credit for the entire revolution in marketing practices after 1900. More recent works on advertising have appeared, but practitioners and academics alike have concentrated on the television era.[22]

The periodical press has had similar treatment. *A History of Canadian Journalism* was published in two volumes, the first by the Canadian Press Association (1908) and the second by W.A. Craick (1959). Once again, the authors were participants, and not surprisingly the heroes here are publishers and editors. There is little sustained discussion of advertising to be found, despite its central importance to the growth of their industry. By contrast, early academic work in the field emphasized the role of technology rather than economics, as seen in W.H. Kesterton's *A History of Journalism in Canada* (1967). More recent academic treatments of the publishing industry have brought a more critical perspective to its history, and among the best of these are works by Paul Rutherford and Jean de Bonville. Nonetheless, while these studies draw direct links between advertising and the changes that overtook the newspaper business, they concentrate on the overt political consequences of these changes, rather than their deeper cultural implications. Since their focus is the newspaper industry, the development of the advertising trade itself is only of secondary concern.[23]

The literature on advertisers is particularly thin. Only one major work has examined an advertiser as an advertiser before 1930, and this is E.J. Hart's consideration of CPR travel publicity, *The Selling of Canada* (1983). The only attempt to draw each of these strands together – the agents, publishers, and advertisers – during the period under review can be found in Leiss, Kline, and Jhally, who provide an excellent sociological overview of the advertising trade. The book's one drawback, however, is its assumption that advertising developed contemporaneously on both sides of the forty-ninth parallel.[24]

This study will attempt a more synthetic approach to the development of the modern advertising trade in Canada. There are three major themes. First, at its core, lies the 'professionalization' of the advertising trade. 'Professionalization' is used here with caution. The rise of professionalism as it has been described by M.S. Larson and Harold Perkin provides a useful model to describe the changes that occurred within the trade from 1890 to 1930, but advertising never became a 'profession' in the strict sense of that term.[25] Professionalism can be seen as a set of institutional structures created by those working in a specific field of enterprise. Those working in recognized professions such as medicine or the law have created unifying organizations, learned journals, educational programs, and barriers to entry that prevent the unqualified or undesirable (as defined by those within the profession) from engaging in 'legitimate' participation. However, there exists a set of ideological premises upon which these institutional structures are built. The 'professional ideal,' according to Perkin, rests upon the inherent value of 'human capital' in place of material wealth; professionals, through trained expertise in a limited field of human understanding, carry within them 'socio-ideological, cultural, intellectual, or spiritual power,' which – if acknowledged by their fellow citizens – confers upon them status and social power.[26] In the case of the advertising trade, a small group of salesmen on the fringes of the publishing industry convinced manufacturers that they were 'experts' regarding its inner workings. Theirs was not the capital of presses, plants, and paper, but of intuition, imagery, and ideas. The strength of an advertising agency was the creative capacity of the men who ran it, both its salesmen and its creative staff.

A study of this professionalization movement also brings to light the contemporary transformation of the publishing industry itself. This is the second theme. The agencies were at the forefront of several trends that found common cause in the creation of mass market periodicals. Publishers were seeking new revenue streams to cover the rising costs of production, advertisers were seeking improved means of communication with the buying public, and the public was developing a growing taste for inexpensive, leisure-time reading. Agencies capitalized on these trends by developing manufacturers into constant advertisers. This in turn increased revenues for periodicals and gave editors the resources they needed to produce newspapers and magazines that appealed to ever-widening audiences.

The third theme that unites the chapters that follow is the Canadian adworkers' relationship to their American counterparts. The American advertising trade gained substantial shape when the first advertising agent appeared there in the 1840s. When Canadian agents began to appear twenty years later, they did so with the American trade in mind. The pattern struck in these early years would never be broken. Innovations in advertising thought and practice would usually appear first in the United States, and Canadian adworkers inevitably adopted the most successful. By 1900 the Canadians were adopting ideas in step with their introduction throughout the United States itself. They never spoke of this arrangement in terms of 'dependence,' nor of 'American-ization.' Rather, they viewed themselves as the fortunate neighbours of a pioneering nation of businessmen. American innovations were simply good business solutions to problems faced on both sides of the border.

Any researcher who studies advertising in Canada faces a difficult task: advertisers, agencies, and publishers, with some notable excep-tions, have been ruthless when disposing of records connected to their marketing policies and practices. What remains in Canada are the annual reports, trade journals, directories, government materials, and other published records, which tend to document the industry as a whole rather than particular advertisers, agents, or media. This need not be a problem. The story that emerges from these records reveals several sectors of an industry consciously working towards common goals. Partisan publishers who fought one another riding by riding in the mid-1800s were cooperating on industry matters by the end of the century. There were several reasons for this change, but the major impetus was an effort to stabilize, then increase, the revenues available from advertising. Met by a newly disciplined press, advertising agents had to organize themselves to plead their case with the publishers. This in turn prompted the major advertisers to join forces, to ensure that their interests were not entirely delimited by the other two. By 1915 every major sector of the publishing industry (save the readers) was actively engaged in mutual negotiations intended to set standards of conduct among themselves. During the 1910s the general public heard tell of advertising conventions trumpeting the virtues of 'Truth in Advertising.' Behind the scenes, these same conventions were draft-ing memoranda that chided adworkers to be honest with one another.

Like any agreement, those of the advertising industry established an operational framework that recognized the competing demands of each sector. In the debates surrounding each agreement can be found a host of arguments presenting the views of many different members of the industry. What emerges are the goals and ideals of those engaged in the advertising trade; the agreements simply enshrined the product of their negotiations.

With these qualifications aside, it is important not to lose sight of individuals. Someone was sitting on these countless committees. Mod-ern advertising and the institutions that shaped it were not products of impersonal market forces, but of individuals with needs and aspirations of their own. If the institutions give us a sense of the industry as a whole and how it functioned in Canada, a knowledge of the individuals involved can give us a sense of the trends and concerns that animated their industry councils.

Chapter 1 sets the stage by describing the various sectors of the industry that are important to the story – the publishers, advertisers, and agents – as they were at the end of the nineteenth century. Advertising as a trade grew rapidly in the last decade of the nineteenth century, and agents were viewed by the publishers with great suspicion, as opportunists interfering where they did not belong and where they were not welcome. Chapter 2 discusses the men and women who worked in the trade by looking at the careers of a select group of adworkers in Toronto; chapter 3 examines the rationale they crafted for their trade. Toronto adworkers were pivotal in this regard, for Toronto was the home of the publications, companies, and trade associations that would set the temper of the Canadian trade. Chapter 4, in three parts, demonstrates how publishers and agents treated with the advertisers to reconfigure the publishing industry in the twenty years after the turn of the century. In large part, this was done through agreements signed by their representative organizations. What they created was a structural framework that systematized the functions of the various sectors in relation to one another.

Chapter 5 looks at the pivotal role played by copywriting in the revamped advertising industry. Through the incorporation of academic psychology, copywriters began to systematize the content of the industry just as the agreements had systematized its business structure. After 1900 three distinct approaches to advertising emerged, whose advocates could be termed the salesman, the artist, and the psychologist. Although all three remained prominent at different firms, a fourth advocate emerged in the 1910s who eventually took precedence over them all, the market researcher. Where the first three had focused upon individual ads and readers, the market researcher looked at campaigns and mass readership. This is the subject of chapter 6. Seen as a 'mass,' readership behaved in accordance with predictable laws, and the market analyst sought to increase the probability of response from campaigns by targeting only the most suitable prospects with pretested copy appeals. The impact of these theories will be traced in chapter 7, where the development of Canadian consumer magazines is examined in greater detail.

Ultimately, the portrayal of Canadian society in these newly fashioned media – primarily the consumer magazines, but also the newspapers and radio stations that learned from them – became increasingly homogenized to fit an anglophone, liberal Christian, middle class. Stewart Blumin argues that middle-class identifications formed around white-collar workers who developed common patterns of social interaction and material consumption.[27] Advertising participated in the construction of this identification. Consistent consumption patterns were integral to the demographic categories formulated by agencies; they were also crucial to media outlets, which used them to establish market niches around which they could construct editorial content. But advertising played upon the anxieties of readers by suggesting that specific products would help them to achieve the status or acceptance they desired. It worked its magic to articulate and reinforce the relationships between lifestyle, status, and material possessions.

Chapter 1

Newspapers, Advertising, and the Rise of the Agency, 1850–1900

You run your newspapers to make money. You are not running newspapers to mould public opinion. That is all guff. That makes me sick. (Laughter)
Roy V. Somerville, speaking to the Canadian Press Association in 1893[1]

James Poole was probably a typical mid-nineteenth-century Canadian publisher. In 1860, in the rural countryside of eastern Ontario, Poole owned and operated the Carleton Place *Herald*, a four-page weekly paper upholding the Liberal cause. It carried his reports of local people and events, stories from around the world brought in by telegraph, and – on every single page – advertisements. He had a good variety of ads. Local people with produce to sell, personal ads, out-of-town financial houses offering investments and insurance, and railways and steamship operators running their monthly schedules all found a spot in his pages. Far more frequent, however, were local retailers and artisans notifying readers of recently acquired goods. Out-of-town advertisers might have come and gone, but the bread and butter of Poole's advertising were the shops within his own community.[2]

Why was Poole typical? Because in the early 1860s, there were some 150 other weekly papers in villages across the province, and another 79 throughout the rest of British North America. By contrast, there were only some 23 dailies. Few of them, weeklies and dailies alike, had circulations over one thousand readers.[3] Journalists such as Poole were more than simple publishers. They were editors, business managers, and pressmen all rolled into one. Newspapering was more than a career for souls such as these with ink in their blood. It was a way of life, like farming or the clergy.[4]

Forty years later, rural journalism found itself the backward cousin of the urban press. As the European demand for wheat and the American demand for pulpwood and minerals grew after 1880, Canada became a favoured destination for hundreds of thousands of immigrants. With them came a host of manufacturers providing consumer goods to a growing working-class population. With these consumer goods came an ever-increasing volume of advertising.

Two groups encouraged this growth in advertising: publishers and advertising agents. Publishers slowly adapted to the emerging industrial economy and left behind the nineteenth-century world of personal journalism. Circulation drives boosted readership and revenues and prompted ever greater investment in new technologies. Much of their new revenue was achieved by increasing the volume of advertising they carried in their pages. What was once a secondary source of income fast became a primary source, and more resources were dedicated to its cultivation among local and out-of-town businesses.

The publishers' enthusiasm for advertising was matched by a new cadre of businessmen, the advertising agents. However, while the publishers were developing a latent economic potential within their own businesses, the agents were essentially outsiders poaching on the publishers' trade. Many had formerly been salesmen in the publishers' employ. As freelance agents, they were still selling publishers' white space, but now they accrued a portion of the profits from this trade to their own accounts.

Periodical Publishing before 1890

Before 1890 Canadian publishers were a remarkably independent lot. There were a wide variety of printing houses in Canada, producing newspapers, magazines, religious tracts, books, and sundry printed items. Despite the commonalities in their trades, they were in no way united as an industry, nor were they inclined to think of themselves as a single industry. Instead, each branch hewed to its own course and was served by its own trade associations and journals.[5]

Even within these particular fields, there were few national organizations to unite members of a trade from every province. The newspapers are a perfect case in point. The Canadian Press Association, founded in 1858, gathered together the publishers of daily and weekly newspapers, magazines, and trade papers, but only those published in the English language in Ontario. Others could join the Eastern Townships Press Association (1879), La Presse Associée de la Province de Québec (1882), or the Maritime Press Association (1888).[6] These groups did not find common cause until the 1910s.

Within each association, there were also felt differences between the publishers of weekly and daily newspapers. Weeklies tended to be the poorer cousins of the big-city dailies, located as they were in smaller towns and rural townships. It was not uncommon for publishers to establish a weekly with the intention of building it into a daily paper. In the mid-1800s success in this line required the prescience to locate in a town on the grow. Where population remained thin and businesses scant, few publishers could turn a substantial profit on a small circulation and few local sources of advertising. Chances were that everyone within reach of the paper would be familiar with the local merchants and craftsmen without notices in the paper. Those merchants who did advertise might have done so as much from a felt duty to the local paper as a desire to place their goods before the public. Such a duty might have been prompted by an obligation to support a partisan organ, or perhaps simply to maintain a voice for their community.[7]

Despite shaky prospects, there was never a shortage of investors in the newspaper field. Reliable statistics on newspapers first appeared in 1864. At that point, the weekly was still the most common format, but most of Canada's larger centres had acquired sturdy dailies. That year, there were 298 periodicals in British North America, of which 226 were weeklies and another 43 semi-weekly or tri-weekly. By 1891, the number of weeklies had more than doubled, while the total number of periodicals had expanded to 837.[8]

Before 1850 most weekly publishers expected their costs to be met primarily from reader sales, either through annual subscriptions or individual copies on the street. A small operation, with perhaps two men, could probably make enough to pay each of them a small competence. The division of labour would not be sophisticated. Likely, the publisher, editor, and business manager would be one man, the compositor and pressman another. Both would share ownership of the business. The latter man would frequently be assisted by an apprentice or journeyman printer, and he too might hope to own a paper or job printing plant someday. After mid-century new mechanized presses began to alter this relationship. While the expertise of business managers was increasingly sought by competitive urban papers, the relative importance of a skilled pressman began to wane. Printers resisted their marginalization through powerful trade unions, but the prestige of business managers grew over time to rival that of the editors themselves.[9]

The dailies were the first to install the new presses. Dailies benefited from faster production runs, which they needed to service expanding readerships. In smaller towns, where there were fewer readers and the paper appeared only once or twice a week, current and future revenue was insufficiently promising to justify an investment in a modern press. Moreover, the urgency of the news was not as pronounced, and more traditional technology sufficed. The daily Fort William *Times-Journal* is a case in point. It kept its hand press until 1899. At that time, its circulation was roughly 250. A hand press could print the entire paper – four pages, 250 copies – in roughly two and a half hours; a small steam-powered press could finish the same run in one half hour. Demand for the new technology was questionable; either press could easily complete the paper overnight for morning delivery. However, the increased speed of the new machine installed in 1899 was decidedly advantageous as the paper expanded to eight pages. With increased traffic between southern Ontario and the Prairies, the port of Fort William expected a prosperous future, especially as the eastern terminus for the Canadian Northern Railway. The *Times-Journal* probably made its investment with that future in mind. It was a safe gamble. Six years later, its circulation had grown to one thousand.[10]

Weekly publishers who did not enjoy a period of growth in the 1890s found other ways to remain solvent. One method reduced the cost of news collection and plate-making by having it done elsewhere. 'Boiler-plates' were pre-set plates of editorial content crafted by print shops and some of the larger dailies. These usually contained undated material such as human interest stories, fiction, or poetry that could be run at any time. 'Ready-prints,' also called 'patent insides,' were full newspaper sheets that publishers bought with both editorial and advertising content pre-printed on one side. When folded, the pre-printed side became pages two and three of a four-page weekly paper. That left only the front page and the back to be filled, usually with the paper's masthead, local news, and advertising.[11]

Party politics also played a significant role in the survival of papers, both weekly and daily. In the 1800s most papers were established to advance either Conservative or Liberal ideals, and men moved between journalism and politics with great regularity. Notable in this regard was Sir Mackenzie Bowell, publisher of the Belleville *Intelligencer*, who served as a member of the federal cabinet and became prime minister in 1894. Late in the century, Liberal and Conservative newspapers were joined by others supporting farm and labour parties. Occasionally, when rifts formed among local partisans, a new paper emerged to champion one party faction against another. W.F. Maclean, a maverick Conservative and member of Parliament, established the populist Toronto *World* in 1880. In so doing, he placed himself in open competition with the high Tory *Mail* and the Toronto-first imperialism of John Ross Robertson's *Telegram*.[12]

The merits of the 'Independent Press' was a subject on the agenda for the Canadian Press Association in 1905. The complete minutes of this discussion are as follows:

> Several members asked: 'What is an independent paper?'
>
> Mr J.H. Thompson: The paper a Tory stops because it is Grit, and a Grit stops because it is Tory.
>
> Mr H.A. James: Is there an independent Liberal or an independent Conservative paper in Ontario?
>
> Several members: No.[13]

Discussion closed.

There were three sources of partisan support for newspapers. The first of these stemmed from the ownership of the papers themselves. The role of partisan backers intensified after 1850, as increased capital was required to purchase the new presses and plants. Previously, it had been possible for men such as William Lyon Mackenzie or George Brown to start a paper on their own resources or with limited financing. Proprietorship allowed them to express their opinions as they saw fit – which both men readily did. Then, their ability to win influence in party councils would have been proportionate to their influence with readers. By the 1870s this relationship was in transition. The capital required to own a paper was beyond the means of most journalists. Josiah Blackburn bought the *Canadian Free Press* in London, Canada West, on his own account for $500 in 1850. To expand the weekly into a daily, he entered into a partnership with his brother in 1853. Twenty years later the paper was reorganized as a limited company. By then, Blackburn was only one of five shareholders, whose combined stock was valued at $60,000.[14]

Under these circumstances, investors had the financial clout to ensure that an editor remained faithful to the party line. This was particularly true where the editor was not a stockholder. However, many owners allowed their editors some degree of autonomy. This approach presumed that readers would not long respect a paper that championed its party at the expense of constructive commentary. A notable example was Sir Clifford Sifton, whose Winnipeg *Free Press* provided a soapbox for editor John W. Dafoe. Similarly, J.E. Atkinson refused to join the Toronto *Star* unless its backers promised him his editorial freedom. In both cases the owners hired men whose party affiliations and political principles were never in doubt. Ultimately, beyond their initial investment, continued support depended on the maintenance of a favourable editorial policy and the depth of the backers' pockets.[15]

The second form of partisan support relied on local businessmen with sympathetic convictions to place advertising on a regular basis. This form of support was more tenuous than direct backing, since advertisers had no stake in the paper's finances. Their main consideration was the paper's circulation. If the paper had competitive numbers, there was no problem. If it fell too far behind its rivals, partisan advertisers would then have to assess their priorities: economic self-interest or loyalty to the cause. Other problems arose when advertisers took issue with a paper's editorial decisions. Pleasing readers did not necessarily please advertisers, and pleasing either could be difficult if the editor supported an unpopular party policy. The Toronto *Empire* foundered after several years spent parroting the Conservative line. Even an unreformed Tory such as Hector Charlesworth thought it represented the worst in blinkered editorial writing.[16]

The third form of partisan support was the least reliable. If the right party was in power, patronage could be sought in the form of government advertising notices or printing contracts. This kind of assistance could not be relied upon, but it kept many a paper solvent when other revenue was scarce.[17]

After reader subscriptions, local advertising, and political patronage, newspapers found their last bit of financing from out-of-town commercial advertisers. Ultimately, this became the most important part of the publishers' revenue. At mid-century, however, it was by far the most neglected. As late as 1890 the publisher of the St Thomas *Journal* declared that such advertising should not have been accepted unless there was vacant space to fill in one's paper.[18] Nothing could have expressed publishers' ambivalence more than the name that publishers gave to it: 'foreign advertising.' In most cases, it actually was 'foreign,' since it was placed by American or British manufacturers. As an expression, 'foreign' did not begin to wane until the volume of national advertising originating in Canada increased after 1900. Even then, the head of Canada's largest agency was still describing it thus in the 1910s.[19]

Before 1900 foreign advertising was placed by manufacturers located outside the immediate region in which the paper was published. For example, McClary's Manufacturing, renowned for their black iron wood stoves, advertised not just in London, Ontario, but wherever their goods were sold. Railway lines and steamship companies publicized their departure schedules. Circuses, theatre companies, and musical shows advertised weeks in advance of their performances to drum up excitement. But far more common than any of these were the patent medicine makers.[20]

More than any other trade, the patent medicine makers are given credit for pioneering the field of national distribution and foreign advertising across North America. Inexpensive to produce, package, and transport, patent medicines were initially sold by itinerant pedlars who travelled through the small towns and rural countryside of the United States and Canada. Sophisticated pedlars learned that the patience of their prospective customers could be profitably lengthened by the offer of free entertainment. What they developed was something of a cross between vaudeville and a travelling circus – a mixture of comedy, music, acrobatics, and freaks presented from their wagons or tents. The master of ceremonies would then use breaks between the acts to introduce a lively sales pitch for the company's medicine. The most skilled orators could make the sales pitch itself into a featured part of the show. These travelling shows found the same audiences that P.T. Barnum found: sometimes earnest, sometimes credulous, but almost always willing to be humbugged in the name of entertainment or the off chance that the concoction proffered actually worked.[21]

The shift from travelling shows to advertising seems inevitable in retrospect. When a show left town, sales could be maintained only if a local merchant carried stock. Without the show, however, the medicine would have to be boosted in some other way. The medicine men already used newspaper advertising to publicize themselves; now they would use it to sell their products directly.[22] In the tradition of their outlandish shows, the advertising of patent medicines was garishly typed, boldly set, and came illustrated with eye-catching cuts. Until the 1890s they were the single largest group of foreign advertisers in Canada and the United States. When the Ontario legislature proposed restrictions on the sale of patent medicines in 1893, the bill was denounced in the publishers' trade paper: 'The country publisher

draws no mean revenue from the general merchant and medicine manufacturer,' opined the editor, 'and he should guard their interests.' The
bill died. When tariffs on American medicines fell some four years
later, it was hailed as 'A Chance for Advertisements.'[23] One medicine
manufacturer in Canada, Senator George T. Fulford, reputedly spent
$1 million in fifteen years advertising 'Dr William's Pink Pills for Pale
People.' His success, and that of others like him, led to the gradual
adoption of these techniques by other industries. The first to do so
were food and clothing manufacturers – paralleling an absolute
growth in consumer expenditures in these fields – but by 1920 almost
every branch of modern commerce had followed suit.[24]

James Poole's business correspondence reveals early glimmers of
these changes, particularly in one set of letters dating from 1856 to
1864. Most were handwritten, asking that a prepared statement be run
in the paper. If the letter came from an individual, payment was generally enclosed; if it came from a business, the client usually asked to be
billed. When reading the letters, there is little perceptible difference
between personal and commercial notices, and the same was true in
print. All parties likely understood the conventions of the day for
newspaper advertising. Most ads would have been typeset and placed
much like the classified ads of the twentieth century. Few clients asked
for larger space or 'conspicuous placement.' William Virgin was perhaps more casual than most, but not untypical when he wrote the
following: 'You would oblige me by advertising the following in whatever form you see proper. A black and white hound with red ears
strayed to my place yesterday[.] [A]ny party claiming him can have
him by paying the advertisement. I think one insertion should do ...
Enclosed is 2/9 for advertisement.'[25]

Here, Poole could write, set, and place the ad entirely at his own discretion. More commonly, clients would have a prepared statement, in
which case the printer would only have to set and place it. In a minority of the letters, the client also indicated a preferred layout. These
invariably came from commercial houses. The dry-goods store of J. & J.
Wylie submitted a handwritten letter whose prepared copy was
drafted in a very stylized fashion. Given this arrangement, the printer
could still play with the size of the type and the justification of the
lines. The Wylies, however, submitted this to replace a previous insertion. Likely they knew how the *Herald* would set it. Similarly, Robert
Watson of the Brockville and Ottawa Railway asked that his copy be
inserted in the 'shape of handbills,' a format that would have dictated

The Wylies' contract with James Poole. National Archives of Canada, MG 24 K 9, Poole papers, vol. 1, file January–May 1856, manuscript letter, 26 May 1856.

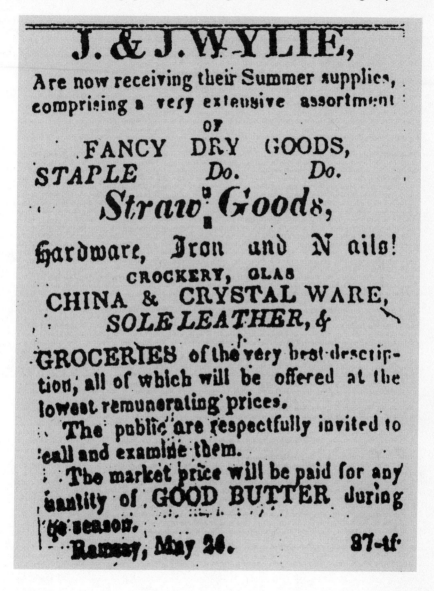

J. & J. Wylie advertisement as it appeared each week, June–September 1856. Carleton Place *Herald*, 28 June 1856.

a specific look to the finished ad.[26] Notably, the only ads that came pre-written and printed in proof form came from foreign advertisers, such as the Provincial Insurance Company of Toronto. Its letter asked that Poole re-create the proof as closely as possible.[27] Over the next four decades, the casual requests of local retailers such as the Wylies would be almost entirely replaced by the more exacting demands of 'foreign' companies from out of town. Such demands signalled the fact that certain businessmen were beginning to take their advertising more seriously than they had in the past.

1895: A Turning Point?

The Canadian economy changed dramatically between 1880 and 1914, and publishers were very much attuned to these developments. From 1871 to 1901 the aggregate value of capital invested in Canadian manufacturing rose more than five times, from $78 million to $481 million, and hundreds of plants opened in the Maritimes, Quebec, and Ontario. Most located in Ontario.[28] In their wake, thousands of Canadians migrated to the industrializing urban centres, and for good reason. The number of jobs increased with the pace of investment. Between 1891 and 1901, while the rural population of Canada grew by roughly sixty thousand, its cities and towns grew by around half a million. At the same time, the annual value of wages more than doubled from $41 million to $113 million. Retailers and marketers were keenly attuned to these developments. On paper, at least, the country seemed flush with disposable income.[29]

With the increase in goods and markets came a perceived increase in the volume of advertising, particularly in the period 1895 to 1905. Although no statistics exist from this period for the advertising trade, several items offer corroborative evidence. Agents identified 1895 as a turning point because that year reputable firms began to outnumber patent medicines as foreign advertisers.[30] Using the balance sheets of five Toronto dailies, economist Thomas Walkom has calculated that total advertising receipts had already eclipsed other sources of newspaper revenue by 1898, when they accounted for 73 per cent of gross revenue.[31] The establishment of American branch plants brought a raft of new consumer goods into the country, and these companies already knew the value of advertising. Since Toronto was at the centre of the country's growth in manufacturing, its papers would have benefited first from increased advertising budgets.

As distribution networks extended outward, advertising followed suit. The establishment of new papers and the improvement of existing ones could be used to gauge investor confidence in local trade conditions. The Fort William *Times-Journal* was an apt case, but so too was the experience of the entire Prairie West. There, the number of dailies and weeklies tripled between 1891 and 1904. These start-ups may have been inspired by the immigrant boom, but readers alone would not have sustained them. Rather, advertisers expanded their publicity with the population, seeking new markets among the new settlers. An officer of the Canadian Press Association estimated that advertising revenue overtook subscriptions as the primary source of income at almost every Canadian paper by the First World War.[32]

Trade paper publishers were also quick to capitalize on the growing interest in advertising. Between 1898 and 1908 at least five new journals began serving the advertising trade in Canada. There was a decided novelty in the focus of their news coverage. When an earlier venture appeared in Toronto in 1893, its subtitle declared that it was 'an aid to all interested in advertising.' Nonetheless, its lead article addressed only retailers, the traditional source of local advertising. Manufacturers, the core group of foreign advertisers, were nowhere mentioned. The reverse was true of *Economic Advertising* when it began fifteen years later. Its editors purposefully set out to attract a readership composed of manufacturers and rarely ran articles on retailing. For agencies, the turning point appears to have been 1902. That year, McKim Limited opened its first branch office in Toronto, and its most aggressive rival there promptly responded with an office in Montreal. Toronto adworkers noted a surge in interest in their work, and two new journals appeared in Montreal. A third started in 1905.[33]

While their industrial counterparts formed trade associations, established standards, and contemplated mergers, publishers remained decidedly individualistic. Their day-to-day operations often involved ruthless competition with cross-town rivals, and they were relatively isolated from the experience of publishers elsewhere. On the surface, it might have appeared that nothing had changed among the rural weeklies. Few publishers could imagine their trade reduced to an impersonal process reorganized like sugar, steel, or cigarettes to fit within the system of mass production. A newspaper was not a standardized product, but an expression of the editor himself and a reflection of the community he served. Newspapers were far too intimate and local to contemplate corporate consolidation.[34]

In their business practices the publishers also evaded standardization. The frequency of publication and the number of pages per issue were entirely dependent on a paper's revenue. More subscriptions and advertising meant that more pages could be run. When George Brown expanded the *Globe* from a weekly to a tri-weekly in 1849, it was not because there was an increase in newsworthy events in Toronto. He was satisfying an increased demand for advertising space. As ad content increased, editors increased their pages to accommodate it. They then increased their editorial content to maintain a respectable ratio of news to ads.[35]

Just as the frequency and page count of each paper could vary, so too could the page size and column width of each paper. This was not a problem for local advertisers since their typesetting was done by the paper itself – note James Poole's work for the Wylies. Alternatively, if the town was large enough to support a job printing plant, an advertiser could get its ad made to order in plate form before sending it to the paper. Foreign advertisers who used several papers and wanted a consistent 'look' for their advertising relied on print shops. However, the lack of standardization among papers increased the cost of plate-making dramatically; each new column size required its own setting.

The rate paid by the advertiser for the space in the paper was open to negotiation. This could vary according to the size of the ad, the frequency of its insertion, and the circulation of the paper. One of James Poole's correspondents avoided all of these questions and simply trusted him to use his best judgment, asking: 'Please advertise the following to the amount of one dollar ...'[36] The value of a publisher's white space was a complex issue. Publishers could have as many as four rates: one for local business, a second for foreign business, a third for government notices, and a fourth, rarely acknowledged but generally understood, for family and friends. To call these 'rates' may be misleading. They were guidelines within which a paper's business manager would operate.[37]

One group of entrepreneurs saw a tremendous opportunity in this chaos: the advertising agents. So long as the papers retained their idiosyncratic production standards and rates, there existed a niche for someone who could assist advertisers in the placement of their notices. This is the opportunity that the agents seized.

The Agent as Opportunist: Robert Moore

'Agents' brokering white space entered the publishing field long before 1900. For much of that time they worked solely as middlemen between those interested in advertising their shops or wares and those who had blank space they wanted to fill. It was a very convenient service. Each town in Canada had at least one weekly paper. To place an ad in any one of them, one would have to know of its existence, inquire after its rates and schedules, draft a contract, make the plates (if one had them made oneself), send them, check that the ad actually ran as instructed on the date arranged, and then pay the bill. Any firm seeking distribution outside of its immediate locale would have to repeat this process with as many papers as it saw fit.

Enter the newspaper's 'solicitor.' Publishers at mid-century did not aggressively pursue advertisers. Since their operating costs were geared towards reader subscriptions, advertising was treated as bonus income. Only when advertising became more lucrative did astute publishers hire representatives to secure it. Once again, the daily papers were ahead of the weeklies. Only dailies could generate sufficient revenue from the sale of advertising space to cover a man's salary. The selling point of any paper over its rivals might be the low price of its line rates or its high circulation. Shrewd advertisers would calculate the value of a paper's rates against circulation. They were also well advised to check for themselves the quality and distribution of the papers being pushed.

A thoughtful entrepreneur might see an opportunity here, and Volney B. Palmer did just that. Palmer set up shop as an independent solicitor in Philadelphia sometime around 1841. As an independent solicitor, Palmer placed ads in any paper for any company that hired him. Like most other salesmen, he took a commission on the business he secured. Palmer's rate was 25 per cent. He would submit the paper's bill to the advertiser, then remit the advertiser's payment – minus his 25 per cent commission – to the paper. This was a logical development from the existing system. It was the paper that had the goods for sale, and it was on its behalf that the solicitor operated.[38]

Palmer inspired imitators. The first in the United States was S.M. Pettingill, one of Palmer's own trainees, who opened his own agency in 1849. In Canada, the earliest agent on record was Robert Moore, who set up in Montreal some twenty years after Palmer, in 1860. Formerly on staff at Montreal's *Commercial Advertiser*, Moore was a salesman with grand ambitions, and he named his office 'The British American Advertising and Circular Delivery Agency.' It was not a success. As yet, Canada had neither the newspapers nor the advertisers to support such a venture.

For the advertiser, agency service was a great convenience. With one agent handling the placement of all of its ads, the advertiser would no longer have to deal directly with the papers. All solicitations could be referred to its agency. As Moore told one potential client, 'I can do your advertising on very reasonable terms, and save you much trouble, time and expense, besides checking any irregularities in the insertions ... From my knowledge of the business, I can work for you better than you can do for yourself.'[39] Moreover, the agent's services were nominally 'free,' since advertisers only paid those rates set by the papers. Doubtless, 'invisible' might be more accurate than 'free.' In all likelihood, publishers raised their rates to compensate for revenue lost to commissions.[40]

Moore's commission was the same as Palmer's: 25 per cent. How this rate was established is not clear. Presumably, this had been the rate the papers paid their own representatives on staff, based upon the cost of selling space relative to other overhead expenses. When John Ross Robertson sold ad space for the Toronto *Leader* in 1863, this was his rate of commission. Hugh C. MacLean earned the same rate working for his brother J.B. Maclean in 1889.[41]

Moore preserved a letter of agreement between himself and a publisher, and it is worth printing it here in its entirety. In February 1860 he wrote:

Receive herewith, Advertisements of the Life Association of Scotland, in three different forms – for insertion in the following manner – No. 1, to be inserted in Monday next, and all next week, when it is to be taken out, and No. 2, put in its place the following week; to be succeeded by No. 3, in the same way, the week afterwards. Then to commence again with No. 1, and to continue in the same succession, till 5th April next inclusive, when the Advertisement is to be taken out entirely, – Insertion in the Weekly Edition to be made in the same manner: – An Editorial notice, which will be sent you, to be also inserted, and copies of the Papers to be delivered at this office, and to the Life Association. The Advertisement must be in the columns of the Editorial page, and nowhere else, or no payment will be made. Your charge for advertising is to be _____. Charge to this office.[42]

Such a contract could have evolved under the in-house solicitation system; the agent simply introduced a middleman. The blank for charges suggests this was a standard form, the rate to be changed to suit the publisher. Note here that the ads were provided by the agency already written and engraved; provisions were made separately for the daily and weekly editions of the paper; the ad's placement on the page was specified; and copies of the paper were to be sent to the agency and client. The last provision allowed the client to check that its ad ran properly. Moore's letter also had the paper run an 'Editorial notice,' in essence a puff piece masquerading as a news article.

Whether or not Moore was the first to offer agency service in Canada, the novelty of his operation remains evident from the problems he faced. One business manager wrote to ask if Moore's commission was to be added to the paper's bill for its space. Another wondered if Moore expected a 'discount' for the client on top of his own 25 per cent commission. As Moore pointed out rather icily to Mr Thomson of the Toronto *Colonist*: 'You seem to be under a mistake with regard to the discount. – As I have been appointed advertising agent for the Life Association, the sole management of advertisements rests with me, and there can be no double discount. The only deduction will be 25%. – If therefore you will agree to insert these according to printed instructions for the sum of $55. less 25%, please do so, but if not be kind enough to return them.'[43] In another case, a publisher frustrated with a delay in payment approached the client. This infuriated Moore, who responded, 'Mr Grant has nothing to do with my business, and you had no right to write him regarding me ... It was a piece of pure impertinence on your part to write to a third party regarding a matter which was personal to you & myself.'[44] To Moore, the role of each player was perfectly clear. He considered each component of the agency's dealings to be a discrete transaction.

Not all publishers found this arrangement troublesome. G.J. Barthe of *La Gazette de Sorel* welcomed Moore's contracts and asked him to be a freelance solicitor for the paper. One wonders if other small-town papers, far from commercial centres and less accessible to advertisers, did not do the same. Never one to let an opportunity pass, Moore accepted the offer, and then offered to collect Barthe's bills as well.[45]

Moore also sought links with other agents, particularly those south of the border. Rather than compete with the Americans on their own turf, Moore offered to exchange his services with agents in Boston and New York City – John Styles and S.M. Pettingill. If they would place business for him in the United States, he would look after their Canadian business. Styles accepted Moore's offer, but no record of Pettingill's answer is available.[46]

For clients, Moore offered two other services beyond print advertising. The most conspicuous of these was postering and the display of show cards. When soliciting business, he claimed to have exclusive right to prime locations in steamers, railway cars, and train stations, as well as the best 'dead walls and hoardings in the City.' His letterbook suggests otherwise. On the same day that he wrote John Styles, informing him that he had agreements with various railway companies to display show cards, he wrote the Grand Trunk Railway requesting this same opportunity. The other service provided to clients was the distribution of circulars. For delivery, he charged $10 per one thousand sheets; to address them before delivery he charged an extra $2.50 per thousand. Considering that circular delivery was part of his agency's name, one wonders to what extent this service was key to his business.[47]

Soliciting clients, placing ads, collecting bills, displaying show cards, delivering circulars, networking with other agents, and later publishing business directories: at mid-century Robert Moore was a jack-of-all-trades, a hustler in business-to-business services. His letters reveal the kind of practices that would later tar the entire industry: haggling over the specifics of contracts to delay payment, attempts to buy editorial columns as well as advertising space, and outright lying to his associates. Regardless, he could not keep his office afloat. Despite the successful models provided by Palmer and Pettingill in the United States, and his own efforts to pioneer agency service in Canada, his company folded in four years. At mid-century, Canada's manufacturing output was not characterized by trade-marked consumer goods, nor did manufacturers have extensive distribution networks. In short, Canada's manufacturers did not need the services Moore provided.

Agency Models

In 1865 changes altered the trade in the United States. That year, George P. Rowell established an agency in Boston with a new rate structure. Competitive pressures were lowering returns from commissions as more agencies were entering the field. Most frequently, agents would rebate part of their commissions to their clients in order to lower the price of their services. Subsequently, their profit margins steadily shrank. Rowell found a way to avoid this problem. Other agents secured their clients first, and then placed their ads; Rowell contracted large amounts of space in one hundred New England papers, and then sold this list complete to advertisers. In short, he became a wholesaler of publishers' white space, a 'space jobber.' He possessed the lowest rates available for those papers, and he could attract advertisers on that basis. Imitators soon appeared who specialized in the papers of other regions and other types of periodicals. Such agents included Lord and Thomas, who contracted space in religious periodicals, and J. Walter Thompson, who did the same with general magazines. Thompson took the new system a step further by securing exclusive access to the publications on his list. Exclusive or not, commissions became irrelevant. Profits were made from the resale value of the white space the agents controlled.[48]

American advertisers eventually questioned the 'closed' contracts of these space jobbers. The papers on an agency list were not selected with an individual advertiser in mind. Rather, they were merely the papers with which the agency had contracts. A.J. Ayer, the founder of N.W. Ayer and Son, exploited this resentment with the introduction of an 'open' contract in 1875. Each advertiser would be offered a judicious selection of media sensitive to its product and distribution network. In so doing, Ayer introduced the concept of advertiser-oriented service into the agency's operations. The agency would not simply be a publishers' representative, nor a wholesaler, but an expert providing the advertiser with objective media counsel. To pay for this service, Ayer readopted the commission system. Despite the allure of service, no agency would have survived had it relied on that alone to amass clients. Advertisers still sought cheap rates, and the agencies that offered them won the contracts.[49]

In Canada, there is insufficient evidence to state which model the agencies followed, be it Rowell's wholesale agent, Thompson's closed contract, or Ayer's open one. Robert Moore clearly contracted for each client on an individual basis. Unfortunately, no other agency records have been preserved from this time period. However, it might be ventured that the space jobbers never held sway in Canada to the same extent that they did in the United States. Few companies apart from patent medicine makers advertised beyond their immediate locales before 1890. Since advertising was traditionally the forte of retailers, most manufacturers were probably happy to leave this expense to them. Further, as previously mentioned, Canadian manufacturers did not produce trade-marked goods in great quantities until the mid-1890s. Without recognizable trade marks, most goods could not be advertised effectively.[50]

The Agent as Broker: Anson McKim

Anson McKim had a better go of it than did Robert Moore. To describe his beginning, however, it is necessary to describe the circumstances surrounding his entry. In 1872 Sir John A. Macdonald surveyed the newspaper field in Toronto and decided that the local Tory organ, the *Leader*, was no match for George Brown's formidable *Globe*. At his suggestion the Toronto *Mail* was formed, which won the support of local Conservatives and forced the *Leader* out of business. Still, the paper was not an immediate financial success. In 1877 it was sold to its chief creditor and a partisan Tory, John Riordan. Riordan set out to re-create the *Mail* with an impressive new building, new presses, new type, and an editorial policy that made it a paper of record to rival the *Globe*. With these changes accomplished, the paper then did something that no one foresaw: it declared its editorial independence from the Conservatives. Rival newspapermen grudgingly acknowledged that the paper's period of 'splendid isolation' represented the best journalism of the day. Readers apparently agreed. By 1892 it had the largest circulation of any paper in Toronto, second only to the Montreal *Star* across the country.[51]

T.W. Dyas was the paper's advertising manager. While Riordan and his editor Edward Farrer expanded the paper's plant and influence, Dyas made the paper profitable through its advertising columns. Since all of the Toronto papers competed for the same local advertisers, he decided to look beyond the city itself. Dyas knew that many American papers had branch offices in other major centres. Such offices gave remote advertisers a personal link to the paper and won substantial contracts. Dyas thought this a good idea, and in 1878 he created a *Mail* office in Montreal. It was staffed by a young man, then twenty-six years old, who had worked at the paper for six years: Anson McKim.

Hired as a special representative, McKim gradually transformed the office into an independent advertising agency. When he arrived in Montreal, he discovered a rival from the *Globe* had preceded him. Neither man found many opportunities in the city, and McKim sometimes went weeks without landing a new contract. His fortunes changed when he reorganized the office along agency lines. Several advertisers wanted to place notices in Ontario centres outside of Toronto. If McKim could secure contracts with several papers at once, he would gain a decided advantage for the *Mail* itself. The *Mail* agreed to this arrangement, as did other Ontario papers. In exchange for this service,

McKim took a commission from each paper, part of which was rebated to the *Mail*. By 1889 the other papers were convinced of the value of this operation, but had grown tired of surrendering a commission to the *Mail*. With their encouragement, McKim left the *Mail* and became an independent solicitor.[52]

Incidentally, McKim's success in Montreal inspired Dyas to open a similar office in Toronto. McKim was not only selling the *Mail*, he was selling a service. There was no reason to believe that advertisers in Ontario would not appreciate this service as well. Instead of hiring another special representative, however, Dyas took the next logical step and opened an 'independent' advertising agency in 1882: the Mail Advertising Agency. Although still connected to the paper, and staffed by one of its former solicitors, it too placed ads in any number of Ontario papers, and sent agents throughout British North America looking for clients.[53]

McKim's success has been credited to his own daring and imagination, but it should not be forgotten that his agency grew out of one of the most respected papers of his day. Where Robert Moore had gone it alone, McKim began with the prestige and credit of the *Mail* behind him, a publisher who was willing to take chances, and a capable mentor in Dyas. Only after seventeen years at the *Mail*, and with the backing of several other papers, did McKim sever this connection. (Even then, the 'Mail' name remained above his storefront until the late 1890s.)[54] However, the apparent success of his agency, and those of men such as Pettingill, Ayer, and Thompson in the United States, inspired other men to go into the trade. Not surprisingly, without the same corporate support that McKim had enjoyed, few succeeded in Canada. City directories for Montreal and Toronto listed agencies throughout the 1870s and 1880s. There were usually four or five in each city in any given year, but few made more than a single appearance.[55] After 1895, however, when the volume of advertising increased, agencies began to survive in most of the regions with rapidly developing mercantile and industrial centres – cities such as Halifax, Ottawa, Hamilton, London, Winnipeg, Edmonton, and Vancouver.

Agency Services

The expanding volume of foreign advertising after 1895 opened many opportunities for new entries into the agency field. Once again, competition sparked innovation, and once again Canadian adworkers would look south for new ideas. Starting in 1900 new types of agency service would transform the typical agency from a small office operation into a modern, departmentalized company employing dozens of staff.

At the root of the agency business remained the solicitation of new clients and space-buying. 'First and foremost and all the time,' McKim's newspaper directory declared, 'it is the business of an advertising agency to promote and facilitate newspaper advertising.'[56] It was their job to solicit supralocal advertisers for the papers. Insofar as the agency system had evolved out of the advertising departments of actual newspapers, this must have seemed self-evident. Regardless, the commission system was based on this premise, and agencies were paid commission on every contract placed, whether new or not. This could be justified because the solicitation process was undertaken at the agency's expense. Long before any ad was placed, before any bill was submitted, the agency was hustling clients on its own time and account. Toronto agent J.J. Gibbons boasted that, in his own shop: 'A corps of intelligent and high-salaried solicitors are constantly working on the non-advertising manufacturers and others, persuading them to become regular advertisers, offering experienced direction to their campaigns, and doing everything in their power to induce them to take up newspaper advertising.'[57] Few newspapers had anything comparable to attract new business.

No matter how much time and effort an agent put into this process, there was always the possibility that nothing would come of it. At times, business could simply be slow. At other times, agencies had to deal with the realities of the market: a competing agency could get the account. A.R. Coffin, an executive with a Nova Scotia printing house, painted a third possible scenario: 'A general advertiser who, in these days, wishes to start in advertising with a fair amount of success has a complete advertising campaign laid out for him, by an agency, which must include all detail ... Then after all the whole proposition may be laid on the shelf for another year, or it has been known that the advertiser would not say thank you to the agency but get a clerk in his office to put into effect the agency's scheme and hold up the papers for the agency's commission.'[58] Coffin knew more than one manufacturer had tried this trick. Understandably, he did not name them in print.

Again, after solicitation, space-buying was the core service agencies provided to their clients. An extensive knowledge of the periodical market was required to do the job effectively, and this became the responsibility of 'media departments.' There were three main groups within such departments: researchers, space-buyers, and checkers. The researchers' task was to know everything about every periodical in the country: where it was published and by whom, its tone and reputation, what market it served, its circulation, its political or religious affiliations, whether or not it carried advertising, and its line rates if it did. Space-buyers would then use this information to maximize the value of each advertiser's appropriation by reaching as many readers as possible at the lowest possible expense. Once the ad was run, it was then the checkers' task to ensure that everything appeared according to contract.[59]

The most difficult information to obtain was invariably the paper's circulation. Most companies wanted their advertising placed in papers that would reach as many readers as possible. In areas with more than one paper, this generally meant they would only select the paper with the highest circulation. Competition among publishers for lucrative advertising contracts led them into a cycle of ballooning estimates and mutual recriminations. Gibbons related the following experience while speaking before the Canadian Press Association: 'I went into one newspaper office in Ontario and inquired about their circulation. One partner told me 1,200, while the other a few hours later told me they were printing 600 and seemed to think they were making splendid progress. In another town the people said the local paper had a circulation of 300; the pressman after thinking it over placed the circulation at 600, while the publisher assured me on his word of honour that the circulation was 900.'[60] Caught between their clients and publishers, agencies had to draft their own estimates. Sometimes, as Gibbons's comments suggest, this was done simply by chatting with the locals and getting a sense of the paper's popularity. The agents requested verified numbers, but were resisted by most publishers. It took the combined effort of Canada's top advertisers to change their minds. That would not happen until the 1910s.

Space rates provided a second bone of contention between publishers and agents. Many publishers had rate cards that they issued once a year for the benefit of their patrons, but they did not strictly follow their stated rates. Competing publishers entered a dangerous spiral of price-cutting to attract agencies looking for the best deal. Agents exploited this practice unabashedly. It was a talking point in their solicitations. An article in McKim's directory was exceptionally frank when it stated that a good agency 'must know the rock bottom rates ... of every publication.' Maxwell R. Gregg claimed to possess 'special facilities for inserting advertisements at the lowest possible rates,' while W.F. Carrier and Company simply stated: 'Our Rates are the lowest procurable.'[61] Clients expected no less, and expected agencies to compete for their business. The Sun Life Assurance Company is a case in point. It wanted to run a brief campaign in 1911 and requested estimates from two different agencies, for the exact same ad in the exact same list of cities. One agency could do it for $2,330.65, the other for $2,011.17. Naturally, Sun Life hired the second agency.[62]

Taken together, solicitation and space-buying were the two core services provided by agencies at the turn of the century; the first was essentially sales, the latter purchasing. Other conveniences were provided to clients, but these were ancillary in nature, and had remained unchanged since the days of Robert Moore: having plates made, sending them out, checking the insertions after publication, and paying the bills.

Copywriting and illustration were not a part of the typical agency's repertoire. It was assumed that clients knew their products best and would prepare their ads themselves. Advertisers who wanted help with creative tasks could find qualified help in two different places. For illustrations, an advertiser could readily call upon a print shop, the bastion of the commercial artist. For ad copy, an advertiser could hire a self-styled 'advertising specialist.' A demand for expert copy services led some fledgling authors to compose ads on a freelance basis. Most would not place the ads they wrote. Rather, they were hired by advertisers who wanted more polished notices than the run-of-the-mill stuff that appeared in the papers, and who placed their ads 'direct.' Thomas Bengough, a veteran Toronto pressman, placed the start of this trend in 1891; three years later he wrote, 'even the old-timers are falling into line.' Some agencies were also known to hire specialists for specific jobs.[63]

The story of Wilson P. MacDonald is interesting in this light. In the 1920s MacDonald was known for a brand of romantic poetry that critics scorned, but adoring fans embraced. While developing his craft, he earned his keep as a freelance copywriter. MacDonald travelled throughout much of Canada and the United States between 1900 and 1918, stopping in towns for two or three months at a time. He rarely stayed longer. He carried with him a stock of pre-written advertisements, which he resold in every new town. When his stock was nearly empty, he moved on. A bachelor living in hotels or boarding houses, MacDonald never had a secretary, let alone a full-service agency under his care.[64]

When the finished ad was needed in plate form, most agencies did not have the facilities to create them themselves. This task too was farmed out to job printing plants. The 1890s witnessed the flowering of these firms in Canada, and Toronto was home to several. Among the better known were Toronto Lithography, Copp Clark, Brigden's, and Grip Limited. Firms of this calibre maintained the skilled labour and equipment necessary to produce a broad range of printed goods, from tickets and handbills to full-size posters. Agencies contracted them for many of these goods, but the most common items sought were plates.[65]

Given the range of expertise at their command, print shops were well positioned to enter the agency business themselves. Since they already illustrated and set advertisements, it was only logical to place them as well. One shop that did so was Diver Electrotype, owned by Frederick Diver. Founded in 1878, it enjoyed a close relationship with the Toronto *World* and produced ready-prints for several weekly papers. These sheets carried a high volume of foreign advertising. About 1897 Diver capitalized on this business by entering the general agency field; he hired a former *Mail* salesman to act as his manager and renamed his firm the 'Central Press Agency.' By 1899 the agency was placing ads nationally for companies such as R.S. Williams Pianos, Salada Tea, and Sleeman's Ale.[66]

The Agent as Corporate Consultant: J.J. Gibbons

The agency scene changed dramatically after 1900, thanks to John J. Gibbons. Like Moore and Dyas before him, Gibbons drew upon American expertise to introduce new services in Canada. While still a teenager, he was hired by the Toronto *News* to become its special representative in New York City. The opportunity acquainted him with several agencies there that offered copy and art services to their clients. They charged nothing for them. Rather, the agencies believed the expense was necessary to enhance the client's advertising – and by extension, to enhance their own reputations within a competitive trade. Gibbons realized that no Canadian agency did this, and in 1899 he returned to Toronto to open a new agency on these lines. In so doing, he established the first copy and art departments to be found at any agency in Canada, and he staffed them with experienced personnel raided from newspapers, advertisers, and other agencies.[67]

Gibbons was not the first to offer these services to Canadian advertisers, but he was the first to bundle them with solicitation and space-buying under one roof. This gave him much greater influence over all aspects of his clients' campaigns. Within three years, his staff was designing plans that achieved thematic and stylistic continuity through every part of a product's marketing, from trade-mark design and packaging to newspaper ads and display cards. The agency's successes were numerous, and culminated in one set of ads designed for Lever Brothers' Sunlight Soap in 1902. Lever found them so attractive, it used them in Great Britain and the United States as well. Lever's contract with Gibbons had been a coup in itself; previously, Lever had worked exclusively with McKim. Gibbons similarly won the McClary contract from J.S. Robertson, a Toronto freelancer.[68] The conversion of these high-profile clients was a portent of things to come. J.J. Gibbons Limited set the pace in Toronto for the next three decades, selling the wares of companies such as Neilson's Chocolates, Northern Electric, Pear's Soap, White Star Steamships, Canada Life Assurance, and Packard Motor Cars. By 1930 Gibbons was providing service to one hundred firms in Canada, the United States, and Great Britain, from offices in Montreal (1902), Winnipeg (1911), and Vancouver (1929). One might note that his staff was either well selected or well trained; several started successful agencies of their own before 1930.[69]

Every agency that sought to expand its stable of clients with prestigious, national accounts was compelled to adopt the full-service approach. At least two other agencies opened in Toronto between 1900 and 1904 offering creative services, and the established agencies quickly took note. The Desbarats Advertising Agency of Montreal admitted as much in 1912: 'In our own advertising business, changes have been the order of the day. The more or less perfunctory service has given way to a really highly specialized one, and we look back to the times that we thought we were giving our customers good service much in the same way perhaps as we will be looking back in another ten years on our efforts today.'[70] It was a costly undertaking, as Edouard Desbarats knew. He decided to incorporate in 1901, after ten years in business. With fresh capital in hand, he immediately acquired greater office space and filled it with copy and art men. McKim began hiring artists after 1900. Four years later he too incorporated his agency and similarly expanded his physical plant.[71]

The increasing costs incurred by these new services led to a desire for greater security among agency owners. A full service agency had significant capital tied up in personnel and plant. By 1904 two agencies were listed in R.G. Dun and Company's credit reference book for Canada. Desbarats was listed with $10,000 to $20,000 in capital assets, and Frederick Diver's print shop and agency was listed at $35,000 to $50,000. Fifteen years later, the Montreal offices of McKim Limited and the Canadian Advertising Agency also appeared, and both rated at $35,000 to $50,000.[72] Freelancers could not say the same. Gibbons had very little patience with men such as Wilson P. MacDonald. Mac-Donald's entire approach to the trade was antithetical to its long-term interests. Whether or not his clients succeeded might have made no difference to him; he would be off to the next town regardless. Further, with no capital investment in the trade, he could afford to undercut the commission charged by other agencies. He tapped the system for its wealth while contributing little of lasting value, and for this he was thoroughly scorned by the full-service agencies. Gibbons decried these 'men that had no office other than their hats.' McKim argued that freelancers were not true agents in comparison with the 'legitimate advertising agency, possessing large capital, thorough equipment, and a staff of trained employees.'[73]

Toronto's Prominence

Toronto emerged as the leading city in the Canadian advertising trade between 1900 and 1914. Montreal remained the centre of Canadian banking and transportation throughout the period under study, but Quebec as a whole lost ground to southern Ontario as a manufacturing and distribution centre. Publishing was among these manufacturing concerns. In 1926 the Dominion Bureau of Statistics stated unequivocally that the 'printing and publishing industry in Canada is centred in Ontario'; 40 per cent of the country's establishments were located there.[74] Toronto, the regional hub of Ontario's economy, benefited most from this concentration, and advertising agencies there flourished.

The influence of Toronto's agencies can be tracked through a number of channels, but census data, city directories, and trade publications provide a rough overview of the number of people involved and the roles they played. Among these sources, the censuses are the most ambiguous, since the census bureau's understanding of 'advertising agent' is not clear. The 1901 census noted that there were 135 'advertising agents' in Canada.[75] What this number represents is impossible to fathom. According to the 1931 census, only 'wage earners' counted as agents, and employers were listed separately. Even then, the census provided two different tallies for the number of agents in Canada.

Demographic tables on 'advertising agents' totalled 2,129, but more comprehensive tables subdivided by specific job descriptions totalled 3,290. It seems likely that the first tally represents only the core occupations of a full-service agency, while the second represents everyone including receptionists and clerks.[76]

These qualifications aside, a few observations can be made. The number of people in the advertising trade rose substantially from 1901 to 1931, with the greatest increase occurring in Toronto. From twenty-three shops in 1900, the Toronto field expanded to more than seventy by 1930. Among these seventy were thirty-six full-service agencies. Toronto's closest rival was Montreal, whose forty-eight shops included twenty-two full-service agencies. Seven of Toronto's number were branches of Montreal agencies, but seven Toronto agents reciprocated with offices in Montreal.[77] Twelve American agencies entered Canada from 1911 to 1930; ten located in Toronto. The city's ascendancy was more evident in the census data. By 1921, 36 per cent of all agency personnel in the country could be found in Toronto, including 35 per cent of all executive and managerial staff. By comparison, Montreal accounted for less than half that, 16 per cent of total staff and only 11 per cent of executive and managerial staff. These proportions remained consistent over the next decade. Beyond Toronto and Montreal, the advertising population of other cities dropped precipitously. After Toronto, with 1,052 adworkers in 1931, and Montreal, with 646, came Vancouver, 205; Winnipeg, 188; and Hamilton, 72.[78]

A number of factors assisted Toronto's ascendancy. Its ready access to water and rail transportation gave its manufacturers a decided advantage in domestic markets and populous sections of the United States. After 1890, its financial control over mineral deposits in 'New Ontario' and hydroelectric power in southern Ontario reinforced its strengths in manufacturing. The Industrial Census of 1880 reported that the total value of production in Montreal was almost $53 million; Toronto, by contrast, claimed only $20 million. Thirty years later, these rankings were reversed: Toronto accounted for $154 million and Montreal, $116 million.[79] Taken altogether, Toronto could boast manufacturers producing consumer goods, a rapidly growing urban population, and a relatively steady supply of industrial wages. By locating there rather than Montreal, a new advertising agency had two clear advantages: it was closer to businesses headquartered in Ontario, and it was closer to the approximately five hundred papers serving the province's growing population (see Table 1.1).[80]

TABLE 1.1
Number of Newspapers in Canada and Newfoundland, by Province, 1891–1930

Province		1891	1898	1904	1910	1915	1920	1925	1930
Prince Edward	daily	3	3	4	4	5	3	2	2
Island	weekly	10	13	12	10	8	6	5	5
Nova Scotia	daily	7	11	12	13	13	13	11	9
	weekly	62	73	62	55	48	50	33	47
New Brunswick	daily	7	9	9	6	8	8	7	6
	weekly	31	37	33	32	32	30	27	26
Quebec	daily	25	17	14	18	23	19	18	19
	weekly	115	114	115	116	109	106	105	133
Ontario	daily	42	55	53	56	56	41	42	42
	weekly	392	464	457	488	449	386	347	344
Manitoba	daily	2	6	8	8	8	6	5	7
	weekly	38	71	87	105	108	96	99	105
Saskatchewan	daily	*0	*0	*1	8	7	6	6	5
	weekly	*8	*16	*41	148	166	171	176	176
Alberta	daily	*2	*1	*4	10	8	6	6	6
	weekly	*8	*16	*27	97	104	110	107	113
British Columbia	daily	9	11	12	15	17	14	18	16
	weekly	17	48	49	68	88	58	67	73
Yukon Territory	daily	0	0	3	1	1	1	1	1
	weekly	0	3	2	2	2	2	2	2
Newfoundland	daily	3	3	3	4	4	4	3	2
	weekly	7	8	8	8	9	9	8	8

*Papers located according to political divisions created in 1905.
Weekly tallies include semi-weeklies and tri-weeklies.
Data from McKim Limited, *The Canadian Newspaper Directory*, 1–24 eds.

These considerations provided sound economic reasons for anglophone agents to locate in Toronto, but they do not explain the dearth of francophone agents in Quebec. Unlike most goods and services, advertising is dependent upon language and recognizable cultural icons to make its point. Advertising in Quebec had to be written and placed in each language to reach both the English- and French-speaking populations effectively. Nonetheless, few French Canadians entered the agency field. At the turn of the century, only three of twenty-three agencies listed in the Montreal City Directory were connected to French surnames.[81]

Notably, the first francophone to establish a successful agency learned the trade in English: Edouard Desbarats. Desbarats came from a printing family and began his career as a representative for the family-owned *Dominion Illustrated News*. He was hired by McKim Limited in 1889 and spent two years there learning the agency business. He then established a rival agency of his own. Despite McKim's prestige and the depth of its client list (one hundred in 1899), Desbarats Advertising developed into a major concern and had clients such as Sun Life Assurance, Tetley's Tea, and Pabst Beer within ten years. Desbarats was a charter member of the agent's trade association and late in life was recognized within the advertising trade as a pioneer.[82]

Fourteen years passed before another agency was successfully launched by a francophone. In 1906 François-Émile Fontaine opened the Canadian Advertising Agency. Among certain members of the trade in Quebec, Fontaine's agency is considered the first French-Canadian shop because it was the first to be staffed entirely of francophones.[83] He began his career selling space at Montreal's *Le Monde* in the early 1890s. *Le Monde* was one of the first French-language dailies to adopt consciously a populist editorial style like that of the English-language penny press. Not surprisingly, it led the development of newspaper advertising among francophones. Fontaine's mentor was the business manager there, Alfred Lionnais. Fontaine greatly admired Lionnais, and considered him 'le premier Canadien français à s'occuper sérieusement de publicité.' The reason for his success was spelled out: 'Elève du Collège Ste-Marie de Montréal, M. Lionnais parlait fort bien les deux langues: c'était une distinction à cette époque. Affable, courtois, spirituel, M. Lionnais avait ses entrées partout, même dans les maisons d'affaires anglaises, moins accueillantes en ce temps-là aux Canadiens français qu'elles le sont aujourd'hui.'[84] Fontaine understood the lesson well. Like Desbarats, he adopted an English name for his business. It did not become l'Agence Canadienne de Publicité, Limité, until 1962. In the meantime, he built up a client list of anglophone and francophone businesses, while specializing in French-language creative services and media-buying.[85]

Fontaine's decision to adopt an English name for his agency highlights the problems faced by a French-language shop. However, if the

TABLE 1.2
Number of Newspapers in Selected Provinces, by Language and Province, 1891–1930

Province		1891	1898	1904	1910	1915	1920	1925	1930
French-language papers									
Quebec	daily	17	8	7	8	10	10	9	11
	weekly	73	55	52	59	57	62	59	84
New Brunswick	daily	0	0	0	0	0	0	0	0
	weekly	2	2	2	2	3	2	2	2
Ontario	daily	1	1	1	1	2	1	1	1
	weekly	5	3	2	7	7	2	4	2
Manitoba	daily	0	0	0	0	0	0	0	0
	weekly	1	2	2	1	3	3	3	1
Total	all	99	71	66	78	82	80	78	101
English-language papers									
Quebec	daily	8	9	7	8	11	8	8	7
	weekly	42	51	55	53	49	43	43	46
New Brunswick	daily	7	9	9	6	8	8	7	6
	weekly	29	35	31	30	29	28	25	24
Ontario	daily	41	54	52	55	52	39	39	38
	weekly	380	452	445	471	434	380	337	337
Manitoba	daily	2	6	8	8	7	6	5	6
	weekly	32	65	80	90	92	78	80	87
Total	all	541	681	687	721	682	590	544	551

Weekly tallies include semi-weeklies and tri-weeklies.
Data from McKim Limited, *The Canadian Newspaper Directory*, 1–28 eds.

prejudices of the anglophone business community provided one obstacle, the demographics of the francophone market provided another. To prepare any campaign was costly, but the returns from an English-language campaign were lucrative given the number of papers printed in that language. An agency working in French had the same fixed costs, but far fewer papers in which to place its advertising. When Desbarats opened shop in 1892, Ontario had 434 papers to Quebec's 140. Of this 140, only 90 served the province's francophones, and only 17 were dailies. This latter number dropped dramatically over the next five years and remained low into the twentieth century (Table 1.2). Quebec was well covered by country weeklies, but they did not attract much foreign advertising. The lesser frequency and lower advertising rates of the weeklies did not encourage agencies to develop this market. An agency working on commission could not earn the profit on five weeklies that it could placing the same ad in one metropolitan daily.[86]

At root, then, there were three key factors impeding the full development of the trade in French Quebec: two languages, considerably fewer papers published in French than in English, and a persistent prejudice among anglophone businessmen that prevented most from hiring a francophone agency. The situation led one Québécois agent to conflate his culture with his ethnicity and ask if advertising was simply foreign to the Latin temperament of the French 'race.'[87] Nonetheless, Desbarats and Fontaine succeeded because they did business in both languages and in every province of the Dominion. It is worth repeating that McKim began as a representative for Ontario papers.

Other cities developed advertising services, but their influence remained regional. When agencies opened in Halifax, Winnipeg, and Vancouver, they depended on local merchants and manufacturers and did not carry contracts with national advertisers located elsewhere. As their local advertisers developed national profiles, agencies from central Canada quickly stepped into the market and either established branch offices or bought out promising local firms.

Vancouver suffered this phenomenon. Print shops and billposters plied their trade there before 1900, but agencies began to appear only after that date. Nine agencies appeared in the next ten years, but all were short-lived. The first to take root was Crawford-Harris Limited, founded in 1915 by two former newspapermen, David Crawford and Frank Harris. Their agency developed a niche serving western companies; by 1929 they had branch offices in Victoria, Calgary, Edmonton, Regina, and Winnipeg. That year, a Toronto office was opened as well to claim a stake in the national trade. By then, however, four agencies from central Canada were already in Vancouver, including McKim and Gibbons. The Crawford-Harris agency affiliated with Gibbons in 1930 and was absorbed completely in 1933. Crawford became a vice-president. The same fate befell Vancouver's second major agency, Eastman Advertising, when Morgan Eastman merged his business with McConnell and Fergusson Limited in 1932. Eastman too was made vice-president – of a renamed McConnell, Eastman and Company.[88] After that, there was no Vancouver-based agency handling national accounts.

FIGURE 1.1
Number of Advertising Agencies in Vancouver, Winnipeg, Toronto, and Montreal,
1890–1930

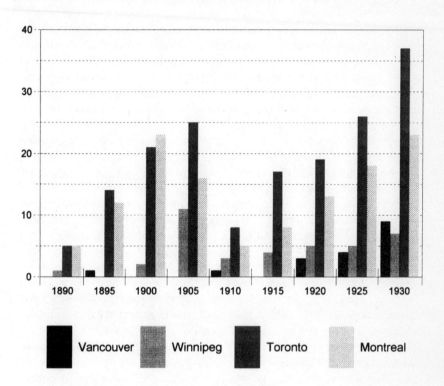

Note: Companies offering advertising services came in many guises in the late 1800s,
but city directories usually listed them all indiscriminately as 'agents.' In 1907 the CPA
drafted a definition of 'agency' that restricted its application to independently owned firms
offering both creative and media-buying services. The figures for 1910 and after are
based upon this definition, which is discussed in chapter 4.
Source: *Henderson's British Columbia Directory* (Victoria/Vancouver: Henderson [1889–
1905]); *Henderson's Manitoba Classified Business Directory* (Winnipeg: Henderson
[1890–1905]); *Lovell's Montreal Classified Business Directory* (Montreal: Lovell [1889–
1905]); *Might's Toronto City Directory* (Toronto: Might [1890–1905]); *Printer and Publisher* 19:11 (November 1910), 45; *Printer and Publisher* 19:12 (December 1910), 46;
Lydiatt's Book (Toronto: Lydiatt [1915–30]).

The tale of Toronto was quite different. An endless procession of volunteers made their way into the agency field. In the two decades prior to 1890 there were usually three to six 'advertising agents' in Toronto in any given year. After 1890 the pace of entry quickened as a host of former clerks, newspaper solicitors, corporate advertising managers, railway card men, billposters, and independent agents clambered for a spot in the growing trade. Few endured. Between 1890 and 1910 ninety-eight different 'agencies' appeared in the Toronto directories; of these, sixty-eight disappeared after one year, while another eight disappeared within two or three years. Almost three-quarters did not survive to see their fifth year.[89] Not all of these agencies fell into the 'fly-by-night' category condemned by J.J. Gibbons, but their rate of attrition was symptomatic of problems in the trade. Their failures tended to sully the reputation of the entire agency field. Still, certain agencies did attain some credibility during this period, such as the Mail Advertising Agency. As previously noted, this agency had the institutional support of the *Mail*, and it remained in business until 1897. Independent agencies would not find real stability until after 1900.

The newspaper world that James Poole had known was not completely forgotten, but its sun was setting. Urban papers such as the *Star* and *La Presse* in Montreal and the *Telegram* in Toronto reached over 75,000 readers daily by 1900. Rural and small-town papers were now, more than ever, thrown to the mercy of a marketplace dominated by out-of-town advertisers and agencies with no personal relationship with individual publishers. Businessmen such as these had little patience for the small circulations of rural papers. At the same time, the largest dailies could command the respect and patronage of advertisers due to the sheer size of their circulations. Weekly publishers could not do the same, and they felt that control of their papers was slipping away to strangers and outsiders.

After 1900, as the number of papers in Ontario peaked and competition reached an all-time high, publishers realized they would have to cooperate to harness the changes that had overtaken them. In time, both the advertisers and the agents agreed that certain restrictions would have to be imposed for the good of the trade, and they participated in the creation of a more stable business environment. Their choices did not harken back to a previous time, but reflected an acceptance of new conditions and practices. Primary among these was the fact that revenues from foreign advertising would soon surpass that from any other source of income the newspapers enjoyed, including reader subscriptions.

In facing these problems, adworkers were forced to assess their roles in this growing trade. If once the field had been characterized by hustlers such as Robert Moore, it was now populated by a wide assortment of companies, with innumerable backgrounds and vastly different services for sale. Out of this diversity, there emerged a core group of agents who became spokesmen for the 'new' trade. All of them were connected with full-service agencies. Their desires, both economically and psychologically, would play a large role in the construction of the modern advertising trade in the years to come.

Chapter 2

Toronto Adworkers

Mr McKim saw only the single elements that make the success of any commercial enterprise. He conceived the business of advertising on precisely the same plane as the business of selling dry goods, or hardware, or railroad supplies. He was a merchant among merchants.

Printer's Ink[1]

From a mere broker of space, the advertising agency has developed into a complete selling organization – being the connecting link between the manufacturer and the consumer.

F.A. Rowlatt, 1910[2]

At eighteen years of age, John C. Kirkwood was obsessed with his career. He didn't have one, but he desperately wanted one. The specific job was unimportant, but his goals were very precise. Maddeningly, they also seemed irreconcilable: genteel respectability on the one hand and fabulous wealth on the other. He yearned for a middle way. Kirkwood resigned himself to a career in teaching and imagined that this would bring him respectability and, at the least, a secure income. However, even these modest hopes were dashed when he was struck down by a severe illness just four weeks into his courses at Queen's University.

While convalescing, Kirkwood consoled himself by writing ads for the family store. It was a revelation; he was seduced by the power of words.[3] He then began to consider the worlds of journalism and advertising and a new career path opened before him: 'I have ... learned that advertising agencies receive on business placed by them 15% ... If in the growth of the agency it could handle $1,000 per week, there would be $150 per ... There is practically no end to the work that a good agency could not secure.'[4] Visions of fabulous riches danced before him. Within months he was working in a Philadelphia advertising agency, learning the trade.

Once an experienced adworker, Kirkwood returned to Canada in 1903 and joined the sales staff at a magazine publishing company. He did not enjoy the work. He was interested in writing, and sales never held the same appeal: 'Soliciting is wearisome and distasteful. Writing [advertisements] – or doing work of [an] ... informing nature – or talking or teaching – is pleasant and commands my best energies.'[5] His meagre interest in sales was further weakened by the politesse it required to close a deal: 'I work with full fidelity, with all diligence, with skill. I have a "prospect." I work on it expectantly, get a good deal of encouragement, and am just within an inch of winning an order when some unforeseeable and insurmountable difficulty or obstacle arises that kills the chance, and makes all my time and effort of no avail.'[6] To his great relief, he was eventually promoted to head copywriter. Here he finally found his niche, or so it seemed. Advertisers clamoured for his touch, and the company asked him to train a small corps of writers to handle the demand for specially written copy. He had finally found security, status, and a substantial salary by the day's standards. Still, Kirkwood's life remained unsettled. To his mind, advertising offered neither respectability nor great wealth.

Kirkwood and his counterparts in agencies, publishing houses, and corporate advertising departments were part of a demographic trend that swept across Canada before the First World War. In the words of American historian Robert H. Wiebe, adworkers were part of an emerging new social stratum, a 'professional middle class' composed of urban, white-collar workers. These workers found their common interests in the exclusive nature of the knowledge and skills that characterized their individual occupations.[7]

In Canada, the emergence of this class has been described by R.D. Gidney and W.P.J. Millar. The class was not entirely new, but after 1890 it was increasingly self-conscious, self-interested, and unified. Further, there was an explosion in the number of occupations seeking status equal to that of the traditional professions, of the clergy, bar, and medicine. Schoolteachers, engineers, architects, social workers, civil servants, and many others professionalized by forming occupational associations, setting standards of practice and codes of conduct, establishing educational programs, and restricting entry into their fields.[8]

The broadening of this class of service-oriented professionals occurred within the expansion of the wider economy. By the 1890s a transcontinental, railway-driven economic infrastructure was in place; by 1914 mass immigration had transformed the country's demographic profile as well. According to economist Kenneth Buckley's estimates, Canada's gross domestic product grew fivefold between 1900 and 1930. The professional middle class grew in step to manage the machinery and distribution systems of the industrial economy.[9]

What drove them, as individuals, seemed to be the same combination of personal ambition and career anxiety expressed in Kirkwood's journals. Kirkwood was at the leading edge of this trend within the advertising trade. Like many others, he readily understood the opportunities that the expanding industrial economy provided. Young, male, Anglo-Celtic, raised in small-town Ontario, and barely out of high school – Kirkwood's ambitions, fears, and career path were in keeping with his contemporaries: eager to join an exciting and financially rewarding new trade, yet equally anxious over the personal costs it exacted and the ambiguous status it conferred. For agents, this problem was especially acute. They were simultaneously self-employed and corporate functionaries; the masters of their own shops, yet the underlings of industrialists.[10] New shops sometimes acknowledged these ambiguities by adopting the term 'bureau' or 'service' instead of 'agency.' Regardless, the lure of a career in advertising remained strong.

The Toronto Advertising Field

Between 1900 and 1914 adworkers in Toronto such as J.J. Gibbons took a leading role in the Canadian advertising trade, much as their counterparts in New York City did in the United States. The Toronto field itself was dominated by the first generation of adworkers to emerge after 1900. They were relatively young and overwhelmingly male, and from their ranks came the top account executives, creative staff, and opinion makers for the next thirty years. J.J. Gibbons was not yet twenty-five when he established his agency. He was not exceptional. Of the 324 men working in Toronto in 1921, three-quarters were aged twenty-five to forty-nine. Two-thirds of the full-service agencies in 1930 were organized by men who could trace their first job to a newspaper or agency between 1895 and 1910; six established their agencies before the First World War. While young men continued to enter the field, this cohort maintained a lock on 53 per cent of the positions in the field in 1931.[11]

It is difficult to generalize about the private life of the 'average' adworker. Census data reveal that most men were married by their mid-thirties. By contrast, the female presence was characterized by young, unmarried women.[12] The problems that these women faced will be discussed in greater detail below, but suffice to say here that they were not encouraged to make advertising a lifelong career. Beyond that, one ventures into conjecture. Adworkers did not appear in businessmen's directories until 1948, by which point most of the pioneers were retired or deceased. None left memoirs, and only four wrote books remotely connected to the trade. Similarly, four Toronto agents left their records for posterity, but only two of them preserved substantial files on advertising. One wonders if they privately suspected that their work was as ephemeral and unimportant as their critics maintained. Perhaps publishers and archivists told them as much.[13]

Still, census data do provide some insights. Toronto adworkers enjoyed a metropolitan lifestyle. Historian Roland Marchand has described the American agent's world as one of streetcars and typewriters, the hustle and bustle of city life combined with constant anxiety over the next deal.[14] In Canada, at a time when almost half the population was rural, the entire advertising trade was located in an urban environment. During the 1920s, 65 per cent of the advertising workforce lived in five of the largest, most highly industrialized cities in the Dominion. Further, they were on the cutting edge of the changes overtaking North American industry, occupying as they did consulting and managerial positions within the economy. Their workplace was the office, and it was populated almost exclusively by white-collar labour, from the receptionist at the front desk, to the clerks handling orders, to the sales staff at their telephones and adding machines.

They were well paid. Judging by census figures, the average starting salary for a young man in his early twenties was $25 per week in 1930, or $1,300 per year. That was no mean sum. It measured favourably against the salaries paid to comparable white-collar workers. The average weekly salary for male journalists was only $26.75, whether starting or fully established; civil servants averaged $31.54. Additionally, while the entry salary was good, those with talent and persistence were well rewarded. An experienced adworker, age fifty, took home $56.32 per week by 1931. Those who worked in Toronto took home the highest average salaries in the business: $68.64 per week, almost $3,600 per year.[15]

There was no set educational attainment for success in the trade. Among the key cohort, there was an exceptionally wide range of backgrounds, from a public school dropout such as copywriter Bertram Brooker to account executive Henry R. Cockfield, a McGill MA. Both became agency vice-presidents. Until the 1920s a formal education in advertising remained a marginal undertaking. It was taught only by private business colleges, correspondence schools, and the night schools of the Young Men's Christian Association. The last was apparently held in the highest regard by Toronto adworkers. When its courses were first offered there in 1913, they were led by E. Sterling Dean, for twelve years a salesman at the Toronto *Telegram* and a recent entrant into the agency field. Even so, employers were not enthusiastic about such courses. One local journal acknowledged the value of the course taught by Dean, but thought the trade deserved better treatment academically.[16] The same editorial commended the development of advertising courses in American universities. Although degree programs in 'Commerce and Finance' were available at McGill and the University of Toronto by that date, instruction in advertising was not offered until the late 1920s.

On-the-job training proved to be of greater significance than education to the key generation. The men who established Toronto's agencies came from many backgrounds, but aspirants had a far better chance of success if they spent time with a newspaper, major manufacturer, or established agency. The first agents all came from newspapers. Anson McKim and his service at the *Mail* springs to mind, but so too does Robert Moore and the Montreal *Commercial Advertiser* and F.-É. Fontaine and *Le Monde de Montréal*. As pointed out in the last chapter, newspaper advertising departments developed in the 1870s and 1880s. At first, these departments were composed of salesmen hired to sell space. Over time, astute publishers coaxed their advertising staff to supply creative services as well. These departments did not wither with the advent of the agency system, but remained the bastion of local advertisers while the agencies developed national accounts.

A second training ground for agents was the advertising departments of major manufacturers. Just as the larger papers had business managers to oversee advertising sales and production, many companies appointed advertising managers to oversee the expenditure of their advertising budgets. This aspect of business practice underwent rapid development after 1890, in tandem with the growth of national advertising and the increased division of labour in large corporations. Initially, the advertising of a company was part of the president's responsibilities. As the company expanded and administrative functions became more complex, this duty was given to the sales department, whose primary concern was the actual distribution of the product or service. If the company adopted advertising on a wide scale, a separate person would then be given the responsibility of managing its advertising: the advertising manager. If his responsibilities expanded to include space-buying, copywriting, agency relations, or strategic planning, then a complete department might grow under his command. Variations in this process occurred from company to company, but this was the general pattern.[17]

After 1900 the most common starting point for new agency heads was the established agencies. Agencies could train newcomers in several different departments. Sales was the key for future managers. It was the salesman's job to generate new business for the firm. Once under contract, he remained the client's link to the army of agency staff that produced its campaigns. This was an important function within the agency, and the term 'salesman' was eventually replaced by the more status-conscious 'account executive.' It was a coveted position; in essence, the account executive managed the agency's relationship with the client, and to do so meant winning the confidence of company presidents and advertising managers – Canada's corporate elite. It was the account executive's skill as a salesman and his reputation as a man that built the reputation of his agency. Former account executives were behind most of the new agencies that appeared after 1920.[18]

This pattern of career development suggests a trade in which personal relationships accounted for a great deal in day-to-day operations. At a time when card rates were not fixed, an ability to cultivate friendly relations with publishers and corporate advertising managers could have financially lucrative benefits. The fact that many of the prominent Toronto agents first worked at the city's top papers only underscores this fact. The *Mail* and the *Globe* were respected commercial papers; the *Star* and the *Telegram* had the largest circulations. Their solicitors became well known among local advertising concerns. Between 1904 and 1913 men with ten or more years of experience left each of these papers to open agencies. In 1915 the advertising manager of the Toronto *News* became the manager of McKim Toronto.[19]

The work environment shaped by these economic relationships was reinforced socially through innumerable clubs. During the early 1930s the trade journal *Canadian Advertising Data* ran a series of short, biographical sketches on agency executives and managers. Family lives, religion, and personality traits were rarely mentioned. In their place, readers found the worthy agent's curriculum vitae and a list of the clubs to which he belonged. Most belonged to two or three. Among these were the select halls of the Granite and National Clubs, as well as the more populist service organizations. There was also the ubiquitous game of golf, which almost every agent played.[20] In 1911 one Toronto trade paper reserved space for the latest news of the 'International Advertising Golf Association,' membership 103. When a luncheon club composed of agency principals formed in 1928, its first order of business was the acceptance of a silver trophy from the *Mail and Empire* – to be awarded annually to the top golfer.[21]

Agency heads had more in common than work, professional networks, income, age, and social pleasures might suggest. Judging by their last names, they were also overwhelmingly Anglo-Celtic by descent. Historian T.W. Acheson has noted that Ontario's industrial elite during the 1880s was dominated by Scots. This group of immigrants came with cutting-edge technical knowledge and ready access to credit; they used these advantages to develop new manufacturing industries in their chosen land.[22] The Toronto publishing industry readily fit this pattern, dominated as it was by newspapermen such as Robertson, Riordan, and Jaffray, and magazine publishers such as Sheppard, Maclean, and Acton. Not surprisingly, those agents whose shops endured recessions and wars were those whose ethnicity reinforced their commercial ties with their industrial clients and publishers. Little wonder then that Edouard Desbarats and F.-É. Fontaine adopted English names for their agencies, even in Montreal. In Toronto, an agency serving a different ethnicity was also cause for a significant name: Dworkin's Jewish Advertising Agency served Jewish businesses in Toronto from 1910 to 1917.[23]

At work, lunch, and play, then, adworkers were surrounded by people like themselves. The entry fees of most luncheon clubs would have excluded those with lesser incomes. The same could be said of the green fees at their favourite links. Underlying all of these pursuits were notions of sociability, public service, and athleticism customarily reserved for the leisure classes, but increasingly claimed by a professional middle class keen to stake out its place in the new urban landscape.[24]

Relations with the American Trade

Regardless of sentimental ethnic ties, the American advertising trade had far more influence over Canadian adworkers than did its counterpart in Great Britain. The Canadians did not consider this influence particularly troublesome. Rather, they defended their cultural borrowing by lauding their own sense of modernity.

Structurally, the Canadian trade took an American shape. In Britain, advertising agencies explicitly served their advertising clients rather than the newspapers. They performed all of the same functions as their counterparts in North America, but they did not describe their work in terms of the sale of white space. Instead, they emphasized the services they provided to advertisers, and they expected to be paid by them rather than the publishers.[25]

Canadian agents rejected this system in favour of the American. Robert Moore had business contacts on both sides of the Atlantic acquainted with the advertising trade, and the same could be said of later agents such as McKim and Gibbons. All three chose the American model, though without more detailed records their reasons can only be imagined. Sheer pragmatism might have played its part. In the 1850s the American agent S.M. Pettingill was already placing ads across the border and listing Canadian papers in his newspaper directories.[26]

This practice was later continued in the Rowell and Ayer directories. By 1894 *Printer's Ink* and other American trade papers were already widely read in Canada and championed the virtues of American advertising. If British agencies developed similar services at that time, they had little profile. Before 1914 most British manufacturers sold their goods in foreign markets through merchant houses, specialized companies that combined wholesale and credit services. These houses handled the manufacturers' goods and advertising as a unit and eliminated the need for British advertising agencies in foreign markets. Sells Limited, a prestigious English advertising agency, began publishing a directory of leading newspapers in the British Empire in 1882, but it made no claims to cover the Dominions comprehensively. Even then, thirty years passed before Sells opened an office in Canada – the first British agency to do so. Both of its branches, in Winnipeg (1911) and Montreal (1913), closed within four years. While agents such as McKim and Gibbons were shaping the Canadian trade, then, the examples before them were decidedly American.[27]

Beyond the trade's structure, Canadian adworkers continued to look south for inspiration and confirmation of their abilities. This was reflected in several ways: American trade news was reported in Canadian trade papers; Americans frequently filled the podium at trade luncheons; adworkers eagerly affiliated with American trade associations before the First World War; pride was taken in every native son who did well south of the border; and, as noted, American trade papers and books were widely read (as one writer put it, 'if *Printer's Ink* is delayed in the mails, there is hell to pay in Canada').[28] The border itself was remarkably permeable. It would be impossible to identify the number of Canadians who worked in the United States during the period under study, but references to them occurred almost monthly in the Toronto trade papers. Some remained there, and some returned to enjoy management positions in Canada.

The Canadians did not view this as a process of acculturation. They were not adopting *American* business practices. They were adopting *modern* business practices. Canadian adworkers believed that new ideas in advertising technique were culturally neutral; brokering white space or writing copy was no more American than brokering stocks or writing cheques. If the Americans had pioneered most of the new ideas in advertising, it could be explained with reference to their dynamic marketplace. The image of frontier capitalism, unbound by tradition or state interference, seemed sufficient to explain why Americans consistently pushed the boundaries of commercial practice. Indeed, this point, with reference to advertising, was conceded not just by English Canadians, but by French Canadians and Europeans as well.[29]

National styles existed, but contemporaries believed that these were expressed in the creative content of advertising, not in its structures or practices. The choice of vocabulary, the tone of voice, the typeface, the style of illustration: all of these – insofar as they revealed particularities of local taste and regionally meaningful symbols – revealed national traits. Wit and erudition, it was thought, were the hallmarks of the British advertisement, just as the garish sales pitch written in hard-nosed 'bluff' was identifiably American. Canadians, ever conciliatory, placed themselves between these two imagined extremes; they strengthened their puffs with practical information, but avoided overtly forward language.[30]

Such stereotypes provided the intellectual foundation for a Canadian advertising trade separate from the American. After 1900 agencies on both sides of the border offered the same services and charged precisely the same rates under the commission system. An advertiser might wonder what value Canadian agencies offered if they simply mimicked the Americans. It would be far better to go to the source and hire one of the top agencies in the United States. In 1916 all of Canada's transcontinental railways were using the same agency for their American publicity: Vanderhoof, Condict, and Eckstrom, of Chicago.[31] From a business standpoint, this made perfect sense. From a cultural standpoint, the Canadian agencies objected most strenuously. American agencies simply did not possess the cultural literacy required to plan successful campaigns in Canada.

C. Truscott Solomon, president of the Toronto agency Advertising Service Company, summed up the prevailing views of agents in 1922. Solomon used the pages of *Marketing* to express his concerns regarding the use of American agencies by the Canadian branch plants of American advertisers. Notably, he quickly dismissed the most frequently cited complaint: the oversights made by American agencies in their creative work, what one adworker termed 'meaningless Yankeeisms.' For example, the use of American spellings, references to holidays that Canadians did not observe, and the prominent display of eagles, stars, and presidents made for frequent smug asides in the trade press.[32] Solomon believed such things were unimportant, mistakes and nothing more. They were merely symptoms of deeper problems that afflicted the use of 'long distance advertising counsel.' Solomon concentrated his attention on two key areas: geographic proximity and cultural sensitivity. First, any client's use of a remote agency was lamentable, particularly when close cooperation or rapid response times were required. Agencies that worked hard for their clients went to their clients, and the most ambitious opened branch offices nearby. Proximity, regardless of nationality, simply meant better service.[33]

Second, cultural sensitivity addressed the success of the client's campaigns. Here, nationality was a decided factor. Solomon charged that American agencies knew little about the subtleties of the Canadian market, things such as the socio-economic make-up of the provinces, their chief industries, and their means of product distribution. *Printer and Publisher* noted that even the vaunted Ayer directory got its facts wrong when listing Canadian periodicals.[34] Such ignorance undermined the most basic agency function: the rational selection of periodicals for campaigns. Similar ignorance was displayed in the creative department. Solomon criticized American companies for using their own copy without revision in Canada. While this might have been cost efficient, it was also misdirected if it failed to account for local differences. It was here that domestic agencies shined, since they were readily familiar with local customs and parlance. An agency 'focused on the Dominion,' as *Economic Advertising* put it, or 'on the ground,' as Solomon's own advertising explained, had an affinity with the markets that advertisers wanted to reach. By dint of birth, education, and loyalties, the Canadian adworker possessed not just the right tools, but something else that could not be acquired: an intuitive feel for the broad cultural matrix of the advertiser's market.[35]

This intuitive feel was most evident in Canadian creative staff. Artists themselves were quite familiar with the competitive pressures of American culture. Well before 1900 writers such as Archibald Lampman and D.C. Scott had argued that Canadians needed to patronize domestic talent if they wished to cultivate a national identity; it was the artist who saw the nation's true spirit and who captured this in tangible form.[36] This line of thinking was easily bent to the adworkers' own purposes. Who better could translate the country's passions and icons into meaningful sales material? The question was answered in typical fashion by an ad for the Toronto print firm Rous and Mann: 'Business has put the artist on its payroll in the last few years, and found that he is a very profitable member of the staff ... His magic touch makes advertising interesting, alluring, profitable ... [Artists] can make your advertisements and printed matter hum with life and selling force.' The advertising manager of Ford of Canada made the connection to Canadian artists explicit: 'It seems obvious that the man best suited to appeal to the Canadian is the Canadian, the man who has born in him this essential qualification: familiarity with Canadian conditions and Canadian characteristics.'[37]

Such sentiments received wide circulation after 1920 thanks to the publicity surrounding the Group of Seven. The Group claimed to have found an artistic style in keeping with the raw, 'new' spirit of the country. While they were keen to have their formal art recognized, they were just as keen to have this style adopted in Canadian commercial art and industrial design. Not coincidentally, six of the original seven painters who formed the Group had developed their craft at Toronto print shops producing commercial art, and all were of the same social background as the typical adworker drawn above.[38] Certainly, the Group's manifesto espoused the same nationalist spirit as the Toronto adworkers. Bertram Brooker – who was intimate with the Group and exhibited with them – ensured that articles on the Group and art in general appeared regularly in the trade paper *Marketing* after 1925. He also had the paper's masthead redesigned by one of its members, Frank Johnston. With the Group's success at an international exhibition that year, advertisers became suddenly boastful in their use of Canadian artists. Prestigious national advertisers such as Eaton's, Birks, and the Canadian National Railways proudly acknowledged that they had supported the young, new artists with their ad appropriations. The Canadian Pacific Railway, which had long used the rugged landscape to sell Canada as a tourist destination, rightfully claimed credit as a pioneer in this regard.[39]

While Canadian agencies relied on proximity and cultural literacy to defend their turf, both arguments were severely tested when American agencies opened branches in Canada. Each American agency tended to staff its new office with adworkers poached from top Canadian agencies and periodicals. The result was an agency with an American brand name staffed by Canadian salesmanship and creative talent. One of the first to arrive was Horne-Baker Advertising, a Kansas agency that opened a branch office in Winnipeg in 1911. Its manager, Charles O. Smith, was recruited from McConnell and Fergusson, a pioneering Ontario agency. Perhaps to signal his importance to the firm, perhaps to give it Canadian credibility, the new office was called Horne-Baker-Smith Advertising.[40]

Eleven other American agencies arrived in Canada by 1930.[41] Nine of these had significant Canadian participation. The other two had conspicuously short lives. Canadian talent was retained in two ways. An agency could simply hire Canadians to staff a branch office, as did Horne-Baker, or it could 'affiliate' with an existing Canadian agency. As an affiliate, the Canadian agency would service the American agency's clients in Canada, but otherwise maintain its own name, books, and roster of Canadian accounts. Such arrangements were mutually satisfactory. Most American agencies did not pursue foreign-based accounts. They simply serviced the foreign branch plants of their American clients. Of course, these plants represented a sizeable portion of Canadian consumer-goods manufacturing. Affiliation mitigated the ill effects of this competition for the Canadian agencies, since it channelled branch plant contracts through them and kept these appropriations in the country. Six American agencies pursued affiliations in the 1920s; they were arranged through direct acquisitions, mergers, and cooperative agreements. Canadians were not always junior partners in these deals. William A.H. Findlay became a vice-president of Lord and Thomas and Logan when he sold out to the Chicago agency in 1930.[42]

This trend within Canadian operations apparently limited the number of Americans who entered the Canadian trade. According to the 1931 census – when ten of Toronto's thirty-six full-service agencies were American branch offices or had American affiliations – only 7 per cent of Canadian adworkers were American by birth, and even less had retained their American citizenship. Among those who had retained their citizenship, none were employers according to census definitions, and the vast majority were wage earners in the agency hierarchy. By comparison, 24 per cent of Canadian adworkers had been born in the United Kingdom, at a time when only one Toronto agency had an affiliation with a British firm. Once again, however, none who retained their original citizenship held positions above 'wage earner.'[43]

The American agencies' willingness to accept Canadian participation in their operations might have indicated their sensitivity towards the criticisms of agents such as Solomon. A representative of H.K. McCann, a New York agency with an office in Toronto, published an article very much in keeping with Solomon's own. In it, L.J. Cunniff addressed the issue of proximity when he stated that 'I do not believe that anyone can live in Milwaukee or Chicago, never visit Canada, and at the same time be able to make the right kind of a list of publications or prepare the right kind of advertisements for use in Canada. No one can get his share of the business from Canada and treat us like poor relations.'[44] His implication was clear: McCann Toronto was not an American agency like the others, but one sensitive to Canadian conditions. In a similar vein, Detroit-based Campbell-Ewald boasted that its Toronto office was 'a Canadian organization – incorporated in Canada – staffed by Canadians – possessing an intimate knowledge of Canadian needs and conditions.'[45]

J. Walter Thompson Incorporated merits special comment, since it entered on two separate occasions and did compete for Canadian-based accounts. Its first entry was conspicuous, but brief. Along with Horne-Baker, it was one of the first American agencies to establish an office in Canada. This was encouraged by Frank G. Smith, a Canadian who sat on its board of directors. In 1911 Thompson himself proudly opened the doors of a Toronto office managed and staffed with experienced Canadian adworkers. It immediately achieved a high profile. Still, when Thompson retired five years later, the new owners quickly dispensed with JWT's foreign business. They decided to re-enter Canada in 1929. Then as before, the new office was staffed with Canadians. Also common to both entries, JWT New York instructed JWT Canada to recruit new accounts from Canadian firms. In this sense, JWT Canada radically altered the nature of the competition between Canadian and American agencies. More will be said about this in chapter 6.[46]

Seven Careers

The lives of seven Canadian ad executives may give some weight to the general sketches drawn above. Although these seven cannot speak on behalf of the entire trade, they were among the most prominent adworkers of their day. Further, they represented every sector of the trade: John E. Kennedy was best known as a corporate advertising manager, J.E. McConnell as an agent, and J.B. Maclean as a publisher. W.A. Lydiatt was active in institutional politics and published a trade journal, while J.P. McConnell, John C. Kirkwood, and Bertram Brooker did what many of their peers did: they moved from job to job, and firm to firm, throughout their lives.

One of the most renowned advertising managers to emerge from Canada was John E. Kennedy. Born in 1864, Kennedy claimed to have served with the North-West Mounted Police as a young man. Certainly, his character seemed to fit the classic image of the Mountie; beyond his broad handlebar moustache, he was a towering figure, physically imposing and intellectually formidable.[47] About 1892 Kennedy entered the advertising trade as a copywriter for the Hudson's Bay Company. He was fascinated by the work and was soon writing letters to *Printer's Ink* debating the finer points of copy style. He gravitated to Montreal in 1895, where he landed at A.E. Small and Company. Small was a clothing manufacturer, and Kennedy was asked to market its ready-to-wear clothing. The campaign he created was a sensation and became legendary in the advertising trade. He then repeated his success with the Slater Shoe Company. In one short year Kennedy had conquered the largest city in Canada. He then turned his eyes south. With companies such as Lydia Pinkham's and Post Cereals, he became one of the highest paid copywriters in the United States, reputedly earning $16,000 in 1904. Booklets outlining his copy style sold in the thousands.[48]

The extent of Kennedy's education is not known. It seems readily apparent, however, that his knowledge of advertising came through on-the-job training, and perhaps his reading of trade journals. In 1910 Kennedy attempted to improve this process for future adworkers when he proposed the establishment of a research institute devoted to advertising. He had in mind an independent body that would operate for the betterment of the trade as a whole. What was needed were comprehensive facts and statistics generated in the preparation and conduct of actual campaigns. By isolating winning strategies and eliminating false assumptions, researchers could inductively construct a solid base of knowledge concerning advertising practice. While the plan was met with interest, it was not immediately taken up. No one was willing to invest the $1 million Kennedy thought was necessary, and few companies were willing to surrender their confidential records to an outside body.[49]

Kennedy, along with McKim and Desbarats, represented the high point of the Montreal advertising trade in the 1890s. At that time, Montreal papers such as the *Star* and *La Presse* were the acknowledged leaders in Canada, and publisher Hugh Graham would become a bona fide press baron. Indeed, one Toronto publisher moved to Montreal and made that city his base throughout the 1890s, despite the fact that he had no press there.[50] Nonetheless, the city's lead was overtaken in the early years of the new century. The torch was symbolically passed to Toronto when Kennedy's successors at Slater Shoe, J.P. 'Jack' McConnell and his brother James Edward, both established agencies in Toronto.

The McConnells grew up in Walkerton, Ontario. After graduation from the local collegiate around 1890, they both apprenticed at the town's weekly paper. Jack, the older of the two, trained as a reporter, and with a promising portfolio under his arm he drifted into Montreal. There he met Kennedy and learned the art of copywriting while they worked together on the A.E. Small and Slater accounts. When Kennedy left for greener pastures, Jack took over as Slater's advertising manager in 1896, at age twenty-two. He then invited his brother J.E. – who had apprenticed as a typesetter – to assist him. Slater's success continued, and the McConnells earned a reputation as top-notch advertising specialists in their own right. *Printer and Publisher* believed that Jack's work represented the best copy in Canada. Offers came from many directions, including the United States, but the McConnells consciously chose to remain in Canada. In 1897 J.E. became the advertising manager of McClary Manufacturing in London, Ontario. Three years later Jack opened his own office as a freelance copywriter in Toronto.[51]

J.E. channelled his experience with Slater and McClary into an agency of his own in 1903. McConnell and Fergusson Limited was a partnership of himself and Malcolm M. Fergusson. Fergusson's career had followed a path similar to McConnell's own. Born in Tillsonburg,

Ontario, he initially worked as a lithographer before training in accountancy. He was twenty-three when he entered advertising as an account executive. Together, McConnell and Fergusson started with clients culled from western Ontario, such as Ford of Canada in Windsor, Penman's in Paris, and O-Pee-Chee Gum, Silverwoods Dairy, London Life Assurance, and McCormack Manufacturing in London itself. They then assembled a list of some eighty national advertisers from across the country. To service these firms, they opened branch offices in Winnipeg in 1907, Toronto in 1910, Montreal in 1917, and Vancouver in 1921. While most of the offices were managed by employees, Fergusson himself took control of the Toronto office, signalling its importance to the agency's national stature. In 1919 the Dun credit agency rated the agency's assets there at $75,000 to $125,000, the highest among Toronto agencies.[52]

From the outset, the service they offered included both copy and art. With their combined experience in copywriting, composition, and lithography, McConnell and Fergusson themselves could offer knowledgeable advice on several aspects of creative work. However, they also possessed a staff composed of talented copywriters, among whom were aspiring writers such as W.G. Colgate and J.E. MacDougall. They also contracted artists on par with Franklin Carmichael to do their illustrations. These policies made the firm a pioneer in full-service work alongside Gibbons in Toronto, and the new agency was held in high regard by agents and publishers alike. Inevitably, some of its employees broke away to found their own agencies. The most prominent was James Fisher, who set up shop in Toronto in 1919.[53]

Jack McConnell eventually joined his brother's agency in 1917. When he started as a freelance copywriter in Toronto in 1900, he could not have foreseen the changes that would follow the opening of J.J. Gibbons's full-service agency. Still, his agency too was lionized in the press as a great advance, since it also resembled the American full-service model. Jack's idea, however, was to offer complete copy and art service without media-buying. To do so he teamed up with three commercial artists who specialized in newspaper illustration. Jack's reputation as a copywriter was well known, but he could not match Gibbons's wider repertoire of client services. Nor did he serve an isolated market like his brother. Rather than compete, he and his partners joined Gibbons in 1902. It was a short but fruitful relationship that firmly entrenched the agency; in six months, McConnell created celebrated campaigns for Tillson's Oats and Christie, Brown Biscuits.

Thereafter, it was fifteen years before he returned to agency work, with McConnell and Fergusson. When he died in 1926, the lustre of his early days at Kennedy's side was still as bright as ever.[54]

Like Kennedy, the McConnells sought to elevate the trade by raising the standards of its practitioners. Jack's contributions came through his pioneering efforts to bring increased planning to the preparation of campaigns. From Slater to his own office to the Gibbons agency, he consistently argued against the haphazard practices that hampered the growth of effective advertising. In this regard, he used the trade press advantageously to publicize his views.[55] J.E. pursued the same goals, but his reforming spirit found an outlet in a variety of trade associations that brought together advertisers, publishers, and agencies. In particular, he was a charter member of the agents' trade association and remained an active member throughout his career. By the late 1920s his agency was also among the first to hire graduates from university commerce programs.[56]

Unquestionably, John Bayne Maclean was the most successful magazine publisher of his day. While not an adworker in the strict sense of the word, the company he created served as a progressive and modernizing force within the Toronto trade. Maclean was born in the small Ontario town of Puslinch in 1862. His father was a Presbyterian minister, a Scottish emigrant who had landed in Canada just six years prior. It was an association the son would cherish. Three times during his life he changed the spelling of his surname to achieve a more 'authentic' Scottish style – moving from MacLean to McLean to MacLean to Maclean. Although he settled on the last version by 1920, his company and its leading magazine were both incorporated while the spelling was 'MacLean.'[57]

His publishing career began in 1882. That year, he started work at the Toronto *Mail* and learned the newspaper business under T.W. Dyas. After five years there, he and Dyas combined to establish a journal serving the grocery trade. The venture endured, and Maclean gradually acquired sole control. Around it he built the MacLean Publishing Company, which possessed nine other trade papers by 1908. Among these was *Printer and Publisher*, a monthly journal serving those who owned and operated the press of Canada.[58] Maclean began the paper in 1892 at the suggestion of the Canadian Press Association. Its pages documented changing trends in Canadian publishing and kept readers abreast of new developments in the United States. Most importantly, it provided a forum for progressive ideas in publishing, and especially

encouraged contributions from those who worked in advertising.
Along with special columns for printers, typesetters, and publishers,
the journal regularly had a column of news and gossip for adworkers.

Maclean was exceptionally open to the practices of American publishing houses. Indeed, he was a member of an exclusive advertising
cabal in New York, the Sphinx Club, whose members included Cyrus
Curtis, Frank Munsey, S.S. McClure, George Rowell, H.J. Heinz, and
C.W. Post. Munsey in particular became a lifelong friend; for a time
they competed for the affections of the same woman. Munsey frequently counselled Maclean on business matters, and his name
appeared regularly in the pages of *Printer and Publisher* as an authority
on press matters. In return, Maclean provided Munsey with valuable
insights into British politics and imperial foreign policy.[59]

Maclean's connections with American publishers paid dividends for
his staff. Like his mentor Dyas, he developed an extensive advertising
department within his own company. Each paper had a business manager responsible for its revenues from subscriptions and advertising.
Then, a host of salesmen scoured the country for advertising contracts.
By 1905 this sales staff numbered twenty-six. To encourage them,
Maclean granted a commission of 10 per cent on new business. He also
held annual 'conferences' that brought them all to Toronto for pep
talks given by himself and select American speakers.[60] About this
same time, he also developed a pool of talent that was responsible for
creative service. In effect, Maclean created an in-house, full-service
agency, drawing upon the successful practices of both Dyas and his
American counterparts. Its early alumni included W.G. Colgate and
Don Tuck, both of whom became prominent in agency and institutional work. But the first of their number were W.A. Lydiatt and John
C. Kirkwood.

William A. Lydiatt's contribution to Canadian advertising was uni-
versally acknowledged by his peers. He got his feet wet early, editing
an earnest little newsletter called *Boy's Own Philatelist* from his parents'
Toronto home in 1897. His career in advertising proper began when he
landed at *Printer's Ink* in New York around 1901. At that point, the
trade paper was still published by the pioneering agent George Rowell. Lydiatt made the most of his short time there, working as a salesman and copywriter for the paper and contributing to Rowell's annual
newspaper directory. He then returned to Canada and joined J.B.
Maclean. Maclean believed Lydiatt's copywriting skills were exceptional and accordingly made him the company's first 'Advertising Spe-

cialist,' a full-time copywriter. He kept this title until 1903, when he left to open his own shop. He closed this when he was recruited by another New York ad agency. Lydiatt never planned to settle in the United States. Rather, he looked upon these trips as valuable training for a future career in Toronto.[61]

After his return in 1911 Lydiatt reopened his shop, established his own newspaper directory, and bought an existing trade journal serving Canadian adworkers. Each of these could have been inspired by Rowell, and he admitted as much with regards to the journal.[62] However, Lydiatt was also driven by a desire to elevate the trade on all fronts. Through his agency he offered new types of service geared to advertisers rather than publishers; through his directory he offered new types of information on markets in Canada; and through the trade journal, *Marketing*, Lydiatt hoped to propagate new ideas in advertising practice. In his own words, he believed that 'there ought to be a co-operative effort to educate some firms to the value of advertising. There ought to be a sustained co-operative effort to awaken an interest in the selling opportunities of the Canadian market.'[63] He lived by what he said. He was a charter member of the Toronto Ad Club, and the first secretary of the Association of Canadian Advertisers – a trade association representing corporate advertising managers – in 1916.

The career of John C. Kirkwood repeatedly crossed Lydiatt's, but his legacy was far more fleeting. Although he contributed to the same trade papers and club movements, he never found a secure position within the trade itself. The reason for this could be traced to his restless search for both respectability and wealth while obstinately remaining in the advertising trade. As previously noted, Kirkwood joined the MacLean Company in 1903, and it was with Lydiatt's departure that he became Advertising Specialist. As demand for this service increased, he was promoted once again and became the first head of a full-fledged 'Department of Advertising Service' within the company. His pay was $20 per week.[64]

Still, Kirkwood's ambitions led him away from MacLean in 1905. By then, he had already lived in nine cities in Canada and the United States. Over the next twenty-five years he travelled between Canada and Great Britain four times more, to solicit for the London *Daily Mail*, to manage the first Toronto office of JWT, to write copy for the St James Advertising Agency in London, England, and to write for Lydiatt's *Marketing*. He regretted leaving MacLean soon after he left. 'Had I but stayed,' he noted in a speech in 1938, 'I too might have been a contributor to the glorious growth of the MacLean Publishing Company, amf [*sic*] might own a stately city mansion, a fine country home, a 100–acre farm in Muskoka, and be a member of the Granite Club, the Hunt Club, other clubs, and might have my name frequently in the news and society columns of Toronto's newspapers.'[65] Despite his own misgivings, Toronto adworkers celebrated his contributions to the trade with a luncheon on his seventieth birthday. It was hosted by J.B. Maclean.

The note struck here, and throughout Kirkwood's private writings, is constant regret. Each new job promised something better. More often than not, it was soon followed by disappointment and rationalization.[66] Contemplating the questionable reputations of certain Toronto businessmen, he wondered if his dream was even possible: 'I do not mean to argue that all unusual earnings and incomes come from ignoble occupations, or by departures from truth and honour, but I do mean to say that, in too many cases – perhaps the majority – unusual earnings and income are possible only at a cost of that which is best in man's nature.'[67] Ultimately, what maintained Kirkwood's sense of self was his Presbyterian faith in God and his sense of patriarchal duty. His wife rarely appeared in his private writings. How she felt about their constant travels can only be left to speculation.[68]

The life of Bertram Brooker was in many ways a fun-house mirror reflection of Kirkwood's. Kirkwood needed advertising; despite himself, he identified strongly with the trade and sought within its confines both status and wealth. By contrast, advertising was almost incidental to Brooker's world. He was, as he put it, 'not particularly proud of being an advertising man, nor especially ashamed of it.'[69] Brooker was a deeply philosophical man who tried to fashion a mystical conception of 'being,' *in toto*. To do so, he shifted restlessly between several media of expression in the popular and fine arts, and threw himself into choral singing, poetry, acting, playwriting, screenwriting, sculpture, painting, pen and ink drawing, and novel writing. He was no mere amateur, and he recorded two important firsts for the Canadian artistic scene: he was the first Canadian to exhibit abstract art in Toronto, and he won the first Governor General's Award for fiction for his novel *Think of the Earth* in 1937.[70] Advertising copy was simply the most lucrative medium of expression open to him. Like an actor playing a part, Brooker sometimes gave the impression that he was merely playing at being an advertising executive, even to the extent of adopting pseudonyms when writing for the trade press and having his alter egos debate among themselves. His son remembered him as someone who strictly separated his life at the office from his life at home. That said, it was a career in journalism and advertising that supplied his sole source of income.[71]

Brooker was born in England in 1888 and moved with his family to Portage La Prairie, Manitoba, when he was eight years old. As a youth, Brooker left school to pursue a rigid course of self-education based upon modern greats in literature, philosophy, and economics. He developed his writer's craft at a string of Manitoba papers, settling finally at the Winnipeg *Free Press* before the First World War. During this time, he also pondered the nature of the trade underlying the newspaper business. Intrigued, he drafted a handful of articles on the theory of advertising, which appeared in *Printer's Ink* and *Judicious Advertising* under the pseudonym 'Richard Surrey.' His ambition drove him to larger pastures, but a fondness for Canada led him to Toronto rather than Chicago or New York. There he continued to bounce between jobs, alternating between editorial and advertising positions at *Marketing* and the Toronto *Globe*. He also did freelance copy work in addition to his day jobs. By all accounts, he was a celebrated copywriter. However, Brooker's insatiable curiosity never allowed him to rest on his laurels. Brooker grappled with every innovation that arrived on the advertising scene. Many Canadian adworkers might have done the same, but Brooker went a step further and published his impressions in leading trade journals. He then drew together all of his articles on copywriting in a book published by McGraw-Hill in 1929, *Copy Technique in Advertising*. An expanding facility in the visual arts allowed him to add advertising illustration to his repertoire, and he published a volume on this in 1930. When the Depression started, he settled into a salaried position at J.J. Gibbons Limited. Coincidentally, this position had been declined by John C. Kirkwood in favour of an editorship at *Marketing*.[72]

There are many common themes that run throughout these careers. Again, it must be noted that these men cannot possibly represent the trade in all of its complexity. Their careers were documented by their contemporaries precisely because they were exceptional. However, their prominence within the trade and the respect they enjoyed reflected the fact that they represented its best aspirations and ideals. Their achievements in Canada and overseas became the achievements of the entire trade, as it yearned to gain national credibility and recognition. Three themes stand out. First, it is immediately apparent these men fit the demographic profile drawn above. Kennedy and Maclean were perhaps ten years older than the first generation of 'modern' adworkers in Canada, but their approach to the trade and their impact upon that generation made them kin with it. Second, American know-how looms large. The prior expansion of the advertising trade in the United States had created a large body of expertise. Kennedy, Maclean, and Lydiatt recognized this fact and exploited it for their own immediate gain. In the process, they sped the modernization of the advertising trade in Toronto; Kennedy's influence could be traced through the McConnells, while Maclean's ad department and Lydiatt's *Marketing* became popular training grounds for new adworkers. With the possible exception of Kirkwood, each man measured his success against American models. Kennedy was the only one of this group to seek his fortune in the United States, but he would not be the last Canadian to do so. Third, there is in all of their careers a search for social respectability. J.E. McConnell's institutional work and Kirkwood's soul-searching are exemplary here, but so too is Kennedy's desire to place the trade on a secure foundation through scientific research. Men such as Maclean, McConnell, and Lydiatt made heavy investments in their trade. They expected their dividends to be paid in social status as well as wealth.

Women Adworkers

The division of labour within the advertising trade intensified following Gibbons's arrival, and this development created a space for women to enter the field. It was a pattern familiar to many employers between 1900 and 1930. As large-scale corporate enterprises became more common, there was an increasing need for staff to handle routine administrative tasks.[73] As these white-collar positions became deskilled, young men avoided those jobs that offered little promise of future advancement. Women, however, proved willing to take them, and at greatly reduced rates of pay in comparison to their male counterparts. Within the advertising trade, the average woman's salary for Canada was 50 to 60 per cent less than the average man's. A standard entry salary for a woman in advertising was $19 per week in 1931; by contrast, men could expect at least $25.[74] By the late 1920s a select handful had parlayed these clerical positions into careers as full-fledged agents. They were the exceptions, however. Most remained members of agency support staff.

As previously noted, the female presence within the advertising

trade was characterized by young, unmarried women. In 1931 women
accounted for 20 per cent of the advertising workforce. Unlike their
male counterparts, most women did not advance through the corporate ranks into more lucrative posts. Judging by the statistics available,
they entered the trade as young women and left upon marriage. Of the
132 women across Canada in essential agency jobs, 93 were under age
thirty-five; 90 per cent of the entire population were unmarried. The
average salary for these women was $30 per week across Canada, and
those in Toronto could expect a bit more; the average there was $37.
There were 666 women in all agency occupations. Of these, 481 held
positions as clerks, stenographers, or running office equipment.[75]

Only one owned her own agency: Margaret Pennell. Pennell began
in the trade as many other women did, working in a media department. She took full advantage of her opportunity. Much of the work
conducted by a media department involved routine clerical chores that
required no decision-making authority.[76] Still, those who undertook it
gained invaluable training, since this information was integral to the
preparation of campaigns. Hired by J.J. Gibbons as a checker in 1904,
Pennell soon switched to data collection and earned recognition for her
insights into media-buying. By 1915 the editor of *Economic Advertising*
had acknowledged her expertise, and she became a frequent corre-
spondent on issues related to Canadian periodicals.[77] In 1927 Pennell
left Gibbons to establish her own agency, Margaret Pennell Advertising. Toronto at that point had thirty-one agencies competing for
national accounts. To position her agency within the field, Pennell
rooted her sales pitch in her gender. Her agency's slogan: 'Advertising
to Women by Women.' This tactic appears to have worked with several
manufacturers whose products traditionally appealed to female consumers. She picked up a dozen accounts within the textiles industry,
and her most noted client produced canned fruits, E.D. Smith and
Sons.[78]

After clerical work and media-buying, copywriting offered women
their next best chance at a career in advertising. As Pennell clearly
knew, their advantage was their gender itself. It was widely presumed
that most consumer goods were purchased by women. Commentators
in the trade press estimated that anywhere from 70 to 90 per cent of
household spending was done by a home-making female.[79] To reach
them through advertising, a 'female' tone of voice was considered best.
An American adworker confessed in *Economic Advertising* that 'there
are too many advertisements written by men and not enough adver-

tisements written by women. The woman knows where lies the human element of the thing that goes into the home, better than any man that lives. It has taken me a long time to admit that.'[80] It was a view the magazine's editor endorsed.[81] Department stores were a step ahead of the agents here. Having long employed female clerks in their departments catering to women, they valued the expertise they 'naturally' brought to selling. It was only logical to have women write the daily advertising puffs, and Eaton's first contemplated a woman copywriter in 1900. One such copywriter was Edith N. Macdonald, also known as 'The Scribe' in the Toronto press. Macdonald began with Eaton's around 1910, and for the next two decades she wrote copy, edited the company newsletter, and produced an anniversary volume on the store itself. One of her many trainees was Byrne Hope Sanders, who began a distinguished career in marketing with Eaton's in the 1910s.[82]

Agencies were slow to follow the retailers' lead. When the agencies first adopted creative departments, they did so to enhance their service to advertisers. Copywriting was sold as a form of technical knowledge best deployed by agents with sales experience as well as literary talent; women were thought to be unqualified. By 1922, however, the number of women working the field brought anxious commentary from W.A. Lydiatt in the pages of *Marketing*.[83] Among these women were Miriam Marshall, Laree R. Spray, and Margaret Ball. Marshall was hired by Toronto agent Thornton Purkis in 1920. When Purkis wanted the effervescent sparkle of a chatty young co-ed for a particular campaign, Marshall was hired upon graduation from the University of Toronto. She subsequently wrote two series of ads for Campagna's Italian Balm. On the west coast, Spray was a freelance journalist. Throughout the mid-1920s a sideline in copywriting proved so successful that she opened her own office in Vancouver. Ball was employed as a copy expert by the Toronto branch of McKim Limited; she also undertook sales and media-buying work. She left the agency when she married one of the firm's directors.[84]

Women adworkers played an active part in the Canadian Business and Professional Women's Club in Toronto, and contributed regularly to its magazine, *Business Woman*. The magazine appeared in 1926 and addressed the interests of women in every rank of white-collar employment, from filing clerks to surgeons. It frequently ran stories on women in advertising, a fact that may reflect two members of its editorial board: Margaret Pennell, and Mabel Stoakley, the secretary-treasurer of R.C. Smith and Son, Advertising Agency. Its first editor was Mary Etta MacPherson, who left to edit MacLean's *Canadian Homes and Gardens*; she was succeeded by Byrne Hope Sanders, who left to edit *Chatelaine*. Also among its contributors was Margaret Brown, then secretary-treasurer of *Marketing*.[85]

By the end of the decade, then, women had found a small but confident place within the advertising trade. Their mood seemed hopeful, and forty-one women adworkers met in April 1933 to create their own luncheon club in Toronto.[86] Pennell was its first chair. Prior to that meeting, writers in the trade press argued that 'The Advertising Agency has a Place for Women' and 'Woman's Day in Advertising is Just Dawning.' Estella M. Place noted the marked advances women had made, not just in agencies, but in periodicals and in corporate advertising departments as well. They were no longer restricted to clerical work, but handling every branch of the trade, including solicitation and management. Indeed, the 1931 census reported that there were nine women in Canada working on their own account in the advertising field. Even Lydiatt recanted for his earlier, alarmist attitude towards women's entry into the business. In 1927 he ran a highly laudatory article on American agency executive Minna Hall Crothers.[87]

Despite this rosy outlook, women still represented only 20 per cent of the workforce employed by agencies in 1931; 72 per cent of them were clerks and stenographers, and their average salary remained far below that of the men. It had taken them sixty years to get a foothold in the trade. Some have noted that it took another sixty years to get its respect.[88]

The key generation that dominated the agency scene from 1900 to 1930 was composed of salesmen and managers who had succeeded in turning a particular set of business skills into a business unto itself.[89] These skills revolved around two things: their understanding of the relationship between media and markets, and their ability to sell this expertise to companies who sought publicity for their products and services. It was the latter skill that built reputations within the industry. Given the necessary amount of time and money to conduct research, anyone could put together a list of newspapers. The reputations of men such as J.J. Gibbons and J.E. McConnell were built on their track records as salesmen and their fiscal responsibility, while copywriters such as J.P. McConnell and John C. Kirkwood tended to remain unsettled. It was the salesmen who sought out the companies with promising products, conceived the possibilities of marketing their wares, and talked these companies into spending thousands of dollars annually on newspapers' white space. For those who set up in the trade before 1914, advertising at its core was a business and not a site of cultural production.

The secondary role given to other tasks within the agency system was reinforced by two trends that emerged after 1910: the increasing division of labour, and the employment of women. First, the very fact that copy and art departments were still rarities in 1905 is significant. Copy was the voice of the ad, that part of the process which actually sold the product. Yet until then most agencies did not offer copy service. It was the domain of advertising specialists, either in publishing houses or freelancing. The agents considered freelancers an economic menace to the trade. When agencies did adopt this service, it did not displace the role of the salesmen within the agency itself. Copywriters were the hired help.

Second, the research done by the media department was considered simple enough that it was classified as routine clerical work. Men grew less inclined to enter this line, preferring one of the skilled jobs in sales, media-buying, or creative services. While this allowed women to enter the agency field, employers did not hire them out of any principle of equality. Rather, these jobs were considered the least skilled and therefore garnered less remuneration. The fact that women such as Margaret Pennell rose above this condescension speaks as much of her perseverance as it does of the broad-mindedness of her employers and clients.

These trends were closely interlinked with those in the United States. Toronto adworkers treated their American counterparts as both mentors and rivals. Through trade papers, employment, and personal contacts, Canadian adworkers constantly looked to the Americans for new ideas and confirmation of their own abilities. Proximity certainly played a role here, but there was another reason for the Canadians' enthusiasm for American publicity. It worked. The commercial culture of the United States appeared to be the most dynamic on earth, the most advanced in the art of advertising. Observing this, a long string of Canadian adworkers looked south to get their advertising education, from Dyas and Maclean to Gibbons and Lydiatt, and beyond. At the same time, they were inclined to distance themselves from American culture, and resisted the entry of American firms into Canada. Canadians insisted that their creative work was as good as anything produced in the United States, and they paraded their awards from American competitions to prove it.[90] Hence, while North America formed a continental market for many ideas, goods, and services, the border remained jealously guarded. For English-Canadian adworkers, British ancestry and political ties to the empire gave this frontier added meaning. This placed them firmly among Canadian men of the day.[91]

By the 1910s it was increasingly possible to view advertising as a lifelong career, if not a 'profession.' The development of full-service agencies was promising; it held out the faint promise of self-employment to adworkers. It also marked their increasing degree of influence in the business world. Account executives dealt with company presidents and handled advertising appropriations worth tens of thousands of dollars. By the 1920s they were also well paid for their services, and individual men gained entrance into the upper echelons of Canadian society.

These developments were in their early stages before the First World War, however. Modern agents were still saddled publicly with an unfavourable reputation created by their forebears in the nineteenth century. It would take the combined efforts of all three sectors of the trade to overcome that legacy. Even then, John C. Kirkwood's doubts were never quite erased. When his son entered university in 1921, he told him to see it through. Remembering his own short time at Queen's, he wrote, 'It has been a lament to me ever since that I went into my earning life a sort of advertiser, and that I have been an advertiser ever since. I want you to avoid my course. I would like to see you equipped by a university training for a different profession. If you have the base of a sound education, the future can take care of itself.'[92] The income and security that Kirkwood sought, he more or less found. The widespread social respectability he craved was more difficult to achieve.

Chapter 3

A Professional Ideal

Suppose we take the advertising man as we find him ... Does he, as I verily believe some rural publishers fancy of Brother McKim, wear horns?

F.H. Dobbin, 1895[1]

St Peter – You say that you were an advertising man while on earth?
Applicant – Yes.
St Peter – This elevator, please.
Applicant – How soon does it go up?
St Peter – It doesn't go up, it goes down.

Anonymous, 1924[2]

Traffic stopped. Crowds gathered five deep on the sidewalk and spilled out into the streets as the exuberant sound of the pipes grew nearer. It was April 1915, and a city at war ground to a halt as a 'monster pageant parade' wound its way through the streets of Toronto. Thirty floats and wagons, decorated to the nines with bunting and flowers, were led by the 48th Highlanders Pipe and Drum Regiment. Scattered throughout the procession, a patriotic corps of diligent Boy Scouts unfurled banners boosting the merits of the Queen City. An even greater spectacle could be found at the parade's end: a carnival of sights, sounds, and speechifying. A massive demonstration of acrobatic stunts was performed by five hundred YMCA boys dressed in colourful outfits, and they were joined by fifty clowns chasing mock elephants, ostriches, donkeys, and horses. Juggling and high-wire acts, flaming hoops, and chariot races completed the show. Musical accompaniment was provided by a massed band of a hundred pieces, the Highlanders joined by the 109th Regiment.

Behind the stage, the masterminds of this affair were members of the Toronto Ad Club, an organization of adworkers from various publications, advertisers, and agencies. The carnival was a patriotic affair intended to raise money for the war effort. It was also a decidedly commercial enterprise. Each of the floats was sponsored by a prominent local business, which got full value for its dollar from the publicity generated by the circus. An audience-participation contest offered a free pair of shoes to twenty lucky spectators, courtesy of Walkerton's Shoes. According to the Toronto *World*, this was the most exciting event of the night.[3]

In many ways, the carnival epitomized a number of trends that had emerged in the Canadian advertising trade over the previous fifteen years. At the dawn of the twentieth century it would have been difficult to identify a recognizable trade connected to advertising. Rather, there was a hodge-podge of business practices developing among a number of companies claiming expertise in the field. Toronto was home to twenty-three advertising agencies in 1900, but there were also newspaper publishers, magazines, print shops, freelance copywriters, and corporate advertising managers offering assistance to anyone who wished to enhance their use of publicity. By 1915 the number of advertising service companies had greatly increased, but the full-service agencies had assumed a leadership role in the trade. They owed their position in no small part to the Toronto Ad Club.

The club itself was a sign of the times. Certainly, it demonstrated that those who dealt in advertising were becoming a self-conscious group of workers with common interests and problems. Men and women were emerging from a wide variety of educational and career backgrounds to develop a new field of commercial expertise. It was a potentially lucrative field, but it was also susceptible to the fickle winds of public opinion. In particular, adworkers laboured under the cloak of a disreputable past woven by the reputations of circus men and patent medicine makers during the previous century. In a marketplace increasingly dominated by specialized labour and managerial expertise, this antipathy did not sit well with white-collar adworkers. Agents could only laugh ruefully at the mindset that condemned them to an eternity of hellfire and brimstone. The ad club was in part an attempt to deal with these problems through cooperation and by participating in worthy causes such as the war effort to elevate their col-

lective reputation in the public mind. The irony of fighting fire with
flaming hoops was not entirely lost on them.

The Toronto Ad Club

At the turn of the century there was a felt sense that disdain for advertising was widespread among the general public. Much of the problem
could be traced to the trade's own excesses: the competition for bill-
board space in cities and countryside alike, the relentless postering of
urban walls and streetcars, and the 'shrieking headlines, shrieking borders, shrieking exaggerations' of the advertising found in the periodical press.[4] In 1904 a movement began in the United States to correct
this problem, and Canadians signed on. In particular, the Toronto Ad
Club decided to boost advertising in the public mind through a series
of campaigns run from 1912 to 1914. Then, for one week before the out-
break of war, Toronto was at the centre of the advertising trade – not
just in Canada, but the world.

The public's disdain could be traced back to the previous century,
and to the practices exemplified by one man in particular: Phineas T.
Barnum. Barnum was an impresario of popular culture who established his career with showcases of hoaxes and freaks. In time he
adapted his talent to the promotion of opera singers and spectacles,
but it was his early exhibitions and his later work in circuses that stuck
in the public mind. Although he used print advertising liberally, he
was not a pioneer in the field; he did nothing to advance that art.
Rather, his expertise was widely diffused in the art of total publicity,
using every media and ploy possible to generate interest in his events.[5]
Historian Jackson Lears has suggested that the novelty of Barnum's
approach was his ability to translate existing commercial practices
onto a mass scale. Certainly, Barnum himself paid tribute to the guileless ways of the medicine men. This he revealed in a celebrated autobiography. Throughout the late 1800s it found a ready audience and sold
in the millions in North America and in Europe as well. *Saturday Night*
held Barnum to be the epitome of the successful publicist, while one
Toronto trade journal, *Economic Advertising*, agreed that Barnum was
recommended reading for anyone entering a career in advertising.
Even after 1940, economist Harold Innis consulted the autobiography
in his work on advertising and communications. Barnum's name was
an icon of successful publicity on both sides of the border.[6]

Whatever his educational merits, the moral quality of Barnum-as-icon became clouded after 1900, when progressive and social gospel idealism cast a shadow over his legacy. Consumers and businessmen grew dubious of the charlatanry of certain commercial practices then common, and in the advertising field these included the wilful trade in hokum pioneered by the patent medicine men. Barnum had identified with them, and the autobiography boastfully exposed his own hoaxes. By the 1920s Barnum's life was no longer an inspiration to the rising young man in advertising, but a cautionary tale, a relic of a past generation lacking in civilized business ethics.[7]

This sea-change in the attitude of adworkers was spurred by the work of two American magazines. In 1904 the *Ladies' Home Journal* commissioned a number of tests on well-known patent medicines. The results confirmed what was long suspected. Many were simply alcohol and water containing little of medicinal value. A select few contained morphine, cocaine, and opium. The magazine printed its results in a series of articles extended over a two-year period. In 1905 *Collier's* joined the crusade. If previously the public had indulged these manufacturers, they did so no longer. American legislators responded to public outrage with the Food and Drug Act of 1906. This legislation forced manufacturers to state the composition of each product clearly on its label. It also restricted the claims that could be made in the advertising of these products. In Canada, the Proprietary Medicines Act followed in 1908, inspired by the same wave of concern as it spilled over the border with the magazines and medicines themselves.[8]

Adworkers in all three sectors were exceptionally defensive in the wake of these events. Agents trying to build up respectable, permanent businesses did not appreciate lingering suspicions that dismissed them as snake-oil salesmen, even though adworkers such as Anson McKim, J.J. Gibbons, and F.-É. Fontaine actually handled clients in this line.[9] Nor did the manufacturers of non-medicinal products appreciate having their publicity associated with the questionable tactics of the circus promoters and medicine men. In the 1910s some insisted that their ads not even appear on the same page with them. Publishers, whose revenues had suddenly increased with the growth of national advertising, had good reason to pay them heed. They could not afford to fan any further public reaction against advertising.[10] Clearly there was an opportunity to cooperate on behalf of the trade as a whole.

The Toronto Ad Club provided a formal means to do so. A small group of Toronto adworkers met in March 1911 to propose an organization that would unite men – no women – from each sector of the local ad trade. A positive response led to a more formal meeting the following month. By May the club was an established fact with fifty members, and by November it boasted five times that. Among these were almost every noteworthy publisher, advertising manager, and agent on the local scene. *Economic Advertising* and *Printer and Publisher* gave it their enthusiastic support, as did the publishers of every Toronto daily.[11] Its first executive included John P. Patterson of Norris-Patterson Advertising Agency, and J.F. MacKay of the *Globe*. Its first president was the advertising manager of Ryrie Brothers Jewellers, and he had the counsel of his counterparts from Office Specialty Manufacturing Limited, Coca-Cola of Canada Limited, and the Dominion Express Company. According to *Economic Advertising*, the selection of an advertiser for president was deliberate. Pride of place in the club was given 'very properly' to the 'buyers of advertising' – a fascinating admission coming from a writer so closely connected to both an agency and a publication.[12] Other members included J.B. Maclean, J.J. Gibbons, W.A. Lydiatt, and John C. Kirkwood.

The club's purpose was laid out in its constitution. Briefly, members sought to achieve four main goals:

1. To develop the science and art of advertising.
2. To encourage the interchange of creative ideas in advertising.
3. To establish a realization of the greater importance of advertising.
4. To promote sociability among the advertising fraternity.[13]

One activity greatly advanced these goals: the institution of a weekly luncheon and lecture series at McConkey's Palm Room, a downtown Toronto taphouse. Here, business and pleasure frequently mixed as visiting speakers from the United States shared the stage with the club's favourite entertainer, Jules Brazil. Brazil, billed by *Economic Advertising* as the 'Toronto midget,' was adopted by the club to be its official 'mascot.' Despite this dubious honour, he was a respected pianist and bandleader and a professor of music at St Michael's College. Beyond the luncheons, the executive encouraged the formation of branches in other Ontario cities and put out a weekly newsletter to keep everyone in touch.[14]

Upon its creation, the club joined a movement already underway in the United States. The Associated Advertising Clubs of America (AACA) had formed in 1904 and was a federation of groups similar to the Toronto Ad Club. From the outset its chief concern had been the 'professional' standing of the trade's practitioners. One of its early presidents, the advertising manager of Coca-Cola Incorporated (USA), stated, 'We have no advertising universities, and only in a few instances are any of our colleges endeavouring to teach even the fundamentals of publicity. Therefore, the advertising clubs have been organized to meet this need of education; hence a good, effective advertising club in any city is an educational institution and a potent influence toward its commercial up-lift.'[15] This influence would be exercised in two key ways. First, individual clubs were expected to foster ethical practices within their own regions by recruiting new members and championing the merits of scrupulous business practices. Second, many clubs also offered night classes to train the next generation properly before they learned the bad habits of the previous generation. (The Toronto club did not, but the YMCA was already offering such classes taught by club members.) Then, once a year, they all gathered at a general convention to discuss matters of common import. The entire movement was rooted in a belief that cooperation and mutual education would elevate the trade as a whole.[16] Apart from these noble goals, the Associated Clubs had no specific program.

Everything changed in 1911 when the Associated Clubs became a fully national organization in the United States. For the first time it incorporated members from every region of the country. The annual convention, that year held in Boston, buzzed with two thousand excited delegates, including twenty from the newly founded Toronto Ad Club. They viewed their new-found solidarity as a sign that they were destined for some greater task than they had known. They were not disappointed. From the convention floor there arose a new cause that gave them a definite purpose and direction: 'Truth in Advertising.' Delegates resolved to reinvent the association as a new force in business ethics; they would throw the fraud and the fake from their midst and elevate their trade to a new level of respectability in the public mind. O.C. Pease, on staff at McKim Toronto, remembered the discussion of the seminal resolution as a 'riot of enthusiasm.' He explained: 'More than two thousand keen, virile men had gathered together for one purpose, to advertise advertising – and it could hardly be otherwise. Ribbons and buttons and banners, party calls, slogans, and songs proclaimed their vigorous allegiance to the cause. That the flood of enthusiasm which was created at that time has lasted up until the present may be judged by the never-ceasing war that has been carried on all over the continent against misrepresentative and fraudulent advertising.'[17] 'Truth in Advertising' became the delegates' new badge, and every session thereafter was dominated by its discussion.[18]

At its core, Truth in Advertising was a philosophical rationalization of the place of advertising in a capitalist economy. Advertising was not a subject discussed seriously by economists, who apparently shared the public's general disdain.[19] It fell to the practitioners themselves to explain what role their trade had within modern business. In essence, they argued that advertising was 'news,' information about products and services that allowed the consumer to make wise decisions in the marketplace based upon all the facts necessary. Such a theory rested heavily upon a classical understanding of economics, whether interpreted by Adam Smith or Alfred Marshall. In its simplest terms, as the quantity and quality of information reaching consumers was augmented, the better their purchasing decisions would be, and the better the economy would perform. 'True' advertising would lead to wiser consumers and by necessity more scrupulous business practices.[20] By the logic of the marketplace, the charlatan and the fake would be slowly weeded out.

Truth in Advertising found practical expression in two different forms: legislation and 'vigilance committees.' The food and drug laws passed before 1910 had regulated only the content and description of consumer perishables. They had done nothing to address the integrity of advertising in general. Inspired by the Boston convention, *Printer's Ink* sought to redress this omission and pushed for legal sanctions on fraudulent advertising. A model statute was drafted, and ad clubs were encouraged to lobby state legislatures for its adoption. By 1914 variations of the statute were enacted in fifteen states.[21]

In Canada, *Economic Advertising* endorsed the model statute in 1913, but it took concrete cases rather than principles to prompt the government into action. In 1912 and 1913, speculators exploited the boom in Prairie settlement by selling land at grossly inflated prices. One sales strategy relied heavily on newspaper advertising in eastern cities. Overly generous descriptions of the lots for sale took advantage of prospects who would not have had the means to verify them. When these schemes were exposed, western political and business leaders were greatly embarrassed and sought means to restore confidence in their municipalities. Ad clubs in Calgary and Edmonton approached an Alberta member of Parliament, R.B. Bennett, to carry the *Printer's Ink* statute to Ottawa. He agreed, received an attentive hearing from the Minister of Justice, and a bill was rapidly prepared.[22] The bill made it possible to prosecute 'every person who knowingly publishes ... any advertisement for either directly or indirectly promoting the sale or disposal of any real or personal movable or immovable property ... containing any false statement which is of a character likely to or is intended to enhance the price or value of such property.'[23] The bill passed with little comment and minor revisions, defended in the Commons by Bennett and the minister with equal fervour. *Economic Advertising* had 'nothing but praise' for the new legislation.[24]

The second manifestation of Truth in Advertising was the formation of vigilance committees. These were volunteer bodies set up by member clubs of the AACA, and they were intended to monitor local advertising. The Toronto Ad Club was no exception. It kept a watchful eye on the local papers, and advertisers were investigated if it thought action was necessary. Still, it could do little even when it did find evidence of fraud. Offending companies were simply asked to change their ways and threatened with public exposure. The false advertising bill leant the authority of the state to these efforts, but in the long run its contribution was questionable. Convictions were exceedingly rare over the next fifteen years. Prosecutors found it difficult to prove intent – that an advertiser had 'knowingly published' a falsehood – and the law rapidly fell into disuse. In 1916 the Associated Clubs reorganized the vigilance committees into the Better Business Bureaus. The Toronto Vigilance Committee disbanded, and a new office on the bureau model was not instituted until 1928.[25]

This situation may explain why the Advertising Bureau of the Vancouver Board of Trade knew nothing about the legislation in 1921. That year, the bureau was considering a municipal statute governing false advertising when it discovered the Dominion already had one. A committee led by Morgan Eastman then examined it and decided that the 'intent' clause had to be removed to make the law effective. A resolution was passed by the full Board of Trade; it was promptly endorsed by ad clubs in Montreal, Winnipeg, Hamilton, and London; and the whole bundle was sent off to Ottawa. The government acknowledged their concerns, but did nothing. As far as it was concerned, there was no public call for such an action.[26]

The last act of the Truth in Advertising movement was played out in Toronto the Good itself. In 1914 the city hosted the annual convention of the Associated Clubs. Soon after its formation, the Toronto Ad Club became intoxicated dreaming of the potential benefits the event would bring. For a group seeking greater recognition from the Canadian corporate elite, nothing could better demonstrate their resourcefulness than successfully fêting two thousand American businessmen. For a group seeking to elevate their profile among the general public, nothing could better demonstrate the scope of their vision and abilities. The first step was to win the Associated Clubs' approval, and they threw themselves into the task. First, they convinced all of the other ad clubs in Canada to back their cause. Then, with a bankroll of $17,000, fifty-four men descended on the 1912 convention in Dallas, Texas. To set themselves apart from the Americans, the entire contingent adopted a Scottish theme: they all wore kilts and sporrans to the general meetings and formal events. To heighten the effect, they were heralded by a rousing set of marches courtesy of two pipers and a drummer from the 48th Highlanders directed by Jules Brazil. While there, the diminutive Brazil struck up a friendship with a 'giant' from Dallas, and the two performed acrobatic stunts together, much to the delight of the crowd. It was a masterful display of publicity, worthy of Barnum himself, and it stunned their American hosts.[27] Following a repeat performance at the 1913 convention, the Toronto Ad Club handily won the nomination for 1914.

When the Associated Clubs arrived in Toronto in June 1914, it marked a significant intersection for Canadian adworkers: the apogee of the Truth in Advertising movement, and their elevation to a recognized place in the North American publishing industry. First, delegates hammered out a wide-ranging set of guidelines concerning the ethical behaviour of practitioners. The results provided some concrete statements that set practical guidelines in the pursuit of advertising 'Truth.' Second, Toronto adworkers were ecstatic simply to host the event. To them, it signalled their acceptance and integration into an international body of advertising practitioners. The highlight in this regard was the convention's decision to revise its name from the Associated Advertising Clubs of America to the Associated Advertising Clubs of the World to reflect the contributions of their Canadian members.[28]

Advertising Advertising

Organization, education, legislation, celebration. These things were worthy endeavours, yet they did little to address directly the core problem faced by adworkers: public antipathy. Ad clubs had fostered a sense of trade unity, night classes provided skills to specific individuals, and legislation threatened the fakers' craft. All of these, however, were matters internal to the trade itself. The Toronto Ad Club constantly fretted over how they might reach the general public, but it took the Canadian Press Association to arrive at an inspired solution. In retrospect, the solution was embarrassingly obvious. They would have to advertise advertising.

The campaign that resulted was a product of the combined efforts of the Press Association and the Toronto Ad Club. In the fall of 1911 a group of publishers within the Press Association wondered how they might encourage a greater use of their advertising columns. Until then, they had largely relied upon direct marketing – special representatives and advertising agents approached advertisers on an individual basis. Now they had a new idea. Nothing would better demonstrate the effectiveness of advertising than actually using advertising itself. With this in mind, the publishers approached agent members of the ad club for their cooperation. The agents readily agreed.[29]

The campaign was intended for the daily papers, so it was thought best to make the most of their market reach. Copy would address all readers in general rather than advertisers alone. That way, the ads would accomplish two things at the same time: they would educate readers in the function and purpose of advertising, and they would have the demonstrative value that the publishers originally had in mind. The major angle, then, became obvious. The campaign would address all of the reasons why advertising was valuable to consumers in their day-to-day lives. It would address its questionable reputation head-on, then shower the reader with a description of the benefits that modern advertising had made possible.[30]

The series was exceptionally self-conscious, both in its tone and its sensitivity towards a diffident public. Each ad was written in the same sober, dignified voice that conjured an almost reverential aura around the subject at hand. At times, the copy read like a sermon rather than a typical newspaper advertisement. This was probably intended. One of its goals was to overcome the lingering association in the public mind with circuses and patent medicine makers. The dignified tone was reinforced by the composition of the ads. The type was clean and modern, balanced and symmetrically laid out, and framed by an elegant border (although swastikas framing two of the ads jar the eye of a later reader). A generous use of white space was evident throughout the series, and no illustrations appeared.[31]

The memory of the past was tackled first. 'For centuries the principle of "Let the Buyer Beware" – "Caveat Emptor" – ruled the world of

Behold
an
Advertisement!

I CAME into being as the spoken language came: slowly, gradually, and to meet an urgent need. I have been worked for evil, but mostly I have worked for good. I can still be worked for evil, but each day it grows more difficult so to do.

I am at once a tool and a living force. If you use me wisely, I am a tool in your employ. If you misuse me, my double edge will injure or destroy you. If you do not use me, I am a force that works ever against your accomplishment of the aims and purposes that animate your business.

I speak a thousand tongues and have a million voices.

I am the ambassador of civilization, the handmaiden of science, and the father of invention.

I have peopled the prairie, and with my aid commerce has laid twin trails of gleaming steel in a gridiron across the continent and stretched a network of copper into the far corners of the globe.

I am the friend of humanity — for I have filled the commoner's life with a hundred comforts denied the king of yesterday.

I have brought clean food, healthful warmth, music, convenience, and comfort into a hundred million homes.

I laugh at tariffs and remake laws.

I have scaled the walls of the farmer's isolation and linked him to the world of outer interests.

I build great factories and people them with happy men and women who love the labor I create.

I have made merchant princes out of corner shopkeepers and piled the wealth of a Monte Cristo into the laps of those who know my power.

I am a bridge that cancels distance and brings the whole world to your doors, ready and eager to buy your wares.

I find new markets and gather the goods of the world into a handful of printed pages.

I fathered the ten-cent magazines and the penny paper.

I am either the friend or the foe to Competition — so he who finds me first is both lucky and wise.

Where it cost cents to hire me yesterday, it costs quarters to-day, and will cost dollars to-morrow. But whosoever uses me had best have sense; for I repay ignorance with loss and wisdom with the wealth of Croesus.

I spell service, economy, abundance, and opportunity; for I am the one and only universal alphabet.

I live in every spoken word and printed line — in every thought that moves man to action and every deed that displays character.

I am Advertising.

Advice regarding your advertising problems is available through any good advertising agency or the Secretary of the Canadian Press Association, Room 503, Lumsden Building, Toronto. Enquiry involves no obligation on your part—so write if interested.

The first advertisement in the 'Advertising Advertising' campaign. Toronto *World*, 12 March 1912.

business.'[32] 'Barnum's "dog-faced boy" is said to have drawn $200.00 a week.'[33] No more. The haggling, trickery, and inflated prices that had characterized the marketplace 'until a decade or two ago' were receding before the bright white light of advertising. If once the merchant could set a different price for every customer that entered his store, now his prices were stated for everyone to see in the pages of the daily press. Advertising was the enemy of obfuscation, the essence of candour itself. Viewed in these terms, it was the merchant or manufacturer who failed to advertise that deserved the public's critical gaze. 'Be Suspicious,' one ad declared, '... of an article with no reputation, no backer, no guarantor.'[34]

One ad nodded to the uproar behind the food and drug laws. While the magazines had exposed the fraudulent practices of the patent medicine makers, Upton Sinclair had similarly revealed grotesque conditions within the meat-packing industry. Here again, advertising could play the valiant knight combatting the evil dragons of yesteryear:

> 'KEEP OUT!' used to hang as a sign on every factory door. The old idea of secrecy in business made it seem a crime to show outsiders processes, materials, and methods of manufacture.
>
> Now the white light of publicity is being let in by those who depend on public favour for business profits and business growth ...
>
> Today, many canning factories, packing houses, bakeshops, and public kitchens welcome visitors, concealing nothing.[35]

Advertising had assisted this process by describing the inner workings of modern businesses and production methods in terms that would reassure the reading public. In so doing, it had participated in the development of great enterprises because untold thousands of people now knew something about the firms with which they dealt: 'The public rewards with its favour and money those who tell it the truth.'[36] For the advertiser, an investment in advertising was not money lost, but capital earned through the confidence and goodwill of his customers.

In the day-to-day lives of readers, advertising represented nothing less than a boon to their entire standard of living. This could be illustrated in several ways. The simplest was through the sheer convenience that advertising provided to the consumer. In its purest form, advertising was information, 'news of merchandise,' that allowed consumers to familiarize themselves with new goods, compare prices between stores, and plan shopping trips that made efficient use of their time. 'Leisurely, in the comfort of your own home,' one ad stated, 'you can plan and decide upon the purchases in view.'[37]

The copywriters placed advertising at the forefront of the revolution in consumer goods. Everywhere one looked, there were new foods and convenience items that were only dreamed of a century before, things such as tinned fruits, breakfast cereals, electric lights, washing machines, vacuum cleaners, refrigerators, and gramophone players. 'Would you be willing to go back to the standards of living that prevailed in 1812?' one of the advertisements asked.[38] The answer was perfectly obvious: of course not. And, as another ad suggested, 'You Can Thank Advertising' for the changes.[39] Only its 'power' had made it possible for scientists and engineers to convey news of their inventions to thousands of people swiftly and economically. This allowed them to capitalize on their ideas and to bring new products into homes of even modest income. Without advertising, such men would languish in obscurity, and their beneficent creations would never have graced the world. 'Science, invention, commerce, are all indebted to its aid. It has raised the standard of living, elevated business ethics, and put us within reach of more real comforts, more real blessings, than we ever enjoyed before.'[40]

On the question of cost, here too advertising proved a boon. Advertising reached thousands of readers every day. If this readership could be translated into consumers, into demand for a product, then it logically followed that sales would increase. When that happened, the fixed costs of production would be shared among greater numbers of units and retail prices would subsequently drop. As such, advertising was not simply a guiding light in a storm of corrupt business practices, not just a convenience for the shopper and a friend to the inventor, but it actually represented an economic utility, a value-added service within the marketplace. When combined with the notions that supported the Truth in Advertising movement – that advertising should make the consumer purchasing decision more efficient – there formed a powerful argument for the existence of the trade within an open capitalist economy. This remained a standard weapon in the adworkers' arsenal whenever the integrity and purpose of their occupation was attacked.[41]

Underlying all of these arguments was an ambivalent conception of the extent of the adworker's influence over readers. On the one hand, the ideal reader was the ultimate authority on all matters related to the marketplace. Advertising could only sell a product once. After that, the consumer would know the product first-hand and either become a repeat customer or not: 'No advertising will offset the bad effect of a dissatisfied buyer.'[42] On the other hand, adworkers betrayed a tremendous self-confidence in their ability to make that first sale. Through careful planning, clever copy, attractive layout, and well-selected media, adworkers claimed an ability to generate interest in any product imaginable. If the product failed, it was the manufacturer's fault, not theirs. If the product succeeded, it could not have done so without the 'power' at their command. Like Adam Smith's deistic invisible hand, advertising was an intangible entity acting in the marketplace. It pointed the way for devout consumers, elevated the worthy businessman, and crushed the fraud and the fake.[43] Further, it was the adworkers who had unlocked the secret of this power, harnessed it, and kept it at their beck and call. Every ad in the series closed with a reminder that 'advice regarding your advertising problems is available through any good advertising agency.'

This reminder brings us back to the ultimate point of the exercise: the campaign itself was intended to increase the total volume of national advertising. By the end of the series a clear message was delivered to the country's retailers and manufacturers. Advertising was imperative for commercial success in the twentieth century. No business was sufficiently unique that it created its own demand. Readers had to be told what was for sale. Advertising was the most efficient means to do this. It was now a highly respectable trade and had a proven track record. The main thing to remember was to advertise constantly, in season or out, lest the competition get ahead. A product was never sold 'once and for all,' since there were always new consumers entering the market, be they maturing children, newly-weds, or recent immigrants.[44] In short, advertisers were counselled to advertise ceaselessly in the daily press.

The series was warmly received by everyone involved. Nine copywriters were selected from five Toronto agencies to produce the twenty ads. Among this group were W.A. Lydiatt (then at Gibbons), W.G. Colgate (Gagnier), Don Tuck (Norris-Patterson), John C. Kirkwood (JWT Toronto), and A.J. Denne (McKim Toronto).[45] The finished ads were offered to every publisher in the Canadian Press Association. The space would have to be donated by the participating papers, but agents had waived their fees for the copy, and the cost of the plates was covered by the association. In total, ninety-three dailies accepted, as did some four hundred weekly papers. According to contemporary accounts, the campaign went some way to achieving their desired ends. The American counterpart to the Press Association, the American Newspaper Publishers Association, followed it closely and then initiated a similar campaign there, while dailies in Philadephia, Chicago, and St Louis ran the original ads. Over the next two years the Press Association and Toronto Ad Club designed and placed three more campaigns, each building on the first. The last ad ran in August 1914.[46]

A number of things came to an end that summer. After the convention of the Associated Clubs, the energies of the Toronto Ad Club began to dissipate. For three years much of its energies had gone into winning and planning the convention. Once it was over it seemed there were no projects of a similar scale to engage the imagination. The Dominion government had already passed the false advertising bill into law, the Canadian Press Association adopted a standard of advertising ethics in June, and in August a newly formed group of advertisers pledged themselves to the cause of Truth in Advertising. Then, as summer itself came to an end, Britain declared war on Germany, and Canada followed suit. The Toronto Ad Club effectively collapsed, and vigilance committees lost members and recruiting committees were formed.[47]

Service to the State

Despite their best efforts, there was still some room for doubt regarding public perception of the trade. At the end of the day, advertising advertising was still ... advertising. Adworkers were still engaged in a promotional scheme. They needed a way to demonstrate their sincerity that was not self-interested. This opportunity was provided by the First World War.

Unlike their counterparts in certain other occupations, adworkers never sought an overt act of the state to substantiate their claims to professional status. There were two ways in which this could have been done. Royal charters conferred a degree of prestige on an organization, while legislation empowered an identifiable core of practitioners to restrict entry into the field. Medicine and architecture embraced these strategies. By contrast, adworkers never lobbied any level of the Canadian state for similar privileges. The state was equally reticent in its approach to advertising. Beyond the Proprietary Medicines Act and the false advertising bill, the federal government did not intervene in the operations of the trade in any direct fashion. Provincial governments were similarly silent.

There were other ways to attain status. Agencies trumpeted their relationships with prestigious firms, and in their solicitations often made reference to brand-name clients.[48] By the same logic, the entire trade gained stature when noteworthy sectors of the economy began advertising on a national basis. One such 'acquisition' was the financial services sector. It was a signal moment when Canada's largest banks and insurance companies entrusted agencies with their publicity after 1908. Adworkers also tried to cultivate clients among the mainstream religious organizations.[49]

Given the relative prestige of the state, it was only a matter of time before agencies began chasing government contracts. Here, however, they ran into the brick wall of political tradition. Advertising was the essential *quid pro quo* of the relationship between the major parties and their newspaper allies. Media-buying was a perquisite of power, and government contracts went only to partisan papers. Further, government ads were official pronouncements and did not require the skills of a trained copywriter. Hence, the two main services provided by agencies were simply not required.[50] Prior to 1914 the government only once adopted a rigorous campaign strategy. At the turn of the century, the Ministry of the Interior used overseas advertising to encourage immigration. This was not a typical government arrangement, however, since all of the contracts went to foreign publishers.

Eventually, extraordinary circumstances compelled the government to rethink its advertising strategy. In the fall of 1914 apple growers faced a pressing dilemma: a bumper harvest, and the loss of traditional markets in Europe. At the same time, there was a mounting panic in the business community since many of its export markets were similarly closed. Bold measures were required. It was proposed that the entire apple crop be sold to Canadians, something that had never been done before. This would allow farmers to salvage the crop and demonstrate that new markets could be found during the war. The federal Minister of Trade and Commerce, Sir George Foster, was struck by the simple elegance of the plan and agreed to subsidize an ad campaign. J.J. Gibbons won the contract, the first government campaign ever given to a Canadian agency. Fourteen thousand dollars bought space in sixty papers for twelve ads. The ads offered a free booklet of apple recipes; there were sixty-two thousand responses. The campaign was heralded as an unqualified success, the dawning of a 'New Era in Advertising.'[51]

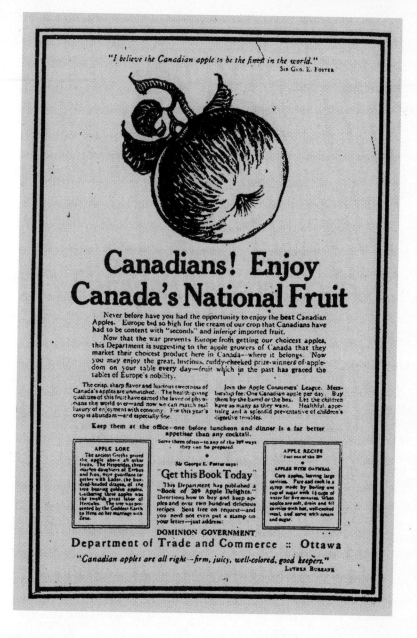

The first advertisement in the apple campaign. Toronto *Star*, 1 October 1914.

The idea for the campaign originated with John M. Imrie, manager of the Canadian Press Association. Imrie was a tireless proponent of modernization within the publishing industry, and he constantly goaded newspapermen to adopt more businesslike practices. A rational approach to government advertising free from partisanship fit well within this wider vision. If successful, it would create a significant new national advertiser. More importantly, it would also demonstrate that advertising had a positive social purpose, used not merely as a means of mass selling, but as a means of mass education. Imrie sought to achieve both ends, and he used the war as a pretext for his arguments. He also had the support of the association's executive.[52]

That Imrie succeeded in breaking tradition may have been due to the state of emergency, but there was room for change within the government itself. Before hostilities broke out, Sir Robert Borden's term as prime minister was marked by his desire to reform the administrative structure of the state. Key here was the removal of patronage considerations from permanent civil service appointments and lucrative contracts. The handling of government advertising appropriations should have closely fit this agenda. When important state information had to be disseminated as quickly as possible, it did not serve well to use partisan papers that were not widely read.[53] Imrie's approach must have found a readily sympathetic audience: 'Our practice in promoting Government advertising has been for me as Manager to present our case direct to the Minister at the head of the Department to be interested and to rest our case on its own merits. There has been no resort to lobbying or third party influence. We have studiously avoided everything of that nature and have encouraged the various Governments to consider the purchase of advertising space as they would any other commodity.'[54] The decision to launch the apple campaign occurred less than forty-eight hours after the meeting with Imrie and it hit the papers eight days later.

Thereafter, the federal government was converted. It launched twenty-nine separate campaigns over the next four years, and following its lead, the provinces began advertising as well. These campaigns, both federal and provincial, had a variety of purposes, but in essence they all exhorted the home population to greater sacrifices. Certain advertisements were aimed at farmers and industrial labour to increase their productivity, while others championed the importance of war bonds. Others again had the daunting task of explaining the Military Service Act to western farmers and French Quebec. Official proclamations continued unabated.[55]

Initially, the two types of advertising most commonly associated with the war – for recruiting and war bonds – were not part of this largesse. Until the passage of the Military Service Act in 1917, recruiting for the armed forces was a function of individual battalions and their civilian auxiliaries. The government baulked at direct financial assistance, and there was no attempt to coordinate efforts nationally. Even Foster, who had endorsed the apple campaign, wavered when it came to recruiting. Any advertising produced was arranged at the behest of local recruiting committees. It helped, then, if such committees had newspapermen and agents on board, as they did in Toronto and Hamilton.[56] Similarly, the private sector had long handled the sale of government bonds, and this arrangement continued during the war. The Minister of Finance, Sir Thomas White, was not keen on advertising agencies. Instead, he had the King's Printer prepare official notices for the press, while the bulk of the publicity was conducted by bond houses.[57]

Advertising agents did not benefit financially from the proliferation of government campaigns. The Press Association asserted that Imrie had solicited the government account, and as such the agencies deserved no commission on its contracts. Exceptions were granted only to campaigns requiring creative expertise.[58] The federal government apparently agreed. Following a meeting with Borden in 1916, the association recorded that 'the introduction of an advertising agency into the relations between the Dominion Government and the press was only a temporary policy adopted with the Apple Campaign because the Department interested felt that it had not at its immediate disposal the facilities for the adequate preparation and illustration of the necessary copy.'[59] Thereafter, the Press Association itself produced most of its campaigns until 1917. J.J. Gibbons lobbied the government relentlessly for further contracts and got nothing, despite offers to bill the government at cost, and despite sample ads produced at his own expense.[60]

Eventually, the agencies used their own trade association to lobby the Press Association for a share of the contracts. In September 1917 they finally got their wish when a joint committee of publishers and agents was struck to advise the government during the fourth and subsequent war bond campaigns, the 'Victory Loans.' Nonetheless, the Press Association controlled expenditures on this committee, and no one agency was entrusted with an entire campaign.[61]

At the end of the day, the trade as a whole gained from the experience of the war. The agents' participation in recruiting committees, government campaigns, and the Victory Loan advisory committee allowed them to demonstrate their expertise in a practical way while working as equals with government and business officials. Further, their contribution was seen to be public-spirited, since their services were often volunteered or provided at cost, something the publishers could not claim. Agents felt a change in the air. Don Tuck, a copywriter with Norris-Patterson Limited, looked at the early results of government campaigns and suggested: 'Here surely is ample vindication as never was known before, of the oft-repeated claim that good advertising backed by good goods or a good cause is able to accomplish little short of the miraculous.' *Printer and Publisher* agreed: 'Advertising, since the war broke out, has come into its own. Its functions and potency have received a recognition never previously accorded them by high-up men – statesmen and government leaders. Likewise, the people have learned much about advertising as a useful force in the economic distribution of news, appeals, and merchandise.'[62] It was an achievement viewed enviously by their American counterparts. *Printer's Ink* ran several articles on Canada's wartime advertising and admonished its countrymen to develop something similar.[63]

Looking back in 1939, two veterans of the Toronto trade remembered the war as a time when the 'cause of advertising' in Canada 'increased a hundredfold.'[64] Certainly, the wartime economy gave the agencies a volume of business sufficient to develop their craft and secure its foundations. Their service to the state drew them out of the wilderness of Canadian capitalism and into the halls of the establishment.

Canadian advertising came of age between 1900 and 1918. For the manufacturer or retailer seeking wider publicity, there were a host of firms in the marketplace offering 'expert' advice, from the freelance copywriters to the print shops and full-service agencies. Within the latter group, the range of services was itself expanding to include everything from the traditional core of media-buying and plate-making to the newest techniques in copywriting and illustration.

Out of this seeming confusion there emerged a core of agents – one generation – who led the efforts to reduce confusion and make the trade a respectable occupation. These men operated the full-service agencies. Earlier agents had operated on shoestring budgets. That was no longer the case. The new shops were developing more sophisticated business practices and advertising services, and the size of their staffs, plants, and credit grew in step. It was their shops that had the most to lose financially if they did not secure their position within the publishing industry. Publishers had run profitable papers long before the advent of national advertising, and advertisers had not yet been convinced that they needed to advertise to reach their customers. As such, it was the agents themselves who most felt the need to reform and standardize the practices of the previous century.

The Toronto Ad Club gave them a collective means to demonstrate their growing expertise and respectability. A trade consciousness was forming among the core group of agency staff – the account executives, media-buyers, and creative people. They could recognize each other and their mutual interests. If once the agency field had been characterized by hustlers such as the disingenuous Robert Moore, now there were the more corporately minded J.J. Gibbons and J.E. McConnell. The ad club allowed them to interact with their peers in publishing and industry on a weekly basis, without the complications of business interfering.

The Truth in Advertising movement, the Advertising Advertising campaign, and their varied war work allowed the agents to render this expertise and respectability concrete. Hand in hand with publishers and corporate advertising managers, the agents drafted codes of conduct that established the ideal behaviour expected from every sector of the trade, in their dealings with each other and with the public at large. Then, the agents articulated a view of the trade as a whole, and the role of advertising within the economy, through the Advertising Advertising campaign. Taken together, these two projects revealed that everyone in the trade was looking at their common occupation from a new perspective, as an integral part of modern business practices rather than as a secondary and occasional undertaking. Advertising was praiseworthy because it played a structurally important role in the functioning of a modern capitalist economy. For industry and the public alike, it could be portrayed as a progressive and enlightening force that made the world a better place to live. The war gave agents an opportunity to demonstrate their beliefs in the public sphere for all to see.

Whether or not the public's perception of their occupation actually improved during this period remains questionable. One year after the AACA convention, as the adworkers' energies were channelled into the war effort, they organized the patriotic parade and carnival to raise money for a Red Cross ambulance. It too was an impressive display of organization and publicity. Despite all of the good that could have come of this event, *Economic Advertising* believed the whole affair had been a little ill-advised: 'Considerable diversity of opinion has been expressed ... and not a few have had no hesitation in claiming that such displays tend to cheapen advertising and lower its dignity. We refer especially to the clown and circus stunts with which the recent entertainment abounded.'[65] Apparently, the public profile of the trade was much more fragile than it appeared. Within the publishing industry, too, there were continuing problems. Eliminating the fraud and the fake would take much more thought and effort than simply passing resolutions at annual conferences. It took fifteen years of negotiations and economic intimidation among all three sectors of the industry.

Chapter 4

The Industry Takes Shape, 1900–1921

The advertising agency is indeed a problem ...

A.R. Coffin, 1908[1]

In 1895 periodical publishing was the job of publishers. Publishers had their differences with Anson McKim and his rivals, but it was they who held the reins of power within the industry. By 1905 this situation was no longer as clear as it had once been. As the volume of advertising increased, so too did the number of agencies. Their appearance was conditioned by a felt need within the marketplace for middlemen connecting advertisers with publishers. By answering this need, however, the agents drew their income from a system that had previously functioned without them. With or without agents, advertisers and publishers would have done business. It became a constant feature of industry discussions to ask just what function the agent performed, and for whom.

Foreign advertising was the catalyst for these debates. Struggling with shrinking margins after 1900, publishers discovered that they had greatly underestimated the potential value of foreign advertising. This realization came hand in hand with a concern that the agents were exploiting the situation by demanding too much in the way of commission. The publishers dealt with these problems in two steps. First, the Canadian Press Association performed a cost analysis to determine a fair price for advertising space in their papers. Second, they examined the agency system to determine its value to the publishing industry.

In performing these tasks, the Press Association became a truly business-oriented organization. Until then, it had largely been a social club. The benefits of membership were defined by the annual summer excursion that was arranged with the cooperation of publicity conscious railways. In a newly focused association, these excursions fell by the wayside, and winter business meetings took their place. At first this change brought a decline in membership. Nonetheless, given the new vigour of the business meetings and the sweeping reforms that were proposed, the numbers lost were soon regained.[2]

The efforts of the Press Association did not go unheeded by the agents. Until 1905 they were a disparate group of businesses. Some had heavy capital expenditures tied up in personnel and plant, while others were composed of little more than a clever writer with a rented office. Some were underwritten by publishers, some by major manufacturing firms, and others by print shops. For those independent full-service agencies that had invested heavily in their trade, the challenges put forth by the Press Association were a serious concern, since it threatened everything they had built. Those with a degree of respect from the major papers formed the Canadian Association of Advertising Agencies to represent their concerns.

Ignored by the publisher-agency agreements, a select group of Canadian businesses that advertised nationally formed the Association of Canadian Advertisers in 1914. For them, the power of the press was in need of redress. First, advertisers had their own interest in the commission system, and resisted attempts to alter it. Second, while publishers had been dictating terms to the agents, an equally contentious issue – reader circulation – had been ignored. Advertisers and agencies wanted audited circulation figures. The papers consistently refused. Once the advertisers were organized, a conflict was not far behind.

While hammering out their positions, Canadian adworkers kept an eye on developments in the United States. Similar problems were met by similar responses, just as the Ad Club movement and Truth in Advertising had touched both countries. Nevertheless, while Canadians were quick to adopt American advertising practices, they were more independent when it came to industrial reform. Sometimes they took the lead. Canadians trade associations achieved a remarkable degree of internal solidarity during the 1910s, and used their high degree of centralization to craft solutions that benefited publishers, agencies, and advertisers.

This was the situation as the publishing industry entered the twentieth century. Three problems stood out. First, partisan pressmen had to bury their political differences long enough to cooperate for the good of their industry. Second, the function of the advertising agencies had to be defined. Third, publishers, advertisers, and agencies had to find some answers to the question of who would pay agencies. The settlement negotiated by their respective associations established the basic structure of the industry for decades to come. The answers also entrenched the fact that the publishers were no longer the independent editor-businessmen they had been in the previous century.

THE CANADIAN PRESS ASSOCIATION

Canadian publishers thought very highly of themselves. If you believed their own rhetoric, they were the primary moulders of the nation's opinion. Historian Paul Rutherford has argued that publishers in Ontario and Quebec developed a trade consciousness through the late 1800s.[3] In part, this meant shucking off the more obnoxious forms of partisanship that divided them. The process began in 1859, when a trade association was first proposed. The idea met with approval, and so was founded the Canadian Press Association. For its first twenty years, the association was little more than a social gathering for Ontario publishers, but it did lobby the government on paper tariffs and postal rates.

In May 1892 J.B. Maclean started *Printer and Publisher* to provide the kind of forum that the association did not: a regular exchange of information on publishing in Canada. Its pages observed changing trends in publishing and new developments in the United States. It provided a soapbox for reformers in the industry, and especially encouraged contributions from those who worked the business side. Given this perspective, *Printer and Publisher* was very well placed to document the changes that took place after 1900. Although it tended to side with publishers rather than advertising agents when disputes arose between the two groups, it was an exceptional journal of record, publishing verbatim (if selected) minutes of the meetings of the Press Association, as well as the full text of agreements and official statements made by the associations involved.[4]

A second journal started in 1908 that specifically addressed the advertising field. *Economic Advertising* was the brainchild of T. Johnson Stewart and T.J. Tobin. The two were joint proprietors of a new agency in Toronto and were keen to publicize it. Although the paper's opening editorial stated that it would provide a forum for the entire industry, its masthead pronounced that it was 'A MONTHLY MAGAZINE published in the interests of CANADIAN ADVERTISERS,' and its content was aimed primarily at advertisers and agencies.[5] Articles explored trends in copywriting, typeface, illustration, and layout, and favoured progressive ideas over the status quo. From time to time, writers looked at other periodicals in Canada to assess their readership and relative merit as advertising media. Still, Stewart and Tobin could not afford to alienate other publications, since these provided their primary source of advertising revenue. Canadian newspapers and magazines used the journal as a means to reach those who placed advertising. Taken altogether, the Press Association, *Printer and Publisher*, and *Economic Advertising* presented a relatively comprehensive picture of the Canadian advertising trade after 1900.

Losing Control of the Rate Card

The role of the advertising agency became a contentious issue after 1895. Until then, it received little consideration. Agents handled 'foreign' advertising, and few Canadian publishers pursued this business themselves. When Canadian agents began placing business for Canadian firms, however, relations between publishers and agents rapidly soured. Publishers wondered if this was an invasion of their own jurisdiction. To make matters worse, agents engaged in a broad assortment of questionable business practices as the competition among them intensified.

Publishers were greatly encouraged by the growth of advertising revenue after 1895, though a perception formed that they were not benefiting as fully as they might. There were two reasons for this. First, the agents had introduced themselves as middlemen, and in the process broke down the traditional links between publishers and advertisers. If an agency had sole control of a company's advertising budget, the agency decided which papers were used and which were not. In principle, agencies did not cultivate business relationships on the basis of personal or party affiliations.[6]

Second, agency commissions cut into publishers' profits. There were few agencies in Canada before 1895. An advertiser that placed its business direct – that is, without the benefit of an agency – paid full card rates for the space it used. When an agent was involved, an advertiser paid the same rate for the space, but the publisher remitted a percentage of the bill to the agent for the latter's commission. When the number of agencies increased after 1895, the amount of commission paid by publishers must have followed suit. Publishers had to face the fact that much of the new business from foreign advertising was subject to commission – that there would always be a disjuncture between the gross value of their pages and the net value that they earned.[7]

This became most pronounced after 1900 when agents closed contracts with established advertisers who had previously placed direct. Most notable was the Canadian Pacific Railway, whose advertisements had been placed direct for some time and whose publicity men were well known among newspapermen. When one agency courted the railway's favour, then, the publishers fell into a jealous rage. There was a whisper of infidelity in such transactions.[8]

Beyond profits and influence, there was a question of jurisdictional import here as well. Some publishers argued that Canadian agencies should not have cultivated any Canadian accounts. To do so obscured their original purpose. It was the role of each paper's advertising department to develop local accounts and the role of agents to develop supralocal accounts. Once the agencies began to solicit Canadian companies, it was only a matter of time before agents billed commission on advertising placed for companies situated in the same city as the paper itself. This was a particularly sore point with papers in Toronto, where many new manufacturers had located. Publishers there felt that stalwart Toronto firms such as Gooderham and Worts could hardly be considered 'foreign.'

Tied to this jurisdictional question was one of rates. Publishers charged foreign advertisers lower rates than local advertisers. This practice was rooted in the notion that foreign advertisers were not dependent on local papers to conduct their publicity. Inducements were expected to win their business. By comparison, local advertisers had to reach a specific, regionally defined market and had little leverage when contracting space with local papers. Agencies, since they specialized in foreign advertising, naturally expected to pay the lower rates no matter where their business originated. As a result, the cultivation of Canadian accounts by Canadian agencies represented a double loss to publishers. Not only would they have to pay commission, but their business would also be placed at lower rates.

The most controversial instance of this practice was the active solicitation of bank advertising, which began in 1907. In the past, individual branches had advertised at the discretion of local managers. Insofar as the initiative was taken locally, such ads were considered the same as those placed by any corner grocer. W.A. Craick, then editor of *Printer and Publisher*, insisted that this kind of advertising remain local. He suggested that even the agencies found it difficult to justify the change: 'It has been pointed out ... that those agencies, which are endeavouring to secure commissions on this class of business, do not demand the commission, but adopt the role of supplicants, pleading for something, which they evidently feel some doubt about their being entitled to. This being the case, it only needs some firmness on the part of the publishers to ensure them against being despoiled of their rights.'[9]

Agencies responded to the publishers' qualms over the local-foreign debate and the solicitation of existing advertisers on much the same grounds. In both cases, the advertiser's decision to hire an agency signalled its ambition to attain a national presence. Although the agencies had not, strictly speaking, developed them as advertisers, the agencies did make them more effective users of newspaper space. And as the agencies repeatedly pointed out, effective advertisers became repeat advertisers. Besides, no firm ignored new markets simply to maintain its status as a local advertiser with its home-town paper.

Anson McKim directly answered Craick's concerns over bank advertising. He did not dispute the fact that business placed by local managers was in fact local advertising. However, his agency was hired by one bank's head office to create a consistent and efficient advertising campaign that would blanket the entire country. The adoption of this service by the bank provided it with better advertising than it had previously had:

> Many local managers look upon local advertising as of little or no value except as a matter of patronage and are willing to put in almost anything to fill the space, leaving it to stand six months or a year without change ...
>
> But the head office of these banks ... have come to look upon advertising as an important factor in a bank's development along modern lines, and ... they want the advertisements written up, set up in type, and submitted to them so that they may know what the bank is saying in its many advertisements. They want to know that their own general plans are being carried out all along the line.[10]

As such, the business had 'naturally drifted' from the local managers to the national office, and by implication into the proper channels, the agents. This, in turn, had fostered a greater appreciation for advertising among·all financial executives, and therefore led to larger ad appropriations. Really, McKim insisted, everybody benefited.

One concrete example of this process was the publication of annual reports. It was customary for banks, trust companies, and insurance houses to issue annual statements in display advertisements. These ads were composed of detailed statistics, and until the turn of the century they were placed only in commercial papers such as the Toronto *Monetary Times* or the Montreal *Moniteur du Commerce*. Agencies had expanded this annual rite to include metropolitan dailies. By having the ads set and checked in plate form, the possibility of embarrassing misprints was eliminated, and the ads could be placed in any number of papers with complete confidence.[11] The Sun Life Assurance Company placed all of its advertising direct in financial papers and Protestant denominational organs until 1908. That year, the company broke its custom and added eleven metropolitan dailies to its list, all in Montreal and Toronto. The next year, the Desbarats Advertising Agency was hired to place the reports, and it recommended a list of dailies that covered the country. Between the financial papers and the dailies, Desbarats's list covered almost forty papers for a total cost of $427.50. The next year, the list of dailies was expanded again for a total cost of $865.11; by 1911 the list of fifty-five dailies alone cost $2,011.17.[12] Even though individual papers may have suffered a loss on the agency commission, the agencies had both expanded the list of papers that received financial advertising and the frequency with which it was placed.

Despite such tangible results, many publishers did not like the pattern that was emerging. Nor was the situation improved by the agencies' questionable business practices, especially their incessant haggling over prices and their tendency to rebate part of their commission to their clients. These practices could be traced to the same source: the intense competition among agencies for clients.[13]

These problems did not affect all papers to the same extent. High circulation papers in metropolitan areas delivered the readership that agents desired and also enjoyed the patronage of hundreds of local retailers and firms. They had leverage that papers in small towns and rural areas did not enjoy. With fewer local advertisers, low-circulation papers could be made or broken by foreign advertising.[14]

As there were few face-to-face meetings between big-city agents and small-town publishers, contract negotiations were conducted by mail. The exchange of correspondence between the two parties, dickering over rates, was often described as endless. J.J. Gibbons claimed that he exchanged fifteen to twenty letters with each publisher to determine his rates. One publisher incensed by McKim described him as 'a most voluminous writer. He writes more than any person since the man who wrote Deuteronomy.'[15] Agents began the process by sending a contract to the paper at a rate far below its stated card rates. A.R. Coffin, a job printer in Truro, Nova Scotia, described such exchanges: 'The agency will ... send out the $50 contract offering the newspaper $5. The cut rate newspaper reasons that it is too big a hoist up to $50, so $40 is quoted back. Next the agency comes up to $10. Then the newspaper says, "Give us $40." The contract passes back and forth several times more, with folios of correspondence until perhaps a rate of $25 is finally agreed on.'[16] Coffin believed this pattern repeated itself wherever agencies operated. More calculating agents included payment with the first contract sent. Some publishers in need of ready cash would accept a pittance rather than risk losing it in a long-drawn-out negotiation.

Another means of inducing lower rates was possible if there were two or more papers in the same market. The agent could start a bidding war. Each paper was asked to ratchet down its rates or surrender the contract to its competitor. Even then, it was not below an agent simply to lie to one publisher about the others' rates. Again, McKim was identified by Ottawa and London publishers as a particularly noxious influence. In this situation, only the active cooperation of the publishers could prevent their undoing.[17]

A third means of lowering rates was more underhanded. When papers drew up their cards, they offered lower rates on extended contracts. The longer the ad was placed, the lower the rates would be. Generally, contracts were divided into three categories: three months or less, three months to six, and six months to a year. It was not unknown for advertising agencies to sign on for a year's contract at long rates, only to withdraw after six months or fewer. When this happened, publishers insisted that the agencies pay at the short rate that applied, but the agencies insisted that they had a contract at long rates.[18]

A fourth method of lowering rates involved payment in kind with the goods advertised. The publisher would be offered a mere sample, and rarely a quantity of goods commensurate with the value of the space used. The shadiest form of in-kind payment came with stock promotions, when shares were offered in exchange for advertising space and perhaps some favourable publicity. Among the certificates for gadgets and gold mines that publishers saw, few would have paid off as handsomely as the stocks that George Brown reputedly refused in 1876. Alexander Graham Bell had to pay in cash like everyone else.[19]

Although these practices were associated with the agencies, some publishers conceded that they themselves were not blameless. When a publisher wanted an advertiser's business, more often than not he would discount his own rates to get it. A short-term loss could be justified if the paper won that client's long-term patronage, or if it prevented the advertiser from going to the competition. The minutes of the Press Association indicate that discounting was a common practice; one agent estimated that some 90 per cent of publishers in Canada did not maintain their cards.[20] In the retail trades, this practice was known as price-cutting; to H.J. Pettypiece of the Forest *Free Press*, it was simply 'deadhead advertising.' The description was apt. 'Deadhead' usually described subscribers who did not pay. The weak financial position created by such advertising not only threatened the offending paper, but also drew business away from papers operating on a rational basis. The strategy could easily backfire. Even if it attracted repeat business, the agent would expect the same rates on every subsequent contract.[21]

Anson McKim grew tired of the publishers' constant knocking. In 1897 he drafted a thoughtful if strongly worded letter to *Printer and Publisher* outlining his opinions on the 'agency problem.' McKim argued that the agent was a businessman like any other. He sought the best price he could get. When publishers stood by their cards, they did not have problems. When they did not, it was incumbent on the agents to seek a lower price.

I can never forget the lesson I had on this point two years ago, when I quoted a fair cash price to a cigar manufacturer for six inches in a list of about 150 papers for a year. He thought the figure too high, so took my list and sent out an offer to each paper of a box of domestic cigars for the six-inch space, on a good local page. Sixty-five papers accepted the offer, and so it is, there are about 200 papers in Canada that will accept almost anything – from cigars to mining stocks – for advertising space if it comes direct from the advertiser, yet when an offer comes from an agent at, say, half their rate payable in cash, they feel that they have been insulted.[22]

Thus, if there was fault to be assigned in the matter, it was the publishers and not the agencies who were to blame. Perhaps with a bit of mischief, he signed the letter 'your very obedient servant, A. McKim.'

Even with mutually satisfactory rates, relations were soured by other means. Most notably, agencies could be decidedly slow in their payments to publishers. This was less true of the major agencies such as McKim and Desbarats than it was of the smaller ones. McKim had one hundred clients by 1900 and maintained a healthy cash flow. Smaller agencies could become financially stretched between major billings. Anxious publishers found little recourse in advertisers; advertisers insisted that they were not responsible for the contracts signed between publishers and agencies. At the same time, some agencies claimed that they could not be held responsible for contracts with publishers if the advertisers defaulted on the agencies. Either way, publishers lost.[23]

Even after an agency accepted a publisher's rate, it was still possible to lower the final amount paid by its client: it could rebate part of its commission to the advertiser. It was widely known that agencies frequently rebated two-fifths of their commission fees. In effect, then, an agency sold the publisher's white space to the advertiser at a discount from the publisher's card rate. The size of the rebate might grow with the size of the contract. On a particularly large one placed for a department store in 1907, it was known that the agency in charge kept only the first 5.75 per cent of the 25 per cent commission. The remaining 19.25 per cent was handed to the client.[24]

Rebating was the agency equivalent of deadhead advertising. The agencies had several ways to justify it. As with the publishers, an agency might undercut its own rates to land a desirable client; a short-term loss was acceptable if it provided a long-term gain. Moreover, it should be remembered that all agencies were not created equal. Few had the staff and expenses of Gibbons and McKim. Smaller agencies and one-man operations could afford to surrender part of their commissions. Rebating allowed these agents to compete with established firms.

Rebating did not please publishers. If the advertiser did not know how the final bill was structured, then he did not know what the publisher's actual rates were and to what extent the agency had included a rebate. This protected the agency's own position in the marketplace. Rebating was a strategic practice; it was not effective if competitors knew each other's rates of commission. Nonetheless, the cumulative effect of discounting and rebating greatly depressed publishers' revenues from advertising. There appeared to be no connection between their printed cards and the actual rates paid by advertisers. Each advertiser that knew of better rates naturally demanded them.

Taken altogether, the publishers felt that they had lost control of a vital part of their business. While revenue from subscriptions and the great majority of local advertisers remained securely within their purview, foreign advertising had been appropriated by an aggressive group of middlemen who were, for all intents and purposes, new to the Canadian scene.[25] Agents created a barrier between the publishers and the largest advertisers in the country, seemingly diminished the revenue earned from foreign advertising, and sullied relations between the various sectors of the industry with their business practices.

Taking Control of the Rate Card

The Press Association decided to reclaim control of the industry in 1904. Its actions were spurred by two developments: first, there was a significant increase in the basic costs of producing a newspaper. From 1891 to 1904 the wholesale price index for wood, wood products, and paper had risen 25.7 per cent.[26] Second, the patience of the weekly publishers had come to an end. There was an increasing number of agencies in Toronto, and the competition among them was intense; it was during this time that agencies began to solicit advertisers who had previously placed direct.

Weekly publishers in the Press Association had complained about the agencies for years, but their meetings had generally ended in shrugs. No paper could afford to take unilateral action to correct publisher-agency relations since it was competition and mutual suspicion that had created the situation. Cooperative action was needed, but that course was more easily prescribed than followed. Members were reluctant to craft a mutually binding agreement through the association. Commiserating over mutual problems was one thing, but no one expected the association to tell its members how to run their businesses. Nevertheless, the apparent surge in advertising in 1902 and 1903, coupled with rising costs, galvanized the weekly publishers in February 1904. After years of discussions and articles in *Printer and Publisher*, J.F. MacKay of the Toronto *Globe* moved that a committee be struck to 'deal with all advertising matter, to draft rules for dealings between advertising agencies and newspapers, to suggest what are fair rates for various classes of papers, to ascertain when possible what agencies divide commissions, and deal with any other matter which the members of the association might wish to refer to them.'[27] The motion passed. The resolution was divided into two parts, separating the issue of card rates from that of agency relations.

The first issue provided a suitable test of their resolve, since card rates were a matter internal to the members of the association. The committee immediately began an investigation of members' rate cards, and assessed income against costs, taking into consideration a judicious margin of profit. It discovered that local advertising was set on a reasonably sound basis. Local advertising was still handled by the papers themselves, and publishers generally knew what rates their markets could bear. Since these rates were higher than foreign rates, and not subject to agency commission, this trade had not been seriously affected by recent trends.[28]

The same could not be said of foreign advertising. The last time the association had discussed rates seriously was in 1891. Then, a suggested minimum scale was adopted based upon the circulation of the paper, the frequency of the advertisement's insertion, and the length of the contract. Many things had changed in the interim. Inflation had taken its toll, as had agency commissions, discounting, and rebating. Many weekly publishers were accepting rates below the cost of production. As a result, the committee made two recommendations: that the minimum rate card be revised for weekly papers, and that rival publishers end the self-destructive competition that had led to their current situation.[29]

These recommendations were highly problematic. In 1891 the minimum rate card had offered publishers a guideline and nothing more. It was not intended to set an industry-wide price floor, and no one enforced it. Publishers remained free to set their own rates. In 1904 the situation was quite different. The revised card was a response to a common economic problem. However, it would only be effective if publishers cooperated and adopted the rates set out. They were reticent to do so – publishers cherished their independence. Of equal concern was the legality of a minimum rate established by a trade association. If publishers united to raise the price of their white space, they risked criminal charges under Canadian combine laws.[30]

To avoid the first problem – damaged pride – the committee made its consultations as inclusive as possible. The initial draft was created by 'leading publishers of weeklies' in the association. Then, several drafts were circulated among the membership before a model card was agreed upon in September 1904. Avoiding the second problem – the appearance of a combine – was more difficult. Members were simply informed that this was a recommended minimum that in no way restricted them from having different rates. The committee suggested that upward revisions would be helpful.[31]

The advertising agencies were sceptical of the utility of this one reform. On the face of it, agencies stood to gain a great deal. If publishers' rates went up, then their returns from commissions would rise in step. However, when *Printer and Publisher* interviewed J.J. Gibbons, the ranking Toronto agent was rather ambivalent. He believed that the Press Association's concern over card rates was a red herring. Yes, the elimination of discounts would probably improve the conduct of the trade. If every agency knew that its competitors paid the same rates, then the ceaseless haggling would end. However, that was a moot point if the paper's rates were out of proportion to its circulation. No agent would pay more for a paper's space than it was worth. If the Press Association sought constructive change, Gibbons suggested that another clause be added to the schedule of rates. He believed that publishers should have been forced to submit audited circulation figures to the association each year.[32]

Despite Gibbons's doubts, the committee reported to the general meeting of the association in February 1905 that the new minimum rates had been 'cordially received' by publishers and agents alike. With slight revisions, the new minimum rates were approved. Members gradually introduced these rates over the next year as their existing contracts with agencies and advertisers expired. It took a great deal of perseverance to implement them effectively.[33] Agents did not expect publishers to stand fast and continued to badger them for discounts. E.J.B. Pense commented at one meeting that 'the agents are hardly fair to the newspaperman, especially if they think him weak.'[34] The solution was simply to stick by the rate, no matter the short-term cost. This meant declining a contract if the agent would not agree to the new card. Those who succeeded in maintaining the price floor found it an arduous task. One publisher stated that McKim had dropped his paper entirely for a time; Pense indicated that he had lost one agency's business for two years before it returned.[35]

A second consequence of the minimum rate reform was the partitioning of the association. The rate card concerned the weekly men, so only weekly men sat on the committee. The practicality of this arrangement became obvious to all. The business of newspaper publishing was sufficiently complex that daily and weekly publishers had developed different concerns; the place of advertising within the industry had simply drawn this into stark relief. Permanent 'sections' were created within the association in 1905, with their own chairs, committees, and reports. While this began as a convenience, it was the first step towards the dissolution of the association in 1920.

The Commission System – Rate of Commission

The next order of business for the weekly publishers was the question of agency relations. This was much more contentious ground. The minimum rate card promised to settle the problems created by haggling and discounting. Now attention focused on the nature of the commission and the agency's great sin, rebating. Discussion settled on two questions: Why was commission paid, and What was an appropriate amount? The association acknowledged that the industry had changed significantly with the tremendous growth of foreign advertising. In time, it also recognized that this phenomenon, and not the agencies themselves, was the source of their concerns. The rate card committee had stated that 'the process of evolution which is going on will some day land the much-abused advertising agency in a position where it can be logically defined.'[36] The new committee would do just that.

Agents positioned themselves within the periodical publishing industry as the servants of the press. Insofar as McKim's agency had actually emerged from a newspaper advertising department this must have seemed self-evident. As such, the payment of commission had not posed a problem. Commission represented the cost of selling the publisher's white space, and the rate was the same paid to newspaper staff. It was rebating that impelled publishers to rethink this situation. Publishers coping with rising costs and wanting a greater share of the largesse from foreign advertising did not appreciate the fact that agents could afford to surrender rebates. If this money was not financing agency operations, then the agencies were billing the publishers under false pretences. If agents could prosper on the equivalent of 15 per cent commission, then they should have received only 15 per cent commission. The remaining 10 per cent should have remained where it belonged, with the paper.[37]

Few publishers suggested the outright abolition of the existing system, despite their condemnation of the agencies. The experience of Frank Munsey gave them all food for thought. Munsey was an American magazine publisher whose marketing innovations set national standards for the industry. At an industry luncheon in 1898 Munsey declared that the commission system was little more than ritual bribery. Although agents claimed to represent the publishers, in practice they represented advertisers and used the promise of contracts as a club to beat down publishers' rates. Munsey declared that after 1 January 1899 he would no longer grant commission to any agency. Those that placed business in his pages would have to be paid by their clients.[38]

The speech caused a sensation in the trade on both sides of the border. *Printer and Publisher* ran a report of the 'remarkable address' in its next issue and offered to send a full transcript to anyone who asked. It also had comments from the advertising managers of three leading papers, including T.W. Dyas at the *Mail and Empire*. Each of them thought that Munsey's outburst was rather extreme. J.F. MacKay, then of the Montreal *Herald*, and C.W. Taylor of the Toronto *Globe* agreed that their own staff could cover the local field, but they appreciated the contracts that agencies brought from outside. Dyas went one step further. His men were capable of covering the whole country, but agency business from outside Canada was gladly accepted. One wonders how his former apprentice, McKim, took the news.[39]

The industry watched Munsey's experiment closely. His partisans were bitterly disappointed. Munsey's revenues dropped precipitously, and in less than a year he admitted defeat. This episode was the final proof for most major publishers that the commission system was entrenched. After that, publishers focused on the rate of commission rather than its mere existence. To alleviate rebating, a reduction was in order.[40]

In the United States, key magazine publishers began the process. They were led by the titles of the Curtis Publishing Company. Cyrus Curtis owned the *Ladies' Home Journal*, the highest circulating magazine of its day. During the 1880s, while the magazine was still in development, Curtis granted an exclusive contract to one agent, J. Walter Thompson, to handle all of its advertising. When the magazine prospered, and other agencies began to clamour for space, Curtis was well positioned to demand concessions. After the Thompson contract expired, the company agreed to contract with other agencies, but only at 10 per cent commission. They accepted. Inspired, other publishers made similar moves. The Quoin Club was a cabal of magazine publishers in New York that included leading titles such as *Harper's*, *Delineator*, *Cosmopolitan*, and the recently chastised *Munsey's*. By common agreement they adopted the 10 per cent commission in 1904.[41]

In Canada, the metropolitan dailies began a similar process. The first to do so were the daily publishers of Toronto, who conspired to drop their rate of commission to 15 per cent. By 1905 publishers in Montreal, Ottawa, Hamilton, and London had done the same, city by city, and outside of the Press Association.[42] As with the rate card, cooperation was essential. Had any one paper unilaterally lowered its rate of commission, it probably would have lost its foreign advertising. By lowering them simultaneously, rival publishers agreed to compete on the basis of editorial content and circulation rather than through business practices that imperilled them all.

The weekly publishers did not follow suit. Although revising the rate of commission was a logical extension of the minimum rate card reform, the weeklies encountered opposition from the agencies that the dailies had not. When J.J. Gibbons discovered their plans, he strongly objected, on two counts. First, he asserted once again that publishers were the primary beneficiaries of the job that agencies performed. Certainly, he felt that they had done 'more to create new business for the newspapers of Canada to-day than all other forces combined.'[43]

Second, looking south, Gibbons surveyed the aftermath of the 15 per cent commission there. Many American agencies had failed, and the survivors had largely forsaken weekly newspapers. All other things being equal, an agency buying space in one large metropolitan daily earned as much commission as it did in five weeklies. After reading Gibbons's article, A.R. Coffin admitted that 'we all know how much cheaper it is to handle one account of $100 than ten of $10 each.'[44] Eventually, the Quoin Club was forced to revise its rate of commission to protect the agencies, elevating it from 10 per cent to 13 per cent, and then finally 15 per cent.[45] Had the weekly publishers in Canada dropped their rates of commission from 25 per cent to 15 per cent, this would have entailed a 40 per cent reduction in agency revenues. Few businesses in or out of publishing could sustain an overnight decline of that magnitude.

Whether or not the weekly publishers were convinced by Gibbons's arguments, the rate of commission was not reduced. They did not meet quorum at the 1905 meetings when it was on the agenda. That said, those members who were present favoured the 15 per cent commission and asked all members to 'endeavour to arrange with their competitors to bring the 15 per cent rate into effect at as early a date as possible.'[46]

At the same convention, a curious anomaly transpired. Trade paper publishers agreed to end all commission on business placed by Canadian agencies. These publishers took the view that 'the agencies are the servants of the advertiser, [and] they should look to their masters for their pay.'[47] One new agency in Montreal made this principle the foundation of its business; by explicitly offering its services to the advertiser, it refused any commission from publishers. M.A. James, then chair of the weekly section's advertising committee, saw in both of these events a sign that the industry was developing a more 'logically defined' role for the agency.[48]

Whatever the merit of this assertion, the MacLean Publishing Company had its own reason to endorse the motion. J.B. Maclean did not deny the importance of agencies in the publishing industry, but he did insist that trade papers were categorically different from other periodicals. They were not read by the general public, but by manufacturers, wholesalers, retailers, and dealers specializing in a particular field of business. Unlike most foreign advertising, each ad that ran in a trade paper was specific to a particular readership. In this way it resembled the local advertising developed by newspapers – even if the community of readers for a trade paper was national in scope – and should have been handled by the paper's own advertising department. In keeping with this belief, Maclean granted agency commissions only on business originating outside Canada. James Acton, Maclean's chief rival in Toronto, stated outright that his company would 'absolutely refuse to do business with any agencies in Canada.'[49]

By 1907, then, three different rates of commission had been adopted by the publishers of the Press Association. The dailies and weeklies accepted that the agencies served publishers, and on this basis rationalized the maintenance of the commission system. Nonetheless, the dailies had united to lower the rate of commission from 25 per cent to 15 per cent to reduce the problems created by rebating. The weeklies, lacking the same financial clout, retained the traditional rate. Meanwhile, the trade papers had rejected the agencies' characterization of their service and declared that the advertiser was the agency's chief client. They sought to end the commission system altogether.

THE CANADIAN ASSOCIATION OF ADVERTISING AGENCIES

The publishers put a scare into the agents. The widespread adoption of the minimum rate card, coupled with a recruiting drive, demonstrated that the Press Association was determined to protect publishers' interests. The agencies decided that they would have to do the same. In the spring of 1905 the presidents of five Canadian agencies met in Toronto to form the Canadian Association of Advertising Agencies. Its principal task was to represent the agencies before the Press Association.

Over the next five years, the agents' association engaged in a series of negotiations with the Press Association. The publishers' concerns continued to be dominated by the same priorities: decreasing questionable business practices while increasing their revenues from foreign advertising. The agencies proposed that both of these ends could be met by building up the competitive advantage of the 'legitimate' agencies. The publishers found this compelling, and the negotiations then focused on what exactly characterized a legitimate agency.

The original composition of the agents' association is worthy of note. Anson McKim, Eduoard Desbarats, J.J. Gibbons, and Frederick Diver ran well-established and progressive agencies. A fifth man, J.H. Woods, was a newcomer to advertising who had earned a sound reputation as a reporter at the *Mail and Empire*. Each of their shops was an independent, full-service company incorporated to service only advertising contracts. Not all agencies could make the same claim, and when their association sat down with the Press Association, it sought to eliminate those other agencies from the field.[50]

At some point after 1890 certain manufacturers began to establish in-house 'agencies.' Whether they hired an agency or placed business direct, advertisers paid full card rates for the space they used. Many companies who placed direct resented this fact and thought they deserved some form of discount equal to the agency commission. They then found a way to circumvent the rules by establishing 'agencies' of their own. More often than not, such an agency was little more than the company's advertising department reconstituted as a separate firm. Its personnel and duties remained unchanged, but technically it qualified for the commission. Hal Donly of the Simcoe *Reformer* stated that there were numerous firms using this ploy in 1906. Publishers frequently condemned the practice, but rarely identified the companies in question. One such agency might have been Eddy Advertising Service, established in 1913. Although it was operated by the grandson of E.D. Eddy, an Ottawa lumber baron, it was underwritten by the grandfather's company.[51]

In-house agencies did not demand copy or art services from publishers. They came with complete campaigns ready-made, unlike local advertisers who relied upon the publisher's advertising department. Not surprisingly, many publishers took this business at net rates. W.A.

Craick was unapologetic about the practice. In a *Printer and Publisher* editorial, he suggested that the in-house agency system replace the independents. Since the independent agencies' revenues increased with the quantity of advertising placed, rather than the suitability of the papers used, they were always tempted to pad their lists. Only with capable, in-house staff could an advertiser be sure that its company's advertising appropriation was well spent on carefully selected media.[52]

The independent agencies cried foul. The main justification for the commission system was the agents' role in developing advertisers. Clearly, companies with in-house agencies were already active advertisers. They simply did not wish to pay gross rates. If this practice became widely accepted the independent agencies would have been driven out of business and there would be no one in the industry with a structural interest in the development of new foreign advertisers. The independents asked the publishers to accept business from advertisers and their in-house agencies only at gross rates.[53]

In its constitution and mandate, the newly formed Canadian Association of Advertising Agencies reflected this debate. In a circular issued to the publishers under McKim's letterhead, they announced that they were coming together 'for the purpose of discussing with the newspaper publishers several important questions of mutual interest, especially the question as to what constitutes a legitimate advertising agency to whom the agents' commission should be allowed.'[54] As well, they were intent on gaining detailed statements of circulation, and any other reforms that would place advertising on a more secure foundation in Canada.

Credit Recognition

While the agencies struggled with the notion of legitimacy, the publishers were equally concerned with the agencies' credit resources. In the heady days of the pioneers, men such as Robert Moore had not taken any responsibility for the financial position of their clients. If the client did not pay Moore, then Moore did not pay the papers. Publishers found this situation intolerable and believed it was the agent's legal responsibility to pay bills on receipt. Despite extracting promises and posing threats, little changed.[55] Papers could only refuse the business of those agents who proved themselves unreliable. By then, of course, money was already lost.

It took the powerful Montreal *Star* to develop a reliable screening system. The *Star* established credit requirements for all agencies placing ads in its pages. As the *Star* was the largest anglophone paper in the country, it was an essential component of most agency lists, and agencies either met its terms or lost access to its pages. Other daily newspapermen held the *Star* in high regard and soon copied its recognition procedures.[56] Weekly publishers found it difficult to do the same. The average weekly had a tiny staff and scant resources; it had little time to investigate agencies. Some agencies brandished recommendations from the major dailies, but there was no way to verify these unless a publisher contacted the recognizing papers.[57]

Two solutions were proposed in 1893. The first would have had *Printer and Publisher* act as a clearing house for agency reports. As an independent publisher, J.B. Maclean was understandably reluctant to do this and face the wrath of the agencies. The second suggestion would have had the Press Association generate a 'blacklist' of delinquent agencies. This would have distributed responsibility for the project among all publishers, but in 1893 there was insufficient interest to make it a reality. By 1905 the situation seemed more pressing, and publishers were quite willing to meet their common problems through cooperation. The daily publishers were a step ahead of the weeklies, and their section of the Press Association established a credit review committee in 1906. It exercised no power, but could only identify fiscally responsible agencies and note which were owned by manufacturers. Publishers were free to use this information in any way they wished.[58]

The gradual accretion of such reforms within the Press Association must have created a sense of anxiety among the agencies. Whether or not all publishers accepted the reforming bent of the association's activities, the publishers of the largest papers in Canada certainly had. The role of the agent was discussed as never before, and this new committee had begun to examine what was and was not a legitimate agency. Little wonder, then, that the agents' association formed when it did. Soon after, it met with the daily men of the Press Association to air their respective problems.

The Daily Section Agreement of 1907

The first meeting of the two associations took place in Toronto in March 1907. Both sides presented their concerns regarding the state of the industry; they also made suggestions to improve their mutual relations. One wonders how volatile the meeting might have been: Craick, reporting soon after, felt that 'the very fact that there was a meeting and that the proceedings were amicable, augurs well.'[59] However dark his fears, his cautious optimism was not misplaced. The next meeting, held the following month, resulted in an agreement that established codes of conduct for both parties. It had the potential to resolve many of the problems that had emerged over the last decade.

There were at least two models for this type of agreement. The Billposters' Association was a collection of Canadian and American companies that produced, mounted, and maintained advertising posters and billboards. Much like the publishers, the billposters set common rates that diminished the possibility of price-cutting among their members. Every advertiser would pay the exact same rate for the exact same service no matter which billposter he hired. United, the billposters met the agencies with great determination. Every agent placing business with a member of the association had to sign the same contract, which stipulated the duties of both parties. Among other things, rebating was strictly forbidden. The other precedent was the Quoin Club. It offered agencies an agreement similar to the billposters'. If the agents agreed to its terms, the publishers would quote only gross rates to advertisers placing business direct and refuse business from non-signing agencies.[60]

The agreement between the daily section and the agents accomplished, in essence, two things. First, it consolidated all of the reforms of the previous three years in one document approved by both sides. Second, it tried to introduce means to enforce the terms of the agreement. The first portion of the agreement dealt with rates. Although no statement of principles framed the agreement, one could have been drafted quite easily; the subtext champions the primacy of the publisher within the periodical industry. Newspapers were the publisher's livelihood. He assumed the financial risks inherent in the ownership and operation of a press, and as such the rates he set were to be held sacrosanct. It was the duty of advertising agencies to accept card rates and to quote them with absolute fidelity to the advertiser. To ensure transparency, agencies agreed to quote each paper's rates separately on the lists they submitted to clients. Discounts, rebates, and any other form of price-cutting would not be tolerated. Any uncompleted, long-term contract would be charged at short rates. All of these conditions defended the price floor.[61]

In return, publishers would protect the role of the independent agencies in the newspaper field and, by extension, reaffirm their acceptance of the commission system. The agreement set out a strict definition of what they would recognize as a legitimate agency:

> 'Advertising Agency' shall mean a person, firm, or company who or which is not a salaried employee of any advertiser, and who or which has an office or offices properly equipped for carrying on as his or their principal business a general advertising business, and who is, by experience and in the possession of financial resources qualified to carry on the business of an advertising agency, and who or which has at least three bona fide new general advertisers or clients, whose advertising is to be placed in Canadian newspapers.[62]

The Press Association would maintain the credit recognition committee. Using this definition, it would determine the legitimacy of each agency in Canada. Only recognized agencies would qualify for commissions. While this definition would not necessarily discourage publishers' advertising departments from competing with the independents, it would discourage manufacturers' in-house agencies. Any savings they might have gained through the commission system were eliminated.[63] No rate was specified for the commission. The daily section hoped that the entire Press Association would sign the agreement. Given the three different rates then in use, it was politic to leave this out.

The emphasis placed on the acquisition of three new accounts may have been imposed at the behest of either side. From the publishers' viewpoint, this clause highlighted the major principle underlying the commission system: that agencies existed to create new business. For the agencies, the wording provided a certain amount of protection as well. It discouraged the formation of new agencies. New agencies frequently sprang from existing agencies, when hired staff decided to establish their own shops. When they did, they often took key clients with them. In 1903 J.J. Gibbons lost one of the largest accounts in the country when the advertising manager of the McClary Manufacturing Company – then, J.E. McConnell – resigned to open his own agency and subsequently carried the contract with him. There was nothing Gibbons could do in this situation, but he tried to prevent mutinies from his own firm by placing a special clause in employee contracts. It stipulated that former employees would not 'for a period of five years ... solicit, execute, or accept any work from any client of his.'[64] Those who refused to sign it were not hired. Under the terms of the agreement, a new agency would be able to place business with members of the association, but it would not be eligible for commission until it had signed three clients that had never before advertised. Without a commission, the new agent would have to rely upon its clients or its credit resources for financing. Once recognition was achieved, however, the publishers would reimburse it for back commission.[65]

The agreement did not apply to local advertising. The publishers emphasized that the agent's field was foreign advertising and not locally operated businesses. Nonetheless, they did concede that the agencies had developed local advertisers into major, supralocal accounts. For the sake of the agreement, the two sides crafted a precise definition of supralocal advertising. The first step was a change in terminology. The word 'general' was substituted for the word 'foreign,' which effectively dispelled the territorial connotations attached to these accounts. The clause stated: 'A general advertiser, no matter where his place of business or head office may be located, is one who advertises in three or more journals in three or more towns or cities in the Dominion, but whose product or merchandise does not constitute the major portion of any local retail store.'[66]

In essence, the two sides tried to pinpoint the difference between the artisan shops of the previous century and the large corporate enterprises that had recently gained a national presence. A tailor who made and sold his own wares in his own shop was a local advertiser; Penman's Limited was a general advertiser. Even then, this definition was extremely generous. Any agency worth its salt should have been able to place its clients' ads in three towns. This clause would only prevent retailers and small-scale artisans from placing their ads in a neighbouring town's paper and claiming the status of a general advertiser.

Section 13 also made another concession to the agencies. It allowed them to claim commission on certain local advertising. Two cases may have inspired this clause. The first was the disagreement over bank advertising. Publishers would grant commission on it if the agencies paid full local rates rather than the lower rates offered to general advertisers. The agreement stated: 'A branch store or office devoted wholly or the greater part thereof to the business advertised, and which is in competition with businesses already in existence and paying local rates, is to be classified as a local advertiser and comes under local rates, with commission to any qualified and recognized advertising agency.'[67]

The second case involved the incursion of Toronto's department stores into suburban markets. Until the 1890s this chiefly affected storekeepers in downtown Toronto, but with improvements in transportation they cast their shadow over outlying regions. Knowing this, department stores placed their advertising in papers outside of Toronto, where they competed with local merchants. Sensitive publishers faced a dilemma. If the department stores put local merchants out of business, few advertisers would remain to support the paper. On the other hand, publishers groused that department store advertising would have been unnecessary if every local merchant actually supported its local paper. Ultimately, the publishers sided with the department stores, but placed upon them the same restriction as they had upon the banks: they would have to pay local rates whether they used an agency or not.[68]

Enforcement proved to be the most difficult aspect of the publisher-agency agreement. There was no positive mechanism to maintain compliance other than enlightened self-interest. Instead, the publishers held aloft an economic club that threatened each agency with derecognition if found in violation of the agreement on two separate occasions. Without recognition, of course, an agency could not claim commission on business placed. This should have been sufficiently forbidding. Meanwhile, any publisher found in violation of the agreement on two separate occasions would be removed from the agreement. On the face of it, this was not much of a threat. The offending publisher would likely lose no revenue by his actions. However, the publisher would no longer be entitled to the list of recognized agencies, and the recognized agencies would not have to curb their less desirable practices when dealing with him. In short, the delinquent publisher was threatened with inconvenience.

One complication remained: the application of this agreement to offshore advertising agencies. American and British agencies would not subscribe to a set of restrictions that did not exist in their own countries. Their domestic industries had credit recognition procedures, but in neither country was the payment of commission tied to specific business practices.[69] This was particularly troublesome with the Americans, since they placed far more business in Canada. Canadian adworkers were always conscious of American practices, but they had taken the lead on this issue and congratulated themselves for addressing a problem still rampant south of the border. Similar agency agreements did not appear in the United States until the 1910s, and even then their applicability was limited to certain major cities. However, as long as American agencies still employed haggling, discounting, and rebating at home, they were not inclined to curtail these practices in Canada. This created a problem for Canadian agencies: agencies based in the United States could now offer Canadian clients cheaper rates. So long as the American agencies could do this, the Canadian agencies were inclined to ignore their commitments to the Press Association.[70]

The Press Association and agents on both sides of the border arrived at a modest solution. The American agents agreed to abide by the terms of the agency agreement on any contracts originating in Canada, paid for in Canada, or for concerns incorporated in Canada. This covered the advertising for both Canadian companies and the Canadian branches of American firms. On all other contracts for foreign-based clients, agencies were free to rebate. The way the amendment was worded, this applied to American and Canadian agencies equally.[71] To indicate their acceptance of these conditions, all foreign agencies were asked to notify the Canadian Association of Advertising Agencies; it would be their signatory to the agreement.

The modest solution did not work to the Canadian agents' satisfaction. The Americans continued to offer substantial rebates to Canadian-based clients that Canadian agencies could not match, with or without the restrictive agreement. In 1911 the Canadian agents' association approached the Press Association for protection in the form of differential rates of commission. For a time, the small city publishers consented. Domestic agencies were developing far more Canadian-based advertisers, and more or less abiding by the agreements. The small city dailies restored the 25 per cent rate of commission for Canadian agencies, but granted only 15 per cent to foreigners. The metropolitan dailies refused to change and granted 15 per cent for all agencies; similarly, the weeklies held at 25 per cent for all agencies. Angry protests from the Americans in 1914 lessened the gap to 20/15, but the principle of differential rates remained well into the 1920s, when the Americans began opening branch offices in Canada.[72]

The Press Association did not have the wherewithal to investigate the credit ratings of agencies based in the United States or Great Britain. Instead, it relied upon the relevant association in each country. In Great Britain, the Incorporated Society of Advertising Agents of England was an agents' group that restricted membership to recognized agencies. In the United States, the American Newspaper Publishers' Association had a committee whose recognition standards were very similar to the Canadians' own.[73] The Press Association adopted the recommendations of both of these lists.

When it was first signed, the agreement bound only the agents and dailies in smaller cities the size of London, Kingston, and Berlin (now Kitchener). By February of the following year, larger papers in Hamilton and Ottawa accepted the agreement and fell in line. Only one metropolitan daily joined at this time, but the association expected every paper across the country would eventually accept its terms. They were not disappointed.[74]

Even before the daily agreement was struck, the weekly publishers were working on one of their own. They established a recognition committee in February 1906, with requirements identical to those of the dailies. The following year a committee was appointed to meet with the agents in September. To their dismay, nothing substantial was accomplished. Despite the ground-breaking agreement signed by the dailies just five months before, each side tried to introduce a new condition that was not in the dailies' agreement. The publishers wanted agencies to stop using papers outside of the agreement, and agencies wanted audited circulation figures. Neither side got its wish, and no agreement was signed.[75]

Despite the failure of these negotiations, the weekly publishers achieved their larger goals the following year. In 1908 the daily and weekly sections combined their recognition committees into a single committee on advertising. In so doing, the weeklies effectively signed on to the dailies' agreement. Although it took another two years to unify their operations completely, the Press Association appeared to have achieved the unanimity it had long sought.[76]

The effect of the agency agreements, and the recognition procedure that they established, cannot be underestimated. Although it has never received attention in the Canadian historiography on the publishing industry, this committee – in its attempts to protect publishers – vaulted the advertising agencies into a new realm of respectability.[77] By agreeing to its terms, the recognized agencies gained a stamp of approval from one of the most powerful instruments of public opinion in Edwardian Canada. Its ownership requirements ensured that major advertisers had no economic advantage over the agencies when dealing with the publishers. Its credit requirements eliminated competition from freelance copywriters and fly-by-night operators, but it also impeded the entry of new agencies. The list of recognized agencies issued by the Press Association in the 1910s severely reduced the number of agencies receiving commission on business; in Toronto alone, a field of thirty was narrowed down to eight in 1910.[78] This new environment gave the recognized agents a degree of stability, which allowed them to consolidate their experience, capital, and list of clients, while expanding their knowledge and services. After that point, there were clearly defined requirements that every new agency had to meet before gaining access to the lucrative trade in national advertising. In return, the papers ensured that the agencies remained dependent upon them, and not advertisers, for their income. If publishers no longer had direct access to national advertisers, it was in their interest to retain some influence with those who controlled the advertisers' appropriations. This became increasingly important over the next ten years as alternative media competed aggressively with the periodical press.

One final consequence deserves mention: the national expansion of the Press Association. Through cooperation, publishers in the association had gained strength. Publishers outside Ontario recognized this and desired a similar organization that would unite them all. In 1905 the Canadian Press Association began a recruiting drive in Ontario; in 1911 it hired a full-time manager to pursue expansion outside the province. John M. Imrie, then editor of *Printer and Publisher*, got the job. He was a typical MacLean employee, and embraced any new ideas and American trends that might have modernized the business of publishing. Cost accounting was his pet project. Once manager, he conducted forty seminars on the subject for publishers across the country. These provided the perfect platform to boost membership, since he could draw an explicit link between a practical business innovation and the association itself. In 1909 the Press Association had 359 members, mainly from Ontario. Two years after Imrie's arrival, the association had swollen to 751 full and associate members, of which over 400 signed the agency agreements. The membership included 99 of the country's 152 dailies, a third of its weeklies, and all of the major trade journals, agricultural papers, and magazines. Almost half of the papers in the West were represented, as were a fifth of those in the Maritimes. Few were French-language. In May 1914 the Canadian Press Association was reincorporated as a 'national' organization.[79]

THE ASSOCIATION OF CANADIAN ADVERTISERS

Advertisers were more or less ignored in the agency agreement. Certainly, they had no place at the negotiations, and the agreement did not address their concerns. In part, this situation was rooted in the agencies' strict insistence that the publisher-agency relation and the advertiser-agency relation remain discrete. More concretely, however, the advertisers as such had no representative association. The Canadian Manufacturers Association brought manufacturers together, mainly to lobby the government on tariff rates and foreign trade. Retailers and financial institutions created their own organizations to do similar work. It was not until September 1914 that the Association of Canadian Advertisers (ACA) was formed. The ACA was the brainchild of B.H. Bramble, the advertising manager of Goodyear Tire and Rubber. At its organizational meeting, the goals of the new body were clearly set out; namely: to investigate the circulation claims of all periodicals, to convince publishers to use uniform rate cards, to eliminate 'unclean' advertising, and to maintain useful statistical records on media outlets in Canada.[80]

Over the next five years, the ACA grew to represent a formidable body of advertisers. There were seventy-seven by 1919, working in both manufacturing and tertiary industries. A partial list would include Canada Life Assurance, Canadian Kodak, Chevrolet, Columbia Graphophone, Dunlop Tire and Rubber, Imperial Oil, Massey-Harris, McLaughlin Carriage, A.&F. Pears, the Steel Company of Canada, and Tuckett Tobacco. Most members had their headquarters in Toronto or Montreal, but a handful came from Hamilton, and a scattering of others came from Winnipeg, London, Ottawa, and the better-known company towns, Windsor and Oshawa. The association established its head office in Toronto.[81]

Circulation Audits

Above all else the ACA wanted publishers to guarantee their circulation figures. This question concerned the agencies as well. Years before, J.J. Gibbons had asked publishers to initiate annual audits through the Press Association. Two problems had always stood in the way: the mutual suspicions of the publishers themselves, and the question of who would pay for the audits.

The publishers themselves were wholly responsible for the doubt surrounding circulation figures. Agencies maximized their clients' advertising appropriations by selecting papers that covered product distribution networks as efficiently as possible. This usually entailed the use of one paper in each town, and each paper's efficiency could be assessed by examining its circulation figure in relation to its rate card.[82] The accuracy of the circulation figure affected the basis of the agency's media plan. However, the competition among publishers led them to overrate their own figures while underrating those of their competitors. Hal Donly pointed to the ridiculous, if unfortunate, effects of this competition:

> It may happen that the circulation statement of one daily newspaper in a certain large city is questioned by the publisher of a rival paper in the same city. It is probable that, previous to this, no advertiser has ever doubted the circulation statement of either paper. Publisher Number One promptly retaliates by casting reflections on the veracity of Publisher Number Two. Publisher Number Two replies by having his circulation records audited, and Publisher Number One immediately does likewise – with the result that the statements of both papers are found to be correct.[83]

Nonetheless, Pandora's box had been opened. Agents and advertisers alike demanded that publishers provide proof of their statements.

Audits did not come cheaply. Publishers assessed their value in relation to their vision of publishing. The majority believed that their product was newspapers and their customers were readers. They could not see the value of a process that added to production costs without adding any apparent value to the final product. A minority of publishers thought quite differently; they believed that their product was circulation and their customers were advertisers. Like any other product, circulation deserved a guarantee. The Montreal *Star* pioneered this view. It began voluntary audits in the 1890s and campaigned for federal legislation that would have made audits mandatory for all periodicals.[84] But most publishers did not simply baulk at the *amount* of these costs. They also refused responsibility for them. If space-buyers did not accept circulation figures as stated, then it was their problem. Space-buyers replied that publications without credible figures would not be used.[85]

The ACA sat down with the advertising committee of the Press Association in May 1915. The advertisers wanted to see if any common ground could be found to conduct joint audits. They found none. The two parties disagreed over two points: how to apportion costs, and the nature of the information to be provided in a circulation report. As a result, the CPA unilaterally issued its own standard reports, less detailed than the ACA desired, and asked its members to use it exclusively when asked for their figures.[86]

Undaunted, the ACA set its own agenda. Before any action was taken, however, a new organization formed in the United States seeking the same ends. The Audit Bureau of Circulations was the product of similar discussions south of the border, but there all three sectors agreed to underwrite the operation of one auditing body. This auditor operated on a non-profit basis. Each company joined as an individual member (rather than as part of their trade association), and paid annual fees relative to the size of its business and the type of service it desired. The Audit Bureau's board of directors represented each sector of the industry. As a result, the bureau claimed a relative degree of autonomy from each of them, and provided a service that was mutually satisfactory. It located in Chicago, Illinois.[87]

Canadian companies were offered membership in the Audit Bureau from the outset. For publishers, fees were geared to the size and class of the papers they operated. A daily with 50,000 to 100,000 in circulation paid $15 per week. For space-buyers, fees were geared to the service desired: $200 bought access to all of the bureau's reports on North American periodicals, $50 to those in Canada alone. To better serve its Canadian members, the bureau set up an advisory board that included publishers George F. Chipman of the *Grain Growers' Guide* and William A.H. Findlay of the Ottawa *Free Press*, as well as John Murray Gibbon of the Canadian Pacific Railway and B.H. Bramble, the driving force behind the ACA. J.J. Gibbons represented the agencies. When the number of Canadian members grew after 1916, the bureau created a vice-presidency for Canada on its executive.[88]

Most Canadian publishers viewed the Audit Bureau with great apprehension. Soon after its formation, the bureau requested an endorsement from the Press Association. The advertising committee quickly discounted the idea. The bureau's membership fees were a tacit admission that publishers were at least partially responsible for the cost of audits. If the ACA went ahead with its own scheme, Canadian publishers would have been able to avoid these costs altogether. Despite the committee's qualms, thirty-six publishers signed up independently for the bureau's service before the end of the year. Among them was the Montreal *Star*. Others waited to assess its operations. Apparently, the bureau earned their trust. It rapidly gained a reputation for high-calibre service. By 1917, 53 out of 125 dailies, representing

78 per cent of Canada's total daily circulation, were members; seven years later almost all the dailies had joined, as had most of the major magazines. The country weeklies, still more dependent on local than national advertising, held off.[89]

When the Audit Bureau opened, the ACA was little more than a list of companies with common goals. Only sixteen corporate advertising managers attended the ACA's founding meeting; fifty-five participated in its first business meeting a year and a half later. The original executive was composed of the advertising managers of companies producing packaged foods, soaps, tobacco, shoes, electrical appliances, and tires. The small number of industries involved reflects how few companies in Canada advertised nationally at that time, but the war also hampered recruiting. Unlike the publishers, this small band immediately cooperated with the bureau. Each would acquire the Audit Bureau reports on its Canadian members and encourage other periodicals to join. In the meantime, they would have their own staff investigate those that did not.[90]

At the same meeting, the ACA formed a circulation and rates committee to undertake the collation of data. It crafted a standard form for the declaration of circulation, then targeted about 250 publications in Canada that ACA members used regularly. By October 1916, only nine months into its mandate, it had the cooperation of 128, of which 71 had also joined the Audit Bureau. Among these were the Toronto *Star Weekly*, Montreal's *La Presse* and *Gazette*, and the country's leading general magazine, *Everywoman's World*.[91]

Under the combined pressure of the ACA, agencies, and Audit Bureau, the publishers were forced to relent and accept the idea of regular and standardized audits. Despite the stand taken by the Press Association, *Printer and Publisher* endorsed the Audit Bureau in May 1916.[92] The circulation and rates committee of the ACA viewed this situation with great satisfaction and reported: 'The publisher who now either refuses or fails to meet such a requirement can reasonably and safely be classed with those who do not desire the details of their circulation known, for reasons which are of no advantage to their advertisers.'[93] Failure to cooperate signalled a publisher whose paper had no advertising value.

The Audit Bureau settled most of the questions surrounding circulation figures. The next problem addressed was the commission system. Here, the advertisers were not as successful. The implementation of independent, standardized audits was essentially a fine-tuning of the industry. A change in the commission system would involve a radical overhaul of the industry's structure.

The Commission System – The Chief Client

As the ACA took shape, a new debate probed the nature of the commission system. The Association of National Advertisers (ANA) was the ACA's counterpart in the United States. Its main goal was the complete abolition of the commission system. Although the ACA did not share its views, John M. Imrie did. As the manager of the Press Association and the editor of *Printer and Publisher*, Imrie was well positioned to champion the abolition of the commission system in Canada.[94]

What had changed since 1907? Some commentators suggested everything. Throughout the 1910s it was commonplace within the industry to assess the changes of the previous twenty years. More often than not, agencies were central to these analyses. The space brokerage was characterized as a nineteenth-century business practice. It was old-fashioned, prone to corruption, inefficient. The 'full-service' agency was identified with the modern, rational world of the twentieth-century businessman.[95] That said, it was becoming apparent that its highly touted services were provided to advertisers, not publishers. J.J. Gibbons and Norris-Patterson Limited did not deny it; they advertised it to the trade. Certain newer agencies in Toronto took this development to its logical conclusion: they operated on a fee-for-service basis rather than the commission system. Selling Service Limited in Montreal emphasized this aspect of its operations in its very name.[96] During the First World War, four Toronto publishers challenged the commission system, and the ACA faced them down. Within five years, they reversed their positions. These two confrontations put in place the final pieces of the industry's structure.

Commentary on the commission question came from many sources. At the annual meetings of the Press Association in 1912 the chair of the advertising committee stated forthrightly that the commission would soon be abolished.[97] W.J. Taylor believed the burden of agency costs should have been borne by those who benefited most, the advertisers themselves. As the system stood, it punished companies that created their own advertising in-house and placed their business direct. Such companies bore all of the costs of copywriting, illustration, and plate-making, but received no discount on rates because they were not recognized advertising agencies. On the other hand, companies that hired an agency to perform these tasks had the service included in the cost of the space. A uniform rate for all space-buyers, be they agencies or advertisers, would create a more just system.

Economic Advertising at this time was owned by Norris-Patterson and edited by one of its copywriters, Don Tuck. Tuck reported a suggestion from the Cleveland Advertising Club, which agreed that agency commissions should be abolished in favour of uniform rates for all space-buyers. However, the club also believed that agencies provided one valuable service to publishers: namely, the assumption of credit risk when placing a client's advertising. This deserved some compensation, and the club thought a discount relative to the value of the service provided was justifiable. It thought 5 per cent or less would be a fair rate. One notable American agency, N.W. Ayer and Son, endorsed this arrangement, as did one of Gibbons's employees, Thornton Purkis.[98]

Tuck had serious reservations with this scheme. The main complaint of American advertisers stemmed from their belief that agents *did* in fact represent the papers. In their opinion, a commission was nothing more than a kickback offered by publishers to secure advertising revenue. This recalled an old accusation: that the media-buying practices of the agents did not serve the best interests of their clients, but maximized their commissions. The ANA wanted a guarantee that agents worked on behalf of advertisers, with no suspicion of divided loyalties. The Cleveland proposal would only enshrine these divided loyalties by having both sides pay the agency.[99]

Another alternative, popular in the United States, did not require a significant alteration in existing practices. Some advertisers insisted that agencies rebate the entire commission to the client. Then, the advertiser would assess the value of the agency's services and pay it accordingly. The commission system was not abolished, but subverted. The agency would still receive a commission for services rendered to the publishers, and the advertiser would not have to pay for agency service on top of the publishers' card rates. However, the agency would be entirely dependent on the advertiser for its income.[100]

The situation in Canada was different. Here, Tuck felt that many agencies still had a difficult time convincing companies that they offered valuable services other than space-buying. ANA members were willing to pay for agency service because they actually acknowledged its value. In Canada, advertisers were slow to adopt copywriting and illustration. Salada Tea was a notable example. It advertised widely, but maintained the same campaign for thirty years: a rectangle two columns wide by three inches deep, which emphasized the name 'Salada' in thick black type. What little copy there was usually drew a trite yet topical connection between the tea and the reader. Illustrations were rare. A puzzled writer in *Marketing* magazine noted that Salada's sales had doubled every decade from 1900 to 1928.[101] Given the apparent success of companies like this, it was difficult to convince everyone that agency service was necessary.

In the summer of 1915 the *Star* and the *Telegram* opened hostilities on the commission system. They unilaterally broke the agency agreement by rejecting its definition of general advertising. This allied them with the *Mail and Empire* and the *Globe*, which had never accepted it. In essence, these papers did not want to grant agency commission on business originating in their own city and declared that all Toronto-based advertisers would thereafter be treated as local advertisers. By eliminating agency commission on this business, the publishers increased their revenues without increasing their card rates. The agencies, however, were forced to bill their clients separately. The publishers knew this was an irritant, but gambled that no advertiser could retaliate and bypass them altogether. Other Toronto papers still granted commission, but their value as advertising media was questionable. John C. Kirkwood found the publishers' arrogance inexcusable and dismissed them as a band of 'Newspaper Napoleons.'[102]

The following year the Press Association tentatively joined the fray. For six years John M. Imrie and W.J. Taylor had worked within the Press Association to end the commission system, and their goal was finally endorsed at the general meeting of the association in 1916. A 'Promotion Department' was created to proselytize the new faith among each sector of the industry. Writing in *Printer and Publisher*, Kirkwood questioned the wisdom of this move and predicted 'a merry war between the agencies and the CPA and the publishers who compose the CPA. In a trial of strength, both sides are likely to suffer losses; and the din and field of battle may even cross the border into Uncle Sam's land, for there are several advertising agencies over there who give business to Canadian publishers; and conceivably they may sympathize with their brethren in Canada.'[103] Kirkwood was right, for there was a battle, but the agencies were not the main contestant. Rather, the publishers were straight-armed by the organized advertisers.

The Toronto situation served as a test. When the 'Newspaper Napoleons' singled out Toronto businesses, companies headquartered elsewhere remained unaffected by their decision. If outsiders had remained neutral, then the papers might have created a useful precedent for the Press Association and its promotion committee to follow. In time, this might have led to the gradual abolition of commission on all forms of advertising throughout the country.[104]

The ACA was not sympathetic, however. It demanded reinstatement of the commission system and boycotted the four papers involved. Most of its members turned to the Toronto *News* and the *World*, but some took the opportunity to explore other advertising media. Billposters, streetcars, and direct mail services gained an unexpected boost over the next year. Although the resistance of some advertisers began to fade after a year, most held on. The boycott endured for two and a half years, after which the newspapers were compelled to readopt the definition of 'general' advertising contained in the agency agreement. The organized advertisers had been quick to exercise their muscle. That they won spoke volumes about their growing influence with the press.[105]

Rather than dividing the advertisers, it was the publishers themselves who were divided by the affair. Their differences culminated in the dissolution of the Press Association into three smaller bodies in 1920. Problems with the agencies had prompted the integration of their regional interests into one national organization; now the increasing competition among dailies, weekly papers, and magazines drove them apart. When that happened, the agency agreement signed by the old association became void. The Canadian Daily Newspaper Association began to draft a new agreement. Once again, the newspapers, agencies, and advertisers aired their concerns. However, when it came to agency commissions, they discovered that their stands had completely reversed since the boycott of the Toronto papers.[106]

At this point, W.A. Lydiatt controlled *Marketing Magazine*. When the commission question was reopened, Lydiatt fanned the flames of disenchantment with the agencies. This did not make him popular with the agents. 'One of your missions in life,' an agent told Lydiatt, 'is to drive a wedge of dissatisfaction between the advertising agencies and their clients.'[107] Although this was his method, it was not his goal. Like Imrie ten years before, Lydiatt took advantage of continuing discontent to advance reforms. Unlike Imrie, he did not seek the abolition of the commission system, but a strict enforcement of the conditions that composed the original agreement drafted in 1907.

Two problems – one familiar, the other new – had emerged to beset publisher-agency relations. First, it was widely known that the agencies were still rebating. Second, publishers were independently raising their rates of commission to secure contracts. Publishers' dependency on general advertising was driven home during the 1910s, both by the boycott and by the number of papers that had simply disappeared. The rise of Canadian mass magazines had also intensified competition for general advertising contracts. As such, publishers resorted to bribery to secure agency contracts – a practice euphemistically referred to as 'special' or 'secret' commissions. Publishers justified themselves with reference to the mantra of free enterprise. The agents were in their employ, and advertisers had no say in their rate of payment.[108]

Lydiatt objected to the rate of commission itself. The rate was based on tradition rather than a close analysis of the cost of selling space. Over the years, the cost of putting out a publication had increased dramatically. This had become painfully evident during the war, when the price of newsprint reached $80 per ton. To compensate, publishers increased their card rates. Since agency commissions were tied to these rates, the agencies received a proportionate increase in their returns. How, Lydiatt wondered, could this be justified? The agency offered the same service regardless of the cost of newsprint. In his eyes the commission system had lost any tangible bearing in the operations of the industry.[109] The agents, either from ignorance or brash impertinence, were completely insensitive to these concerns. In October 1920 the agents' association formally asked for a general increase in the rate of commission. They notified publishers through a circular letter.[110]

That same week, the ACA responded with a bulletin of its own. Two years after having broken the Toronto publishers on the commission question, the advertisers themselves began to doubt its value. In 1916 the ACA was little more than a list of companies. By 1920 it had a lot more experience with the workings of the industry. This experience offered the advertisers an important lesson: marketing strategies did not have to rely solely on print media. However, so long as the agencies were paid by the publishers rather than themselves, they could expect the agencies to favour print over billboards, streetcars, and direct mail.[111] Their answer was to remove any possibility of divided loyalties from the structure of the system by placing the agents under contract to themselves. Towards this end, the ACA bulletin posted in 1920 asked members to consider the following resolution:

RESOLVED that we authorize the Agency Relations Committee to lay before the three Press Associations a suggestion with regard to advertising payments; this suggestion being, that the Association of Canadian Advertisers would be favourable to the said Publishers billing the Advertiser at the present net rates ... instead of the gross rates as at present, leaving it to the Advertiser to reimburse the Agency according to what he judges to be the value of the service rendered.[112]

This had been a common practice in the United States for some time.

The agents' association objected most strenuously. In yet another circular to publishers, the ACA resolution was reproduced alongside a slate of criticisms that focused on the advertisers' motives rather than the logic of their arguments. Indeed, the agencies' principal claim alleged that the ACA was simply attempting to bastardize the existing system. The agencies parroted once again the notion that they served publishers and should be paid by them. If publishers agreed to bill advertisers at net rates, they would grant commission to firms that did nothing to develop new business. In essence, the advertisers asked for nothing more than the right to institutionalize rebating, which the publishers had opposed for thirty years.[113]

The proposed system would also destabilize the agencies' financial structure. If the agencies' rate of pay was not fixed by an industry standard, then every contract would be subject to negotiation. Quality and type of service would be pitted against the cost of delivery. The entire industry would be set back to the competitive days of the 1890s. Then, margins had tumbled as agents haggled for clients, and clients demanded the lowest rates possible. Agents found this difficult to conceive in a trade that had become reliant on creativity and talent rather than sheer negotiation. The fragile shell of professionalism that the agents had so diligently constructed was now in danger of being smashed.

The agents closed with a threat. The circular commented in alarmed tones: 'The ACA wants the paper to allow the full commissions to the advertiser direct, and the advertiser will then determine how much of the commission he will pass on to the Agencies; the advertiser paying only for the work it does for *him*.'[114] In other words, the agents suggested that no one would develop new advertisers if the publishers paid no one to do so. How hard the publishers laughed at this assertion before tossing the circular away cannot be told. That agencies would have stopped pursuing new clients must have seemed like a patent absurdity. But the publishers could have had an equally gay time with the notion that the proposed system would give commissions to advertisers. With the gradual adoption of cost accounting, publishers had learned to incorporate commissions only after they had ensured a rate that covered their own costs. Billing the advertisers at net rates would cause no more hardship to the publishers than billing the agencies at gross rates.

Considering the fact that the agents were then seeking higher commission rates from the publishers, the ACA proposal might have been a ploy to forestall further increases in their costs. Despite his own preferences, Lydiatt acknowledged that no system would likely be perfect, and the existing system did create successful advertising. Further, it would prove difficult to change the Canadian system if the United States and Great Britain did not make similar changes. Canadian publishers would face stiff opposition it they refused commission to domestic agencies while granting it to those offshore.[115]

In the end, the arrangements negotiated in 1907 remained intact, as they would into the 1930s. The agencies did not get a hike in the rate of commission, but neither was the whole system abolished as the advertisers had wished. Nonetheless, the dailies' association and the agencies failed to negotiate a new agency agreement. The American agencies were still rebating, the American Newspaper Publishers' Association had never enforced restrictions against it, and as such the Canadian agents refused to accept any new agreement that tried to do so in Canada. Instead, the dailies arrived at an understanding with the agents' association: recognition procedures remained in place, and publishers were still intent on ending rebating, but they found themselves obliged to ignore it. The weekly and magazine publishers did the same.[116]

The advertising agency that had emerged in the late 1890s had complicated the business of periodical publishing. In the discussions over minimum rates as much as those dealing with legitimacy, rate of commission, and the chief client, agencies were central to the problem at hand. Early on, the agencies gained an upper hand on publishers. With dozens of new papers opening in every province west of the Maritimes, agencies with lengthy lists of clients had significant leverage when buying space. Through a variety of means, both above and below board, they did so. They were reined in only when publishers united to reassert control over their rate cards, and by extension their own businesses and industry.

The publishers' ideological model of the newspaper was still decidedly Victorian. Despite their experiments with modern forms of industrial cooperation and organization, they held fast to the sanctity of editorial independence. By cooperating on matters concerning agency relations, publishers believed they could set the ground rules for a fair competition of intellects in the editorial pages of their respective papers. If they successfully put this view to the agents, they were less successful in conveying it to the advertisers themselves. The creation of the ACA and the Audit Bureau sounded the death knell for personal journalism. Thereafter, the delicate balance between subscribers and advertisers tipped in favour of the latter. Populist papers such as the Toronto *Star* and the *Telegram*, and inoffensive, middle-of-the-road journals such as the Southam holdings, based their success on high circulation figures and the bottom line supplied by advertisers. Overtly idiosyncratic papers such as W.F. Maclean's *World* eventually failed. So too did the labour press.[117]

The reform process both paralleled and broke with events in the United States. The explosive growth of American national advertising preceded that in Canada. However, American agencies worked both sides of the border, and Canadian publishers were soon familiar with their practices. Because of this, publishers across North America began their reforms simultaneously. Canadian publishers differed from their American counterparts, however, in their degree of cooperation and centralization. Each trade association in Canada had two or more counterparts south of the border. Even after the Press Association broke up in 1920, its three successor bodies enjoyed a degree of national solidarity within their respective sectors that was not matched by trade associations in the United States. Indeed, a decade passed before the Canadian Association of Advertising Agencies had an American counterpart. Canadians observed the 'chaos' of the American advertising trade and tried to avoid similar problems through industrial cooperation. This allowed them to craft innovations of their own, and to institute reforms nationwide while the Americans did so piecemeal. Their highest achievement was the agency agreement.

The advertising agency emerged after 1920 both stronger and weaker. Insofar as its services were legitimated and protected by the three new press associations, it was far stronger than it had been in 1900. On three different occasions it had been within the publishers' power to minimize the agencies' importance within the publishing industry. By defining a legitimate agency as one with no business interests other than the solicitation of advertisers for the press, the Press

Association had tried to ensure that the agencies would remain dependent on the press for its income. Nonetheless, it also created a stable environment in which agents such as McKim, Desbarats, Gibbons, and their peers could invest in personnel and plant with some assurance that they would not have their revenue base undercut by publishers' or advertisers' in-house ad departments.

Canadian adworkers habitually noted that their industry was ten to twenty years behind the Americans. Perhaps the brokerage agencies of the 1860s and 1870s had provided their counterparts with a similar sense of security. Agencies such as Ayer, Thompson, and Lord and Thomas, which had exclusive control of dozens of publications, had no competition for their lists. Blessed with secure profit margins, their only concern was the solicitation and maintenance of new clients. It cannot be a coincidence that these three agencies emerged from the nineteenth century among the leaders in the United States. Agencies in Canada occasionally had exclusive claim to certain publications (for example, Desbarats was the sole agent for *Canadian Magazine* in the late 1890s), but none had such a broad number at their command.[118] McKim probably carried a list of papers with which he worked on a regular basis, a list he might have developed while working for the *Mail*. However, nothing suggests that these papers refused business from his competitors. Thus, the benefit of the 1907 agreement: it eliminated competition from in-house agencies that had an 'unfair' credit position based upon their parent companies' resources, and from freelancers who had an 'unfair' price advantage based upon their limited overhead. The agencies that remained were independent and service-oriented. To be sure, there was still competition among them. By protecting their access to the top publications, however, the agreement tried to ensure that this competition would be rooted in the provision of better service rather than lower prices and falling margins.

If the agreement made the agencies more secure, it also weakened their ability to manoeuvre within the market. In the nineteenth century, agents had operated in an unrestricted free market. Regardless of their capital or talent, men such as Robert Moore could open agencies, engage enormous contracts, and close in the wink of an eye. Agents knew they could badger small-town publishers for endless discounts and advantages because they controlled advertisers' appropriations. That changed. Publishers, unwilling to let outsiders exploit their partisan rivalries, closed ranks and forced a code of conduct on the agents. They also made it extremely difficult for fly-by-night operators to enter the field. When new agencies applied for recognition from the Press Association in the 1910s they were expected to have assets in excess of $10,000. Those with marginal credit were asked to post bonds with the association. When the Hamilton Advertisers' Agency was established in 1913 its bond was set at $5,000.[119]

H.E. Stephenson and Carlton McNaught argue that the advertising agent was the catalyst behind the transformation of the publishing industry at the turn of the century.[120] It would be more precise to argue that the agents were in the right place at the right time – that they recognized that an opportunity existed within the industry and stepped in to exploit it. The opportunity in itself was created by the increased volume of national advertising, and this could only be provided by the advertisers.[121] Further, it was the publishers who confronted the organizational problems created by the increased volume of advertising, and it was they who rationalized its effects on the industry and established a workable framework to contain it. When the advertisers finally took stock of their position, they dramatically reoriented the reform process to assert their roles as the chief clients – of the agencies and the publishers alike. The agencies were sidelined insofar as the structure of the industry was concerned, destined to play whatever role they were given. Where the agencies would exercise the most influence was not in the industry's structure, but in its content – in the advertisements themselves.

Chapter 5

Copywriting, Psychology, and the Science of Advertising

Today, we advertising men ... take as much pain in analyzing the methods which produced the results as we did in writing the ads.
Economic Advertising, 1910[1]

'The Man at the Tee Box.' Here was the perfect image of the advertising man as he wanted to see himself. Cresting the hill, rising above the landscape and gazing out over his domain, he stands with arm outstretched, confidently pointing the way. He dominates the scene while another figure, ostensibly his equal but currently marginal, scurries about in vain. A man, square-jawed and clear-sighted, clean-shaven and impeccably dressed, he cuts a sporting figure on the sunlit green.

What more could the status-hungry adworker crave? Golf was the trade's unofficial sport, the arrivistes' mark of distinction. For A.J. Denne, it provided a bankable metaphor describing the agent's service, and perhaps the trade's 'arrival' itself. Denne drew a direct comparison between the advertising agent and the golfer surveying the greens from the tee. The man at the tee box offered his playing partner an unbeatable combination of vision, training, and experience that would lift his game out of the rough. The parallel was obvious. The adworker, with his 'straight, unhampered vision,' offered expertise in all facets of the advertising game.

Denne's portrayal of expertise was novel, but his goal was not. It was part of a long, continent-wide tradition of salesmanship angling to sell the manufacturer on advertising. With the emergence of the full-service agency came a raft of literature from the United States and Canada unlocking the secrets of successful copy. There had been copy

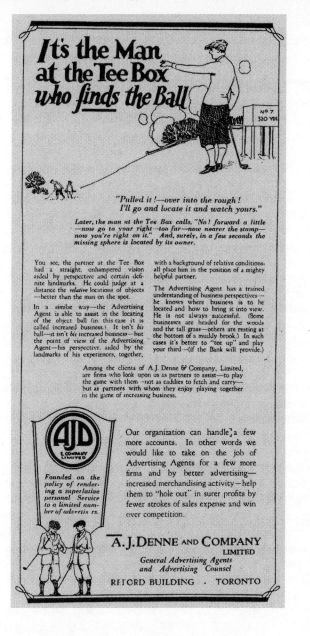

From *Marketing* 22:1 (15 January 1925), 21.

before then, of course. Indeed, there had been very successful copy, some of which had gained international notoriety. For the most part, this copy had hinged upon gimmicks: slogans, reiterated statements, or short poems featuring the product's name. It was the handiwork of people not trained in advertising, who simply used their common sense to intuit public response. That changed when adworkers started to question if there were not higher principles governing the more successful campaigns. Why did reiteration work? What made some slogans more effective than others? What made any ad resonate with thousands of readers? In their attempts to answer these questions, adworkers developed a theoretical approach to advertising. They wanted to systematize its content just as they had systematized its structure through standardized rate cards and agency agreements.

Theories came from many quarters, from the United States and Canada. In this respect, Canadian adworkers participated as equals with their American counterparts. Two groups in particular had an economic interest in the project: publishers and agents. Publishers found it useful to extol the benefits of copywriting, since it helped to generate interest in the product they had to sell. Once the agencies began to provide copy services, they too pushed their own variety of expertise. What set the full-service agencies apart from the space brokers, print shops, and in-house agencies was their ability to create advertising that generated reader response. When selling this service to advertisers, they had to articulate their view of copywriting and demonstrate their expertise in this line of service.

After 1900 a third group – academic psychologists – entered the discussion. Psychology as an academic field separate from philosophy developed between 1870 and 1920, precisely the years of advertising's rise to prominence. In retrospect, it seems inevitable that the new tools of experimental psychology would be turned upon the human response to advertising. The results of these experiments – all American – were published in a number of journals and books, some aimed at the advertising trade and others at an audience of fellow academics. All of them, from the modest findings of Harlow Gale to the sweeping mind-control theories of John B. Watson, promised to improve the efficiency of advertising.

Canadian adworkers grappled with the results of these studies. They learned of them through trade papers, luncheon meetings, and innumerable books. At the end of the day, they decided that the specific findings of the psychologists were not as important as the approaches to copy they advocated, either implicitly or explicitly. In many respects the specific findings of the psychologists sounded remarkably like the sort of things that a previous generation of publicity men had known intuitively. However, the psychologists' approach to advertising copy exposed an angle that copywriters had not previously explored in depth: in privileging the cognitive responses of readers, the psychologists made the consumer, rather than the product, the focus of their theories on advertising. The man at the tee box had found his ball.

Copy before 1890: Three Styles

Conventional wisdom has it that there were three broad styles of advertising in the 1800s: the traditional announcement, the Barnum style, and the Powers style. When theorists emerged in the United States and Canada after 1890, these three styles offered a focal point for discussion. Theorists pondered the factors underlying their relative success, dissected their assumptions, and then moved towards a more rarefied understanding of the art. Most advertising before 1880 took the form of a politely phrased announcement. Advertisers made it known that particular goods or services were available, and readers were asked to give them their kind consideration.[2] From this basic announcement, the other two styles developed, each privileging one of the advertisement's two basic functions: publicity and edification.

The Barnum style looked to advertising to gain attention for its message. The end goal was rapid and widespread publicity, and this imperative overruled everything else, including a sense of traditional propriety and plain-spoken truth.[3] Barnum himself described advertising as a catalyst, intended to induce a response that would multiply in the public at large: 'I saw that everything depended upon getting people to think, and talk, and become curious and excited over and about the "rare spectacle." Accordingly, posters, transparencies, advertisements, newspaper paragraphs – all calculated to extort attention – were employed, regardless of expense.'[4] Translated into cold type, this enthusiasm was manifest in an expansive use of space, brash layouts, a liberal use of ornamentations and cuts, and a disorienting variety of typefaces. These ads were more like proclamations shouted by the town crier rather than polite announcements. These were techniques developed among the patent medicine men. Barnum himself acknowledged that he did not invent them; he simply took them as far as they could go.[5]

Barnum coupled these techniques with an intimate understanding of his audience and the entertainments they enjoyed. One such attraction was an ingenious piece of taxidermy, a monkey's head invisibly grafted to the body of a fish. Barnum billed it as final proof of the existence of mermaids. It was one of his most notorious hoaxes, exposed only after thousands had seen it, and late in life he felt the need to explain his actions: 'I used it mainly to advertise the regular business of the Museum ... I might have published columns in the newspapers, presenting and praising the great collection of genuine specimens of natural history in my exhibition, and they would not have attracted nearly so much attention as did a few paragraphs about the mermaid which was only a small part of my show.'[6] If Barnum had done nothing but insult the intelligence of the people he claimed to serve, his reputation would have been questioned long before the turn of the century. Barnum and the medicine men offered their audiences something that they wanted: entertainment, amusement, diversion. In his autobiography, Barnum half boasted, half justified his actions: 'It was my study to give my patrons a superfluity of novelties, and for this I make no special claim to generosity, for it was strictly a business transaction. To send away my visitors more than doubly satisfied, was to induce them to come again and bring their friends.'[7] This too was a lesson well learned from the patent medicine men.

The Powers style stood in direct opposition to the Barnum style; it sought to inform rather than bamboozle. John E. Powers was the advertising manager of Wanamaker's, a Philadelphia dry-goods store that had pioneered the department store concept in the United States. Wanamaker's was known for innovative marketing techniques. Among other things, the price of each item in the store was clearly marked, and the same price was asked of all customers. There was no haggling, and no favours based on the customer's standing with the clerks. Wanamaker's cultivated the same transparency in its print advertising. Powers's copy style did not play to the curiosity or desires of the readers – at least, not overtly. Rather, his copy was brief and factual and proffered reasons why the item would be useful. Such reasons could include the readers' vanity, but just as frequently appealed to their sense of frugality or convenience. In one catalogue, Powers stated of a line of paint: 'This isn't much of a paint, but it is cheap, and good enough for hen houses and things like that.' Perhaps not surprisingly, the paint sold very well to people with hen houses and things like that. Powers's style became legendary and earned the sobriquet 'reason-why.'[8]

The difference in tone between Barnum and Powers could not have been more stark. To the extent that the Barnum style played to the gullibility of its audience, there was a degree of condescension in its view of humanity. The public were rubes, at best coauthors of their own illusions. Powers was more inclined to see the public as customers. Customers, seen within the intellectual framework of classical economics, had interests of their own that they sought to maximize in every commercial transaction. They were not to be misled, but assisted in the formation of their purchasing decisions. For classical economists such as Adam Smith, the essence of the ideal commercial transaction was not mystification, but clarification. For the economy to run efficiently, the consumer had to have access to relevant information and make proper decisions. The Powers style suited this outlook admirably.[9]

The differences between the styles can be overstated, however. Department stores such as Wanamaker's had a great deal in common with spectacles such as Barnum's American Museum or London's Crystal Palace. The emerging consumption patterns of an industrialized, urban society that led to the acceptance of the one led just as easily to an acceptance of the other.[10] Both were dependent on high-volume traffic to maintain profitability, and both were dependent on novelty and consumer satisfaction for repeat business. In their architecture as well as their layout, department stores focused on display no less than the spectacles. In this sense, they could go the spectacles one step better: the customers could sate their tactile desires by actually handling the objects on display and then purchasing them.

Now, consider for a moment that most Toronto adworkers of the late nineteenth century were not college graduates. Perhaps their understanding of the marketplace was influenced by an acquaintance with Adam Smith. However, it seems more probable that their views of human nature were shaped by the prevailing religious faith of the day, Protestant evangelicalism. Canadian evangelicals of the late nineteenth century did not view the individual as an essentially rational and forthright being. They viewed the individual as a frail vessel, weak by nature, inclined to sin without the saving grace of an other-worldly God. Only through an intimate acceptance of Jesus Christ could one overcome a sinful nature. Evangelicalism's defining ritual was the conversion experience, the intensely emotional 'release from sin' that was sometimes described as a second birth. While this view of human nature acknowledged the power of human agency, it was a limited power; it required the constant attention of a faithful will.[11] Seen from within the evangelical belief system, the Powers style flattered the human condition by idealizing the power of human rationality. It might have offered an approach to copywriting, but its take on human nature was one-dimensional. The same could be said of the Barnum style, though by contrast it elected to exploit human weakness.

With that in mind, it is worth noting the advertising practices of two of Canada's most prosperous merchants during this period, John Mac-Donald and Timothy Eaton. MacDonald, based in Toronto, owned one of the largest wholesale operations in Canada. In a booklet issued to his staff in 1876, MacDonald counselled them to 'avoid all extravagant expressions in selling. If the value is good, your customer will not have difficulty in discovering it; prudent men dislike boastful utterances, as well as the undue advocacy of one's wares.' Three years before, the wholesaler had recorded in his diary a set of business principles that would 'add to your business largely every month, every week, every day.' They were framed by one belief: a business should be conducted 'on the principles of God's Word, which contains the grandest commercial maxims in existence.' His approach to salesmanship, then, might have been informed by a considered assessment of 'human nature,' but it seems equally informed by a desire to live by God's will and not bear false witness.[12]

Timothy Eaton, also a devoted Methodist, offers a contrast to this austere approach to salesmanship. Eaton arrived in Toronto in 1869 when he left his small-town grocery for a dry-goods store in the city. The business developed into a thriving department store with the timely adoption of retailing practices by then common in the United States. An advertising department was established in the 1880s to handle all of the store's newspaper ads, and Eaton made clear what he expected to see:

Tell your story to [the] public[,] what you have & what you propose to sell –

Promise them not only bargains but that ev[er]y article will be found just what it [is] guarantee[d] to be –

Whether you sell a first-rate or a 3rd rate article the customers will get what they bargain for –

If you humbug do it right – let it be a genuine humbug – that no-one

but yourself will see through & that they will conjecture – use no decep-
tion in the smallest degree – no – nothing you cannot defend before God
or man.[13]

The first three paragraphs encourage a keen sense of honesty. Like
Powers and MacDonald, Eaton wanted simple, straightforward descriptions of his goods, even if that meant calling a third-rate item third
rate.

Eaton's reference to humbug may seem out of place given the rest of
his advice and his religious convictions. Perhaps at heart he was still
the small-town shopkeeper; he had no objection to what Sam Slick
might have called the 'soft sawder.' Eaton seems to refer not to trickery,
but to puffery, to salesmanship. He wanted his goods described hon-
estly, but at the same time he wanted them to be desirable. If they possessed qualities beyond what was empirically observable, those too
were acceptable talking points. So long as the qualities described could
bear scrutiny – so long as they did not inspire 'conjecture' – then they
were within the bounds of truth, and justifiable, and could rightly be
deemed a 'genuine humbug.' Eaton had found his own compromise
between the Barnum and Powers styles that also reassured his conscience: the satisfaction of respectable consumer desires *was* a reason-
why.

At the turn of the century the evangelicalism of MacDonald and
Eaton was in flux and adapting to the changing landscape of a modern
industrial society. Among a clerical and lay elite in Toronto, progressive theology was ascendant. The traditional evangelicals' concern for
personal salvation was becoming obscured by the pursuit of social
salvation, an attempt to cure the ills of society before converting the
individual. Temperance and Sabbatarianism were exemplary in this
regard, but so too was the Laymen's Missionary Movement. Formed in
1907, it brought together Methodist businessmen who donated their
organizational expertise to worthy Christian charities. Among its
members were Joseph Flavelle, then owner of the Toronto *News*, and
H.H. Fudger of the Robert Simpson Company, Eaton's chief rival. Historian Phyllis Airhart argues that such associations attempted to rein-
terpret the religious values of the past for the new society; the Laymen,
for example, actively introduced business considerations into the operation of local charities. Nonetheless, still implicit in its goals was a
desire to evangelize the world. Whether or not these associations succeeded in their particular aims, they could sate a member's nostalgia

for a traditional sense of piety, and perhaps 'restore a sense of Christian community' in a competitive and industrial urban world.[14]

It was during this time, as Daniel Pope has noted, that the Associated Advertising Clubs of the World initiated its Truth in Advertising campaign. Its opaque definition of truth, struck in 1913, was strikingly similar to Eaton's: 'We believe that agents and advertisers should not issue copy containing manifestly exaggerated statements, slurs, or offensive matter of any kind.'[15] Three years later, the Association of Canadian Advertisers would similarly resolve that they were opposed to: 'All advertising that is fraudulent or questionable, whether financial, medical or any other; ... that is "blind" or ambiguous in wording and calculated to mislead; that makes false, unwarranted, or exaggerated claims, ... all advertising that makes remedial, relief, or curative claims, either directly or by inference, that are not justified by the facts of common experience; and any other advertising that may cause money loss to the reader or injury in health or morals or loss of confidence in reputable advertising and honorable business.'[16] Not the absolute 'truth,' perhaps, but nothing that would inspire 'conjecture.' In Toronto, the most vocal proponents of truth in advertising were those youthful adworkers who had emerged from small-town Ontario, joined the ad clubs, and enthusiastically reformed the trade. In 1914 they adopted not only the fervour of the evangelicals, but their very pulpits. During the Toronto convention of the AACW, there were 'a number of sermons by advertising laymen in Toronto churches, representing nearly every shade of religious belief, even the Roman Catholics and Hebrews taking advantage of this splendid opportunity for propagating the gospel of truth and honesty.'[17] One wonders, then, if their idealism was informed by the same pangs of conscience, the same religious impulse, that had animated MacDonald and Eaton, Flavelle and Fudger. If so, the Truth in Advertising movement was not simply another ploy to professionalize the industry, but an attempt to Christianize it through the application of evangelical idealism. Their attempts to recruit the church as a client tend to reinforce this interpretation.

By the late 1800s, then, there were three recognized styles of advertising copy, exemplified by the traditional announcement, the Barnum style, and the Powers style. Each was informed by a view of human nature, but none of them offered a very complex reading of the typical consumer. Indeed, the Barnum and Powers depictions of consumer behaviour were little more than cartoon caricatures in comparison with the sophisticated view of humanity presented by the church. Though advertisers adopted these copy styles, they did not necessarily accept the sentiments that informed them. Instead, they continued to pursue a more satisfying explanation of readers' responses to advertising.

The First Writings on Advertising

During the 1880s numerous writers appeared ready to advise neophytes in the mysterious world of advertising. They comprised two groups, publishers and agents, and both took up their pens for the same reason: to demonstrate their expertise in the arts of publicity. At this time, it was customary for advertisers to write their own copy. As competition escalated between publishers for advertisers, and between agencies for clients, copywriting became a means for both groups to court the advertisers' favour. Publishers could argue that they offered more than just a good advertising medium; the advertising placed in their care would be well written and designed to ensure maximum notice. The full-service agencies, their media-buying credentials well in hand, could use the talents of a copywriter as a trump card during solicitations. The promise of well-crafted copy might suffice to close a deal.

Publishers included columns on advertising in their newspapers or magazines. Agents published specialized trade papers. In the United States, this became a cottage industry in the 1890s. The agent who pioneered the space brokerage, George Rowell, established *Printer's Ink* in 1888. Its early success spawned numerous imitators, some little more than newsletters boosting the fortunes of their parent companies. They all attained a degree of notoriety within the trade, and among the more reputable could be included *Profitable Advertising* (1890), *Fame* (1896), *Judicious Advertising* (1896), and *Mahin's Magazine* (1901).[18]

Canadians followed these trends. Newspapers and magazines frequently filled their empty space with treatises on good advertising practices. Throughout the 1890s they were joined by a modest domestic trade press when *Canadian Advertiser, Biz, Printer and Publisher*, and *Business* were started. By 1901 one freelance copywriter commented that 'with the number of trade and technical papers devoted to advertising, there can be little excuse for any newspaper publisher not getting abundance of suggestions ... The woods are full of them.'[19] These early journals revealed a trade developing both consciousness and expertise. Its expertise drew heavily upon past experience rather than theoretical knowledge.

18 Economic Advertising October, 1910.

The Tariff
or
Advertising?

The fallacious theory of the manufacturer who believes that a tariff wall is sufficiently adequate to protect him against foreign competition, reminds one of the Chinese soldiers, who, not more than a generation ago, wore armor to protect them against the onslaughts of a modernly-equipped foe.

Imagine antiquated armor stopping modern projectiles shot from a Maxim or Krupp gun.

Imagine the passive tariff wall attempting to offset the active, intelligent, and well-directed efforts of the foreign advertiser who is spending thousands of dollars to develop a market in Canada.

If the possibilities of the Canadian market are great for the American Advertiser, what must they be for the Canadian Manufacturer?

We have made a study of the Canadian market in all its aspects and we are prepared to discuss the matter with any one really interested.

Write us or call.

GAGNIER ADVERTISING SERVICE

Saturday
Night
Building

TORONTO
ONTARIO

Demonstrations of agency service became a means to secure clients in an increasingly competitive market. *Economic Advertising* 3:10 (October 1910), 18.

Each new paper that hit the news-stands declared its advertising policies and rates within its first few pages. Quickly thereafter it would also explain why it, and it alone, should have been entrusted with the thoughtful merchant's advertising. The Montreal *Star* offered the following advice on its editorial page in January 1869: 'The value of an advertising medium may be determined by the extent of its circulation. Wide publicity is the requisite of the general advertiser, and the cheap popular journal suits him, with its circulation of thousands, rather than the more pretentious morning daily with a tithe of its number of readers.'[20] Hugh Graham's *Star*, along with *La Presse* of Trefflé Berthiaume, and John Ross Robertson's Toronto *Telegram*, pioneered the penny press in Canada.[21]

Advertising advice was becoming more sophisticated by the time E.E. Sheppard founded *Saturday Night* magazine in 1887. Sheppard ran not one, but eight full columns on the art of advertising. The prospective advertiser first received the usual advice on media-buying, though this time the medium was a pretentious weekly and not a popular daily. Why should advertisers choose *Saturday Night*? To reach extremely worthy readership: 'Had he [the advertiser] taken the trouble to ascertain just which papers his customers read, he might very easily have dropped the others, profiting thus by a direct reduction of the amount expended, without in any way lessening the volume of his business. There are some people, like Barnum, whom it pays to advertise in everything from a comic weekly to a poultry journal, but the average advertiser should pick his advertising medium with the same caution that a thief picks a pocket or a woman a set of false teeth.'[22] By using *Saturday Night*, the wise advertiser saved money otherwise wasted by advertising promiscuously in every medium available.

Having dealt with media-buying, Sheppard's later columns focused primarily on advertising's 'mechanics,' its layout and design. He also broached the subject of copy. Readers sought their favourite items in the same part of a paper or magazine with each issue. The same was true of advertising, when readers sought the ads for their favourite stores. Sheppard believed this habit could be heightened and exploited if the advertiser encouraged it. For example, curiosity could be stimulated by changing the copy or illustration with each insertion. People read the papers for news; they expected no less novelty from their ads. If the same ad was run without change over a long period of time, readers would eventually glance past it. Sheppard suggested that copy be written around timely appeals, such as seasonal needs. Blankets were a good bet for winter, gifts at Christmas. Sheppard did not explain his reasoning here, but presumably such appeals envisioned the consumer's needs, and did not simply itemize the retailer's stock.[23]

The first trade journal of Canadian advertising – entitled, aptly enough, *Canadian Advertiser* – appeared in 1893. By this time the flood of literature on copy had begun in the United States, and this Toronto magazine rode the tide, with twenty pages chock full of advice on copy, type, and layout. Its discussion of media was far more catholic than that of Graham or Sheppard, covering shop windows, posters, and show cards, as well as periodicals. It was probably the product of Diver Electrotype, later renamed the Central Press Agency. Although no one connected to the magazine was named, its address was that of the Toronto *World* building, where Diver was housed, and six pages at the back catalogued electrotypes for sale.[24]

In its first issue, its editor claimed to be an experienced journalist working with an 'advertising expert.' He boldly declared that 'the art of advertising may be acquired by much study; for advertisers are not born, they are made.'[25] This would have come as quite a shock to P.T. Barnum. Although he credited advertising for his success, he claimed not to have a system when composing it. Rather, 'I often seized upon an opportunity by instinct, even before I had a very definite conception as to how it should be used, and it seemed, somehow, to mature itself and serve my purpose.'[26] *Canadian Advertiser* would have none of this. Barnum might have been a success with such slipshod tactics, but the advertiser of the 1890s could no longer do the same. 'There are certain essential elements which form the basis of this art,' it asserted, 'and these must be thoroughly absorbed into the advertiser's brain before he can become a master in his art.'[27] The magazine would be a fountain of wisdom kept fresh by the outpourings of experts. The age of the agencies and freelance copywriters was dawning.

Canadian Advertiser had advice on media-buying and mechanics, but it also ventured boldly into the realm of copy style. After some familiar commentary on the value of timely themes and well-planned designs, it addressed the problems that arose when searching for the proper tone of voice. Above all else, the editor advocated simplicity: 'All advertisements should be in as few words as possible, and the language should be plain, business-like and straight forward. All high-falutin, bombastic vaporings must be avoided, and every advertisement must appear to be truthful.'[28] These words echo those of Powers and Eaton. Short, simple, practical: this was the essential message.

There was, however, a new consciousness underlying this advice that was not evident in the earlier writers. Certainly, they had advocated trustworthiness and clarity, but *Canadian Advertiser* pushed its analysis one step further and added a literary perspective to copy. Atmosphere could be suggested by the wording of the copy, and this atmosphere had to be used to good advantage. The editor insisted that the advertiser not talk about itself or its business. Instead, it should focus attention as much as possible on the people reading the ad and address them in a familiar voice, the 'conversational style which speaks directly to the reader and never says "we" where it can say "you."' 'Such an advertisement,' he argued, 'talks to the consumer, mentions his wants and tells him where they can be satisfied.'[29] The hints that lay within Sheppard – to privilege the consumer's desires over the product itself – were now explicit.

There are other echoes here, of Sam Slick. It was the mythical pedlar's talent to simulate the spontaneity of a sincere interchange, to win the confidence of his marks, and exploit this to make a sale. *Canadian Advertiser* understood this ploy. Advertising had to re-create in type the same sense of easy familiarity that customers expected from their local shopkeepers – clearly, since it was for the local shopkeeper that most newspaper advertising was then written. Advertising, the editor stated, 'tells the reader just what the clerk or his master would tell the consumer across the counter.'[30] The shopkeeper had a reputation to uphold, and his roots were firmly planted in the community. He had to cultivate the goodwill of his clientele, and to do this he had to be as trustworthy in his advertising as he was in his store. Contemporary portrayals of the itinerant pedlar charged him with more underhanded practices. Harold Innis recalled of his youth in Otterville, Ontario, that 'they were often foreigners and in the country districts referred to as "Italians." The writer has strong reminiscences of abuse heaped on the head of a pedlar who followed the trail of defective articles traded by a forerunner.'[31] The shopkeeper's salesmanship could no more mimic the pedlar's reputed techniques than those of the medicine makers and circus promoters. Though more cautious, however, the shopkeeper's final intent was not much different. Once cultivated, the confidence of the clientele was still turned to advantage. With the cool tone of reason, the carefully written ad of the shopkeeper 'often creates wants where those who possess them were not aware of their existence. It appeals to their common sense and convinces them by its logic.'[32] Trustworthy, if not necessarily truthful; plain spoken, but consciously contrived; providing service to clientele while cultivating their unbidden desires: this was the model advertising propounded by *Canadian Advertiser* in 1893 and repeatedly described in the pages of *Biz*, *Business*, and *Printer and Publisher* thereafter.

Beyond the mainstream press and trade magazines, agencies also issued pamphlets and books outlining their copy strategies. The most famous copywriter to emerge from Canada during this period was undoubtedly John E. Kennedy. Kennedy landed in Chicago in 1903. There he made the acquaintance of Albert Lasker, an account executive with Lord and Thomas Advertising. Although a salesman, Lasker understood the importance of good copy and wanted a means to formalize the process of writing. Kennedy had precisely this: a proven approach to copywriting encapsulated in a simple formula. Advertising, Kennedy asserted, was 'salesmanship in print.' As Stephen Fox has noted, there was nothing novel in Kennedy's ideas; they were essentially those of Powers twenty years before.[33] In words that closely paralleled *Canadian Advertiser*, Kennedy argued that advertising had to convey the same information to the masses that a salesman would to an individual in order to strike up interest in the product and close the deal. Lasker was apparently thunderstruck by this revelation and trained all of the copywriters on his staff using Kennedy's ideas. In the time-honoured tradition of all major agencies, he then issued a publication boosting the firm's expertise – in this case, a series of pamphlets outlining Kennedy's approach.[34]

If the Powers style became formalized in Kennedy's writings, the Barnum style was rehabilitated by Ernest Elmo Calkins, an American agent. Calkins's approach to advertising emphasized the evocative possibilities of illustration.[35] Towards this end, he pushed his creative staff to consider the effect of each advertisement taken as a unit. Beautiful imagery, balanced layout, and a literary approach to copy could create unforgettable advertising by suggesting an atmosphere in association with the product. The finished ad would not appeal directly to reason, but to the emotive sensibilities and imagination of the reader. Calkins believed that many readers leafing through their favourite periodicals were not always looking for edification, but rather diversion; advertising beautifully composed could arrest attention and tap into their open state of mind. Calkins and his partner Ralph Holden put these ideas to the test on many accounts. Their most notable creation was the Arrow Collar Man – a staple of men's clothing ads for decades to come. J.E.H. MacDonald advised his students at the Ontario

College of Art to pay special attention to them, while Bertram Brooker voiced an impish protest: 'We are so fed up on the Arrow Collar type of male beauty that an oasis – however homely – almost brings tears of welcome to our eyes.'[36] Calkins was a regular contributor to advertising trade journals, and in 1905 brought together his ideas in a book entitled *Modern Advertising*.[37]

Behind these scattered sources of advice – from the mainstream press, trade papers, and books – there did lie an understanding of human behaviour. Few would have called it 'psychology.'[38] That a person's curiosity could be aroused by novelty, that a reader's eye could be attracted and held by a graceful composition, or that a consumer had to be personally interested in the goods for sale would have been considered common sense. The same knowledge of 'human nature' informed the pedlar's craft, Barnum's publicity, and the editorial policies of the penny press. Copywriters wrote from personal experience and imitated ads that had captured their own imaginations. Kennedy and Calkins formalized the assumptions and practices of generations of publicity men in terms recognizable to modern businessmen, and the enthusiastic new generation of adworkers read their treatises by the thousands. This was the environment the academic psychologists entered after 1900.

Academic Psychology

Until the late 1800s the academic study of the human mind and its operations took place within the halls of philosophy departments. Usually referred to as 'Mental and Moral Theory,' it was taught by men trained in the classic texts of John Locke and Immanuel Kant. Such works might have been grounded in the empirical tradition of the Enlightenment, but their primary data were drawn from the introspection of the philosophers involved. Their evidence was intangible. It gained its veracity through the sympathetic understanding of their readers, who were asked to look inside themselves to confirm the author's words. By the mid-1800s certain scholars believed this form of research was exhausted. A new approach was sought, more positivist, founded upon real-world experimentation and verifiable results, something that would provide hard, demonstrable evidence of theoretical models. The first person to do this was Wilhelm Wundt, who established a psychological laboratory at the University of Leipzig in 1879.[39]

Wundt attracted students from Europe and North America. To his dismay, not all of them pursued traditional philosophical questions. Despite his new methods, Wundt himself was still engaged in the metaphysical discussion of the human mind. Real-world applications seemed unthinkable; decades might pass before a proper synthesis along scientific lines could emerge. However, students such as John M. MacEachern, Harlow Gale, and Walter Dill Scott would not wait. Each of them attended to problems of applied psychology rather than the theoretical interests of their teacher. MacEachern, a Canadian hired by the University of Alberta in 1909, was drawn to industrial psychology and eventually became active in that province's eugenics program. Harlow Gale and Walter Dill Scott, both Americans, chose to study the effects of advertising. Wundt tried to discourage them from their unphilosophical interests, but decided their orientation to practical ends was a particularly North American trait.[40]

In 1896 Harlow Gale became the first academic psychologist to study the assumptions underlying advertising practices by using human subjects in laboratory experiments. His interests covered both the mechanical composition of advertising and its content. On the mechanics side, Gale started with a relatively common question: What made an advertisement noticeable? To answer it, he contrived experiments that tested the placement of advertising on a typical magazine page. Each subject was asked to sit in a dark room. Then, a card divided into four equal parts was briefly illuminated. After the light was turned off, the subject was asked which quarter of the page first attracted his or her attention. The test was repeated with a series of different cards, with a number of different subjects. Gale found that in most cases, subjects preferred the left side of the page to the right, and the top to the bottom. In other words, most people scanned the page as they would have read it.[41]

Gale's work on content was similarly innovative. These experiments tried to identify copy appeals that best captured the reader's interest. In these tests, Gale created a set of fictitious brand names for the same product, then had an ad set for each one, in the same style and type. Each ad featured a different talking point: the age of the firm, a celebrity endorsement, the price of the goods, or a description of their virtues. Individual subjects were asked to rank the products according to their impressions of the ads. Taking these scores as his data, Gale then assessed the effectiveness of each appeal. This technique, which became known as the 'order of merit' test, seemed to offer concrete assistance to copywriters.[42]

Gale included gender in his analyses. When questioning human subjects, he tabulated responses from men and women separately. In one experiment, he tried to determine which factor had the greatest influence over purchasing decisions: personal experience, a friend's recommendation, or advertising. The result, to his mind, was unexpected. Among men in his sample group, 31 per cent were primarily influenced by advertising, and among women, 35 per cent. Gale considered the difference negligible. 'We were rather surprised,' he wrote, 'that these trials did not show a comparatively larger proportion for the females in favour of advertising, as professional advertisers had told us they counted more on the women than on the men.'[43] He was similarly surprised in his order of merit test to see that men and women were influenced most by the same copy appeals. Both groups claimed that references to the age of a firm and the reliability of its goods were more compelling than its prices or attractive illustrations. His experiments did suggest some differences. The colour red caught women's attention best, while men were drawn to black; and women more than men were drawn to ads in which the illustrations had little relevance to the products being sold. However, the small size of his sample groups defied definitive explanations. Gale believed these findings might be useful to advertise products that were gender-specific. Otherwise, his conclusions about advertising in general were silent on the subject of gender.

While Gale's work inspired other psychologists, it did not capture the imagination of the advertising trade as did Walter Dill Scott's. The medium selected by each man might explain this difference. Gale presented his work in a series of research papers, which he had printed independently in Minneapolis, Minnesota, in 1900. Scott's ideas first appeared in a trade paper published by a reputable Chicago advertising agency. The interest sparked by these articles led to their republication in book form, as *The Theory of Advertising* (1904).[44]

Scott's book was a short, accessible, and well-illustrated piece of writing. In fifteen concise chapters he outlined what psychologists knew about the movement from reading to buying, and he explained how this movement could be directed. The key was the way in which ideas became associated. From laboratory experimentation, psychologists had shown to their satisfaction that three laws held in this process: first, that 'the idea next to enter the mind is the one which has habitually been associated with ... the one present to the mind.' Second, 'If two things have been recently connected in the mind, when one is thought of again it suggests the other also.' And third, 'If my present thought has been associated with a thousand different objects, that one will be suggested with which it has been most vividly associated.'[45] The application was obvious. The successful advertiser was one who forged a vivid association in the minds of readers between an everyday need and its product. The task of the copywriter was to make this association as vivid as possible, so much so that all other associations would be secondary to that of the product.

To create an effective association was one thing, to impel the reader to act was quite another. Scott described two means to do this. The first was the power of suggestion. Basically, Scott believed humans were highly suggestible creatures, and the mere idea of an action would usually bring it to fruition. He explained this process with reference to Ouija boards and hypnotism. In both cases, ideas were planted in the participant's mind to the total exclusion of all others. Under exceptionally focused conditions, participants were induced to bring about a desired end with apparently no conscious participation on their part. To apply this idea in advertising, the copywriter would have to demonstrate the benefits of *using* the advertised product. The ad could not dwell upon the product in isolation, but had to conjure in the minds of the readers an image of themselves with it. At its best, the association would be so vivid that the reader would not link the activity to any competing product.[46] A most effective way to do this would be through the use of an apt illustration, and Scott devoted six chapters to perception, apperception, and mental imagery.

The second means was the 'direct command.' This was a much more difficult method to use successfully because it directly confronted the reader's own inclinations. The reader who was told to 'Use Pears' Soap' or 'Drink Coca-Cola' could well answer 'no' and be done with it. Any copywriter using this type of pitch would have to be extremely judicious in his choice of words. It would be necessary to cloak the ultimate purpose of the ad: 'No one would be willing to admit that he had used Pears' Soap simply because he had read the command, "Use Pears' Soap." It is, however, quite probable that many persons have used Pears' Soap for no other reason ... We are perfectly willing to obey as long as we are unconscious of the fact. But let any one see that he has been commanded and his attitude is changed; he becomes obstinate instead of pliant.'[47] Scott believed that this obstinacy was more likely among the upper classes than the lower. The lower classes were accustomed to taking orders.

Both of these methods attempted to manipulate the conscious decision-making process of the reader. Scott believed that an idea
implanted in the mind could prejudice the outcome – the purchasing
decision – at a preconscious stage in that process. Suggestion did this
by encouraging the reader to participate in the formulation of that preconscious idea. The constructed image of the reader with the product
was expected to condition his or her ultimate decision, and conse-
quently influence future purchases. By contrast, a direct command
attempted to implant the ultimate decision itself. Either way, the ideal
advertisement would pre-empt the conscious thought patterns of the
reader. By definition, anything less would be an unsuccessful advertisement in Scott's mind: 'Actions performed as a result of a conscious,
deliberate determination would not be said to be suggested. Ideas
gained by a conscious, voluntary process of reasoning would likewise
not be said to be suggested.'[48] Hence, the ideal result of either method
would find readers responding to advertisements as if under hypnosis.

It was this assured outcome that psychologists hoped to achieve
when they applied their expertise to advertising. In the introduction to
his book, Scott set out the following program: 'In this day and generation we are not afraid of theories, systems, ideals, and imagination.
What we do avoid is chance, luck, haphazard undertakings ... We may
be willing to decide on unimportant things by instinct or by the flip-
ping of a coin, but when it comes to the serious things of life we want
to know that we are trusting to something more than a mere chance.
Advertising is a serious thing with the businessman of today.'[49] Scott
noted the enormous sums invested in publishing and advertising. This
industry needed the assurance provided by a scientific understanding
of its workings, and psychology, according to Gale and Scott, was the
science of advertising. Without it, everything was built on a foundation
of sand.

Unlike Harlow Gale, Scott did not examine the possible differences
between the cognitive responses of men and women. Nothing in his
language suggested that there were any. Rather, in the custom of the
day, Scott used masculine nouns and pronouns – he/his, man/man-
kind – when describing all psychological phenomena. Tellingly, in a
chapter on individual 'Differences in Mental Imagery,' he focused on
questions of social status rather than gender. He acknowledged that
the lived experience of readers would affect their perception of individual advertisements, but he did not specifically identify gender as an
important variable. Rather, 'a man's occupation, his age, his environ-

ment, etc.,' Scott wrote, 'make a difference in his manner of thinking, and in the motives which prompt him to action. In appealing to people we ordinarily think of these conditions and formulate our argument in accordance with these motives. That is to say, we address ourselves to a particular social or industrial class.'[50] Reading between the lines, one might conclude that the same held true for gender. If more women than men bought baking soda, presumably it was not due to any biologically determined cognitive process, but to differences in their lived experience. Still, Scott remained silent on this point.

The work of Gale and Scott was developed most rigorously within the school of psychology known as 'behaviourism.' Its most vocal proponent was John B. Watson, a psychologist at Johns Hopkins University in Baltimore, Maryland. While studying rats, Watson rethought Wundt's approach to laboratory results. As previously noted, Wundt used his experiments to test hypotheses concerning intangibles, things such as cognition, emotions, the mind. At root, then, his studies remained metaphysical, since his categories of analysis were informed purely by introspection. Even a concept such as 'mind' was at best mercurial; the only thing that could be known with certainty was the existence of the brain. Similarly, the cognitive processes that fascinated Wundt were estranged from anything material and verifiable. Rather than study these, Watson concentrated on the human animal and its activities. Instead of a science of mind, he demanded a science of behaviour, which acknowledged only empirically observable phenomena. Watson called this approach 'behaviourism.' With it, he expected psychology to discover the causal factors behind human actions. The practical applications of such knowledge would be almost infinite.[51]

Although Watson himself did not publish on advertising in the 1910s, a number of other behavioural psychologists did. The most prominent was Harry L. Hollingsworth, a professor at Columbia University in New York. Around 1910 he began searching for the fundamental drives behind consumer behaviour using the order of merit test. If it were possible to categorize and rank copy appeals according to their effectiveness with particular product types and markets, then all of the guesswork would be taken out of copywriting. His work on this and other questions was supplemented by the behaviourists Edward K. Strong, Henry Foster Adams, and Daniel Starch, all of whom published extensively throughout the 1910s.[52] By contrast, other schools of psychology remained aloof from advertising research. Freudian psychoanalysis was particularly noticeable by its absence given its desire to map the subconscious mind. Perhaps this is why adworkers paid it little heed. Among the American trade papers, it was a rare article that even mentioned Freudian concepts. It seems not to have penetrated the Canadian trade press at all.[53]

The behaviourists shared Scott's ambivalence towards gender as a category of analysis. Most incorporated it into their studies, but found that men and women provided similar results regarding the mechanics of advertising – things such as winning attention, the effects of colour, and long-term memory. Henry Foster Adams surveyed two decades of research and declared that few real differences had been found. Those differences that did exist were ascribed to culture rather than biology. A study on copy appeals demonstrated his point. Although adworkers and popular opinion agreed that women were more emotional than men, Harry L. Hollingsworth's research suggested the exact opposite where advertising was concerned: that men were more attuned to emotional appeals than women. Subjects were given fifty generic copy appeals and asked to rank them according to their persuasiveness. Both groups gave high marks to copy that emphasized healthfulness, cleanliness, and scientific design. After these, however, women were inclined to favour efficiency, safety, and durability. By contrast, men were drawn to ads suggesting an aura of modernity, the cultivation of family affection, and sympathy towards household pets. Hollingsworth described these results in terms of their social orientation: women favoured appeals that emphasized the products' usefulness to them personally, while men favoured appeals that emphasized the products' ability to enhance social acceptance. He believed that these responses were informed by one of two things: either temporary motives connected to the experiment itself, or to variations in 'sex experience' – the very real differences distinguishing the lives of contemporary men and women. Many of the appeals used in the experiment could have been associated with household goods that women were more likely to use than men. Either way, he did not believe the results stemmed from biological sources. It was a conclusion that his fellow behaviourists working in advertising shared.[54]

In Canada, there was no original work done in advertising psychology. Before 1920 only three philosophy departments had had research psychologists on staff. The University of Toronto employed two of Wundt's students – James Mark Baldwin (1889–93) and August Kirschmann (1893–1910) – but neither took an interest in advertising. The same was true of John MacEachern at Alberta, and the behaviourist William D. Tait at McGill. The development of psychology as a discipline separate from philosophy did not take place in Canada until the mid-1920s. Even then, Canada's academics concentrated on social psychology rather than commercial or industrial applications, a concentration well in keeping with the social gospel tendencies of the contemporary social sciences. Scholar Ernest F. Scott neatly summarized the prevailing mood when he curtly dismissed commercial research, writing, that 'in such arts as advertising and business method, the born rascal will do better than the psychologist every time.'[55]

Adworkers Respond to Academic Psychology

Canadian adworkers found much to discuss in the ideas of the academic psychologists, and after 1908 the trade press gradually revealed the growing influence of psychological thought. However, the interest in academic psychology among adworkers was particularly focused during two distinct periods. The first occurred after a revised edition of Scott's book appeared in 1908, and tapered off before the First World War. The second period followed the hiring of John B. Watson by JWT New York in 1920.

Stephen Fox offers a way to place the adworkers' discussion of academic psychology in some context. In his biographical history of the American advertising industry, *The Mirror Makers* (1984), Fox argues that there are two fundamental streams in copywriting: hard sell and soft sell. Hard sell corresponds to the Powers style, or the 'salesmanship in print' championed by Kennedy. It was characterized by its frank acceptance of the business transaction intended by the ad itself. It spoke of quality, price, efficiency, convenience, health, and any other factors affecting the purchase decision that privileged practicality over sentiment. Soft sell was its polar opposite. Soft sell dodged the transaction and entreated the public to look favourably upon the advertised product, regardless of its utility or price. This corresponded to the ideas of Barnum and Calkins.[56]

Reading Scott's book on suggestion and association, Fox argues that academic psychology endorsed the soft-sell approach. It is difficult to believe that Scott had this in mind. The psychologists did not intend to engage in an ongoing dispute among admen. Rather, as Merle Curti has argued, they sought to find the underlying principles that made *all* advertising work, not simply one style or another. The various theories regarding reason-why and humbug were merely gleaned from the writers' experience.[57] In place of these rules, psychology offered a way to develop campaigns in accordance with the needs of the imagined reader. The copy written could take any one of a variety of tones and styles. Even Scott endorsed the use of 'reason-why' copy with particular products. A key example was the piano. In the late 1800s pianos became a widely regarded middle-class status symbol. The piano was an investment in prestige, an imposing piece of furniture, and an indication of cultured accomplishment. Piano manufacturers knew this well and tended to stress these intangible benefits of ownership. Surely this was a suitable case for Scott's theory of suggestion; it clearly justified the scores of ads featuring well-dressed, admiring visitors cooing over their hosts' new upright. But here was Scott's reply: 'A piano is primarily not a thing to look at or an object for profitable investment, but it is a *musical* instrument. It might be beautiful and cheap, but still very undesirable. The chief thing about a piano is the quality of its tone. Many advertisers of pianos do not seem to have the slightest appreciation of this fact.'[58] The product might well be endowed with the magic of prestige, but the manufacturer still had to offer some reason why its name stood above the rest. The cold reality of the hard sell intruded into every advertisement. The appeal had to be tailored to the needs of the readership as well as their desires.

The difference between academic psychology and the reason-why style lay not with the copy itself, nor in its conception of human nature, but in its desired effect upon the reader. Scott's pursuit of hypnotic certainty directly opposed the Powers style and its faith in consumer acumen. An ad by Powers offered news; it conveyed information about the product and reasons why it should be purchased. If these reasons were pride or insecurity rather than efficiency or convenience – that is, if they appeared to be emotional rather than purely rational – then so be it. However, the ultimate decision regarding the product's utility was necessarily the consumer's to make, in full consciousness. Scott's theory of advertising challenged the reason-why approach only on this point. Powers privileged a conscious decision-making process, while Scott favoured the inculcation of pre-rational ideas and behavioural conditioning. The difference was often oversimplified as a conflict between reason and emotion.

The theories of Kennedy, Calkins, and Scott were readily available through numerous publications. Beyond the books and pamphlets they had authored, their ideas were also represented in the Canadian and American trade press. Due to his citizenship, Kennedy's activities were noted in *Economic Advertising*, which gave a ringing endorsement to his Lord and Thomas pamphlets.[59] The same paper regularly printed articles written by Calkins himself. Scott had an impact in other ways. He was never mentioned by name, perhaps because he was associated with a particular Chicago agency. Nonetheless, the discussion of psychology mounted in the Canadian trade press and Toronto luncheon rooms after a revised edition of his book appeared in 1908.

When *Economic Advertising* itself began in 1908, it landed thick in the middle of the debate aroused by Kennedy, Calkins, and Scott. T. Johnson Stewart, the new journal's editor, declared: 'The mission of this publication is to help advertisers and publishers alike to eliminate all waste in advertising ... As a rule our merchants and manufacturers are investing too little in systematic advertising ... Spasmodic advertising, it does not matter how big the investment, is not scientific, and cannot be economic. Haphazard advertising is nearly always wasteful.'[60] Scott's manifesto echoed through these passages. If advertising had been unsuccessful in the past, then the fault lay with ill-conceived plans. Advertisers needed better-written copy and a more judicious selection of media. The key words for Stewart were 'systematic' and 'scientific.' Advertising had to be placed upon a basis that would allow for greater assurance of a profitable return.

On the matter of copy, Stewart advocated appeals to emotion and appeals to reason. He believed that the reading public could well be swayed by both, though 'the majority of mankind' was generally won by an appeal to their sentiments. By way of example, Stewart did not point to any one advertising campaign, but to the temper of a church congregation. 'You never knew a cool, logical preacher to have a crowded church. The popular preacher appeals to the emotions of men and women. Incidentally, he may be logical, but crowds who attend his services are not enticed by his nice reasoning.'[61] Still, Stewart expected a sales pitch in the midst of this emotive copy. A painting may provoke powerful emotions, but never sell anything. Stewart seemed to favour a compromise between Kennedy and Calkins: reason-why copy with a focus on human sentiment. 'That the selling argument will be more and more used by advertisers goes without saying,' he stated in one editorial, but this selling argument could not rely on the hard sell associated with Powers.[62] Rather, 'The writer who can most vividly picture the little personal features of goods, their beauty, the good standing which will be produced by their possessor, their exclusiveness, their distinction from common wares, has learned a lesson that has business value. Telling how long an article will last, how strong it is and how well put together, is all right, but all these are points of a material nature. While giving attention to this side, don't overlook the personal side – the pride side – sentiment.'[63] Like Eaton, *Canadian Advertiser*, and Kennedy before, Stewart urged the copywriter to think about the reader and to demonstrate through the text an understanding of his or her desires. Stewart, however, put a remarkable new emphasis on the social stature imparted by goods. The advertiser was no longer selling something that offered to gratify practical or even personal desires. Now the goods carried a symbolic value for those who did not purchase them as well.[64]

For all the suggestions advanced in its pages, *Economic Advertising* did not fully endorse the adoption of psychological approaches to copy. Rather, it tended to use the new vocabulary supplied by psychologists only to relate the old wisdom of the trade. Where past advertisers had 'hammered home' their sales message by repeating the same slogan week after week, now they spoke of 'conditioning' the reader's mind through 'systematic' advertising.[65] Similarly, an article in *Printer and Publisher* could now speak of 'creating desire' rather than putting over the sales message.[66] For all of their talk of science, the new advertising intellectuals had to admit there was very little that was scientific about copywriting itself. The only 'scientific' aspect of their work was space-buying, where circulation figures could supply a measure of mathematical conviction to their decisions regarding media. However, no one suggested that there was anything comparable to assist in the preparation of copy. Systematic, longingly 'scientific,' but ultimately not psychological: this was Stewart's approach to advertising in 1909.

Stewart found a curious rival in George French, the editor of an American trade paper called *Profitable Advertising*. French was an experienced agency man, active in institutional work and a moving force behind the Association of National Advertisers in the United States. He contributed numerous articles to *Economic Advertising* and *Marketing* and became a regular columnist when he moved to Montreal in 1929.[67] In 1909 French editorialized that all of the talk about the 'science of advertising' was essentially bunk. He took particular aim at the work of men such as Gale, on the mechanics of composition. '[A] good advertisement, or a good piece of printing,' French believed, 'depends for its beauty, its strength, its pulling power, upon the very same prin-

ciples that make a good painting ... The painter goes about the preparation of his canvas exactly as the advertiser or printer should go about
the task of "laying out" his work. This is composition in art; and it is
composition that the advertiser must study.'[68] These aspects of advertising had been studied by adworkers and compositors long before
Gale and his ilk arrived on the scene. As the Toronto print shop Rous
and Mann knew, 'The artist makes even such a drab subject as a cook
stove a most desired possession. His magic touch makes advertising
interesting, alluring, profitable.'[69] French believed that academic psychology offered little in the way of new ideas. A better training in
advertising could be afforded by a study of fine art, a suggestion that
could have come straight from Calkins.

Although Stewart did not endorse the adoption of psychological
theories, he felt compelled to respond to these comments. By identify-
ing the 'science of advertising' strictly with psychology, French had
attacked the basis of Stewart's journal. However, because the science
he so eagerly sought did not yet exist, Stewart found it difficult to
frame his objections. He made this frank admission:

> The science of advertising is no more fallible than any other science extant
> ... There is no ultimate and final knowledge. Nor has there been a single
> instance in the whole history of advertising, as far as we know, where the
> counsellor's predictions have been more than approximately correct.
>
> But because we cannot predict the exact results of any advertising cam-
> paign we may plan and engineer, it does not follow that we are unscien-
> tific or that nine-tenths of all advertising is a gamble. Because we cannot
> altogether eliminate chance in any line of business, it would be utterly
> foolish to solemnly declare that all but a tenth of the business on the globe
> was speculative, pure and simple.[70]

References to the fallibility of science and the lack of ultimate knowledge, combined with a warm embrace of the scientific spirit, betray a
familiarity with American pragmatists such as Charles S. Peirce or
John Dewey. And yet, in the very next paragraph, Stewart scorned academic psychology, dismissing it as the 'vaporings of savants, who
never wrote an ad., or never sold an inch of space in all their lives.'[71]
One wonders, then, why he would champion the spirit and not the
reality of the contemporary 'science of advertising.'

Part of the problem may have been the businessman's general suspicion of academia. The businessman fancied himself a man of action,

carrying heavy responsibilities for personnel, plants, and investments; the academic was a mere spinner of theories without much connection to the real world of commerce.[72] Walter Dill Scott had participated in a few profitable campaigns, but Harlow Gale had not, and his methods came under close scrutiny. In particular, his lab conditions were criticized for their inability to replicate a real-world reading experience. Subjects who were momentarily focused on a dimly lit page in a dark room might have recognized the sensation of reading in a lightning storm, but it is doubtful this matched anyone's notion of leisure-time reading. If Gale had allowed his subjects more than a fleeting glimpse of each page, his results might have been different.[73] One of Gale's deficiencies became evident among newspapermen in 1910. Based on his lab results, Gale found his subjects' attention was first drawn to the upper left corner of each page. As a result, Gale believed this was the optimum placement for any ad. In practice, editors used the top left corner for news and built up their advertising matter from the bottom right. That way, news was the first thing that most people saw as they turned the page. Then, scanning down, the last thing that fixed in their minds was an advertisement. This suggested that the optimum position was the bottom right corner. Describing this arrangement technique to the Canadian Press Association, J.R. Bone of the Toronto *Star* implicitly suggested that Gale's findings were, psychologically speaking, completely wrong.[74]

A second impediment for advertising psychology may have been the academics' own hesitations. As reported in *Economic Advertising*, the most promising applications of psychological discoveries to advertising problems were always part of a dimly perceived future. In February 1911 the journal ran a speech by Charles S. Ricker, chair of psychology at Harvard University. Ricker could have coined the summation to any number of articles when he stated that in 'a few years psychologists will reduce to an exact science the method of composing advertisements so as to obtain answers.'[75] Statements such as this might have sparked the interest of ambitious young copywriters, but it offered nothing concrete in the way of methods. Once again the adworkers' quest for professional authority and credibility was frustrated by unmet expectations.

In the end, then, one has to wonder if Stewart's fascination with science was not more of a general outlook than a practical program. Stewart's 'system,' as it appeared through his columns, amounted to this: place emotive copy in well-selected publications as frequently as possi-

ble, whether the general business climate is good or bad. Advertise
your goods with the right pitch, all the time.

Despite Stewart, there were many agents in Canada who flirted with
academic psychology. W.A. Lydiatt, in his directory of Canadian periodicals, recommended certain books that he considered mandatory
reading. In 1918 the list included Scott's *Psychology of Advertising* and
Hollingsworth's *Advertising and Selling*.[76] McKim Limited revealed
more than a passing knowledge of Scott's book when it claimed in its
1911 directory that it had 'dug deep into practical psychology, and
learned how to attract, convince, and sell to the prospective buyer by
means of the printed advertisement.'[77] After Woods-Norris Limited
bought *Economic Advertising* from Stewart and Tobin, it ran several articles on the benefits of applied psychology, and in its own ads boasted
that 'proper analysis of the buying public' was a featured part of its
service.[78]

Herbert N. Casson, a partner in H.K. McCann Detroit and Canadian
by birth, felt that academic psychology had provided at least one useful thing: a scientific framework to understand and describe reader
behaviour. This gave adworkers more convincing means to assure
their clients that their money was not being wasted. Further, they
could reassure themselves that their efforts were truly effective. In the
meantime, despite their fondest wishes, it was impossible for adworkers to predict or guarantee the results of the campaigns they created.
Stewart addressed this issue by arguing that Canadian advertising was
still 'emerging from cloudland.' The 'science of advertising' had provided rudimentary tools to take the guesswork out of their trade.
Beyond that, trust and patience were the orders of the day.[79]

The trade's interest in academic psychology was piqued again after
1920. That year, JWT New York hired John B. Watson as an account
executive. Watson introduced the agency to research techniques that
gauged consumers' impressions of specific products. However, while
such research provided valuable data about consumer attitudes, it did
not prescribe actual copy. It was one thing to know how a sample
group felt about a product, quite another to persuade millions of readers to buy it. Watson's methods were tested with his handling of the
account for Cheseborough-Pond, a manufacturer of women's beauty
products. Historian Deborah J. Coon has argued that the ads produced
under his direction were indeed consistent with his psychological
manifesto. Still, none of the ads struck a new note in style or approach.
The copy appeals employed had been used for years, by other adver-

tisers and other agencies. Advertisers did not need a psychologist to suggest that status envy, yearnings for romantic love, and celebrity endorsements could sell beauty products. Once again, it appeared that the 'science,' or theories spun in the name of science, had simply served to validate long-established techniques.[80]

Still, the imaginations of Canadian adworkers were once again sparked by the possibilities of academic psychology. Over the next decade, Canadian psychologists found a new and eager audience when they were invited to speak to the advertising trade. Three members of the philosophy department at the University of Toronto – George Sidney Brett, James W. Bridges, and Earl MacPhee – hit the luncheon circuit during the 1920s. None, however, worked in the field of advertising psychology. Brett was not even a psychologist. Bridges did research into the human personality, and eventually landed in the Faculty of Medicine at McGill; MacPhee was active in the mental hygiene movement, but left academia for a management job in industry in 1929. Their speeches to adworkers had none of the propaganda value of Watson's broadsides. Rather, they offered the usual blandishments on the utility of psychology, sentiments expressed in countless trade paper articles. For example, Bridges appeared at the annual meeting of the Association of Canadian Advertisers in 1923. The gist of his talk: an adworker approaching a new campaign should first ask five questions – Who is the consumer? What appeal will sell the product to him? What is the best way to present that appeal? What media should be used? and What place has advertising in the general scheme of business? Doubtless, few took notes. A year later, Brett spoke before the Canadian Weekly Newspaper Association. In his opinion, 'about 90 per cent. or more of the matter printed in publications devoted to business psycho-analysis was valueless, other than it served to give an idea of the enormous complexity of things. The formulas given, as a rule, cannot be put into actual practice.' He then asked his audience to advertise responsibly and to stick to reason-why copy. Perhaps this explains why no psychologist wrote for the Toronto trade press or did consulting work with an agency before 1930.[81]

If the psychologists themselves were less than helpful, this did not deter Canadian adworkers in their quest for psychological insights. In 1923 a minor skirmish erupted around 'forward association,' an affectation among copywriters that placed adjectives after their nouns in expressions such as 'the tea supreme.' One letter writer told *Marketing* the practice was assinine, 'an example of what the psychologists do for us when they start meddling with advertising.' Nonetheless, the same writer used his understanding of basic human behaviour to treat the issue at hand. Even if useful findings and reliable methods were not forthcoming, it was increasingly apparent that 'psychology, or rather the application of the study of human nature to advertising, is a vital and necessary part of marketing.' This was the belief of T.D. Rimmer, of McConnell and Fergusson. His thoughts found greater explication in a letter from W.A. Dutton, of R.C. Smith and Son, Advertising. 'Most of us agree that the obvious aim of all advertising is to sell goods,' Dutton wrote, 'and to do so an effect has to be produced upon the mind of the reader to bring about a favorable response or reaction. That being so, any step taken to intelligently comprehend or measure advertising responses must admittedly fall into the realm of psychological endeavour.' By dint of their very trade, adworkers were necessarily psychologists. For Rimmer and Dutton, to have an understanding of 'psychology' was simply to have an understanding of 'human nature.' The terms were apparently interchangeable.[82]

Had academic psychology changed the adworkers' conception of human nature? Merle Curti believes it did: adworkers once held a positive view of humanity, as rational beings responsive to reason-why copy. Academic psychology had prompted more cynical thinking, which viewed humanity as matter in motion prone to manipulation. This account seems unlikely, particularly if the first generation of modern adworkers had their view of human nature shaped by the Sunday school texts of their youth. Evangelicals acknowledged the existence of sin and the weakness of the human will in the face of temptation. The new psychology resonated powerfully with these ideas, where original sin and temptation were reconceptualized as deep-seated instincts and mechanistic responses to external stimuli. For adworkers, it might have appeared that the language of religion had simply been replaced by the language of science. Human nature was understood to be no more and no less rational than it had ever been.[83]

The language of science offered one benefit that the language of religion could not. Evangelicalism had a moral standard of right and wrong. Even if temptation was a fundamental part of being human, surrender was a sin. The behaviourists recognized no such problem. Behaviour predicated on the instincts or external stimuli was part of the natural and unquestioned order. The adworker was given wide latitude to exploit whatever human sentiment or weakness would best sell the product at hand. This rendered any objection to the Barnum style irrelevant and greatly eased the conscience of some adworkers. For example, W.A. Dutton's comments, quoted above, came in the midst of a discussion on the ethics of advertising. The same concerns that had troubled the Methodist merchants of the 1870s and the Truth in Advertising movement in the 1910s were still nettlesome in the 1920s. Dutton's description of advertising psychology was designed to reveal the moral neutrality of their work. As he put it, 'The veriest dabbler in psychology knows that it is provable that most emotions are fundamental, and as such are inherent and permanent. That being so, how can an appeal to these fundamentals be considered unethical? Motherhood, love of home, love of children – all such fundamental sentiments are emotional and instinctive rather than intellectual, and, therefore, can a copy appeal directed towards such orderly and proper sentiments be deemed anything but ethical?'[84]

At the end of the day, copywriters did not find that their work had changed much in the wake of academic psychology. George French, no doubt familiar with John B. Watson's agency work, could comfortably repeat in 1926 the impressions he had had in 1909. The consumer attitude survey was a useful new addition to the agency's arsenal of weapons, but all of the rest of the theoretical posturing was still bunk. Whether the information made available to creative staff was intuitively held or survey-generated, there still existed an unbridgeable gap between theoretical strategies and creative product. The final ad was still a fallible product of human minds and hands. There was nothing scientific about creative tasks.[85]

The foremost Canadian writer on the subject agreed. Bertram Brooker took great pleasure lampooning Watson's adventures in advertising. In the short story 'Mrs Legion's Affections,' a former account executive – Illingsworth by name – describes to his companion Linscott the downfall of an 'old-established' New York advertising agency. The end came when it tried to sell a new flour with an endorsement campaign featuring the average American housewife. 'Not simply *an* average woman, Linscott, but *the* average woman,' Illingsworth explained. A partner in the firm had suggested that census and market data be used to identify the demographic position of the 'average small-town American family.' Then, Illingsworth continued,

he said we ought to strike some psychological average. He said he knew a professor at Columbia who could do it for us. You know the ways things like that are done – a series of questions and the answers 'rated' according to a formula figured out in advance – the idea being to find a woman with average mentality and average emotional reactions ... The answers would be compared with the 'mean' or 'average' established by the Columbia professor, and we could truthfully say ... that we had scientifically selected *'the perfect average of American womanhood.'*[86]

The average American woman turned out to be Daisy Newman, a married mother of one in Mimico, Ohio. She readily agreed to work on the campaign, and was soon embracing the high life in the Big Apple, where she captivated every executive at the agency. Enraged, her jealous husband sued the lot of them for alienation of affection. The agency became a laughing stock, its reputation effectively ruined. The agents had tried to seduce the average American woman, and in turn had been seduced themselves – not simply by Mrs Newman, but by their own blind faith in the 'science' of psychology.

Brooker's wider journalism – in trade papers such as *Marketing*, *Printer's Ink*, and *Advertising and Selling* – revealed a fascination with the creative process behind copywriting. In one of his more notorious articles, entitled 'Shunning Shakespeare,' he exchanged barbs with an American counterpart over the choice of language used in ads aimed at popular audiences. Brooker favoured language that was expressive, clear, and precise. The tone of voice he adopted never spoke down to his readers, and if a particular word carried connotations that no other word could, he would use it no matter how uncommon the word might be. In short, Brooker favoured a highly literary approach to advertising without endorsing trivial embellishments.[87]

Brooker believed that wording was crucial because advertising's purpose was to graft meaning onto the products or services being sold. Each person's life was not guided necessarily by true or false facts. In contrast with the advocates of reason-why copy, Brooker did not believe that people could calculate the best response in every situation according to a cold and sober analysis of the information on hand. Rather, everyone freighted their analysis with values, and it was these values that governed their individual responses. In Brooker's words, the key was 'significance – the *view* imposed on facts by the individual observer according to his particular position or relation to the facts observed.'[88] The truth of the claims made in any ad were irrelevant. It was the significance of the claims and their mode of expression that carried the sale. Timothy Eaton might have called this a 'genuine humbug.' For Brooker, the appearance of truth carried more persuasive power than truth itself. An ad for pipe tobacco clarified his point. In it, a notorious Hollywood vamp claimed that all of her leading men smoked the advertised brand. The public had largely dismissed the ad because none of the characters portrayed by her leading men were pipe smokers: 'You see, it may be true that she wrote it. It may be *true* that in private life her fiancé did smoke a pipe. But these truths have little or no significance because both she and her fiancé *made signs* in thousands of movie palaces that make them out to have been of quite a different character. You see, known character counts more than truth.'[89] Advertising appeared in a world that the copywriter could not control, where meaning was fluid and individually interpreted. The copywriter had to pay attention to the suggestive value of words and construct his ads in such a way that they triggered the reader's values. The reason-why reliance on conscious decisions and the behaviourist reliance on conditioned responses could both be faulted. Both held mechanistic views of 'human nature' that failed to account for the fact that 'life is not *subject* to mathematics.'[90] The trade's search for scientific certainty was doomed from the start.

Given his interest in copy, it was inevitable that Brooker would comment on the theories proffered by the psychologists. He did so in 1930, in a book that knit together themes from several of his articles. To prepare himself, Brooker surveyed every book on advertising psychology that he could get. His conclusion? No one else should ever have to do the same. To Brooker's mind, psychology had one great advantage: it asked copywriters to think about the consumer's needs and aspirations, the consumer's values. To write copy that would engage the reader's attention, it was not enough that the copywriter simply describe the product. It was not enough to relate the care in its manufacture, its unique qualities, its beneficial effects, or its price. These aspects of the product reflected the concerns of the manufacturer and distributor. To engage readers' attention, the copywriter had to evoke something that would be of interest to the readers: the readers themselves. Brooker demonstrated what he meant:

People need soap.
People *want* good complexions.
Why do they want good complexions?
To attract the opposite sex – to retain the love and admiration of their relatives and friends – to achieve popularity!
Do you see what happens when you start to *ask questions in the right*

order? You are led immediately away from your product and your own business to where the prospect lives.[91]

Thus, insofar as psychological theories asked copywriters to think in terms of how their creations played with the readers, they were on the right track. Unfortunately, all they offered were abstractions, not concrete suggestions upon which to construct a campaign. Brooker returned to his example to make his point:

> Take Popularity for instance. It isn't enough for you to know that people want to be popular. You ought to know why people want to be popular ...
>
> Popularity is an abstract term, and that won't do in advertising.
>
> You must discover what they will *get out* of popularity in terms of living![92]

The advantage of academic psychology was not a prescriptive set of rules governing the writing of copy. Rather, it suggested a habit of mind that led one to ask the right questions and to seek useful information before starting the creative process. Psychology informed the copywriter, not the copy.

In their depth of analysis, Brooker's writings on copy and advertising set him apart from most of his contemporaries in Canada. Nonetheless, he was not dismissed for his ruminations – he was in high demand. During the time that he wrote *Copy Technique* he was a consultant with McKim Limited. The year that it was published he was courted by J.J. Gibbons Limited and a rising new agency known as Cockfield, Brown. Five years later he was hired by MacLaren Advertising, where he retired as a vice-president in 1955.[93]

The full-service agency changed the complexion of advertising in Canada. The ground upon which the agencies competed shifted, from a focus on rates to a focus on copy. Where the space brokers relied on a knowledge of rates and circulations, the copywriter had to craft a new rhetoric of expertise to sell his service. Copy was still a novelty at the turn of the century. The appearance of American psychological studies on advertising could not have been more timely.

Psychology offered adworkers three things. In very practical terms, it offered a basic training for rookies in the advertising trade. Barnum and Powers had an intuitive feel for the mind of the public, but few had their talents. Hundreds of people tried their hand at advertising once the trade began to flourish. For many without practical experience in writing or sales, the sudden raft of psychology texts must have provided valuable guidance. For those with experience, the works of Gale, Scott, Hollingsworth, and their peers confirmed their best instincts. On these two points alone, Stewart, French, Casson, and Brooker were willing to accept that psychology had contributed something useful. For French, psychology was simply a way 'to do systematically, and with certainty of successful results, that which we have been doing blindly and wastefully.'[94]

Second, psychology did this by challenging copywriters to consider the reader. This may seem an obvious point, but it was novel at the time. The style of advertising prevalent before 1880 was phrased as an announcement. Ads may have noted the availability of the product, its quality, or its price; they may have noted the competence and efficiency of the manufacturer, or the cordiality and prestige of the retailer. The focus was on the product, its manufacture, or its distribution. By examining the cognitive processes of the reader, psychology asked the copywriter to think in terms of the prospective consumer. Although there were campaigns that had done this prior to Gale, the debates surrounding advertising psychology made the importance of the reader-consumer, either male or female, explicit. Again, this was something that could inform both the 'emotion' and the reason-why styles.

Finally, the trade's interest in psychology, particularly before the First World War, meshed well with the larger movement towards its elevation from a suspect commercial practice to an indispensable and professional component of modern business. From 1904 to 1914 publishers had demanded fixed rates of commission from agents, and advertisers and agencies had demanded audited circulations from publishers. In these demands, there was an economically motivated drive to reduce the risk of financial failure and a widespread attempt to eliminate the uncouth, the dishonest, and the unnecessary underside of the trade. Each sector sought to place its respective tasks on a firm business basis. In their flirtation with psychology, adworkers revealed a desire to systematize the content as well as the structure of the business. They sought a scientific demonstration that what they did had an impact on the affairs of commerce, that what they did really mattered in the way they thought it did. With the findings of the academic psychologists, even novice adworkers gained some assurance that they were experts in persuasion and that their expertise was rooted in something tangible and verifiable.

'Canada's National Advertiser' as the 'Man at the Tee Box.' *Marketing* 20:8 (19 April 1924), 247.

Taken altogether, the Ad Club movement, the agency agreements, and the discovery of psychology represented three manifestations of the same urge: the desire to attain higher status for the advertising trade. It would be a misnomer to call this professionalization. None of these attempted to divorce advertising from its place in the world of commerce and place it among the learned professions. However, just as the Advertising Advertising campaign provided a philosophical rationale for the existence of the trade within the economy at large, psychology provided a scientific rationale for copywriting techniques. Even if the reading public remained oblivious to these events, they were crucial to the trade's own self-respect.

An ad for the Toronto *Star* made this plain with a single illustration – 'Canada's National Advertiser' was portrayed perhaps as he wished to see himself: hovering in the clouds, godlike, an aloof and paternal being remote from the teeming throng of humanity. The *Star* would be the Advertiser's prophet and missionary. The *Star* was one with the throng; it walked among the masses and understood them. At the same time, it was filled with the Advertiser's vision, and its efforts were bent to the Advertiser's will. An ad in the *Star* would awaken the masses, foster a new consciousness, and lead them to the Advertiser's door. Here once again, in his most flattering, his most vain representation, was the Man at the Tee Box.

Chapter 6

Market Research and the Management of Risk

Advertising, of course, is no longer the haphazard affair of years gone by. It has been reduced to a science. It is in the hands of experts, men and women who have devoted years to the study of the popular appeal and who know how to construct announcements that will strike the imagination of the public.
Canadian Advertising Data, 1928[1]

Joseph Tetley and Company began importing a high-quality blended tea into Canada in 1889. When it did, the English company asked a Toronto agent to handle its introduction, someone who knew the Canadian market. Tetley asked Timothy Eaton. Eaton gladly shared his knowledge of conditions around Toronto. Tetley's tea, he felt, was of a very high calibre. Such teas were not found in Ontario in large quantities. Quite the opposite – Eaton felt the country was 'full of rubbish' where tea was concerned, so much so that the general public could not even recognize a good tea. In his Toronto store, Eaton wrote, 'We have opened a little stand for brewing tea ... Our Canadian people have not this previous knowledge, and give some very funny expressions when they taste it. They enjoy the fragrance arising from it when infused, but cannot give any definite opinion whether they like the taste or not, having never tasted the like before.'[2] Here was a classic problem in marketing: how to introduce a new consumer product into an existing marketplace.

Tetley and Company proposed one solution. It wanted to introduce a second-grade blend with a lower price alongside the flagship line. This would establish a foothold for the Tetley name in the market for lower-grade teas and gradually draw converts to the higher-priced blend. Eaton demurred. The lower-grade tea would simply obscure the advantage of the higher-grade tea. Brand loyalty would be developed only with difficulty. 'The moment you drop the quality,' he asserted, 'you lose the confidence of the people, and unless you have a superior quality to talk about[,] it is next thing to useless to say a word about it.'[3] If Tetley and Company followed its plan, Eaton would not invest any of his own money in its advertising.

Eaton's alternative was very simple. The public had to be told that the Tetley name stood for a high-quality tea. There were two ways to do this. First, the tea stand within the store was introducing shoppers to the new tea and handing them trade cards and leaflets to take home. This could be continued. More important, however, would be advertising. Although he traditionally used the daily press to advertise his store, Eaton wanted to place Tetley ads in an American group of magazines known as the Butterick quarterlies. These magazines ran dress patterns that appealed to fashion-conscious women, and he owned their Canadian rights. With this one decision, Eaton consciously made women tea drinkers the target of the campaign. He also proposed a second campaign informed by his impressions of the tea stand. Although many of 'our Canadian people' were indifferent to the tea, Eaton found that 'the English-speaking or Old Country people appreciate it very much, it reminds them too what they have been accustomed to drink in England.' Here was an opening. He would capture the patronage of English immigrants while cultivating the tastes of the native born. Again, he would pass over the dailies in favour of weeklies 'largely in the country where Old Country people are located.'[4]

In the space of two letters, Timothy Eaton demonstrated why he was the leading retailer in Ontario. He was conscious of existing products that the new product would have to overcome. He was also conscious of the investment required to create a niche for the product. In the tea stand he had a vehicle to introduce shoppers to the new item and survey their responses to it. From their responses, he devised a strategy that would overcome consumer resistance in a way that would start with a sympathetic audience. This strategy hinged upon a recognition that the market was not a monolithic mass, but divided by gender and ethnicity. To reach these markets effectively, he had a knowledge of the relevant media. In his use of trade cards and circulars we might wonder if he was not also consciously targeting a specific class of consumers, a class that did not read newspapers and fashion magazines. With the Butterick rights, he also achieved a degree of forward integration in his selling practices by controlling an important source of consumer information. As great as his understanding of retailing was, it is also readily apparent that Eaton had an exceptional grasp of marketing.

'Marketing' is a concept that describes the movement of goods between the producer and the consumer. This involves every aspect of that movement, from the obvious material components such as packaging, transportation, and retailing, to intangible components such as the consumers' knowledge of a product and their attitudes towards it. A marketing strategy will take into account every relevant aspect of this movement. Its goal is to get the goods to the widest suitable market at the lowest per-unit cost. Seen in this light, advertising forms only one part of a larger process. It is asked to fulfil only the ideological aspects of the marketing strategy. That said, advertising is undeniably that strategy's most visible component.[5]

Twenty-five years after his handling of the Tetley account, a new group of service providers within the advertising trade would consider Eaton's technique outmoded – a relic of a previous, unscientific age of commerce. This group conducted market research, a new set of business services that handled the same kinds of questions that Eaton had, but with far greater concern for method. A market researcher might have wondered if Eaton's shoppers were truly representative of the tea-drinking public. That researcher might also have wondered how Eaton identified clientele from the Old Country. For that matter, how did Eaton know that more British immigrants lived outside the city than in the city itself? And would they really drive sales until the rest of the population tried the new tea? These were the kinds of questions that market research asked. Rather than working from impressions and assumptions, the researcher would offer something decidedly more concrete: facts. And such facts would be offered in the guise of cold, hard numbers. No longer would managers have to base crucial decisions on their impressions and guesswork concerning the market for their goods. Now, the market could be studied in depth and all of the relevant information could be placed at their fingertips. Theoretically, marketing decisions would become a matter of calculation.

The rationale and techniques of market research were slow to emerge. They did not spring forth fully formed, but developed in response to the needs of publishers and advertisers. Nor were these groups entirely responsible for the techniques to which they laid claim. Rather, they drew upon developments in a variety of fields encompassing economics, statistics, sociology, and psychology. As with psychology, most of the innovations in market research emerged first in the United States. However, they were implemented almost simultaneously there and in Canada.

Manufacturers: The Development of Marketing

In the last half of the nineteenth century there was no discernible set of practices known as 'marketing' among manufacturers. Rather, the term was used in a generic sense to describe the movement of farm produce. It was adapted to industry only after 1900, as innovations in sales techniques mounted within publishers' and manufacturers' sales departments.

Prior to 1890 manufacturers were primarily concerned with the production of goods. In a consumer goods economy dominated by small-scale manufacturing, distribution outside of local markets was the realm of wholesalers. Wholesalers rationalized the process of storage and transportation. With their credit resources and warehouses they improved upon local economies of scale by dealing in several product lines in several industries. Nonetheless, manufacturers were rarely pleased with these arrangements. Historian Alfred Chandler argues this situation became particularly acute among certain manufacturers in the United States during the 1880s as they adopted technologies of mass production and were no longer confident that the wholesalers could adequately dispose of their wares. One man who worked in the Canadian wholesale trade at the turn of the century, C.L. Burton, noted that the mediating role of wholesalers conferred a great deal of power on a few men: 'It is difficult to appreciate the power of the wholesaler who ruled our world within the lifetime of men like me. The wholesaler told the manufacturer what to make. The wholesaler told the retailer what to sell. He was the kingpin of commerce. The public took what it was offered.'[6] Burton may have overdramatized the extent of the wholesaler's power, but his concerns were those of a great many working in both retailing and manufacturing. Such firms sought to limit the middleman's power or eliminate him altogether.[7]

The manufacturer's efforts were assisted by a strong corporate identity. Many common staples were sold unpackaged and without labels prior to 1890. Since consumers had little idea who produced the goods they bought, they could rarely request them by name. This allowed wholesalers to fill their lines from the cheapest available sources, and led to the conditions described by Burton. When consumers became aware of a particular brand, and demanded it, then the manufacturer gained more control over the price and distribution of its wares. The conscious development of brand names and trade-mark symbols, then, was a strategy purposefully intended to bridge the gap between manufacturers and consumers. The 'Christie Girl' was a perfect example of this phenomenon, created for Christie, Brown and Company by J.P. McConnell and J.J. Gibbons Limited. With her sparkling white dress and doe-eyed smile, she was 'the symbol of biscuit purity.' According to a puff in *Economic Advertising*, the Christie Girl was 'representative of the 300 girls employed in the brightest, cleanest, and most modern biscuit factory in all Canada.'[8] In this case the trade mark was an image of the ideal producer herself. By 1905 trade journals and business textbooks were encouraging more of the same and spinning theories on the creation of memorable names for new products. McKim Limited did its part, asserting: 'Many a business which was once at the mercy of a few big jobbers is now, thanks to trademarks and advertising, in an absolutely secure position through its hold on the goodwill of consumers.' J.F. MacKay of the *Globe* agreed: 'The business of the future is to be a war of brands. The customer will buy the goods he can identify by their trade-mark.'[9]

With a recognizable brand name, a manufacturer could appeal to consumers over the heads of middlemen. The most direct means to do so was through catalogues, trade cards, and advertising, and contemporaries attested to the growth of these tactics after 1895. With the parcel post system or door-to-door salesmen, the middlemen could be eliminated altogether. Still, retailers remained the preferred means of product distribution, and here too brand-name advertising was effective. Trade papers linked businesses united by a common trade and allowed manufacturers to familiarize hundreds of retailers with their products. Little wonder, then, that over a dozen trade paper publishers appeared in Toronto between 1895 and 1920, producing almost one hundred titles in every line of trade imaginable.[10]

Advances in marketing practice such as trade marks and advertising itself set the stage for market research. It was the function of market research to provide concrete information for the preparation of marketing strategies. While psychology offered a new perspective into the creation of advertisements, it was quintessentially subjective in its orientation. Insofar as it asked copywriters to write from the consumer's perspective towards the product, it asked copywriters to think in terms of the *individual* consumer. The market, on the other hand, was composed of *millions* of consumers, all with their own needs and aspirations. Market research promised to condense this mass into a body of readily comprehensible information. It analysed populations in terms of quantifiable characteristics and described the results via statistics.

Market researchers were not the first to grapple with the statistical analysis of large populations. The intellectual and practical antecedents of their trade can be found in the nineteenth-century development of statistical theory and social surveys. During the late 1800s statistics became a powerful resource to those challenging the policy options of governments. Churches, labour groups, public health advocates, and voluntary organizations used social surveys to reveal new aspects of modern life, where the statistical machinery of the state – developed for censuses and to track trade patterns – did not look. Within universities, statistics were incorporated into several disciplines in the emerging social sciences. Most academics adopted quantitative data analysis for much the same reason: they were seeking a scientific foundation for their research. Further, many of the key academics advancing statistical analysis were committed to the same social reform movements pioneering the use of surveys. Among them were British mathematicians active in the eugenics movement, Francis Galton and Karl Pearson, who developed the first reliable theories regarding correlation in the 1890s.[11]

A similar combination of empirical research and practical application led to the formation of the first departments of psychology. The research and test methods employed in psychological research frequently depended on information acquired through survey methods. While statisticians concentrated on the mathematical manipulation of statistics and the integrity of their formulas, psychologists developed their own theories on the ability to control factors affecting data at their source. In particular, they problematized the wording of survey questions and debated the relevance of sample size in the acquisition of representative data. On these questions, American scholars took the lead during the 1910s, using as a point of reference the pioneering work of Harlow Gale and Harry L. Hollingsworth.[12]

Economics provided the other vital link between the emerging social sciences and the study of markets. Here too American scholars took a leading role. A handful of political economists considered the role of distribution in the national economy during the 1880s. Their attention eventually turned to the institutions that managed distribution – firms such as credit agencies, wholesalers, railways, and retailers. The field gained wider acceptance after 1890, and two universities led the way: the University of Wisconsin and Harvard University. Researchers at Wisconsin investigated the marketing problems faced by the state's agricultural sector in the 1880s. At Harvard, the study of industrial marketing came into its own with the foundation of the Graduate School of Business in 1908.[13]

Market research drew upon all of these movements and disciplines, a fact made evident in the work of Paul T. Cherington. Cherington taught marketing at Harvard when the graduate school opened. He was also active in the foundation of the Bureau of Business Research in 1911, created to develop quantitative measurement techniques specifically geared to marketing problems. Practitioners greeted this work with enthusiasm, and the Associated Advertising Clubs of America asked him to produce a book on the role of advertising in the distribution process. He produced two: *Advertising as a Business Force* (1913) and *The Advertising Book – 1916* (1916). Each volume was an anthology of articles drawn from American trade papers; each article detailed the problems of a different manufacturer; and each author was a corporate manager or advertising agent. Neither book focused on advertising. Instead, they wandered widely over the entire process of product distribution, from packaging, trade marks, and shipping, to wholesalers, retailers, and sales staff. The articles revealed a wide knowledge of surveys, statistics, sociology, and psychology, which may indicate corporate America's growing interest in university graduates. All of them stressed the necessity of fully investigating the marketplace before successful plans could be drawn. One difference stands out between the two books, however. In 1913 research was described as a novelty; three years later it was an established practice at prestigious firms.[14]

This conjunction of interests occurred primarily in the United States. Throughout the period under study the most sophisticated statistical work in Canada was found within the federal civil service. Although Canadian academics and adworkers were aware of the new developments, private sector investment in market research was slow to appear. Most Canadian adworkers remained spectators to the discussions highlighted by Cherington. Meanwhile, the Dominion government began integrating the statistical work of its various ministries into one agency in 1912. The move was intended to cut costs while enhancing the statisticians' expertise and productivity. With this hope in mind, the new 'Dominion Bureau of Statistics' was told to explore new services. Robert H. Coats, its first director, eagerly complied. The bureau aggressively developed a niche for itself within government operations and cultivated relationships with outside organizations as well.[15]

The new bureau inherited its core mandate from the office it replaced, the Census and Statistics Branch. To this was added the collection of data on resource industries, agricultural production, power generation, transportation and communication, external trade, employment, and prices. In short, the bureau tracked every major macroeconomic trend of consequence to the Canadian economy. Coats explained that 'the fundamental purpose of statistical centralization lies in the fact that its great subjects, such as production, trade, finance, population, etc., are not separate and distinct, but are closely interrelated ... The statistics of the country, therefore, must be framed to illustrate these relationships.'[16] When he wrote this, Coats had in mind the legislator seeking to draft government policy. Nonetheless, there was an obvious dividend to be earned by serving the interests of the business community. It was not coincidental that the bureau was housed in the Department of Trade and Commerce. Coats wanted to provide a monthly review of national statistics that would be of 'a marked service to the business community.'[17] It began in 1928 as the *Monthly Review of Business Statistics*.

From a marketing standpoint, there was a major drawback to the bureau's information. All of its statistics privileged production and transportation. It contained no data regarding retailing and consumption. Coats's definition of 'marketing' hinged upon its origins in the distribution of agricultural products – no small matter in the Canadian economy. Those who desired information on the consumer markets for processed foods and manufactured goods, however, found the process of extracting useful information from its reports somewhat frustrating. As a reporter for *Marketing* put it, Coats's mind 'does not run to jam.' Rather, his bureau was engaged in a much larger project: 'It is concerned with building up a logical, exhaustive, and perfectly co-ordinated scheme or system of statistics from which jam manufacturers, and the 397 other types of manufacturers included in his classification of trades, can all dig for information with fair prospects of getting what they want.'[18] The bureau, no matter how sophisticated its operations, could only supply marketers with the base statistics for their studies. Every study it undertook had to be justified on the basis of its utility to the government. It could not initiate ad hoc projects for every company that wanted industry-specific research done. Further, all of the statistics the bureau handled were of strictly material objects: people, farms, factories, exports, investments – anything of a quantifiable nature. It could not measure intangibles, such as the attitudes or intentions of consumers. This was not a failing, but a product of the bureau's mandate as a government department. That anyone found fault with this indicates that new questions were being asked, and that a new field of business services had opened.[19]

Periodicals: Readership, Demographics, and Market Segmentation

At the forefront of market research were North America's periodical publishers. Although manufacturers, wholesalers, and retailers were consciously developing more sophisticated marketing practices, they had not given much thought to market research prior to 1910.[20] In this regard, publishers had more at stake. As competition intensified among American periodicals after 1890, publishers there sought means to differentiate their products in the eyes of advertisers. At first this was accomplished with broad claims regarding a paper or its readership. After 1900 sceptical advertisers prompted publishers to substantiate their claims. Ever watchful, Canadian publishers quickly took up the new strategies.

Periodicals with large circulations had an easy task when selling their space to advertisers. They could rightly assert that advertising in their pages reached the greatest number of readers, and thus gave advertisers the greatest exposure possible for their money.[21] This was a safe pitch. Before 1900 space-buyers generally wanted to reach the largest possible audience at the lowest possible price, in each town where their company did business. Periodicals could effectively promote themselves to national advertisers using little more than their location and their circulation figures as talking points. The Montreal *Star* had the best time of it; it had the largest circulation of any Canadian periodical. Others had to be more creative in their use of this appeal. Witness the Vancouver *Sun*, proudly proclaiming that it was 'The FIRST PAPER in Canada's FOURTH CITY.'[22]

If a periodical's circulation was nothing to brag about, a publisher could sell it in other ways. At the turn of the century it was common to emphasize a periodical's quality and special appeal. Its heritage might be trumpeted, or its production standards, or the reputation of its editorial staff. The type of people who read a periodical might also pro-

Quality of the periodical itself as a talking point. *Canadian Newspaper Directory*, 4th ed. (Montreal: McKim, 1905), 79.

REACHES THE WEALTH,

BRAINS AND CULTURE

OF CANADA.

The Sheppard Publishing Co.

Publishers, ---Saturday Night Building, Toronto   Limited

Elite readership as a talking point. *Canadian Newspaper Directory*, 3d ed. (Montreal: McKim, 1901), 48.

vide an indication of its quality. Publishers and editors always had some impression of their audience, or at least the ideal reader to whom they addressed their articles. Certainly, E.E. Sheppard had a high opinion of *Saturday Night* readers. The accuracy of this impression was crucial to the periodical's longevity. Letters to the editor could have focused this impression; the subscription list should have done so as well. Even if subscribers' names were not familiar, the neighbourhoods indicated by their street addresses would have been revealing of their affluence or social standing. Further, every periodical published was geared to a specific constituency. Most newspapers had an editorial mandate defined by party affiliation and social class; magazines by religious faith or hobby. Publishers, then, had a variety of ways to demonstrate the quality of their products to advertisers quite apart from circulation figures. Nonetheless, the qualities that sold a periodical to readers did not necessarily interest advertisers. Scrupulous

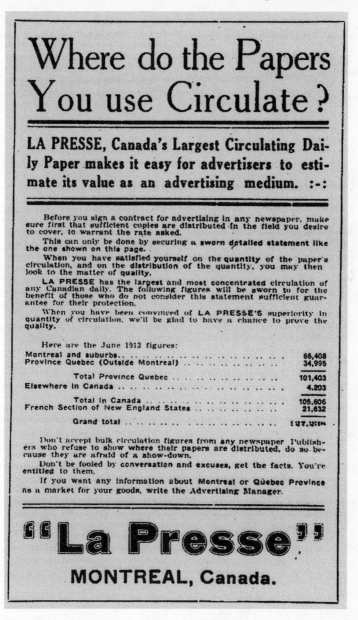

Territorial coverage as a talking point. *French Periodicals* (Montreal: Canadian Advertising, 1912), 39.

THE CANADIAN NEWSPAPER DIRECTORY.

LA PATRIE

reaches daily more than 85 per cent. of the total
purchasing power of the French population.

Advertisers who desire a share of
the growing trade of the Province
of Quebec must cater to existing
conditions. All advertisers who
are using LA PATRIE and
LE CULTIVATEUR are
reaching the French people of the
city and province—who can afford
all the necessaries and most of the
luxuries advertisers have to offer.

Quality and quantity of circulation makes the paying medium,
La Patrie having both- it pays.

A. McKim & Co., Advertising Agency, Montreal and Toronto

THE CANADIAN NEWSPAPER DIRECTORY.

Over Two Hundred Thousand People

out of 330,000 speak French
in Montreal : the local or general
advertiser cannot reach the best
or monied element of this great
majority except through LA
PATRIE : nor can he cover the
province without LA PATRIE
and LE CULTIVATEUR
(weekly). The latter goes into
30,000 rural homes every week.

LA PATRIE

(all editions) goes into more than 115,000 homes
weekly—an average of nearly half a million readers.

A. McKim & Co., Advertising Agency, Montreal and Toronto

Language as a talking point. *Canadian Newspaper Directory*, 4th ed. (Montreal: McKim, 1905), 110–11.

advertisers were not looking at the quality of a periodical per se, but at the quality of the readership itself. Once publishers understood this, their strategies changed dramatically.

After 1900 publishers' emphasis on quality and gross circulation lost ground to descriptions of their readership consciously portrayed as markets.[23] These markets were identified by four main characteristics: territorial coverage, language, class, and gender. This breakdown mirrored the concerns of advertisers and moved from purely material considerations towards more ideological considerations in the segmentation of the market. The geographical coverage of the periodical was the primary concern, simply because no firm advertised where it had no distribution.

The language of periodicals was a particular concern in Quebec. Few periodicals were published in French outside of that province during the period under review (Table 1.2, page 47). There, however, advertisers of products who wanted comprehensive coverage of the province had to advertise in two papers in several regions. An enigmatic ad for *L'Evenement de Québec* asserted that 'QUEBEC is very definitely *NOT* a one-newspaper market!' but one wonders if its perceived competition was the English-language Quebec *Chronicle* or the French-language *La Presse* in Montreal.[24] One English-language publisher, noting its absence from the francophone market, created a companion for its flagship magazine in 1919; advertisers could buy space in *Everywoman's* and *La Canadienne* with one appropriation.[25] After 1910 the scene became more diversified when recent immigrant groups began publishing in their own native tongues, neither English nor French; these papers appeared simultaneously in several parts of the country. For the sake of economy, space-buyers gauged the consumer spending power of a language group before using its papers. Every periodical, of course, was adamant that its readership was crucial to the advertiser's market.[26]

Once region and language were dealt with, social standing offered another means to narrow the target audience. Publishers treated the social standing of readers as a reflection of their disposable income. Generally speaking, the more costly the goods to be sold, the narrower the market for them would be. Wise advertisers chose those publications whose readership most closely resembled their customers. The demand for common necessities such as soaps, razors, hosiery, and hairbrushes cut through class divisions, and so the manufacturers of these products preferred those mediums with the greatest circulation. Popular dailies such as the *Telegram* and the *Star* were obvious choices in Toronto. On the other hand, upmarket versions of these same items – say, a gentleman's gift shaving kit with a handcrafted leather case, or a silver brush and comb – were more often advertised in periodicals appealing to those with higher incomes. The *Mail and Empire* assiduously courted Toronto's financial elite and chose not to compete for the mass audience sought by the *Telegram* and the *Star*. It advertised itself accordingly.[27]

Gender offered an alternative means of segmenting the market. In the 1890s advertisers and publishers began to believe that in the typical urban family, composed of a breadwinning male and a home-making female, the latter partner exercised the majority of daily consumer purchasing decisions. The food her family ate, the clothes they wore, the cleansers she used, and the furnishings they enjoyed, all were purchased during the homemaker's daytime shopping excursions,

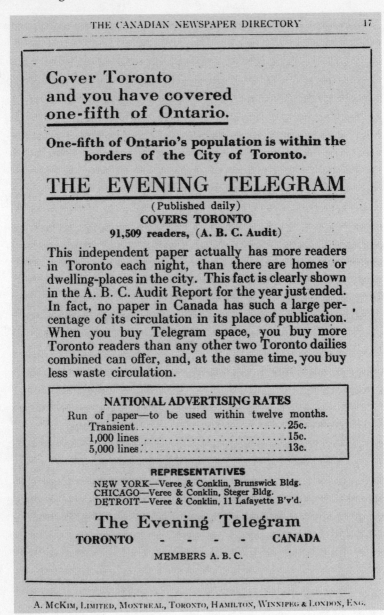

Saturation coverage as a talking point. *Canadian Newspaper Directory,* 15th ed.
(Montreal: McKim, 1920), 17.

The income of elite readers as a talking point. *Canadian Newspaper Directory,* 5th ed. (Montreal: McKim, 1907), 6.

without her husband. Many copywriters geared their advertising specifically to women rather than an all-inclusive mass readership. Hence, an ability to reach women became a decided advantage for periodicals. Literary magazines, with their cultivated notions of belles-lettres, had long enjoyed a female readership schooled to appreciate such things. They were joined by the 'domestic' or 'household' magazines in the late 1880s. These newer magazines had romantic fiction and florid illustrations, but they focused on the practical aspects of housekeeping, child-rearing, recipes, and sewing. Newspapers, to entice women readers, developed new sections modelled after these domestic magazines. Some women were contemptuous of this narrow reading of their interests, to little effect. Katherine Coleman was one of these critics, but she became Toronto's first woman editor when she created the women's page for the Toronto *Mail* in 1889. The popularity of her writing, and the page itself, inspired imitations at several other papers by 1900.[28]

As the volume of advertising increased, individual ads could be lost in the shuffle. Publishers tried to limit this effect by placing ads alongside news of interest to those most likely to purchase the featured product. In effect, they mimicked the physical organization of the department store, and departmentalized their editorial and advertising content.[29] Cigars, typewriters, and automobiles might be advertised in the financial section; concerts, lectures, and books in the entertainment section. Departmentalization reinforced the gendered division of the modern newspaper. If it seemed that more men than women read the sporting pages, then those pages were a good bet for the ads of items gendered 'male.' For the makers of items gendered 'female,' the women's section was an useful innovation. By 1910, then, a periodical's ability to reach women, men, or both groups was a decided asset when selling space.[30]

The publishers' use of market segmentation in their sales efforts gradually emerged between 1900 and 1910. As it did, publishers also learned how to substantiate their readership profiles with statistical data. Drawing upon census data, it was possible to describe the circulation area in terms of population, native tongue, ethnicity, and gender. From the census of occupations and the *Labour Gazette* they could estimate the relative social standing of the local workforce, and perhaps its average disposable income. Drawing upon their own subscription lists and circulation data, they could also calculate their own effective coverage of this population. This kind of analysis required

20   Economic Advertising   March, 1911

Everything for Women

Or the Home, Should
be Advertised in the

Canadian Home Journal

Women buy 80 per cent. of the necessities and luxuries for the home. Then the only logical way to
secure their trade is to advertise in a publication
read by women.

Most women delight in reading good fiction or something about fashions, household duties, or children.
That's why the "Canadian Home Journal" is read
with interest by thousands of Canadian women, that
have no time or desire to thoroughly read other
publications.

Value of Advertisements Carried Doubled in One Year

In one year this magazine has climbed from the bottom
to the top of Canadian publications, AND THE VALUE
OF ADVERTISEMENTS CARRIED HAS DOUBLED.
A shrewd advertising solicitor can secure advertising contracts, but a renewal is only given on results.

Every Large Advertiser Has Renewed Contract

This is surely a proof that they are obtaining
satisfactory results.

CANADIAN HOME JOURNAL

59-61 John Street   -   -   -   Toronto, Canada

Gender as a talking point. *Economic Advertising* 4:3 (March 1911), 20.

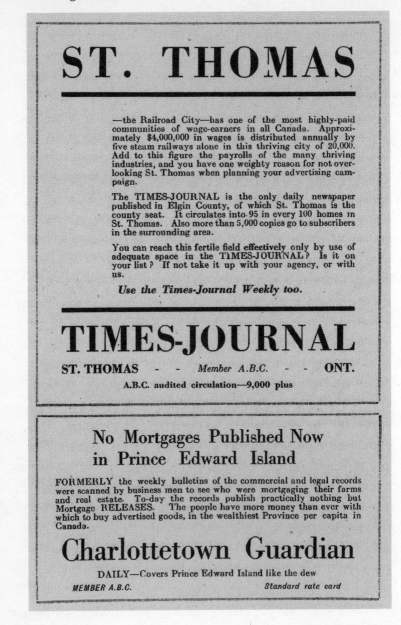

ST. THOMAS

—the Railroad City—has one of the most highly-paid communities of wage-earners in all Canada. Approximately $4,000,000 in wages is distributed annually by five steam railways alone in this thriving city of 20,000. Add to this figure the payrolls of the many thriving industries, and you have one weighty reason for not overlooking St. Thomas when planning your advertising campaign.

The TIMES-JOURNAL is the only daily newspaper published in Elgin County, of which St. Thomas is the county seat. It circulates into 95 in every 100 homes in St. Thomas. Also more than 5,000 copies go to subscribers in the surrounding area.

You can reach this fertile field effectively only by use of adequate space in the TIMES-JOURNAL? Is it on your list? If not take it up with your agency, or with us.

Use the Times-Journal Weekly too.

TIMES-JOURNAL

ST. THOMAS - - *Member A.B.C.* - - **ONT.**

A.B.C. audited circulation—9,000 plus

No Mortgages Published Now in Prince Edward Island

FORMERLY the weekly bulletins of the commercial and legal records were scanned by business men to see who were mortgaging their farms and real estate. To-day the records publish practically nothing but Mortgage RELEASES. The people have more money than ever with which to buy advertised goods, in the wealthiest Province per capita in Canada.

Charlottetown Guardian

DAILY—Covers Prince Edward Island like the dew

MEMBER A.B.C.   *Standard rate card*

Readers' aggregate income as a talking point. *Marketing* 14:4 (April 1920), 218.

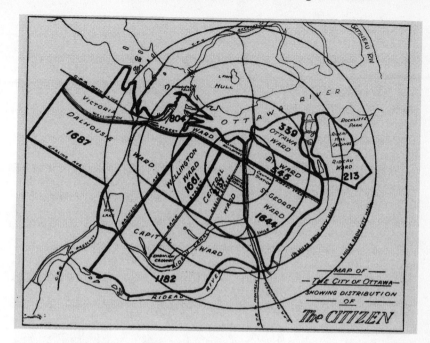

Chart designed by the Advertising Department of the Ottawa *Citizen*. *Printer and Publisher* 23:3 (March 1914), 67.

no sophisticated training in mathematics or statistics. Nor did it require any survey techniques. The raw data were readily available. What it required, as noted above, was a fundamental shift in thought. Publishers had to predict the needs of advertisers and offer them services specifically designed to satisfy their desires within the pages of their periodicals. It also meant, again, that publishers had to sell the quality of their readership rather than the quality of the periodical itself.[31]

In 1910 the Curtis Publishing Company took these developments to their logical conclusion. It established its own research department to collect published statistics and to develop a unique database on its own readers. The idea for this department had come directly from its sales staff. If detailed readership data could be generated for each of the company's magazines, the salesmen believed their job would be

greatly enhanced. Without this information, they were selling something that was often vague and elusive: abstract circulation figures and
the publisher's impressions. With it, they would be able to sell something that was far more concrete: real-life consumers, described in
quantifiable, easy-to-grasp terms. Although Curtis Publishing did not
originate the idea of research, it became the industry's acknowledged
leader with this development.[32]

Few Canadian publishers had the financial resources of Curtis Publishing. Indeed, probably few American publishers did. Nonetheless,
its research department soon focused the industry's attention on
research practices. By 1914 it had become a hot topic of debate in the
pages of *Printer and Publisher*. The editor posed a crucial question: Was
it important for an advertiser to know the socio-economic standing of a
paper's readers? The answers he received from publishers – curiously,
no advertisers were asked – indicated that they were extremely vexed
over the whole issue. It also indicated that publishers from Nelson,
British Columbia, to Moncton, New Brunswick, from the major Toronto dailies to the smallest weekly paper in Iroquois, Ontario, were
contemplating it. Cost was their main concern. At that point, few yet
wanted to carry the expense of something that offered no apparent
added value to their white space. F.S. Jawfs of the Calgary *Farm and
Ranch Review* believed that research was 'interesting, no doubt, but this
kind of thing has become a fetish with some publishers and advertising men.'[33]

Others were more enthusiastic. If market data sold white space, then
research was an investment worth making. This was the thought of
M.R. Jennings, publisher of the Edmonton *Journal*. It was also the
thought of several space-buyers. McKim Limited had been an early
convert, and declared in its 1911 newspaper directory: 'To "Make It
Pay," this agency has made a close and detailed study of Canada as a
nation of buyers and an equally close study of advertising mediums.'
Margaret Pennell, a media planner at J.J. Gibbons Limited, reviewed
the solicitous letters of publishers and was dumbfounded that many
still did not supply market data in 1915. 'There are hundreds of facts
that are of interest: the number of homes in their town, the assessment
of property ... the industries and the number of men they employ – get
in touch with storekeepers, find out what the public are buying,' she
advised. The *Mail and Empire* concurred and stated in a 1920 ad that,
though costly, 'there is probably nothing done by the Advertising
Manager or Space Buyer of more importance' than the provision of

'detailed information as to the class of subscribers.' For its part *Printer and Publisher* fully endorsed the new practices.[34]

Advertising Agencies: Demographics, Media-Buying, and Copywriting

The development of the demographic approach to readership offered advertising agencies two advantages over their traditional preoccupation with gross circulation figures. First, media selection could be placed on a more rational foundation. Second, if the character of a periodical's readership could be categorized economically and demographically, then it was assumed that something specific could be said of its culture. That being the case, copywriters would be far better informed when drafting appeals.

The first documented agency to acknowledge these points was JWT New York. In the latter part of the nineteenth century J. Walter Thompson had been a leader in the development of magazine advertising. After 1900, however, his agency was slow to develop copywriting and art departments. The introduction of these services at Calkins and Holden and at Lord and Thomas made them the rising stars in the American trade. JWT caught up only after 1916, when Thompson retired and sold the firm to a new group of investors led by Stanley Resor.[35]

Stanley Resor's approach to advertising was informed by recent developments in the social sciences as well as the publishing industry. Resor believed that human behaviour was not usually guided by rational considerations, but by the unpredictable and irrational desires of each individual. This unpredictability was troublesome. Copywriters had to conceive their audience simultaneously as individuals and as mass. The written ad required sufficient intimacy to appeal to the ideal reader, adrift in quiet repose. However, the success of the ad would be measured by the volume of responses it generated. Any one appeal or copy style might well work with the copywriter's ideal reader, but ultimately fail with most actual readers. This risk had to be eliminated. So long as the ideal reader was an imagined figure, this risk would always remain. However, conceiving the reader as part of a 'mass,' Resor believed it was possible to observe broad patterns in human behaviour and to identify appeals that would resonate with a statistically predictable percentage of readers.[36]

There were studies supporting this belief, and some were rooted in the work of the academic psychologists. Particularly important was the work of Harry L. Hollingsworth. Using the order of merit test, he ranked the persuasiveness of fifty generic advertising appeals among two groups of female subjects and one group of male subjects. Each subject was asked individually to rank the ads; a group ranking was generated by averaging the individual results. Hollingsworth then compared the rankings of individual subjects to their group's ranking, as well as the group rankings to one another. He was quite excited by the results. The correlation between individual responses and their groups was quite strong, as was that between all three groups.[37] The application was obvious. The opinions of small groups of subjects seemed to be representative of wider public opinion; not of all people, perhaps, but of a significantly large proportion of all people. As a result, it should have been possible to perform similar research to identify copy appeals for specific products, copy appeals that would resonate with statistically significant parts of the entire population.

By 1921 psychologists had connected Hollingsworth's central argument with discoveries in other academic disciplines. Even in its fundamental irrationality, it seemed, humanity was still predictable. Walter Dill Scott, in a revised edition of his book on the psychology of advertising, put the matter in clear and precise terms:

> Human choice has always been assumed to be unknown, to be the one indeterminable factor in the universe. In spite of all this we have come to see that human action is governed by known laws and that by carefully studying the nature of society and the influences at work prophecies may be made with certain limits which are sufficiently accurate for all practical purposes. Under given political, social, and industrial conditions the number and character of crimes remains constant ... The wise merchant knows to a certainty from the political, social, and industrial condition of the country that there will be increased or decreased demand for individual lines of goods. Despite all the uncertainty of human choice he knows that there are certain conditions which determine the number who will choose his commodity and take the pains to secure it.[38]

Demographics, as it had been developed by sociologists and criminologists, could supply a critical new tool to the adworker's handbag.

Stanley Resor advanced his ideas at JWT prior to his purchase of the firm. One of his initiatives was a statistical analysis of the U.S. population based upon its segmentation by region and retail distribution networks. When combined with a standard newspaper directory, such information assisted media-buyers immeasurably. Instead of simply looking at papers' gross circulation figures, they were able to assess each paper's influence by comparing its local coverage with the accessibility of retail outlets. JWT published this data in a booklet entitled *Population and Its Distribution* (1912). Met by a keen audience of advertising personnel, the book was periodically updated and reissued over the succeeding years. It was also copied by rival agents. One of these was John Lee Mahin. Soon after JWT's booklet appeared, Mahin began to issue an annual volume entitled *The Advertising Data Book*, covering much the same ground.[39]

While JWT's book took advantage of published statistical records, the agency's staff also required information that was not readily available. As with Curtis Publishing, Resor expected his research department to develop new data of its own. Paul T. Cherington was its first director. It was a good fit, since Cherington shared Resor's conception of the typical consumer: fundamentally irrational and individualistic, but conforming to broad-based trends. Under Cherington's command, the department conducted its own analyses of circulation coverage, as well as consumer attitude surveys. The first set of results assisted media-buyers and commercial travellers, while the second assisted product designers and copywriters. The agency's account executives could also plan marketing campaigns tailored to each client's product and the relevant features of the market.[40]

It should be noted that several other American agencies undertook market research before 1920. Although figures are unavailable, the number of agencies involved was sufficient to trigger a rift in publisher-agency relations. Market studies could be expensive, but most agencies did not bill their clients separately for this work. They simply absorbed the cost, as they had done when creative services were introduced. Publishers baulked at this arrangement, since it demonstrated once again that the rate of commission was far too high. If nothing else, it was definitely out of proportion to the services provided to the publishers themselves. The agencies responded that any service that increased the effectiveness of advertising would only improve the publishers' profit margins in the long run. In 1912 the magazine publishers in the Quoin Club acquiesced and increased the rate of commission to cover the agencies' increasing costs.[41]

Marketing Magazine

W.A. Lydiatt was one of the first Canadian agents to champion market research. From 1907 to 1911, while Curtis Publishing and JWT made their forays into the new field, Lydiatt worked for agencies in both Philadelphia and New York, including N.W. Ayer and Son. He returned to Canada brimming with new ideas. After a short stint with Gibbons Limited, Lydiatt went solo in 1913 offering services substantially different from anything else then available in Canada. His new agency not only counselled clients on media and copy, it also provided statistics and advice on markets, merchandising, and distribution. His prominence in Toronto – as an active club man and later publisher – raised the profile of market research considerably among all sectors of the advertising trade.[42]

Like many an agent before him, Lydiatt publicized his firm through publications. His first effort appeared in the spring of 1914, a newspaper directory entitled *Lydiatt's Book: What's What in Canadian Advertising*. Its contents went well beyond the standard periodical data featured in competing directories. The most striking difference was an extensive set of statistical data drawn from the Canadian censuses of individuals and industries. Here could be found population figures arranged by province, occupation, and religious faith; trade statistics on imports, building starts, and bank clearings; figures on agricultural production; and estimates regarding retail outlets in Canada organized by province and goods handled. In short, he supplied the same kinds of information that periodicals were beginning to include in their sales materials, and that JWT and Mahin were issuing in their data books. Lydiatt believed: 'Advertisers are coming to appreciate the importance of statistics to the success of their advertising plans. The most successful advertisers, those who advertise with the least waste and greatest effectiveness, have learned to base their methods and their selection of media on a careful analysis of the statistics relating to their markets.' In very simple terms, he suggested: 'Statistics should show the advertiser where to find the people he wants to reach, the number of possible customers, and the likely sale for his goods in a given territory – how these markets can be reached with the greatest economy of advertising and selling expense.'[43]

Apparently, others agreed. The directory brought him to the attention of the Association of Canadian Advertisers, and in 1915 he became its first secretary. It was Lydiatt who guided the association through its battle with the Toronto 'Newspaper Napoleons.' Though he decided to close his consultancy when he took this job, he continued to publish the directory. By the late 1920s *Lydiatt's Book* had become an established authority, cited by account executives at JWT New York as well as academics in *The Encyclopaedia of Canada*.[44]

Lydiatt left the association in 1918 when he bought *Economic Advertising*. When he did so, he revised the journal's mandate to cover all aspects of modern distribution. Looking at other advertising trade papers, he found that most were owned by agencies. This was a problem. Given that agencies were dependent on the periodical press for credit recognition, their trade papers had an unfortunate tendency to boost print media uncritically. Although print advertising was an important part of any marketing strategy, it could not be considered in isolation. However, it took a keen eye to find any discussion of direct mail, billboards, or other alternative media in the trade press. Lydiatt, conscious of a movement towards integrated marketing practices, addressed his paper to all aspects of 'the selling problem': 'Its aim should be to promote efficiency in selling – in all the things which enter in to the sale of manufactured goods. This phase of its editorial character should predominate. Advertising should be recognized as but one, even if a most important, means of selling.'[45] To make this change perfectly clear, Lydiatt changed the masthead from *Economic Advertising* to *Marketing and Business Management*. Readers and staff shortened the title to *Marketing*.[46]

The trade paper became an informal school of marketing and attracted a talented cast of adworkers to its staff. Among the most notable were Bertram Brooker, Val Fisher, John Landels Love, and Margaret Brown. Beyond these four, it also retained a number of contributing editors with wide reputations in the field. Among these could be counted John C. Kirkwood, then writing copy for an agency in London, England; Charles Stokes, assistant advertising manager of the Canadian Pacific Railway; Herbert Casson, by then a noted management consultant; and George French, the former editor of *Advertising and Selling*. Brooker, it may be noted, controlled the publication from 1924 to 1928, but he did not alter the course set by Lydiatt. If anything, he enhanced the journal's discussion of statistical analysis.[47]

Lydiatt's own commitment to market research was evident in his enthusiasm for the Dominion Census. The population statistics in *Lydiatt's Book* were all derived from the 1911 census, which pre-dated the formation of the Dominion Bureau of Statistics. In 1921, after the next national tally had been taken, Lydiatt grilled the new agency on its handling of marketing-related issues. His reporter peppered R.H. Coats with questions on just one theme: 'How the census can help us sell.' To the reporter's dismay, nothing notable had changed from previous years. Despite valuable statistical information related to population and production, the selling field remained a weak point. The Retail Merchants' Association of Canada had approached Coats on this matter and had lobbied for a census of retail and wholesale firms as sophisticated as the census of industry. Coats replied that such a costly program would require a parliamentary mandate – which the industrial censuses had had.[48]

Although no byline appears on the article, its style is unmistakably that of Bertram Brooker. Four years after this interview with Coats, Brooker claimed that he had inspired a revision in one of the bureau's statistical series. One of its tasks was the regular calculation of total bank clearings – the total value of all cheques written on personal accounts. These figures should have indicated aggregate consumer spending power. Late in 1924 Coats arranged to log all cash withdrawals from personal accounts as well. The resulting statistics, it was hoped, would more accurately reflect consumer spending power. In his annual report to the minister, Coats made this the most significant event of the year.[49]

Brooker's piece on the census highlights a curious aspect of *Marketing* magazine: while Lydiatt continuously cajoled businesses to adopt the marketing outlook, it was Brooker who wrote most explicitly on the subject. As noted in the previous chapter, he took a pragmatic approach to the function of psychology in the creation of advertisements. Briefly, he believed that psychology asked the copywriter to think about each product from the point of view of the consumer rather than the producer. Beyond that, it provided no sure rules; 'psychological' facts could not be fed into a copywriting black box from which completed ads would emerge. By contrast, Brooker believed that market research provided the data that were sought: the demographic details necessary to visualize the ideal consumer. Psychology and market research would work best if they worked together, if psychology supplied the copywriter's approach and market research supplied the data.

Brooker's articles on market research relied upon two sources of statistical information: government-generated data and privately commissioned surveys. Despite its silence on consumption patterns, the census was still a rich source of information on the market itself. In an article entitled 'A Statistical Picture of the Average Canadian Consumer' (1924), Brooker demonstrated how population data and trade statistics on basic commodities could be used to generate 'per capita' numbers regarding individual consumption habits.[50] One concrete example was the tobacco industry, where taxation laws made available statistics on the number of cigarettes 'released from bond for consumption.' Assuming that the vast majority of smokers were males over the age of fifteen, Brooker divided the number of cigarettes released from bond by the male population over fifteen and arrived at a figure he believed was the average per capita consumption of cigarettes in Canada. With that figure, a manufacturer could then use its own production figures to estimate its share of the market. This technique could be repeated wherever suitable trade statistics were available. For example, the Department of Labour reconstructed the Canadian working-class diet by calculating per family consumption of basic foodstuffs.[51]

Survey research generated a different set of data. Where census and trade statistics provided quantitative information on the aggregate volume of the market, survey returns offered qualitative information regarding the rationale behind select marketplace decisions. In 'Millions of Dollars to Unearth' (1924), Brooker identified two different means of conducting such surveys: dealer questionnaires and reader contests in popular periodicals. In the first instance, retailers would be asked for their impressions regarding consumer responses to a particular product. By contrast, contests that asked readers to write their own advertisement for a given product provided direct access to the ultimate consumers. This latter method was fraught with difficulties, however. Any ability to control the size of the sample was beyond the researcher. Moreover, the tone of the responses might be coloured by readers' expectations of what constituted a winning entry – all based on notions derived from reading previous ads. At that point, researchers could suffer from consumer 'feedback' as their own ideas became endlessly recycled. Still, researchers hoped that such surveys and contests would allow them to glimpse beyond the surface of their average consumers, and ever so briefly into their minds.[52]

Out of this assortment of statistics and responses, Brooker believed that a composite picture of the target audience could be drawn. Lydiatt championed the use of statistics as concrete expressions of market size and demand. Brooker always noted that statistics simply indicated passing trends in public opinion or human behaviour. In 'Markets Are

People!' (1925), he lamented the fact that too many managers and account executives forgot this fact when drafting their plans. Referring to J.A. Hobson's thesis in *Work and Wealth* (1914), Brooker asserted that individuals were not rational economic actors; they did not fulfil Adam Smith's belief that all human actions were based upon a strict economic understanding of personal costs and benefits. For this reason, he believed that no campaign could be structured upon an expectation of how consumers *should* respond to a product under ideal conditions. Rather, every campaign had to be based upon an understanding of how consumers actually *did* respond to products in the real world. Nothing could be taken for granted. A sound marketing policy required sound research, and due to the ever-shifting nature of human wants, research would have to become an ongoing process.[53]

The gospel of marketing research, advanced in the pages of *Marketing* and countless American trade publications, books, meetings, and conventions, began to have an effect. Throughout the 1920s several Canadian agencies developed market research capabilities within their existing media departments. One of the earliest to advertise these services was Norris-Patterson Limited, the former publisher of *Economic Advertising*. In 1921 it offered to conduct 'market investigations and research work' for its clients. 'Waste in advertising,' it stated, 'can be easily averted by calling in a reliable agent at the inception of a new product. The agency should cooperate with the manufacturer from the choosing of the name to the determining of the selling policy.' In 1925, it hired an associate editor from *Marketing*, John Landels Love, to head up its research staff.[54]

Love was not the only writer from *Marketing* to find work in this line. Lydiatt left the journal in 1924 to re-establish his consultancy. No records remain of this company, other than one lone mention in *Lydiatt's Book*. In 1925 he listed himself among the Toronto agencies, but not the following year. Did he offer market research services? Given his efforts to encourage them, it would be hard to believe otherwise. Did he find any clients? None were named in the directory. Did he fail due to a lack of interest? Unfortunately, it is impossible to know. In 1926, however, he dropped the consultancy to open a job printing plant called Swan Service, and two years later he returned to Marketing Publications. He ran both the printing plant and the press until his retirement in 1954.[55]

A more successful research firm was established by Val Fisher. Fisher was an English adworker who had formerly published his own

WASTE IN ADVERTISING can be easily averted by calling in a reliable agent at the inception of a new product. The agency should coöperate with the manufacturer from the choosing of the name to the determining of the selling policy.

Some services we perform for our clients

1—Invent suitable names for new products.
2—Design packages and containers.
3—Conduct market investigations and research work.
4—Prepare plans and estimates for all kinds of advertising.
5—Write copy and buy art work.
6—Set the advertising in type.
7—Provide electrotypes, stereotypes and mats for newspapers and magazines and dealer advertising.
8—Check up the advertisements.
9—Plan, write and place trade paper advertising.
10—Supply dealer helps and follow-up matter.
11—Design window and counter-cards, etc. ..
12—Offer at all times expert advice and coöperation toward the solution of advertising and merchandising problems.

"It's all in the Service"

NORRIS-PATTERSON
LIMITED
ADVERTISING
TORONTO   MONTREAL

Marketing and merchandising advice as agency services. *Marketing* 15:4 (15 February 1921), 134.

trade journal in Great Britain. Moving to Canada after the war, he joined *Marketing* as a contributing editor in 1924. At the same time, he undertook freelance research work for assorted clients. After two years he left the journal to concentrate solely on research and established the Canadian Business Research Bureau in Toronto. According to its ads the bureau offered a wide array of sophisticated market studies, including surveys. It remained in business until at least 1935.[56]

Brooker, too, answered the call. Brooker left the journal in 1928 to nurture a budding career in the fine arts. He kept his hand in advertising by working freelance for the next two years, but the stock market crash and subsequent business slump forced him to change course. He was quickly hired by J.J. Gibbons Limited, which asked him to set up its first 'media and research department' in December 1930. The link between media-buying and market research was clear in the very name of the new department.[57]

Case Study: Marketing to Albertans

The William Findlay Company was the crowning achievement of its founder, William A.H. Findlay. Findlay had worked in advertising for almost thirty years, mainly as a newspaperman selling white space to advertisers and agencies. Born in Bracebridge, Ontario, in 1876, he got his start with the Barrie *Examiner* and then moved into the big time of the major metropolitan dailies with the Toronto *News* under Sir John Willison. He earned an enviable reputation as an advertising man while there, despite the ailing condition of the paper itself. He was an active member of the Toronto Ad Club and engaged in the implementation of market research at his own paper. Perhaps sensing its inevitable demise, Findlay left the *News* to become the business manager of the Ottawa *Free Press* and the *Journal* when P.D. Ross owned both those papers during the 1910s and then moved to the Toronto *Globe* from 1919 to 1922. Back in Toronto, he found himself in the midst of the advertising boom. The agency scene had clearly eclipsed the newspaper game, and Findlay sought to capitalize on his years of experience. He first became a director of McKim Limited in 1922; he then opened his own agency in 1926.[58]

Many agencies opened in Toronto in the 1920s, but few did so with the fanfare of Findlay. He was intimately acquainted with most of the country's leading advertisers and agencies – the opening of his agency would have received polite notices in the trade press, as well as word-of-mouth promotion. If he had merely wanted to announce the formation of his new agency, he could have done so quite modestly. He did not. His first ad to the trade was a bold, full-page splash in *Marketing* that featured classical lettering, photographs, and a liberal use of white space to provide air and clarity. The message, both explicit and implicit, was plain: the firm was not a brash new upstart, but a credible proposition – one that had a pedigree rooted solidly in Findlay's own personal experience and reputation. The ad featured portraits of the agency's four key executives, supported by brief career puffs. Most prominent among them was Findlay himself, a paternal figure overseeing his younger associates. Despite their youth, however, they too came with impressive credentials, filled out with long years in the newspaper industry or by university educations.[59]

The agency's second ad moved beyond the personnel of the firm and discussed its approach to marketing strategy. Here was the experience and expertise of the agency laid bare, the collective wisdom of the four executives applied to current, practical conditions within the Canadian economy. 'The William Findlay Company,' the ad stated, 'is an organization of trained men with personal knowledge and experience, and possessing statistical information on market conditions in all parts of Canada.' To this data was added 'personal investigation of the West, as well as much enquiry from well-informed sources.'[60] In truth, this would not have suggested a level of service much different from any other major agency. It was not their methods, however, so much as their conclusions that were remarkable.

Canada, the ad stated, was traditionally divided into five 'marketing zones': the Maritimes, Quebec, Ontario, the Prairies, and British Columbia. Indeed, an ad for the Canadian Daily Newspaper Association had used this division as a talking point just seven months before.[61] The Findlay Company's research drew this into question. New conditions were working to alter the existing movement of people and goods within the country, so much so that a new alignment of marketing zones was emerging: Alberta was casting off its Prairie identifications and integrating with the coastal economy of British Columbia. Several trends indicated that this was already well underway. Geographic proximity had already privileged the development of economic and social ties between the two provinces. However, the people of Alberta were also beginning to develop cities, and presumably a lively urban culture would eventually put them out of step with their rural counterparts in Saskatchewan and Manitoba. Their new dancing partners would be found where they were sending increasing amounts of their business: in the port cities of Vancouver and Prince Rupert.[62]

Throughout the 1920s, as Vancouver began to realize its potential as a western outlet for Canadian goods, Albertan farmers began to reroute their shipments away from Winnipeg and the long trip to the Atlantic in favour of the shorter haul to the Pacific. In five short years, the ad noted, the volume of Alberta grain handled by Vancouver had increased from half a million bushels to fifty-four million. In light of this, the Alberta Grain Pool had contracted elevators there and in Prince Rupert. This traffic encouraged a corresponding increase in trade in the other direction. Salesmen, jobbers, and other representatives of Vancouver industry began to view Alberta as an extension of their own sales territories in the British Columbia interior. So too had its agricultural sector, keen to sell more fruits and vegetables. Only one impediment slowed these developments: a rather inconvenient set of mountains. A solution lay in the steady improvement of transportation systems. Both provincial governments were actively building motorways into the Rocky Mountains. They further agreed to make a joint representation on railway freight rates to the federal government. Taken altogether, these trends seemed to indicate strengthening ties between the two provinces at several levels: economically, socially, and politically.[63]

There was one practical consequence to be drawn from this insight: any company with distribution in Alberta or British Columbia would now have to adjust its marketing plans. This could entail any number of changes if that company's goods were sensitive to regional variations in consumption. It could mean that packaging, lines of distribution, and choice of retailers would have to be reconsidered. It might also entail a new strategy with respect to the creative work in advertisements and the selection of media used. Who better to advise the company than the agency that had pointed out the problem? With its keen insight into the country's economy, the Findlay Company claimed that it was able to 'co-relate advertising to selling in that definite manner that makes selling methods more effective and adds to the returns from advertising.'[64]

If the first ad had been a bold statement of self-congratulation, the second ad was nothing less than a declaration of war. *Marketing* was geared to the advertising trade in Canada. To have challenged the alignment of marketing zones was to call into question the basic assumptions underlying media-buying strategies. In particular, it

MARKETING *for* NOVEMBER 27th, 1926   355

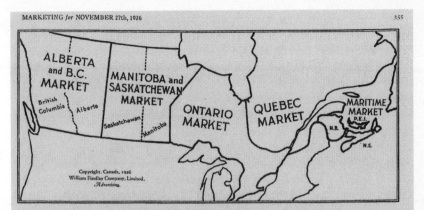

The NEW alignment of Marketing Zones

Of the grain crop of 1925, 54,000,000 bushels were exported through Vancouver. Of the crop of 1920, but half a million bushels. The new Government elevator at Prince Rupert will handle 50,000 bushels per hour. It has been leased to the Alberta Grain Pool.

British Columbia has developed in Alberta her nearest and one of her best markets for fruit fish and early vegetables; and Alberta, in British Columbia, her nearest and one of her best markets for meat, poultry and dairy products.

Salesmen for many British Columbia houses cover Alberta, and salesmen of Alberta houses go down through the Crow's Nest country and other sections of British Columbia.

In the case of equalization of mountain freight rates before the Dominion Railway Commission, the two Provinces combined their arguments.

The good roads systems have been extended till they meet in the mountains. Thereby both Provinces benefit by a motor tourist traffic of great magnitude which comes from the United States, and is increasing year by year.

CANADA is commonly divided by manufacturers, distributors and advertising authorities into Marketing Zones, or trading territories; as follows:—(1) Maritime Market [Prince Edward Island, Nova Scotia, New Brunswick]; (2) Quebec Market; (3) Ontario Market; (4) Prairie Market [Manitoba, Saskatchewan, Alberta]; (5) British Columbia Market.

New conditions, which are becoming more emphatic every day, point to a re-alignment of these zones or marketing territories. Geography and the economic and social relationship which is developing between the two most westerly provinces cannot be denied.

Attention must be given, also, to the change in the character of agricultural operations in the West. The word "Prairie" does not imply the diversified and intensified farming methods which are becoming more prevalent. It does not assign adequate importance to the cities and towns.

Manufacturers and distributors who will now consider Alberta and British Columbia as one trading territory and Manitoba and Saskatchewan as another, will be in line with the most recent development in the internal trade of Canada.

The *NEW* alignment of Marketing Zones would be:—(1) Maritime Market [Prince Edward Island, Nova Scotia, New Brunswick,]; (2) Quebec Market; (3) Ontario Market; (4) Manitoba and Saskatchewan Market; (5) Alberta and British Columbia Market.

The boundaries of any Marketing Zones, or trading territories are elastic. There is much over-lapping in any case. Personal investigation in the West, as well as much enquiry from well-informed sources, warrant us in believing that the *NEW* alignment more correctly reflects marketing conditions in that country.

WILLIAM FINDLAY COMPANY, LIMITED, *Advertising*, is an organization of trained men with personal knowledge and experience, and possessing statistical information on market conditions in all parts of Canada.

Thus it is able to co-relate advertising to selling in that definite manner which makes selling methods more effective and adds to the returns from advertising. It invites interviews with advertisers who seek better advertising. There is no obligation upon you if you request us to see you in your office, or come to see us in ours.

WILLIAM FINDLAY COMPANY, LIMITED, *Advertising*, TORONTO 2
Telephone ADelaide 4295, Bank of Hamilton Building, Rooms 726, 727, 728, 729, 730, 731 and 732.

questioned where Albertans would place their civic loyalties – and more importantly their brand preferences. If they had to identify with one metropolitan centre, would they choose Winnipeg or Vancouver? If they read one weekend paper, was it to be the Winnipeg *Free Press* or *Grain Grower's Guide*, or the Vancouver *Sun* or *Farm and Home*? Did they see themselves as pioneers or entrepreneurs? By following this line of questioning, it becomes apparent that the ad also challenged the marketing strategies of Prairie periodicals.

It should not have been surprising that many readers were driven to comment. One company created its own ad mimicking the layout of the Findlay ad, with all three Prairie provinces emphatically recast as a single market.[65] *Marketing* itself fielded responses, and many correspondents addressed the ad as if it had been an editorial piece. The editor noted their passion and presented the most provocative letters in a series of articles over the next three months.[66]

The letters came from two main groups: representatives of western media outlets, and space-buyers. Typical was the response of W. McCurdy, the business manager of the Winnipeg *Tribune*. McCurdy's business was directly in Findlay's line of fire, and he responded to each point from the original ad in great detail. It was, he felt, a terrific contribution; it had certainly drawn attention to the West as an advertising field. Nonetheless, McCurdy felt that 'Mr Findlay has attempted the impossible when he endeavours to establish that the province of Alberta should be separated from the sister provinces of Manitoba and Saskatchewan.'[67] To carry his argument, he answered Findlay's statistics with his own. For example, if 54 million bushels of wheat had passed through Vancouver, it was worth noting that 92.6 million had passed through Winnipeg. It was also worth mentioning that the grain shipped through Vancouver was still handled by companies headquartered in Winnipeg. Really, he wondered, which city was the true metropolis?

A response to McCurdy's question came from a predictable source: R.W. Brown, his counterpart at the Vancouver *Daily Province*. The static details of the last year's harvest were almost irrelevant; the fact of the matter was that Alberta and British Columbia were in the process of forming a dynamic partnership. The two provinces, Brown argued, 'are largely complementary one to the other. Their natural resources are different. What the one lacks, the other in large measure is able to supply. Fruits, green vegetables, and lumber products that are grown in abundance in British Columbia are required in Alberta, which, in exchange, sends beef, dairy products, wheat, and fowl. The list might easily be extended.'[68]

Other commentators echoed the arguments made by these two writers. E.H. Macklin of the Winnipeg *Free Press* and space-buyers Ashdown Hardware, Case Threshing Machines, and Edgar M. Rutter all sided with McCurdy in his criticisms of the original ad. Meanwhile, O.L. Spencer of the Calgary *Herald*, as well as advertisers Parkhill Bedding and Babson Brothers, sided with Brown in favour of it.

Two other responses bear mention. Outside of the letters to *Marketing*, a number of ads for media outlets addressed the same issue over the next six months. Of these, one for the Calgary *Farm and Ranch Review* and one for the Winnipeg *Free Press* took direct aim at the Findlay Company's claims. The *Farm and Ranch Review* agreed that Canada's marketing zones could be reorganized, but insisted that the new zone was not Alberta and British Columbia; rather, it was Alberta and western Saskatchewan. Eastern Saskatchewan was still in Winnipeg's orbit, but the rest of the Prairie West was now looking to Calgary for leadership. 'The character of agricultural operations, geography, and the economic and social relationships separate these zones distinctly,' the *Review* argued. 'This is to be expected from a territory so vast that over 1,500 miles is the distance from one end to the other.'[69] No magazine could hope to offer valuable service to every class of reader throughout the entire Prairie West, but if one looked closely enough one would find that certain periodicals dominated in each zone. Naturally, the *Review* itself was the ideal medium to reach people in Alberta and western Saskatchewan.

The *Free Press* took exception to this. Its ad, briefly described above, mimicked the Findlay Company ad by redrawing the map of Canada with a single, bold circle around the entire Prairie West. (Curiously, no one placed Kenora and Thunder Bay within Winnipeg's influence.) Once again, the boundaries of the zone were relevant to the wise advertiser's media buy. As the ad noted, 'Whereas in most of these zones, the advertiser has a choice of a number of excellent mediums from amongst which his problem is to choose those best suited for his purpose, there is no such problem in the Prairie Zone. In this zone, the Free Press Publications are so complete in their coverage that they are the immediate first choice as the foundation of any advertising campaign.'[70] Evidence was marshalled to support this contention. The weekly *Free Press Prairie Farmer*, it was claimed, reached one-third of all farm homes in the three provinces. Advertisers liked it as well as readers; it carried more advertising than any other western weekly.

Regardless of their authorship, all of the letters and advertisements that responded to the Findlay Company ad revealed a common trait. None of the writers took issue with the agency's basic methodology. They all rooted their arguments in the same set of economic and demographic considerations that had guided the Findlay Company. Statistics regarding imports, exports, and the grain trade featured prominently in all of their arguments, as did population figures and estimates of the relative wealth of each province. Since they failed to disagree on these terms, writers took issue either with the agency's specific facts or with its interpretations.

A second point of agreement: all of the writers implicitly accepted that a region's social and cultural attributes were rooted in its economy. The heart and mind of a region – its loyalties and identifications – followed its economic interests. At bottom, the zoning question simply asked if Alberta's economic interests were tied more closely to Vancouver or Winnipeg. A simple answer to this simple question, however, would suggest something quite complicated about the culture of the province. Economic statistics might reveal the buying power of the market, and demographic statistics might reveal its size, but taken together these data also revealed something of the character of the market. Using this, one could suggest effective copy appeals or select apt media. The Findlay Company ad made vague allusions to the cultural consequences that might follow in the wake of Alberta's increasing prosperity – particularly if its population continued to migrate to the cities. A population with a growing taste for urban comforts would not long be satisfied with homespuns. The letter writers drew a similar connection between economy and culture. T.A. Torgeson's own line of thought suggested that it was a direct causal link. He wrote of the three Prairie provinces: 'The residents of these provinces will always engage in the same occupations. The products of the land are the same. The trend of thought of these provinces is along the same channel. This is particularly noticeable in their politics.'[71]

The link between economy and culture caused problems for those who examined the facts too closely. This was the case with G.M. Bell, of the Calgary *Albertan*, who acknowledged that a provincial economy could not be seen as a monolithic entity. If Alberta was viewed from a producer's point of view, it would clearly be identified with its two easterly neighbours. Those engaged in trade and commerce, however,

Map of the Five Principal Marketing Zones of Canada

ADVERTISING
In the Prairie Zone

FOR purposes of marketing and selling manufactured products, Canada is naturally divided into five principal marketing territories—usually referred to as the Maritime, Quebec, Ontario, Prairie and Pacific Zones.

Because each of these zones is individual in its tastes, temperament, wants and needs, and distinct in its merchandising requirements, each one presents to the manufacturer a separate problem in the distribution, selling and advertising of his merchandise.

But, whereas in most of these zones, the advertiser has a choice of a number of excellent mediums from amongst which his problem is to choose those best suited for his purpose, there is no such problem in the Prairie Zone. In this zone, the Free Press Publications are so complete in their coverage that they are the immediate first choice as the foundation of any advertising campaign.

The Winnipeg Free Press, with its Free Press Prairie Farmer weekly, has the largest circulation in the Prairie market, in both the daily and farm paper fields. It circulates as no other paper does in this zone. The daily Free Press goes into 90% of Winnipeg English-speaking homes, beside covering an outside small-town area larger than the whole of Southern Ontario. The weekly Free Press Prairie Farmer reaches more than one-third of all the farm homes in the three Prairie Provinces. In consequence it carries the largest volume of advertising of all the papers in the whole of Western Canada, exclusive of daily newspapers.

The Free Press
WINNIPEG

Ask Your Advertising Agency

Marketing 26:8 (16 April 1927), inside front cover.

would more likely look west as time passed. Bell was the only writer to suggest that, ultimately, civic identifications might be a matter of personal choice, though he stopped himself before explicitly suggesting that these identifications might be class based.[72] No one suggested how language, ethnicity, or gender factored into the equation.

Even if the categories of analysis could be agreed upon, problems could still afflict the interpretation of research results in the creative departments of advertising agencies. Few heeded Bertram Brooker's warning that economic and demographic information expressed through statistics and maps could only suggest what entire populations felt about the consumer goods that surrounded them. Regardless of the accuracy of the research techniques, at the end of the day they still had to be interpreted by human beings, and these human beings still had to craft advertisements from the results. In the process of interpretation, creative staff in Toronto, Montreal, or New York were still limited by their own perceptions and experiences of modern life. This was particularly true of ads targeting rural Canada and Quebec. Once a year *Marketing* ran special issues on two key Canadian markets – farmers and French Canadians – and every year another writer familiar with each field had to ask when copywriters were going to stop dredging the barrel of hackneyed stereotypes for their appeals. An ad for the Calgary *Herald* revealed this tendency with astonishing irony. Addressing space-buyers through the pages of *Marketing*, the *Herald* asserted that Calgary was no longer a frontier town dependent on one source of revenue. Instead, it was a growing city, prospering from the development of mixed farming, lumbering, oil, and manufacturing. Blue-chip American advertisers now recognized this fact and placed their ads in the *Herald*. One of these was Kellogg's cereals, and one of that company's ads was reproduced to illustrate the *Herald*'s point. The dominant image in the Kellogg's ad was a cowboy astride a bucking bronco.[73]

Market Research in Canada in the 1920s

The Findlay episode offers an important qualification to a discussion of market research in the 1920s. While its assumptions and practices may have been widely employed, the quality of the research itself remained inconsistent. This prompted doubts about its utility and slowed its implementation at many firms. Nonetheless, there was a steady trend towards more sophisticated and continuous research. This trend was capped by the establishment of the first research departments at Canadian agencies as the decade closed.

As previously noted, J.J. Gibbons Limited did not have a full-fledged market research department until it hired Bertram Brooker in 1930. The fact that such a prominent agency lacked this function provides a clear indication that agents were reluctant to take it up. Toronto agent A.J. Denne, in 1927, believed that agencies such as Norris-Patterson were actually foolhardy to offer services beyond creative work and media-buying. To his mind, market research was solely the responsibility of manufacturers.[74] He was in good company. The largest agency in Canada proudly defied the trend. H.E. Stephenson and Carlton McNaught, both connected with McKim Limited in 1940, believed that market research reached 'extravagant' heights during the 1920s. Their agency 'never yielded to the illusion that creative work can be guided by "scientific" yardsticks,' and so it chose not to imitate the 'spasmodic' efforts of its competitors with things such as consumer attitude surveys.[75] Despite their protestations, however, its media-buying department routinely gathered basic audience and demographic data. At this basic level at least, ongoing research efforts had become entrenched at most major agencies by the early 1920s.

Although few Canadian agencies offered research services, manufacturers who wanted research conducted did have a limited but growing number of options. Publishers' advertising departments remained a constant source of detailed market information, though the scope and quality of this information was relative to the periodical producing it. And, as noted, the Dominion Bureau of Statistics was beginning to consider consumption a suitable field of data collection by 1926. Canadian firms that wanted more in-depth information also had three other alternatives: they could conduct the work themselves, hire an academic researcher, or hire an American advertising agency. Due to a lack of records, it is difficult to suggest how many companies chose the first option in the 1920s. In 1967 a survey was conducted of the marketing practices of advertisers with a national presence in Canada. Of the 302 companies that participated, only nine had created research departments before 1934.[76]

The second alternative was similarly unpopular before 1930. Canadian adworkers, unlike their American counterparts, were slow to cultivate links with academia. There was no research institute on par with Cherington's adventure at Harvard. This was no doubt due to the Canadian tendency to resist specialization in the humanities and social sciences. The academic study of marketing began among American economists in the 1880s. In contrast, Canadian universities began hiring full-fledged political economists – with chairs separate from their colleagues in history and philosophy – only at the turn of the century. Then, scholars were largely preoccupied with political history and theory. The introduction of statistical work in the field of economics was not accomplished until the 1910s by scholars such as O.D. Skelton at Queen's, and at this early date their interests were not yet geared to the problems of individual businesses. They shared the same preoccupations as their cohorts in the Dominion Bureau of Statistics: macroeconomic trends, fiscal policy, and a concern for production rather than distribution. An academic treatment of industrial marketing did not appear in Canada until the publication of *Canadian Marketing Problems* by political economists at the University of Toronto in 1939. Marketing, if considered at all, was usually considered within the realm of agriculture.[77]

One prominent exception emerged from this general pattern. Humfrey E. Michell was an instructor in political economy at Queen's who began studying agricultural movements in the 1910s. His work led him to examine Canada's distribution systems, including credit institutions and retailers. Unlike many of his contemporaries, Michell popularized his findings among businessmen as well as academics. In 1919 he moved to McMaster University (then still in Toronto), and found two different outlets for his ideas. The first was a political magazine, the *Canadian Forum*. In tandem with Gilbert E. Jackson of the University of Toronto, Michell used quantitative analysis to write a monthly column on 'Industry and Trade,' which ran from 1920 to 1927. Then, in 1923, he opened a private consultancy that offered 'business forecasting' services. By looking at patterns in trade and production statistics, Michell issued predictions on the performance of the Canadian economy over given periods of time. Whether or not Michell thought of this work in terms of 'marketing' cannot be said, but his bureau was never listed with advertising agencies in any of the standard directories. A failed prediction in 1927 led to the end of his column and the consultancy. After that, his academic work returned to the fore.[78]

The third alternative that manufacturers enjoyed – hiring an American agency – became much easier during the 1920s, when several American agencies opened in Canada. Among these was Stanley Resor's reorganized JWT. Resor had pulled the agency out of Canada when he bought it in 1916. In the late 1920s he clearly wanted to return. Account executives and creative staff in the New York head office held weekly seminars on topics of current interest. Almost every year from 1927 to 1932 one session featured a Canadian issue.[79] Every time, the speaker excitedly related the large volume of trade between Canada and the United States as if he were the first to have discovered it. Nonetheless, by the time JWT established a Montreal office in 1929 it already had placed branches in eight European capitals and two African cities.[80]

JWT did not completely abandon Canada between 1916 and 1929. Its American offices continued to place advertising in Canadian publications for their American clients, though Resor was uncomfortable handling them. Since the agency did not have a permanent presence in the country, it had not developed the same in-depth data on the Canadian market as it had the American. For this reason, Resor turned down a Canadian campaign for Simmons Mattresses, and was denied Canadian campaigns for two of its biggest American clients: General Motors divided its ads between the Toronto offices of Campbell-Ewald and McCann, while Fleischmann's Yeast gave its work to Bowman Hoge. Resor decided to re-enter Canada via Montreal in 1927, and he demanded that the office conduct the same quality market research that JWT was known for in the United States. Cherington's research department was soon testing its media-buying strategies by looking at the Ontario periodical market.[81]

JWT Montreal was managed by Robert J. Flood. American by birth, Flood was an accountant with experience in transportation law. In the summer of 1929 he put together a research department and initiated the first Dominion-wide market survey ever conducted in Canada. With the data from this and the periodical survey, Flood sold the merits of the Canadian office to JWT's American-based clients and won Fleischmann's back into the fold. He also won Canadian-based contracts. Resor had turned away the Dominion Rubber Company in 1927; now Flood was recruiting the likes of the Canadian Marconi Company.[82] The success of the operation seemed manifest, and in November 1930 Flood bought full-page ads in the trade press to announce that JWT Canada had opened a second office in Toronto. Both branches would offer:

MARKET RESEARCH · COPY · PLAN · ART
MEDIA · PRODUCTION · SALES ANALYSIS
IN RADIO, NEWSPAPERS, MAGAZINES, DIRECT MAIL
AND OUTDOOR MEDIUMS THROUGHOUT THE WORLD.[83]

The largest agency in the United States had arrived in Canada, and it had brought all of its weapons with it.

Canadian agencies responded to this invasion in a number of ways. Some had steeled themselves by affiliating with American agencies. Agencies keen to maintain their independence chose a different option: to compete with the Americans on their own terms. The most celebrated in this regard was Cockfield, Brown and Company. Cockfield, Brown was a new name in the late 1920s, but its principals had been active in the trade for some time. Henry R. Cockfield had been the president of the Advertising Service Company of Montreal and Toronto, while G. Warren Brown had held the same position at National Publicity Limited of Montreal. In December 1928 the two companies merged. Montreal was chosen for the head office, and a branch was maintained in Toronto.[84]

Brown and Cockfield believed the agency needed a research department to be competitive. In 1927, speaking before the Canadian Association of Advertising Agencies, Brown noted that ever more clients were demanding some degree of marketing counsel in addition to the usual gamut of agency expertise. Anyone reading *Marketing* should have noticed this trend. Stories had appeared on a study of macaroni use by the Hamilton Advertising Agency, the market for home appliances by the Hoover Company of Canada, and the reactions of modern consumers to corsets by the Harold C. Lowrey Organization.[85] To Brown, the trend was clear and inevitable. An ability to conduct market research was no longer just a useful advantage, but a necessary tool in the design of campaigns. Evidently, Brown had already undertaken market research at National Publicity two years before its merger with Advertising Service.[86]

The man hired to organize the research department at Cockfield, Brown was W.W. Goforth. Goforth was a professor of economics at McGill University and a recent graduate from Toronto's program in political economy. He assembled a staff unlike that seen at any agency in the country to that point. In the first year he hired a McGill law student, two Harvard MBAs, one Oxford graduate with experience at National Publicity, and three veterans of the federal government's Tariff Board. Others with similar levels of education or experience were hired on a contract basis to collect data across the country, including academics such as Gilbert Jackson from his alma mater.[87] Over the next four years Goforth's department conducted market surveys for companies such as Campbell's Soup, Jantzen swimwear, and Molson's; it also did audience research studies for the Kingston *Whig-Standard* and radio station CFCF Montreal. A highlight was a highly touted market survey for the federal Department of Fisheries on fish products. It was published under the crown imprint in 1932 and held up as an example of what objective, 'scientific' research could accomplish in the commercial world.[88]

Henry King, the Oxford graduate on staff, later wrote that the agency had had the market research field to itself from the day it opened until 1932. That year, a renegade staff member from its Toronto office formed Canadian Facts Limited, a research firm that specialized in radio audience ratings. King's opinion notwithstanding, it is readily apparent that Cockfield, Brown never had the field to itself. Cockfield himself acknowledged that competition existed in 1930. The 'modern agencies' were all seeking 'economists, statisticians, marketing experts, and even engineers, cost accountants, and lawyers.'[89] JWT Montreal's highly visible research operation opened the same year as Cockfield, Brown, in the same city. Nonetheless, it is also readily apparent that Cockfield, Brown had the most sophisticated research department of any Canadian agency at that time, one that consciously mimicked the American model. One has to wonder if Brown and Cockfield were not perfectly aware of Resor's plans and initiated the merger to protect their own interests.[90]

One might also emphasize here that Cockfield, Brown's initiatives did not mark the beginning of market research in Canada. Rather, the agency consolidated a set of assumptions and practices that had developed piecemeal over the previous thirty years and institutionalized them within a permanent department. In doing so, however, it cleared the way for future developments in the field. In particular, it too foresaw what Bertram Brooker had seen: the necessity of combining quantitative economic and demographic data with the qualitative findings of the psychologists.

'No Sybilene sorceress of old with her leaves of divination ever had a more absorbed audience than has the modern society diviner with her tea leaves! Deep in the hearts of nearly all women, and a great many men, is an incurable desire to pierce the veil of the Future and to know what Fortune has in store. The tea cup seance is not taken too seriously by any, but its appeal is irresistible and the sibylline prophecies are listened to with an amusement that does not quite disguise the lurking belief that there may be "something" in the pronouncements of the oracle.'[91] So wrote J.D. Neill, the sales manager of Thomas J. Lipton of Canada, Limited, in 1924. Lipton made its name selling low-priced, pre-packaged tea in the 1890s.[92] Thirty years later it decided to expand its sales horizon with the introduction of a second line, a higher-grade tea sold at a premium price. Trouble was, the market was already occupied by Tetley and Company, among others. In its time of need, Lipton sought help. But it did not turn to its distributor, as Tetley had approached Timothy Eaton. Rather, it turned to a market researcher.

The report that followed pleased the manufacturer greatly. Not only did it suggest that the market for a premium tea was still open to expansion, it also suggested that this market encompassed women from a wide variety of income brackets. With that, the planning wheels were set in motion. A strategy was sought that would appeal across all classes, and particularly to women. It had to justify the higher price of the tea and distinguish it from its competitors. Further, the company wanted to do this without the aid of sales premiums – a prize that could be earned by saving coupons from every package – since it was thought such a ploy would detract from the elite character of the tea. The result was a masterstroke of marketing. The tea would be associated with the oriental art of cup reading. The possibilities were tremendous. Little or nothing had to be said about the flavour of the tea. Rather, every leaf would be imbued with the power of magic, the fantastic possibility of seeing into one's own future.[93]

Around this idea, the entire marketing strategy was planned. Print advertising would be used as a matter of course, but the company also prepared a thirty-two-page booklet on how to read leaves. A copy would be included in every package. According to Neill, this was not a sales premium, so much as an entertaining and frankly informative extra provided for the benefit of the tea drinkers. It was a winning formula. Before launching the full campaign, Neill tested its appeal with a cup reading tent at that year's Canadian National Exhibition. As hoped, it drew a broad range of curious fair-goers, and the booklet was eagerly snapped up. The print campaign, along with dealer display cases, trial-size packages, and a special price offer to retailers, began that fall.[94]

One might wonder how different the Lipton experience was from that of Tetley. After all, Eaton too had done his research, if only through a tea stand. Nonetheless, the differences were marked. Lipton, also an English company, had set up a permanent office in Canada to handle the local market. Where Tetley had delegated its marketing responsibilities to its distributor, Lipton's sales manager played a key role in its research and implementation procedures. Eaton's copy had relied on the intrinsic, material merits of the tea, while Neill allowed a supernatural aura to be woven around a mass-produced, pre-packaged product. The greatest difference, however, was in their research. Eaton's marketing strategy, no matter how successful, was ultimately based on his own experience and intuition. Neill was guided by a statistical understanding of the market discovered through planned research and fortified by testing in the field.

Behind this change was an urgent desire to reduce the risk involved in the selling function of modern industry. Managers guiding multimillion-dollar companies wanted to base their decisions on something more concrete than intuition. Market research seemed to provide this assurance by adopting the tools and theories of the emerging social sciences and putting them to work in the commercial world – first to improve media-buying practices, then to inform creative work. This was no more evident than at JWT New York and Cockfield, Brown, where leading academics found part-time work as corporate consultants. Demographic statistics seemed to give adworkers the practical, 'scientific' foundation that they had vainly sought in psychology alone. Now they had the means to comprehend the whims of the mass and to direct their production and salesmanship accordingly.[95] The adoption of these tools also allied professionalizing adworkers with an institution that enjoyed a recognized level of social attainment and respectability.

It was not the agencies, but the publishers who first developed these practices with advertising in mind, and they did so to influence media-buying. Once again, American companies pioneered the new ideas, but Canadian companies adopted them with an enthusiasm dimmed only by their smaller economy of scale. Where psychology had asked advertisers to think of readers as individual consumers making individual decisions, publishers armed with market research asked advertisers to think of readers as mass markets. Unlike individual consumers, these mass markets had identifiable divisions and common interests, identifiable aversions and desires. With quantifiable measurement techniques, later market researchers learned how to investigate these interests and desires, to select likely territories for sales campaigns, to pick the most effective media for particular products, and to pre-test campaign strategies on sample audiences. In retrospect, there was a manifest logic behind the gradual development of the researcher's tools, from intuition, to publishers' readership profiles, to demographic data, to consumer surveys. With each added layer the researcher was ostensibly one step further removed from sheer guesswork and one step closer to the inner desires of a composite, typical consumer.

The skirmish over Alberta's identification suggests that the basic economic and demographic approach to marketing had become well entrenched among all sectors of the advertising trade by the mid-1920s. This was true even if individual companies resisted the creation of their own research arms. To their minds, the culture of a region could be understood through a close examination of its economy and demographic statistics. At the same time, this approach offered wildly differing results. Indeed, research findings commissioned by the periodicals sounded remarkably like sales pitches crafted by a previous generation of business managers. How to explain the fact that the *Herald*, *Albertan*, and *Farm and Ranch Review* each believed it was the best medium to reach Albertans, based on a sober analysis of the same market research – never mind that the Vancouver *Sun*, Winnipeg *Free Press*, and Winnipeg *Tribune* wanted to make the same claim? As adept as they were at collecting information, it appears that market researchers were equally adept at finding the best statistics possible to support a desired end. If that could not be achieved, then a new marketing zone could always be invented in which the chosen periodical would be the acknowledged leader.

These ambiguities – and the difficulties inherent in reading bald economic and demographic data for cultural characteristics – prompted the advertising trade to combine psychological approaches and market research. These approaches were in development after 1910 but did not become fully accepted until the 1930s. Where broad numbers might have provided some context and direction for a marketing campaign, surveys and polls provided the kind of qualitative data regarding cultural characteristics that proved to be more welcome to creative staff.[96]

Ultimately, it did not matter who conducted these studies, be it the manufacturer, agency, research bureau, academic, or publisher. Agencies believed that manufacturers had come to accept this new way of thinking about the buying public and subsequently sought the benefits that research could bring. The readers of high-circulation newspapers and magazines would no longer be seen as a community of readers sharing a common political outlook, civic identity, or literary interests.

They had became a mass of demographic numbers reconstituted as predictable markets. Their hopes, fears, desires, and even their identities were now the grist of the marketing strategist and the advertising copywriter.

Chapter 7

The Canadian Market, Magazines, and the New Logic of Advertising

It remains to be seen whether or not ... Canada will produce magazines or other publications which, in point of circulation, will cover the cities and large towns of the Dominion in the way that the 'Ladies' Home Journal,' 'Saturday Evening Post,' 'Munsey's,' and other American publications cover the United States.

W.J. Healy, 1908[1]

W.J. Healy had good cause to ponder this question. He oversaw the advertising revenues of the highest circulating periodicals in Canada, the Montreal *Star* and its weekend edition, the *Family Herald and Weekly Star*. Both had circulations over 100,000. No Canadian magazine came close. With no competition from a strong consumer magazine in Canada, both papers dominated the field in national advertising, as well as the Montreal field in retail advertising. Magazine circulation was so fragile that most national campaigns began with a list of daily papers stretching from coast to coast and relegated magazines to a secondary role, serving specialized markets where needed.[2]

The fragility of native magazines had never provided an accurate view of the market for magazines in Canada. Readers above the forty-ninth parallel had long purchased American magazines in quantities that far outstripped what Canadian publishers produced. After 1900 these quantities increased dramatically. Had any Canadian publisher tapped into this market, the periodical landscape might have changed suddenly and dramatically.

Five years after Healy's comments, this scenario came to pass. Canadian magazines appeared that seemed capable of attracting a vast number of these readers. The population itself was expanding. At the same time, it was also becoming increasingly urban and dependent on store-bought goods. American publishers were cultivating a growing audience for consumer magazines and supplied ample examples of successful formats and formulas. Then, with the new market research tools developed by academics such as Paul T. Cherington, it became possible for publishers to identify emerging trends in the Canadian marketplace and to respond to them with topical magazines of their own. The change began with the adoption of reader profiles by publishers' advertising sales staff. This event prompted a reconsideration of the relationship between magazines and their readerships. It did not occur overnight. Nonetheless, the conception of readers as patrons gradually lost ground to a conception of readers as consumers. Publishers reoriented their magazines' editorial and financial structures around the concept of consumer markets. Every policy adopted by such magazines ultimately had to be justified by its service-value to advertisers.

American Magazines in Canada

Canadian magazines were never the only choice enjoyed by anglophone Canadians. Throughout the nineteenth century, the market was dominated by British and American periodicals. Indeed, it would be no exaggeration to state that the market was shaped by the presence of these periodicals, and that Canadian offerings merely filled limited roles not served by their imported counterparts.

It is difficult to assess the actual number of newspapers and magazines that entered Canada before 1930. Reliable circulation figures for American periodicals did not become available until 1914 when the Audit Bureau of Circulations was formed. In its reports it isolated the regional distribution of every periodical's circulation and treated Canada as a unit. W.A. Lydiatt drew upon these figures and issued a list of the top-selling American magazines in Canada each year after 1916. These figures, however, could not provide an overall picture of the number of magazines entering the country. The only agency that kept statistics on this subject was the federal Ministry of Customs, which administered the country's tariff laws. It tracked the annual dollar value of periodicals entering the country rather than their absolute number. Nonetheless, these statistics can provide the basis for an educated guess.[3]

The annual value of American magazines entering Canada grew relatively slowly before the turn of the century. Indeed, this value declined between 1889 and 1894. This dip corresponds with the price war fought among *Munsey's*, *Cosmopolitan*, and *McClure's* on their home turf. Before Frank Munsey reduced the price of his publication to 10¢ in 1893, the average price per issue for a consumer magazine was 25 to 35¢. Hence, the *dollar value* of magazines entering Canada dropped in the early 1890s – and bottomed out in 1893 – but the *number* of magazines probably increased. Where one dollar represented three or four magazines in the 1880s, it usually represented ten by 1900. In terms of the absolute number of magazines entering Canada, then, the customs figures probably understate the true magnitude of the increased American presence. This consideration makes the figures after 1900 all the more remarkable. From 1900 to 1921 the average annual rate of growth in the value of American magazines entering Canada was 16.4 per cent (Figure 7.1).

British magazines provide an interesting contrast to the American imports. From 1900 to 1915 the value of British magazines entering Canada tripled. There are two possible explanations for this. First, the increased sale of American periodicals certainly indicated that Canadians had become magazine enthusiasts. No doubt this benefited all publishers, American or otherwise. Second, the period also saw a significant increase in the number of British immigrants to Canada, who probably sought news of the home country. Either way, not even the war sustained this demand. The importation of British magazines was inconsistent throughout the 1920s. While the value of their imports stagnated, their share of the Canadian market in foreign periodicals was destroyed. In 1900 they held a 20.3 per cent share, which compared respectably with the 79.0 per cent held by the Americans. In 1920 the British barely scratched 1.7 per cent out of a market smothered by the Americans' 98.3 per cent share. French magazines played almost no role in these statistics, although they usually accounted for the third largest share. Total imports from countries other than the United States and Great Britain represented 0.7 per cent of the total in 1900 and less than 0.1 per cent twenty years later. *Lydiatt's Book* never bothered to include information on European periodicals. Their reach as advertising media in Canada was negligible.

Given the dollar value of imports from the United States, one could estimate that some 17.5 million magazines entered Canada in 1921 alone.[4] This number compares favourably with the estimated total for

FIGURE 7.1

Total Dollar Value of Newspapers and Magazines Entering Canada for Home Consumption, by Country of Origin, 1890–1930

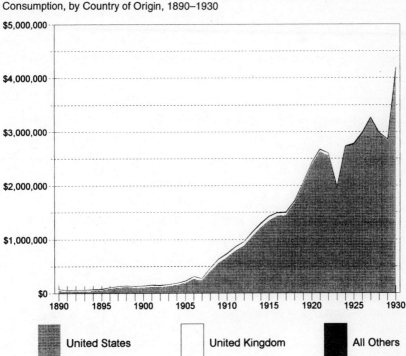

Note: Individual values for the United States, United Kingdom, and all others for 1896 are estimates based on aggregate total dollar value and ratios derived from the surrounding years.

Source: Canada, Department of Customs, *Tables of the Trade and Navigation of Canada* (Ottawa: Queen's/King's Printer [1881–1932]), and Canada, *Dominion Year Book* (Ottawa: Queen's/King's Printer [1898–1932]).

the ten top-selling American consumer magazines in Canada for 1921: 10,698,160 (Table 7.1). The comparable figure for Canadian magazines for the same year was 14,024,128 (Table 7.2). This may reflect favourably on native publishers, but it should be remembered that after these ten there was no other consumer magazine published in Canada with a circulation above 25,000. Even then, the list has been padded with one fraternal organ and one religious paper, both of which made valiant

TABLE 7.1
Ten Highest Circulating American Magazines in Canada, and Estimated Value of Circulation, 1921

Title	Annual subscription ($)	Issues per year	Average circulation per issue in Canada	Estimated total annual circulation	Estimated total annual value ($)
Ladies' Home Journal	1.50	12	84,452	1,013,424	126,678.00
Saturday Evening Post	2.00	52	64,386	3,348,072	128,772.00
Cosmopolitan	3.00	12	62,433	749,196	187,299.00
Redbook	2.00	12	55,598	667,176	111,196.00
Butterick Trio*	1.40	12	54,406	652,872	76,168.40
Pictorial Review	2.50	12	52,991	635,892	132,477.50
Women's Home Companion	2.00	12	52,639	631,668	105,278.00
Collier's Weekly	2.50	52	43,630	2,268,760	109,075.00
Good Housekeeping	3.00	12	31,865	382,380	95,595.00
McCall's Magazine	1.50	12	29,060	348,720	43,590.00
Total				10,698,160	1,116,128.90

*The Butterick Trio was composed of three quarterly magazines: Delineator, New Idea, and Designer.
Canadian circulation figures: Lydiatt's Book, 9th ed. (Toronto: Lydiatt, 1922); subscription rates: N.W. Ayer, American Newspaper Annual (Philadelphia: Ayer, 1922).

TABLE 7.2
Ten Highest Circulating Canadian Magazines in Canada, and Estimated Value of Circulation, 1921

Title	Annual subscription ($)	Issues per year	Average circulation per issue in Canada	Estimated total annual circulation	Estimated total annual value ($)
Everywoman's World	2.00	12	106,167	1,274,004	212,334.00
MacLean's	3.00	24	76,478	1,835,472	229,434.00
Canadian Home Journal	2.00	12	55,407	664,884	110,814.00
Northern Messenger	0.75	52	54,455	2,831,660	40,841.25
Jack Canuck	3.50	52	49,441	2,570,932	173,043.50
Western Home Monthly	1.00	12	43,319	519,828	43,319.00
Saturday Night	4.00	52	36,221	1,883,492	144,884.00
Veteran	2.00	12	33,918	407,016	67,836.00
Christian Guardian	2.00	52	32,186	1,673,672	64,372.00
National Pictorial	1.00	12	30,264	363,168	30,264.00
Total				14,024,128	1,117,141.75

Circulation figures: *Lydiatt's Book*, 9th ed. (Toronto: Lydiatt, 1922); subscription rates: *Canadian Newspaper Directory*, 15th ed. (Montreal: McKim, 1921).

attempts at mainstream acceptance: *The Veteran* and *The Christian Guardian*. Without their 2 million copies in annual circulation, the Canadian list would lose its edge. In terms of revenue, it lost regardless. The Canadian circulation of American magazines was strictly bonus revenue. Their overhead costs – barring paper, ink, and distribution – were recouped in the United States before any copies were shipped for export. The Canadian circulation of Canadian magazines had to cover the entire cost of production and distribution. As such, the $1,116,128.90 earned by American magazines dwarfed the profits made by their Canadian counterparts in 1921.[5]

Canadian Attempts at Consumer Magazines

There was one other major difference between the rise of the American consumer magazines and those in Canada. South of the border, a large number of national advertisers had emerged in the pages of the daily press before the magazines themselves came into being. Literary journals such as *Atlantic* and *Harper's* did nothing to develop this advertising. Rather, it was the agent J. Walter Thompson who convinced them that advertising would not detract from the prestige of their editorial content.[6] Even then they were reluctant to alter the tone of their periodicals by encouraging increased patronage from advertisers. Quite the opposite – they restricted the number of pages of advertising that could appear in each issue and relegated these pages to the back of the magazine, presumably where they would do the least harm.[7] Cyrus Curtis and Frank Munsey exploited this situation by offering manufacturers media willing to serve the advertiser's interests. Their editorial content did not reflect a desire to attract an elite, intellectual audience interested in belles-lettres. Instead, they aimed at the largest audience possible, an audience connected by its need to purchase the kinds of commodities that manufacturers advertised.[8] The editorial content was no less topical or political, but it was far less pretentious in its literary reach. It was middlebrow rather than elite, and never pretended to be otherwise.[9] To advertisers, the appeal of their circulation alone was perfectly rational and economic. Rather than placing ads in dozens of newspapers, an advertiser using one magazine such as the *Ladies' Home Journal* could confidently expect to reach a significant percentage of American homemakers in every region.

Many Canadian publishers hoped to re-create the success of their American counterparts, but they did not enjoy the same base of advertisers from which to draw support. Even if a literary journal such as *Saturday Night* had wished to replicate *Munsey's*, there were too few advertisers to support a reduced cover price. A weekly number of *Saturday Night* averaged thirty-two pages in the late 1890s. By contrast, *Munsey's* and the *Ladies' Home Journal* regularly carried over one hundred pages of advertising alone. There were two routes open to Canadian publishers withstanding the American competition. The first option was to maintain the status quo and shrug off the rising number of imports as an inconsequential fad. The second option was to craft a Canadian magazine in a format popularized by the Americans.

Among those magazines that stood their ground was *Canadian Magazine*. *Canadian* was the monthly standard of a book publishing firm – the Ontario Publishing Company of Toronto.[10] Among other things, Ontario Publishing produced textbooks for the provincial school system. Whether its editors were attempting to live up to its educational reputation, or simply trying to compete with *Harper's*, the magazine was self-consciously literary from its start in 1893. In the same year that *Munsey's* led the respectable consumer magazines into the 10¢ arena, the cover price of *Canadian* was a solid 25¢. Certainly, nothing was scrimped on materials. It was printed on heavy-stock paper in digest size, its pages included a smattering of half-tone photographs, and advertising was kept strictly to its back pages. This advertising was removed completely when year-end volumes were bound for sale. The cover itself epitomized tradition: a bold, solid black masthead framed by double lines – sturdy, balanced, and symmetrical. Like many of its contemporaries in Canada, its masthead and ornamentation remained unchanged from month to month, save for the date of issue.

Through its first thirty years, the magazine changed remarkably little. Two competent editors, John A. Cooper and Newton MacTavish, guided it through the tremendous surge of American imports and the appearance of Canadian imitations. (Cooper, incidentally, had come to the magazine after serving as the first editor of *Printer and Publisher*.) In essence, each editor clung to the tradition of belles-lettres established by *Harper's* in the 1860s. The Canadian market had only just become capable of sustaining this kind of magazine in the 1890s, both in terms of an audience and a supply of contributors to keep the magazine fresh. Nonetheless, it was its orientation towards an elite, highbrow readership that ultimately led to its decline. As a traditional literary magazine, it never cracked the top fifty periodicals sold in Canada. With a small but loyal readership, its appeal to advertisers was the apparent prestige of that group – presumably men of affairs and professionals – and its longevity.[11]

The easiest way to compete with the Americans was to follow the second route: to imitate them. As writer Fraser Sutherland has noted, this was usually done by taking American formats and filling them with Canadian content.[12] One of the most enduring in this regard was a magazine created in 1906 by John A. Cooper himself, entitled *Canadian Courier*. *Courier* was to *Canadian* what *Munsey's* had been to *Harper's*: a streetwise weekly magazine dealing with many of the same topics and issues as the older, more sedate monthly journal, but with a lighter touch. The prose was less academic, the cover and look of the magazine incorporated more use of white space to give it an airier feel, and photographs formed a more integral part of the fare. Its twenty-four pages were printed on good quality bleached paper, and it was generously sized. It immediately appealed to advertisers and soon had contracts for various foods, office supplies, and home products, as well as the perennial advertisements found in the middlebrow magazines: insurance, banks, and books.[13]

Beyond its content and materials, *Courier* also offered advertisers better service. In a major shift from the traditional journal, Cooper adopted one of the new techniques of the American magazines: he integrated editorial and advertising content on the same page. While newspapers had always done this, the literary journals had kept the two strictly separate. The new general magazines of the 1890s had dropped this practice in favour of running them side by side. Eventually, this developed into the practice of 'tailing': running the end of an article through the thickets of ads at the back of the magazine to generate reader traffic. *Courier* kept the front of the magazine free of advertising, then integrated or tailed its articles into the back. This kind of attention to the needs of advertisers was crucially important in the development of the mass magazines to follow. Few things better signalled the shifting of editorial attention from subscribers to advertisers.[14]

The differences between *Canadian Magazine* and *Canadian Courier* could not have been more stark.[15] The *Canadian* remained just as it had been, a fact highlighted by the two magazines' ads in McKim's directory for 1915. The *Canadian* ad relied heavily on its prestige, and practically concluded that some advertisers' goods might not be up to the standards of this lofty publication. 'If your product is worthy of introduction to the permanent homes of Canada,' it intoned, 'you will find the "Canadian Magazine" a profitable medium.'[16] Meanwhile, the *Cou-*

rier drew attention to its regular editorial departments, which closely paralleled emerging consumer patterns. Manufacturers of pianos, sheet music, pianolas, phonographs, and recordings would have appreciated the 'Music' section, while other businesses would have found comfortable niches in one of the 'Motoring,' 'Travel,' or 'Women' sections.[17] In 1917 the editor even included a list of national advertisers in the magazine itself and recommended that readers patronize them. If readers could not readily find the brand names mentioned, then the editor would be happy to send them instructions on how to get them.[18]

Advertisers had a reason to prefer the *Courier* over the *Canadian*, and apparently readers did as well. By 1910 the *Courier*'s average circulation per issue was 25 per cent greater than that of *Canadian*. In 1919 the *Courier*'s circulation more than doubled that of its elder competitor. This statistic is all the more remarkable if one considers how frequently the magazines were issued. The *Canadian* was issued only once a month, and sold 17,250 copies. The *Courier*, issued twice a month, sold over 90,000 copies monthly.[19]

Another magazine that took the American route was the *Home Journal*, established by James Acton. Acton was a Toronto publisher whose trade journals rivalled those of J.B. Maclean. In 1905 he broke new ground by plunging into the consumer field with the *Journal*. In the space of two years its circulation grew to 20,000, a significant number for any magazine then sold in Canada.[20] However, with a format little different from that of its American model, it offered nothing to set itself apart. Its circulation stalled, and twice it changed hands by 1912. The second person to buy it was Harold Gagnier, another trade paper publisher, who had recently acquired *Saturday Night*. Rather unsubtly, Gagnier rechristened the *Journal* as the *Canadian Ladies' Home Journal*.[21] The Curtis Publishing Company did not look kindly upon it and immediately filed suit for copyright infringement. Gagnier retreated and settled out of court. Thereafter the magazine was called the *Canadian Home Journal*.[22] It remained a stalwart national entry in the magazine wars until 1958.

This tendency to imitate specific American magazines did not serve Canadian publishing houses particularly well. *Canadian Courier* and the *Canadian Home Journal* provided modest success stories, but several others were not as fortunate. Among these were *National Monthly* (1904–6), *Maple Leaf* (1922–6), *Canadian Pictorial* (1906–16), *Canadian Collier's* (1908–11), *Canadian Century* (1910–11), and *Vie Canadienne* (1918–19). A profusion of national tags in the mastheads is immediately noticeable. It points to a persistent belief among publishers that merely by being 'Canadian' magazines would attract readers. Apparently, the failure of these self-same magazines did nothing to discourage such hopes. There were a few success stories beyond the *Courier* and the *Home Journal*: *Canadian Motorist* (1914), the *Canadian Forum* (1920), and *Canadian Homes and Gardens* (1922) have all survived into the present day in varying forms, though only the last could claim to be a consumer magazine. *Canadian Motorist* was adopted by the Canadian Automobile Association to become its chatty promotional newsletter, now called *LeisureWays*. The *Forum* survived the Great Depression as an ally of the League for Social Reconstruction and the Co-operative Commonwealth Federation.[23]

Canadian Collier's deserves an honourable mention. It was not simply a Canadian imitation of the American magazine, but a Canadian edition owned by the American publisher. Peter F. Collier had made his name producing bargain-priced editions of classic books in the 1870s. He added to this success in 1888 when he started a breezy, well-illustrated paper entitled *Collier's Weekly*. During the 1890s it slowly gained a reputation for its unique combination of muckraking journalism, top-notch commentary, and quality illustrations and photography.[24]

The magazine that set up shop in Toronto offered the same brand of progressive journalism and short fiction as its namesake. Indeed, more often than not, it offered the *same* progressive journalism and short fiction as its namesake. H. Franklin Gadsby, a St Catharines writer, was the Canadian editor. Despite the introduction of some Canadian material, he drew heavily upon the editorial content and advertising of the American edition to fill its pages. Their covers were the same, and the volume numbering remained synchronized – there was no first issue to launch the 'new' magazine. Nonetheless, the Canadian material gave the magazine a very high profile. One series of articles featured biographical sketches of native sons who had become 'Captains of Industry'; another asked selected premiers and lieutenant-governors to peer into the future of their respective provinces. Noted francophone journalists such as Olivar Asselin provided occasional pieces on Quebec, and during its first few months of publication these articles appeared in French untranslated.[25] Other articles and poetry were written by the likes of Bliss Carman, George F. Chipman, and Hector Charlesworth. Perhaps the most provocative piece the magazine ran was a contest. In 1909 it offered $100 for the best English-language lyrics written for Calixa Lavallée's national hymn, 'O Canada.' This contest proved so popular that some two hundred versions entered circulation, and six of these gained widespread popularity.[26] Despite this response, Gadsby's editorial policies were not to last. After a year, his name disappeared from the title page and was not replaced. Canadian contributions waned after that. The same year, Collier died and left the publishing house to his son Robert. Robert ambitiously set his sights on the industry-leading *Saturday Evening Post* and reorganized the American *Collier's* as a lower-quality, 5¢ paper. By coincidence or design, *Canadian Collier's* closed soon after.[27]

Everywoman's World

The true success story in Canada before 1920 was undoubtedly *Everywoman's World*. *Everywoman's* was founded in 1913 by a new Toronto firm, the Continental Publishing Company. Continental was formed by a partnership between Isidor Simonski and Charles C. Nixon. Of the two, Nixon had the more extensive background in publishing and took a more public role in the magazine's promotion. He had served as the managing editor of *Farm and Dairy* before joining the Gagnier organization to work on its trade papers. Simonski came to publishing from a background in marketing.

The idea for the magazine had come to Simonski while advertising a flavouring essence through existing Canadian magazines. After the campaign was over, he analysed the response rate from each periodical and discovered that the cost of obtaining any one response ranged from 40¢ to $1.19. This was appallingly high, too high to be justified by the retail price of the product. He traced the problem to his media selection. The product was mainly of interest to women, yet the proportion of women reading any one of the magazines on his list was no more than 60 per cent. Clearly, he thought, there was room in Canada for a new periodical that spoke only to women. The name selected was a clever alteration of *Everybody's*, a popular American magazine then part of the Butterick empire.[28]

The term 'national' had two different connotations depending on who Simonski and Nixon were addressing. When talking to readers, *Everywoman's* status as a 'national' magazine conjured up visions of a community of readers both widely inclusive and deeply patriotic. Inclusivity was important, in the sense that every woman, regardless of her station or creed, could feel that she was participating in something national in scope simply by reading the magazine. Certainly, it was priced within reach of many homes, at 10¢ per copy and 50¢ for an annual subscription. Patriotism, meanwhile, was a moral imperative that any reasonable Canadian publisher would strive to fulfil. It was a common mantra among all of the consumer magazine publishers of the day, and it was a rhetorical tool that *Everywoman's* used well. A Dominion Day editorial in 1920 waxed on the substantial contributions that magazines made to the task of nation-building. 'Something nationally human,' it pronounced, 'must be built upon what politicians, railway builders, manufacturers, and bankers laid down.'[29] Magazines reaching from the Pacific to the Atlantic could supply the cultural content necessary for a country built of capital and steel.

The word 'national' meant something quite different when publishers spoke to advertisers. A national magazine was everything that a daily newspaper or a country weekly was not: nationwide in its circulation, potentially exclusive in its readership, and geared towards the delivery of advertising rather than news. *Everywoman's* joined with five other publishers for a cooperative ad campaign in 1921. One ad argued quite explicitly that 'the people in any one centre would not be aware that your advertising was being displayed in all the other centres' if one used newspapers, 'and this aspect of national advertising is of the utmost importance – the impression that your goods are on sale everywhere. It is precisely this idea of national consumption which builds national prestige for your product.'[30] *Everywoman's* was not published to fulfil readers' interest in things domestic; *Everywoman's* was published to serve advertisers who wanted to reach all Canadian women with one appropriation.

Nixon himself made this point explicit in *Economic Advertising*. To the question 'Are Women's Magazines Justified?' Nixon replied with a decided yes. His reasons, however, paid no mind to the growing strength of women's voices within Canadian society, nor did he care to provide them with a forum of their own. Full justification could be found in the simple fact that women controlled household spending. Nixon pointed to a recent study done by the Home Economics Department at the University of Wisconsin that claimed 90 per cent of household expenditures were made by women. With or without statistics, this belief had long been held by publishers in the United States. Nixon felt it was insufficiently appreciated in Canada. 'Women folk are the ultimate buyers of almost all of all kinds of merchandise for food, shelter, and clothing, and to a great extent also of so-called luxuries,' he wrote. For that reason alone, a medium was necessary that would provide advertisers with a single, direct introduction to their homes. That a magazine such as *Everywoman's* could also give its reader 'vital information about her everyday needs and desires, and which also entertains, elevates and points her to new fields of freedom and accomplishment,' was a notable side effect.[31]

Simonski and Nixon's efforts paid off. Within a year *Everywoman's* had the highest circulation of any Canadian magazine. Within two years, it became the first to attain a circulation of 100,000.[32] Part of this success may be due in part to the magazine's own policy of advertising advertising. Nixon relied heavily on printer's ink rather than salesmen to reach manufacturers. In the summer of 1915 he cut a deal with Norris-Patterson Limited that gave him the entire first page of *Economic Advertising* – a page previously reserved for the paper's lead editorial – through the coming fall and winter. Then, month after month, Nixon used this space to barrage prospective clients with endless facts, describing the location, size, spending power, and influence of the magazine's readers. Two years on, Nixon struck again with the first four-colour ad in *Economic Advertising* to demonstrate the effectiveness of colour printing.[33]

In his own pages Nixon constantly drew attention to the advertising columns. Where other magazines opened with an inspirational message from the editor proclaiming a new star in the magazine heavens, *Everywoman's* had a message from its advertising manager. Tucked among the peonies and ribbons of an artfully set page came a sober essay on the economics of publishing and the beneficence of the magazine's advertisers. If readers enjoyed the magazine, Nixon submitted, there was something they could do to ensure its survival:

> Perhaps our interested people who get 'Everywoman's World' this month can best show their appreciation for this great Canadian enterprise by writing to and patronizing the advertisers whose advertisements appear in this issue. Advertisers have been rather timid about taking space in this medium, thinking that you might not favor 'Everywoman's World.' We would be glad if in addition to writing to any of our advertisers ... if you would write to us pointing out other advertisers whom you would like to see as advertisers in 'Everywoman's World.' This will all help us to make 'Everywoman's World' better and better for you.[34]

Nothing was said of the magazine's stories of love. Readers with favourite recipes or household tips could keep them to themselves.

What the editors really wanted was a clear demonstration that their advertising columns were read.

A regular feature that began that month made the circle of editorial and advertising columns complete. 'The Romance of Modern Business' drew brief biographical sketches of well-known manufacturers and their leading products. All of them became famous through the same measure: advertising. Readers of the Valentine's issue in 1914 were treated to the story of Waterman's Fountain Pen. An unquestionably useful item, it had languished in obscurity until its inventor had a chance meeting with a quick-witted advertising man. A union ensued, and their progeny were multitude. The story concluded thus:

> It has been shown that through the force of national magazine advertising a large industry was created. But there is another side ...
>
> There is a broad, ethical mission to the development of an industry such as the L.E. Waterman Company. Thousands of people are served, office and written work is facilitated, time is saved and life generally is made easier and happier for many the world over.[35]

This was advertising dressed as romantic fiction, complete with an instructive message and wrapped in a convenient package.[36]

The appearance of the new magazine made news in *Economic Advertising*, which announced that *Everywoman's* was the first 'low-price, high-quality' journal of its kind in Canada.[37] The comment was not made lightly. The *Canadian Home Journal* frequently patronized the advertising columns of the advertising trade paper. Clearly, the editor saw in the new magazine something that made it categorically different from its predecessors. It might be suggested that it was the first consumer magazine produced in Canada.

MacLean's Magazine

When J.B. Maclean entered the general magazine field, he did so with all of the guile and reserve that characterized the rest of his business. Rather than starting a magazine from scratch, as Acton Press and Continental Publishing had done, Maclean bought an existing niche-market magazine and allowed it to develop a new editorial voice, though always with the understanding that it would become something geared to the mass market. In 1905 Maclean bought *Business Magazine* from the Toronto bookseller and advertising agent J.S. Robertson. Robertson had established the magazine ten years before to supply local businessmen with articles of interest on commercial affairs, particularly on the subject of advertising.[38]

Maclean wanted a magazine that would appeal to the new corporate employee of the twentieth century: urban, white-collar, ambitious, well educated, and engaged in the affairs of the world. When he bought *Business*, Maclean was primarily acquiring its subscription list and the goodwill of its readers. Robertson had targeted those whom he believed were buyers of advertising, precisely the kind of progressive business people that Maclean wanted to reach. This was the same market that the popular *Saturday Evening Post* had developed in the United States – not the social elite, and not the urban working class, but go-getters running their own small businesses, professionals, and managers finding their niche in the new corporate structures of monopoly capitalism. Maclean's magazine would not be a trade paper for white-collar workers. Quite the opposite, Maclean had in mind a consciously home-oriented magazine, more akin to an agricultural journal such as *Farm and Home* than any of his own papers. Initially, Maclean kept Robertson's masthead, but he attached a telling subtitle: 'the Home Magazine of the Busy Man and His Family.' 'Busy Man' had a good ring to it; Maclean made that the new title with the third issue. Despite the new masthead, however, Maclean knew that women were an increasing segment of the urban, white-collar workforce, and he considered them a part of his potential readership from the outset. Taken together, these readers composed the 'leadership families,' which he described as 'the most cultured and prosperous homes in Canada, homes which influence the buying habits and practices of the communities in which they are found.'[39]

The magazine began as a digest of other periodicals, particularly those from the United States and Great Britain. Canadian material was not a priority. The editor reviewed the British and American press for the best new writing on politics, business, and society, then reprinted it for the benefit of Canadians. The idea was pitched to readers as a convenience, saving them both time and money. Occasionally, an original piece written in Canada would appear.[40]

To build up the magazine's circulation, Maclean had two advantages. First, he had Robertson's subscription list, and this he honoured with the new magazine. Second, he had extensive lists of his own, one for each of his ten trade papers. These lists comprised the very market that Maclean wanted to develop: literate urbanites engaged in commerce and industry. A letter was sent to each one, describing the new magazine and asking his or her indulgence of a subscription, sight unseen. According to company advertising, this campaign met expectations.[41]

For advertisers, the appeal of the new magazine was the subscription list that Maclean had put together. Here was a magazine that reached a decidedly attractive market. Its readers should have occupied a higher income bracket than most periodicals, and they should have provided a ready market for consumer goods. Further, it was not a trade paper aimed at a reader distracted by the hustle and bustle of workaday life. It was intended for quieter moments, after hours, in the privacy of the home. Better still, the subscription list was genuinely national in scope and made no appeals to readers on the basis of gender, ethnicity, party, or faith. In the terminology of the day, it was purely a 'class' magazine. The appeal apparently worked. By 1911 the magazine boasted nearly one hundred pages of advertising per issue, carefully segregated from the editorial matter. The February number had seventeen pages of advertising at the front and another eighty pages at the back.[42]

Over its first six years, Busyman's slowly increased the amount of original Canadian material it carried. This may well have been prompted by competition from the Saturday Evening Post, Canadian Courier, and Canadian Collier's; they all tried to appeal to the same market. In terms of sheer numbers, the Post was the clear leader in North America – although it is impossible to state how well any American magazine did in Canada before the Audit Bureau began to supply statistics by regions. So long as Busyman's continued to run reprints from other sources, however, it competed head-to-head with its more polished counterparts. With greater amounts of Canadian content, it slowly created its own niche within the consumer magazine market: Canada itself. Nationalist sentiment might have suggested this strategy, but prudence could also have played its part. In the same year that he bought Business, Maclean was offered two American magazines: Women's Home Companion and Farm and Fireside. Between them, they had a monthly circulation of 1.2 million in the United States and Canada. Maclean chose to purchase the lowly Business, circulation fifteen hundred, instead.[43]

In 1911 Maclean's understanding of American publishing practices, American magazine design, and Canadian content came together. That year, Maclean refashioned the journal-sized Busyman's digest into a standard-sized magazine entitled *MacLean's*. The magazine now rigorously pursued new material from Canadian sources, increased its use of illustrations, and adopted a four-colour cover. From 1913 to 1917 it also appears that Maclean elected to run *MacLean's* on a deficit in order to build its profile. The magazine weathered five successive deficits during this time. Given that Maclean enforced strict austerity measures during the war, these losses – and their relatively consistent values despite great fluctuations in revenue – can only be seen as deliberate.[44]

Beyond Maclean's deep pockets, the magazine was also helped by the appointment of a new editor, Thomas B. Costain. Costain had joined the company in 1911, when Maclean put him in charge of *Hardware and Metal*. His editorial talents quickly became evident, and he was soon promoted to the chair of the company's flagship magazine. Together with Maclean, Costain slowly crafted a recognizably distinct and competent mixture of muckraking journalism, light fiction, and Canadian nationalism.

The editor did not always agree with his publisher on the magazine's overall direction. Costain was inclined to infuse the magazine with serious commentary; he had in mind articles on J.M. Keynes's analysis of the Versailles Treaty and the lingering tensions between French and English Canada. Maclean insisted that the magazine strive for a lighter rather than a more serious tone.[45] In one gentle rebuff of his editor, Maclean wrote that the magazine needed:

> articles that will interest the great majority of Canadians, and interest them so effectively, that they will talk to every one they meet about the article ... We don't want to discuss problems of any kind at the present time in MacLean's, but to give the most informing, the most exciting, the most curiosity arousing specials we can secure from Canadian writers on Canadian topics, and after that the same class of matter from American, British, and other publications ... It is not what you and I like best, but rather what the readers like best that we must give.[46]

After a tour of the western provinces, Costain came to agree with his publisher. He had spoken with hundreds of people at luncheons, meetings, and while travelling by train, and he concluded that the magazine had a definite following: 'I believe, however, that in order to make them really look forward to the magazine we must provide them with considerable entertainment. I base this on the fact that everywhere I heard references to certain features. Unquestionably the most popular thing that we have been running this year from the Western standpoint is the series of Bulldog Carney stories.'[47] Maclean had learned to give his readers what they wanted, at a price they were willing to pay. It was a strategy maintained over the next two decades.

While these strategies brought in readers, it was up to the sales staff to bring in advertisers. Like *Everywoman's*, the magazine relied heavily on a demographic interpretation of its readership. It took time for the company to develop the statistical facility of Simonski and Nixon, however. Throughout the 1910s MacLean Publishing relied more upon the quality of its editorial content and the sheer size of its readership to sell its white space. Nonetheless, it remained convinced of the quality of its readership as well. One 1918 ad claimed that 'over 65,000 families – 300,000 individuals ... read MACLEAN'S – men and women who form the very foundation of Canada's commercial and social structure – men and women to whom others naturally look for guidance'; a later ad asserted that they were 'the live progressive Canadians in each province.'[48]

Urban, white-collar workers were key to this perception of the readership. The company's flagship paper had to have an aura of quality, something that would reflect and reinforce the reputation and status of its namesake. Moreover, the readership had to have sufficient disposable income to buy advertised articles and services. Managers and professionals were *MacLean's* ideal readers because they were 'the people who represent the most important proportion of the consumer purchasing power in Canada.'[49] They were not simply a national audience, they were a 'national market,' and national magazines openly asked advertisers to 'Cater to Classes.'[50] Managers and professionals were not the kind of people who shopped by price alone, but sought out products that emanated quality – the kind of products that did not scrimp on advertising, but used the four-colour, glossy pages of consumer magazines. 'It is the tendency of the *mentally alert* to get the best goods for the right price,' an ad declared in 1921. 'They are the *particular* shoppers who recognize and continue to purchase good brands because of their standard quality and price ... These *particular* shoppers are usually magazine readers.'[51] In producing a magazine that appealed to these readers, *MacLean's* actively constructed a community of middle-class shoppers who would be key to the marketing plans of national advertisers.

In the 1920s MacLean staff began to develop more intensive readership analyses. Indeed, they were manipulating census data, cross-

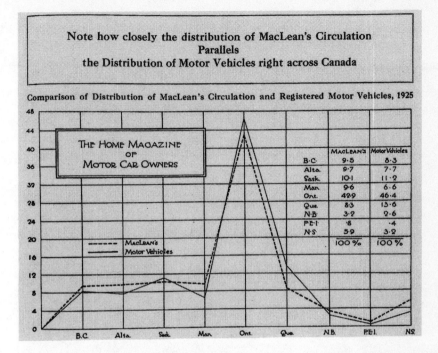

Note how closely the distribution of MacLean's Circulation
Parallels
the Distribution of Motor Vehicles right across Canada

Comparison of Distribution of MacLean's Circulation and Registered Motor Vehicles, 1925

THE HOME MAGAZINE
OF
MOTOR CAR OWNERS

	MacLean's	Motor Vehicles
B·C·	9·5	8·3
Alta.	9·7	7·7
Sask.	10·1	11·2
Man.	9·6	6·6
Ont.	42·9	46·4
Que.	8·3	13·6
N·B·	3·2	2·6
P·E·I·	·8	·4
N·S·	5·9	3·2
	100 %	100 %

MacLean's
Motor Vehicles

MacLean's 1928: Detailed Analysis of Distribution (Toronto: *MacLean's*, 1928),
37. National Archives of Canada, MG 31 E 97, Arthur Irwin papers, vol. 18,
f. 25.

referencing it with subscription lists, and conducting supplementary
surveys by 1927. One such survey of 1,694 subscribers discovered that
each issue was read on average by four different people – half women,
half men – a figure that suggested to the MacLean staff that it actually
was the family paper they had long believed it to be. This information
appeared in *MacLean's 1928: Detailed Analysis of Distribution* (1928). This
fifty-two-page booklet was a painstakingly detailed readership study
of the location and spending habits of the magazine's readership. Key
here were charts that revealed the extent to which its readers were on
the cutting edge of Canadian consumption patterns. A line graph illustrated the rate of automobile ownership by province across the country. Then, superimposed, was the rate of subscription to *MacLean's*. The
near identical lines implied that the two groups represented were one

and the same; automobile owners *were* regular readers. This was only good news for advertisers, since it illustrated a sure way to reach elite consumers. The brochure argued: 'Because of the very much higher cost of automobiles in Canada, ownership of a motor car is not only evidence of purchasing power but also of a desire to buy. It is an accurate "Yardstick" of the Canadian market, and of the exceptional market offered by *MacLean's Magazine* for every kind of merchandise.'[52] The same technique was repeated with several indicators of income and consumption, including income-tax payment, telephone ownership, and electrically wired homes.

It was a formula that worked. Such was the success of Costain's editorial direction and the company's growing marketing savvy that its American rivals took notice. In 1921 Costain was made assistant editor of the *Saturday Evening Post*, where he became heir apparent to its legendary chief, George Horace Lorimer. When he left *MacLean's*, it was second only to *Everywoman's* among Canadian magazines. By 1930 it was the head of its class, outsold in Canada only by the American *Pictorial Review* and the perennial weekend papers, the *Family Herald and Weekly Star* and the *Star Weekly*.[53]

The Newspapers Respond

The appearance of magazines such as *Everywoman's* and *MacLean's* did not sit well with the publishers of Canada's newspapers. American magazines had affected neither their subscription bases nor their advertising revenue. Canadian magazines did. The aggressive cultivation of advertisers by Simonski, Nixon, and Maclean was a new phenomenon. Nixon's sales pitch to manufacturers did not portray the magazine as a useful supplement to newspaper advertising, but as an effective replacement. Agencies such as Desbarats noticed and were enthusiastic about the media choices they now had when buying space.[54] Newspapers countered these developments with a host of arguments in their advertisements to the trade, but their most potent weapon was the circulation strength of their weekend editions.

Weekend papers were Saturday editions of the large metropolitan dailies. In the United States, these papers were usually issued on Sundays and featured articles and stories of a less newsy character than that found in the same papers from Monday to Friday. Serialized fiction, children's pages, comic strips, travel writing, lengthy political discussions, and perhaps a rotogravure section, characterized the pages of the popular Sunday papers. Due to Canada's persistent Sabbatarianism, its publishers shied away from Sunday print runs. They issued their papers on Thursday or Saturday instead.

American weekend papers at the turn of the century resembled consumer magazines. Their Canadian counterparts resembled farm papers. Competition between the metropolitan dailies of the 1860s prompted some publishers to look beyond their native cities into the wider province for readers.[55] While outlying districts offered greater circulation, the cost of obtaining these readers could be prohibitive. The weekend edition offered a tidy solution to this problem. With a higher price and a greater print run than a daily paper, the weekend edition could be profitably marketed to a rural population. George Brown of the Toronto *Globe* enhanced his farm appeal by gearing his editorial content to the supposed interests of a rural readership. In 1863 he bought a floundering monthly entitled *Canada Farmer* and made it the basis for his own weekend paper. The result was the *Weekly Globe and Canada Farmer*.[56]

George Brown was not the only publisher to employ this tactic. In Quebec, it was undertaken by French- and English-language papers with equal zeal. Farmers' editions were started at both of the major French papers in Montreal, *La Patrie* in 1880 and *La Presse* four years later. The daily *Canadien* made its ambitions perfectly clear when it named its Saturday edition *Le Cultivateur* (1884). The grande dame of the field, however, was the *Family Herald and Weekly Star*, the weekend companion of Hugh Graham's *Star*. Founded in 1869, the *Family Herald* became a popular institution whose readership attended its weekly ministrations of sensible advice and romantic fiction for over eighty years. By the 1890s it had an average weekly circulation of 70,000, and individual issues occasionally broke the 100,000 mark. In 1926 it became the first periodical in Canada to break the 200,000 mark, and it enjoyed a readership spread from the Prairie West to the Maritimes. Until the Second World War, it had the highest circulation of any periodical in the country.[57]

The *Sunday World* and its cross-town rival, the Toronto *Star Weekly*, were not aimed at the farm market. Both papers embraced the urban working class and courted the growing number of families located in the suburbs surrounding Toronto after 1900. The *World* was the older paper, owned by William F. Maclean. The *World* and its Sunday edition – the only one in Canada – served a steady diet of sensationalist news in the style of the American yellow press. By all accounts, it perfectly suited Maclean's own personality.[58]

The Toronto *Star* under Joseph E. Atkinson emerged as a voice of new liberalism. Atkinson took the editor's chair in 1899 when the paper was a distant sixth in a six-paper town. He rapidly rebuilt the paper according to his own vision, and after ten years it became the top Toronto daily. All that remained in terms of competition was the weekly field, where the *Sunday World* snapped in the wind like a red flag before the bullish editor. When it started in 1909, the *Star Weekly* offered a bookish selection of fine arts and cultural reporting, along with the usual selection of commentary and fiction. While this definitely set it apart from the *World*, it placed it against *Saturday Night*, and won few readers away from either. This changed in 1910, when J.H. Cranston was appointed editor. With Atkinson's blessing, Cranston introduced more photographs, comics, colour rotogravures, short pieces, and humorous stories; he also began to budget lavishly for better-known writers. By the time he was done, the paper looked nothing like the one he had inherited. In 1920 the *Star Weekly* overtook the daily in circulation and became the third ranking Canadian periodical. Only the *Family Herald* and the daily *La Presse* topped it.[59]

From the advertiser's perspective, the line separating the weekend papers from the emerging consumer magazines was fine indeed. Atkinson himself equivocated in his own description of the *Star Weekly*, and MacLean Publishing saw it as a rival for national advertisers.[60] Both the papers and the magazines sought the widest readership possible by offering what was essentially entertainment rather than news. Both skirted around the more contentious issues separating Canadians to offer articles geared to lifestyle and recreation. In terms of specific content, this meant current movies, popular writers and their novels, home decorating, fashions in clothes, recipes, sports – things that occupied readers in their leisure hours rather than their workaday lives. Of course, each provided a leisure-time activity itself. The newspaper was a literary cigarette, the magazine a cigar. Weekend papers were definitely the poorer cousins of the periodical press, printed as they were on regular newsprint, typeset with standard linotype, and sold without binding. Photographs and colour printing appeared, but the quality of these was limited by the quality of the paper itself. Weekend papers were, at bottom, newspapers – and they looked like it, cheap and ephemeral. The pages of the best magazines, such as *Everywoman's*, were presented in stylish fonts on high-grade paper and bound for the ages. Where the weekend paper might serve a fecund variety of tasks by the end of the week, the magazine retained a place of honour in the reader's parlour or den, a sign of distinction as surely as a well-selected piano.[61]

Ultimately, there was perhaps one difference that media-buyers recognized when choosing between them: where a consumer magazine could target a specific national market very efficiently, the weekend paper blanketed an entire region regardless of its internal market segmentation. Both types of circulation were useful to advertisers, depending on the product and its marketing strategy. Despite their quibbling, papers and magazines both continued to attract advertising dollars.

The Traditional Magazine Genres Respond

If the new consumer magazines had an effect on the newspapers, they had an equal effect on the traditional magazines. The consumer magazines had evolved out of the domestic and literary magazines of the nineteenth century. Those that succeeded in making the transition were those that expanded their horizons from the respectable, middle-class readership of the Victorian era to the more broad-based, new middle class of the early twentieth century. Those periodicals that clung to their traditional editorial voices and traditional markets retained those markets, but they grew increasingly marginal as the readership of the consumer magazines vaulted past 100,000.

Instructive on this score was the fate of *Canadian Courier* and *Canadian Magazine*. As previously noted, *Canadian* was getting along with 17,500 readers per month in 1920, while John A. Cooper's magazine attained a circulation of 45,000 twice monthly.[62] The *Courier's* numbers were impressive, but even it was rapidly losing ground to *Everywoman's* and *MacLean's*. Where *Courier* offered a section devoted to women, *Everywoman's* offered an entire magazine – reaching at least 100,000 readers every month. Once *MacLean's* created the same-scale audience for a general magazine appealing to men as well as to women, the days of the traditional literary journal, and its middlebrow progeny, were numbered. While Maclean sold advertisers on the merits of his 'leadership families,' Cooper described his magazine in the following terms in *Lydiatt's Book*: '*Canadian Courier* – bringing the East and West together in a compact, interesting, compelling review of Canadian Events – set out to enlarge the common understanding and expand National Sentiment throughout the Nine Provinces.'[63] Space-buyers may have admired his coast-to-coast patriotism, but he offered them nothing in the way of market information. Apparently, readers preferred *MacLean's* as well. In 1920 *MacLean's* had a circulation of 65,000 per issue, twice a month, and it appealed to the same well-informed, patriotic audience as the *Courier*.[64] Cooper called it a day, closed out his magazine, and joined the Toronto advertising agency of Smith, Denne, and Moore.[65]

Perhaps it is ironic that *Canadian Magazine* outlasted its breakaway editor and his upstart magazine. It did not have long to gloat, however. *MacLean's* continued to rise, and broke 80,000 circulation within three years. *Canadian* hovered at 15,000. The next year, 1924, it was finally revamped as a consumer magazine. *Canadian* adopted all of the innovations that the *Courier* and *Busyman's* had almost twenty years before: it increased its size, added four-colour printing, adopted a glossy cover, and placed the illustrations on an equal footing with the text. To attract advertisers, it also decided to integrate the editorial and advertising content. The changes were not well received by its traditional readership, and the more alienated among them left. Its owners decided to cut their losses, and in 1926 sold it to Hugh MacLean.[66]

MacLean changed the magazine yet again. When he bought it, he was well aware that he would have to compete with his brother J.B., and Hugh was nothing if not competitive. He immediately struck a blow at 'Jack's' company by hiring one of its rising editors, Joseph Lister Rutledge. Together, MacLean and Rutledge crafted a magazine that would rival *MacLean's* both in its content and its service to advertisers. Within four years, the magazine had a monthly circulation of 91,000, a distant but respectable showing against *MacLean's* and its twice-monthly 164,000. Over the long run, however, English Canada only needed one magazine of this genre, either for readers or advertisers. The Depression highlighted this fact. *Canadian* carried barely a third of the advertising linage of *MacLean's* in 1938, and projected losses of $34,000 for the following year. It folded soon after.[67]

Canadian's transformation from a literary journal into a consumer magazine did not signal the end of serious periodical writing in Canada. There were two havens for the readers of this genre: university journals and a new breed of political magazines. University journals had existed for some time and were very much in the same format as the *Canadian Magazine* of old: digest size, with few illustrations and a predilection for political and social commentary and belles-lettres. Such journals included *Queen's Quarterly* (1893), the McGill *University Magazine* (1901–20), and *Dalhousie Review* (1921). Unlike *Canadian Mag-*

azine, however, these journals were not market-driven. They were not private enterprises run for profit, but the standard-bearers of academic institutions keen to maintain a connection with the outside world. The genre was able to ignore the marketing imperative precisely because these magazines did not rely on advertising to pay their bills. Rather, they took in what advertising was available, had higher subscription rates than most other magazines, and submitted their operating deficits to their universities. The exception proved the rule. The McGill magazine was published commercially after the university stopped funding it in 1906. It failed in 1920.[68]

The second group mentioned, the political magazines, tried to respond to the demands of the market while retaining a serious, literary tone. The *McGill Fortnightly Review* (1920–1), *Onlooker* (1920–2), *Canadian Forum* (1920–), *Willison's Monthly* (1925–9), and *Canadian Mercury* (1928–9) each tried to craft a similar paper, a hybrid of the serious journal and the modern consumer magazine. Each entry came in a large magazine format, with modern dress in masthead, typeface, and layout. Nonetheless, all of them remained subdued in their use of illustrations, preferring to run woodcuts or reproductions of contemporary artwork rather than photography.

Willison's was the magisterial soapbox of its namesake, Sir John Willison. In his youth, Willison had earned a reputation as a talented journalist, and he became editor of the Toronto *Globe* at age thirty-four. After twelve years there, Willison grew tired of the ceaseless partisanship of the daily press. Together with Joseph Flavelle, he bought the derelict Toronto *News* in 1902 and remade it as a politically independent evening paper seeking an upmarket readership. It was the worst marketing decision imaginable, and the paper was crushed in the competition between its popular evening counterparts and its upmarket morning rivals. After six years it was sold to a partisan Conservative. Willison, still editor, was enchained again. The magazine was his last attempt, at age sixty-nine, to write serious and independent political commentary. Everything about it reflects a rarefied conception of politics, from the clean symmetry of its cover and the roman lettering of its typeface, to the sober and institutional tone of its advertising. Following the style of the London *Times*, none of the articles was signed – a signal statement of the periodical's self-assured sense of authority. Looking at the ads, from companies such as Eaton's, Simpsons, and the Canadian Pacific Railway, as well as several banks, insurance firms, and trust companies, it is readily apparent that none of them used hard-sell methods in the magazine. All of them ran glosses on their firms *as* important Canadian firms. One wonders if they were placed out of courtesy and respect to an aging warrior. Willison's former business manager at the *News* was then president of McKim Limited; Willison's son worked for McConnell and Fergusson. Few of their clients ever bought space in other political magazines. It is impossible to gauge the value of its pages or the size of its readership, since the magazine never revealed these figures to the newspaper directories.[69] Death took Willison in 1927, and creditors took the magazine in 1929.

None of *Willison's* peers rose above its meagre existence. Willison, having left the *Globe*, the Liberals, and the Conservative press behind, provided an independent conservative voice in his magazine. During its last year, the magazine faced some competition from a younger group at the *Canadian Mercury*. H.L. Mencken's notorious *American Mercury* enjoyed a sizeable vogue in the late 1920s among a class of cranky young intellectuals.[70] The *Canadian Mercury* was a none-too-subtle imitation that attracted the same class of readers and contributors in Canada. Among these could be counted the iconoclastic copywriter Bertram Brooker, as well as poets Dorothy Livesay, A.M. Klein, and Leo Kennedy.[71] The *Mercury* did not last long; both it and *Willison's* were eclipsed by their 'new liberal' counterpart, the *Canadian Forum*. Begun in 1920 by faculty members at the University of Toronto, the *Forum* struggled along with the same cluster of advertisers to which most of its peers had resorted: book publishers and other firms desiring to reach the dusty halls of academe. The *Forum* was the only one to survive the period, perhaps because its brand of liberalism was in its ascendancy.[72] That said, it was never financially self-sufficient. It survived the 1930s not as a truly market-dependent magazine, but as an associational organ for a left-wing think-tank, the League for Social Reconstruction. Even then, it took generous cash donations and business advice from wealthy members to keep it afloat – including Carlton McNaught from McKim Toronto.[73]

Similarly, religious periodicals carved out a new niche for themselves in the 1920s. At the height of Protestant influence in Ontario, between 1880 and 1920, there were several periodicals representing each denomination. There were also several Catholic magazines. Advertisers had traditionally used these in Canada in the absence of a national, middle-brow magazine. It was generally assumed that their subscribers were nothing less than the most upstanding members in their respective communities, 'the leadership class.'[74] It was they that advertisers of new consumer goods and luxury items most wanted to reach. The *Presbyterian* told advertisers: 'It has a select constituency and it selects the advertising it admits ... There is not an influential Canadian Presbyterian home that this paper does not enter and its readers read and use the advertisements because they trust to the integrity of the paper.'[75] The respectability of a religious paper reflected well on the advertiser. Presumably, no such editor would allow his pages to be sullied by charlatans and quacks.

The arrival of *Canadian Courier, Canadian Collier's,* and *MacLean's* threw a wrench into the accustomed business of the religious periodicals. The directors of the *Westminster* traced a sizeable drop in ad revenue in 1911 to secular competition. Leaving faith aside, the new consumer magazines appealed to demographically similar groups defined by their income and social standing. Advertisers who did not identify their markets with denominational labels could have used one appropriation in place of seven or eight and probably reached the same number of readers. Advertisers also could have avoided any appearance of religious prejudice; the whisper of bigotry inevitably hounded an advertiser if it used any one religious paper to the exclusion of the others. Sun Life Assurance stopped using them altogether by the mid-1920s. The Vancouver Board of Trade diplomatically referred to them as 'donation' media and did not counsel its members to use them for business purposes.[76]

As a result, denominational organs went through a long period of adjustment after 1905. They could either compete with the new magazines on their own terms, or withdraw from the fight and concentrate solely on denominational matters. The *Christian Guardian* chose the former route. Created by Egerton Ryerson in 1829, the paper had been the voice of the Methodist establishment for eighty years. Around it had been built one of the largest publishing firms in the country, which became the Ryerson Press in 1920.[77] Throughout that time the *Guardian* was a sternly Protestant weekly newspaper, printed on full-sized newsprint with no illustrations. Its masthead was a wrought-iron work of Victorian gothic type, its front page nothing but news and commentary on topics religious, social, and literary. By 1910 Ryerson would no longer have recognized it. Reduced to the size of a small magazine, it sported a front cover in keeping with contemporary trends, a ruler-straight box framing a different inspirational passage each week. The masthead appeared above it in a simplified gothic shadow of its previous self. With these changes in place, the weekly retained a minimum

circulation of 20,000 until 1920. At that point, inspired by the success of
MacLean's, it changed again, this time to a full-size magazine with
colour covers. It then embarked on a twofold campaign to increase its
revenues. First it targeted readers by pitching itself as a wholesome
Christian paper for the home, Methodist in origin but ecumenical in
spirit. It then targeted manufacturers by touting its new advertising-
friendly façade as well as its audited circulation. Its readership rose to
40,000 during the campaign, but only half of the new readers stuck
with it. Circulation levelled out at 30,000.[78]

This was the magazine inherited by the United Church of Canada. In
1925 the Methodist Church of Canada, the Congregational Church of
Canada, and roughly two-thirds of the congregations of the Presbyterian Church of Canada came together to form a 'united church' representing the mainstream of liberal evangelicalism. In this spirit, *New
Outlook* was created to supersede each of the concurring denomina-
tions' own organs: the *Presbyterian Witness* (1848–1925), *Canadian Con-
gregationalist* (1854–1925), and the *Guardian* itself. The new magazine's
editor and printing house were those of the former *Guardian*, and it
continued to hold the same conception of its ideal reader: nationalist to
a fault, socially conscious, politically engaged, and welcoming of most
faiths. The new magazine looked like an explicitly Christian *MacLean's*.
It was printed on newsprint, but was a full-sized quarto page and wore
a heavy-stock cover. Its layout inside was smart and clean and bright-
ened by a liberal use of white space and photographs. Both Lydiatt and
McKim felt comfortable listing it with general magazines as well as
religious periodicals. Its own title, of course, made no reference to religion at all, while its subtitle declared only that it was 'A Paper for the
Whole Family.'[79]

Despite its best efforts, *New Outlook* never achieved the same success
as *MacLean's*. This may be explained by the fact that *MacLean's* already
existed, and the broad-based consumer magazine could not have been
reinvented as a denominational organ. After 1926 there was also the
redesigned *Canadian Magazine* with which to contend. Moreover, the
churches themselves were losing members throughout the 1920s.
Church membership in Canada did not keep pace with population
growth and fell away in many urban congregations. It should have
surprised no one if their magazines suffered a similar fate.[80]

Beyond these two market-oriented reasons, a third, more cultural
reading presents itself. One might wonder if the ethical prescriptions
implicit in the magazine's editorial stance were conducive to the atmo-

sphere of consumption encouraged by magazines such as *Every-woman's* and *MacLean's*. There was no special department set aside for cooking, sewing, or practical housekeeping tips, no sections devoted to spectator sports, music, or automobiles. It would have been difficult for the advertising manager of any religious paper to solicit appropriate advertisers for regular columns on daily Bible readings, overseas missions, or spiritual growth. (Not that they didn't try: Canadian Pacific enticed readers to 'See this World before the Next.')[81] The encouragement to consume that pervaded the editorial matter of the magazines simply was not present in a religious paper devoted to personal piety and self-sacrifice. Readers of *New Outlook* were asked to consider each act of their daily lives as service to God, to seek spiritual growth, and to participate in church groups and voluntary societies. They were not encouraged to keep up with the Joneses. Asserting the importance of other-worldly priorities did not establish the atmosphere sought by manufacturers desiring greater concern for material interests. Indeed, it did little to entice middle-class subscribers.[82]

Despite its failure to secure a wide audience, *New Outlook* eventually recognized the loyal audience it did attract. It was a costly undertaking to publish a quality magazine, and without sufficient advertising it strained the resources of its publishing house. In 1931 *New Outlook* ran a deficit of $20,253.30 on ad revenues of $21,906.92. By contrast, Ryerson's Sunday school publications had no advertising, but enjoyed a profit of $53,573.25.[83] This was not an exceptional year for *New Outlook*; the magazine ran deficits annually. In 1938 its format was changed, and it became in essence the official gazette and newsletter of the United Church. While it did not drop its interests in current events altogether, its commentary on issues concerning secular society and politics assumed a secondary role within its pages.[84] Like *Canadian Magazine*, it could not compete with *MacLean's*. Instead, it resigned itself to the same role that its counterparts serving other faiths had previously accepted. Magazines such as *Canadian Baptist* (1854), *Canadian Churchman* (1868), *Presbyterian Record* (1876), and *Catholic Record* (1878) had all made this transition. The gradual waning of animosity among the mainstream churches had removed the need to interpret the world through sectarian lenses, and secular periodicals now covered the world's affairs to the satisfaction of readers. If once the church organs had offered literary and political fare, they now merely reported the decisions of church councils, recent appointments, and new ideas in fund-raising.

Two genres resisted the move to consumer-oriented general magazines: the trade papers and the agricultural press. Of the two, the former proved much more resilient. Beyond the MacLean Publishing Company, Hugh C. MacLean Publications, and Harold Gagnier's Consolidated Press, Toronto was home to at least seven other trade paper publishers with three or more papers during the 1920s. Several more published only one, such as W.A. Lydiatt and *Marketing*. Most of these papers relied on circulations between 1,000 and 7,000 subscribers. Readers may not have been numerous, but they tended to be corporate executives and managers. For this reason alone, the trade papers served a purpose for advertisers. They held their readers by providing a news service that in no way competed with consumer magazines.[85]

The agricultural press was another matter. Farming was never simply a business, and the papers that served farmers and their communities rarely confined themselves to the business of farming. Agricultural papers addressed all matters affecting the household economy of the farm, both inside and outside of the home. Those editors who had domestic columns were very well situated to attract the advertising for many household items after 1890.[86] They were no doubt aided by the fact that the rural population of Canada was numerically greater than the urban population at that point. If advertisers wanted to reach breadwinners and their families, farm papers offered them a sure place to start. As previously noted, this was a fact embraced by many of the largest urban dailies, who designed their weekend editions to be agricultural papers.

After 1900 a number of publishers in the agricultural field adapted just as John A. Cooper had with *Canadian Courier*. One of the highest circulating farm papers throughout the period was the monthly *Journal d'Agriculture et Horticulture*. The journal was the official organ of the Council of Agriculture of the Province of Quebec and published two editions monthly, one in French and the other in English. The council served as an executive body for all of the local agricultural societies in the province and had semi-official status through an affiliation with the provincial Department of Agriculture.

The *Journal of Agriculture* began in 1898 and had the look of a contemporary trade paper. In particular, its masthead resembled those of the MacLean Publishing Company at that time. The title was superimposed over placid scenes of Quebec farm life, its bold, three-dimensional lettering beaming out towards the reader from a hidden point on the horizon like the morning's first sun at daybreak. Inside, the editorial content covered every possible angle of farm life and every major form of farming; it offered the latest news in crop management and animal husbandry, as well as maintenance tips for machinery and the farm itself. The 'Women's World' section offered advice on domestic matters such as sewing, canning, and candle-making. The journal carried photos and cuts, but they were not significant other than as illustrations for the articles they accompanied. In sum, the journal was practical, straightforward, and edifying – concerned more with the serious business of running a family farm than the quality of life of the family itself.

As an official organ of the Council of Agriculture, the journal was mailed automatically to every member of a local agricultural society in Quebec. Advertisers usually discounted the circulation of fraternal newsletters because they assumed that readers were indifferent to them. In terms of news or entertainment value, such publications were negligible, and eminently disposable, no matter how polished their editors tried to make them.[87] Advertisers did not think this of the *Journal of Agriculture*. Its instructive articles made it useful to farmers whether or not they read its coverage of the council and its affiliated societies. In the 1910s it enjoyed the largest circulation of any French-Canadian periodical save for the daily *La Presse*. In 1913 its French circulation stood at 90,000 while its English circulation was 9,000. If one sets aside the *Family Herald and Weekly Star*, it had the largest circulation of any farm paper in Canada.[88] Not surprisingly, then, it was filled with advertising. In the February 1913 issue, advertising covered five pages at the front, eight pages at the back, both inside covers, the back cover, and most noticeably of all, the front cover itself. Advertisers included all forms of farm-implement makers as well as consumer durables and foods: effervescent salts, machinery, seeds, stock feed, rifles, oil lamps, potash, stoves, tobacco, fencing, hand tools, concrete, Kodak cameras, indoor plumbing, and Post Toasties all publicized themselves in its pages.[89]

The journal continuously adapted itself to changing conditions in the periodical market. The look of the journal was modernized in 1914 when the cover was altered to reflect new fashions in consumer magazines. Its masthead was no longer a cluttered pastiche of pastoral scenery; now its title was printed in a stylized roman type on a plain white background. Elegant, certainly, but it carried none of the symbolism of the farm that had characterized its predecessor. Beneath it, the advertisements for shingles and paint were removed. There now appeared the box design that became common among popular magazines in the 1910s.[90] Inside, the topics and tone of its articles remained fundamentally unchanged. As the editor stated in his brief explanation to readers: 'The Journal of Agriculture stands for progress not only in all lines of farming but also in the production of a high grade, artistic magazine, which will be both instructive and pleasing to the reader.'[91] Quality of content would not be sacrificed for the quality of the package. Otherwise, the journal also adopted several standard techniques to appease advertisers. By 1920 it no longer segregated its editorial and advertising content, but tailed its longer pieces into the back.[92]

The way in which the *Journal of Agriculture* adapted is notable in itself. Like its approach to editorial content, its approach to format and design was above all pragmatic. Rather than resisting the changing tides of the magazine industry, it incorporated new ideas one at a time. Essentially, it adopted only those ideas that made it more visually interesting or offered better service to advertisers. In this way, it probably avoided the situation faced by *Canadian* in 1924 when that magazine radically altered its format and design only to lose thousands of readers. Instead, the *Journal of Agriculture* managed to retain a great proportion of its readers throughout the 1920s, despite urbanization and the rise of French-language consumer magazines. By 1930 the journal had lost only 25 to 30 per cent of the circulation it had in 1913. This placed it well behind the weekend farm editions of *La Presse* and *La Patrie*, but among magazines it remained second only to a Jesuit religious paper, *Le Messager Canadien du Sacré-Coeur* (1892).[93]

A number of agricultural papers appeared in the Prairie West that challenged the *Journal of Agriculture* for supremacy. Most followed in format and design the same pattern as their Québécois counterpart. Among the most successful were the *Farmer's Journal and Home Advocate* (1866), *Nor'-West Farmer* (1882), *Canadian Thresherman and Farmer* (1903), and the *Grain Growers' Guide* (1908). Among this Winnipeg quartet may also be placed the *Farm and Ranch Review* (1905) of Calgary. Some were associational organs, such as the *Grain Growers' Guide*, but most were the products of independent publishing houses. Regardless of their affiliations, all of them sought to cultivate sizeable readerships and maintain profitable operations. The *Grain Growers' Guide*, the most political of the group, was no different. Under the able direction of George F. Chipman, the *Guide* became one of the most recognizable voices of western Canada, quoted by rival papers across the country for its astute editorials.

The *Guide*'s format appealed to the progressive, commercial farmer of the new West. In terms of status this readership did not identify itself with country bumpkins and rubes, but with the solidly respectable middle class. That said, it was not a middle class that expressed solidarity with the inhabitants of Canada's eastern cities. This was Chipman's niche; his columns articulated the political and cultural frustration of westerners, and he crafted an editorial identity unique from eastern periodicals.[94] His defence of reciprocity with the United States, which defied eastern manufacturers (and advertisers) who opposed it, was only the most notorious of his stands. Founded in 1908, the *Guide* gradually built up its circulation over the next decade, reaching 29,000 in 1913 and 75,000 in 1920. Among all Canadian magazines, it was topped only by *Everywoman's* and *MacLean's*.[95]

Advertising writers in *Printer and Publisher* and *Marketing* argued that the readership of the agricultural press was composed of thoroughly modern consumers. Although the western farmer's opinions were not those of his industrial counterpart in Ontario or Quebec, he nonetheless shared the same interests in the political, economic, and religious questions of day. The farmer also shared the same taste in consumer goods.[96] An American advertising manager writing in *Economic Advertising* was dumbfounded by just how few of his peers appreciated this. G.B. Sharpe wrote: 'That the farmer has more surplus money than the average city clerk and mechanic, we must all admit ... That he can best be reached through the farm papers, in fact, *cannot successfully be reached in any other way*, and that he is worth interesting, is also a fact that seems not to have percolated to the inner consciousness of many of our national advertisers.'[97]

The farm papers themselves set out to re-educate them. *Canadian Farm* advertised itself by suggesting that, through its pages, manufacturers would be 'Discovering a New, Big Field for a Product.'[98] *Rural Canada* bluntly told advertisers that it would reach 'the greatest, most responsive market there is.' It deftly handled its knowledge of markets and market segmentation to argue that farm women and their families needed 'a great home journal edited exclusively for her and their own peculiar farm and home interests – a great, Canadian, National farm paper.'[99] The *Guide*, asserting that advertising agents knew their markets and used the best media, simply listed the names of ninety-four agencies that had used its pages in 1919.[100] One might also note the Advertising Service Company in this regard. In 1928 it appointed a director of 'Agricultural Markets Advertising.' The man hired to fill this post was a former minister of agriculture for the province of Alberta.[101]

The burgeoning market in farm papers eluded J.B. Maclean. He created *Farmer's Magazine* in 1910 to build a national agricultural companion for *Busyman's*. While it offered the full slate of MacLean Company services to advertisers, it never attained wide circulation. This failure might be traced to its inability to develop a unique or compelling presence in a competitive market. Readers would have found nothing to differentiate its coverage of national affairs from that of their local newspapers, let alone *Canadian Courier* or *MacLean's*. Nor could it overcome regional differences in agricultural production and markets in its coverage of farm news. After twelve years of constant losses, Maclean folded the staff and subscription list of *Farmer's* into *MacLean's*. When he did, he justified it with a fascinating argument: 'The automobile has made it convenient for farmers to drive ten, fifteen, or twenty miles into the best shopping centres where they buy first-class merchandise, attend public meetings, and in other ways keep themselves abreast of the times just as do the best of the town and city people ... This means that the time has come when they are asking for and will appreciate a good magazine such as *MacLean's* ... the time had come when Canada's rural denizens no longer wanted special treatment.'[102]

According to Maclean, Canadian farmers wanted the same mix of topical articles, short fiction, and consumer advertising as their urban countrymen. Not only that, they wanted it in the same package. Perhaps. After this date, *MacLean's* became the biggest circulation magazine in the country. But dogging its every step were the *Guide* and *Nor'-West Farmer*.

After 1905 Canadian magazine publishers reoriented their editorial and business departments around the new logic of advertising supplied by applied psychology and market research. Not all magazines embraced this transformation. A notable group of university, religious, and trade papers held to their traditional formats. Nonetheless, those pursuing increased advertising patronage either adopted the services and circulation-boosting techniques that advertisers wanted, or they bowed out. The appearance of *Canadian Courier* was the first sign of things to come; *Everywoman's* was the future arrived.

A certain view of the magazine industry has emerged in the history of Canada's culture. This view portrays an industry under siege, barely capable of resisting the invasion of American magazines that swept across the border.[103] Nationalist intellectuals and business people organized in the 1920s to protect their economic interests in the face of this competition. Believing that their work was crucial to the formation of national consciousness, they asked the federal government to intervene on their behalf. Above all, they sought a protective tariff that would have increased the cover price of American magazines and allowed their own products to compete where it counted: on the newsstands.

Canada had an astonishingly wide and vital periodical publishing industry both before and after the market was transformed by national advertising. The only components of this industry that did not meet the expectations of their publishers before 1905 were the literary and consumer magazines. Until that date, until Canadian advertisers sought national media that covered the country, these genres did languish in the shadow of their American counterparts. After that date, however, Canadians developed the skills, capital, and marketing orientation required to produce magazines that were competitive with the American genres they consciously mimicked. Publishers such as John A. Cooper, Harold Gagnier, Isodor Simonski, and J.B. Maclean were important in this regard. Nonetheless, it should not be forgotten that theirs were not the only periodicals produced in Canada. While these four crafted magazines that found a wide appeal in the large, urban centres of central Canada, there emerged in Quebec and the West numerous farm papers that doubled as domestic magazines. Add to these the weekend papers, political and artistic magazines, academic journals, associational organs, and religious papers, and there emerges a great variety of periodicals serving markets large and small.

The publishers behind the tariff lobby of the 1920s were the publishers of the consumer magazines. Chief among them, offering both staff members and financial backing, was J.B. Maclean. A lobby group opposed to a tariff also formed, and it was led by the publisher of the *Grain Growers' Guide*, George F. Chipman. The difference between the two camps may have simply reproduced traditional regional politics, a protectionist central Canadian manufacturer facing down a free-trade western farmer. However, their stands were well rooted in the underlying structure of the industry in which both participated. Chipman and his peers supplied periodicals that had evolved in the communities they served, be it the academic tone of the *Journal of Agriculture* in Quebec or the barber-shop pragmatism of the *Guide* itself. They were started by people intimately familiar with farming and rural life, who recognized the markets to whom they spoke. Similar points could be made of the religious, fraternal, and other associational periodicals. The consumer magazines were not similarly inspired. They were formed to reproduce the success of a genre of magazines that had developed in another country with a different social and economic structure. They had to construct the audience they intended to reach, and for this reason they were constantly dependent on its whims and desires. They needed market research to know who their audience was. When these publishers compared the circulation figures of their own magazines to those of their American rivals, they had good reason to be disappointed. In most cases, an American magazine of the same genre outsold its Canadian counterpart in Canada itself.

The content of the Canadian consumer magazines made them vulnerable. Their editorial voices tended to emphasize an urban, modern world of new technologies, convenience goods, and ample leisure-time distractions. Much of their cultural content was cosmopolitan in nature, offering cars from Detroit, movies from Hollywood, songs from New York, fashions from London or Paris, and art from the Continent. The emerging culture of industrial society was relatively homogeneous, and media such as magazines, cinema, and radio made this culture widely recognizable – if not yet widely available. Toronto and Montreal were not centres in this network of creativity. If a magazine that discussed such things was available from New York, London, or Paris, it probably made sense to buy it rather than a pale Canadian imitation. This was true even if the topics discussed were completely foreign to Canadian sensibilities, even if the specific goods advertised were hopelessly unavailable. Perhaps the greatest lesson that the Canadian publishers of consumer magazines had to learn was this: that their competitors' products were not necessarily bought for their news value or even their relevance to the workaday lives of their readers. They were often bought simply for their entertainment value. Appeals to the supposed higher moral qualities of Canadian magazines or their patriotic value were useless. Such was the lesson that Maclean taught Costain, and Cranston discovered with the *Star Weekly*.

By contrast, the political economy of farming in Canada was significantly different from that in the United States. Periodicals that offered insightful discussions of farm life, as well as recipes and short fiction, pictures and humour, found readers in every province of the Dominion. Their publishers did not seek tariff protection because they could compete against the Americans without it. Unlike the consumer maga-

TABLE 7.3
Ten Highest Circulating Canadian Magazines in Canada including Farm Papers, and Estimated Value of Circulation, 1921

Title	Annual subscription ($)	Issues per year	Average circulation per issue in Canada	Estimated total annual circulation	Estimated total annual value ($)
Everywoman's World	2.00	12	106,167	1,274,004	212,334.00
Le Journal d'Agriculture	1.00	12	89,153	1,069,836	89,153.00
Grain Growers' Guide	1.00	52	81,959	4,261,868	81,959.00
MacLean's	3.00	24	76,478	1,835,472	229,434.00
Nor'-West Farmer	1.00	24	71,462	1,715,088	71,462.00
Canadian Home Journal	2.00	12	55,407	664,884	110,814.00
Northern Messenger	0.75	52	54,455	2,831,660	40,841.25
Farm & Ranch Review	1.00	24	50,016	1,200,384	50,016.00
Jack Canuck	3.50	52	49,441	2,570,932	173,043.50
Farmer's Sun	1.50	104	46,207	4,805,528	69,310.50
Total				22,229,656	1,128,367.25

Circulation figures: *Lydiatt's Book*, 9th ed. (Toronto: Lydiatt, 1922); subscription rates: *Canadian Newspaper Directory*, 15th ed. (Montreal: McKim, 1921).

zines, the farm papers did not simply re-create successful *genres* found elsewhere. Rather, they re-created – either intuitively or intentionally – the successful marketing *formulas* of the American consumer magazines. Perhaps better than Cooper or Collier, Chipman knew who composed the largest mass market in Canada. Further, he had a large group of advertisers who wanted access to that readership. By matching a set of advertisers with an existing, self-defined market, the *Grain Growers' Guide* and its rivals were more successful as consumer magazines than most of the actual consumer magazines themselves. If one includes them in the portrait of Canadian consumer magazines drawn in Table 7.2 (page 233), a decidedly different impression of the Canadian magazine market emerges. The five top-selling farm papers displace five magazines from the list (Table 7.3). Further, the total number of Canadian magazines in circulation more than doubles the American top ten. As such, the farm papers cannot be dismissed from the ranks of Canadian magazines before 1930. They were a popular, nationwide collection of periodicals that reflected the realities of the country's economy, society, and culture through the eyes of its rural citizenry. By focusing on the national appeal in their pitch to readers, so-called mass magazines such as *MacLean's* simply boxed themselves into a niche market: Canada itself.

Conclusion

*Among the constructive economic forces in business, alongside the engineers,
the architects, and the manufacturing experts, the genuine and experienced
Advertising Agency takes its place.*

McKim Limited, 1923[1]

*Every now and then somebody compares us advertising men unfavourably
with doctors, lawyers, engineers, and other earthworms of that sort ... They say
that these professional men are welcomed and their pronouncements weighed
with much gravity in the counsels of the mighty. Personally, I doubt it ...*
    *It's the bunk! But there is one place, it seems to me, where advertising
men might learn something. And that is the theatre. And especially, the
vaudeville theatre.*

Bertram Brooker, 1925[2]

Bertram Brooker could afford to be flippant. By the mid-1920s advertising had achieved a certain cachet within the publishing industry,
and advertising agents were riding what was probably the largest volume of appropriations ever seen in Canada. It was both curious and
revealing that he should compare himself and his peers – even in this
backhanded fashion – to the learned professions, as opposed to, say,
skilled tradesmen or businessmen. Clearly, Brooker was having some
fun at the expense of his readers by exposing their yearnings for a
respectable public image while distancing themselves from the past. A
less charitable analysis might conclude that he was picking at a scab.
Little wonder, then, that he published this piece under a pseudonym,
'Mark E. Ting.'

There was no doubt about it, however – advertising agents had successfully turned an opportunistic, marginal nineteenth-century trade into a service-oriented, vital twentieth-century economic sector. They alone were not responsible for the dramatic changes that had transformed the economy, the publishing industry, and the very nature of the periodicals themselves. Despite the claims of agents such as H.E. Stephenson and Carlton McNaught, the nineteenth-century media-buyers had not led the movement to national advertising as it occurred after 1900.[3] Rather, a younger generation of entrepreneurs, who understood the changes taking place in the American publishing industry, opened their agencies just as the national distribution of consumer goods became a reality in Canada. These young agents refashioned the idea of client service and forced the older agencies to adapt or bow out of the field. In the wake of J.J. Gibbons, the older space brokerages of Anson McKim and Edouard Desbarats adapted; J.S. Robertson and Frederick Diver eventually bowed out.

Most of the new ideas that surfaced in the Canadian trade were developed first in the United States. Publishers and agents such as J.B. Maclean, J.J. Gibbons, and W.A. Lydiatt consciously adopted techniques they had learned while working in the United States themselves, and it was they who cultivated the interest of Canadian advertisers in the new services. There was no resistance to their implementation, and no apparent desire to follow a British model of advertising practice instead. Rather, Canadian adworkers greeted American innovations as the rest of the world did, with great enthusiasm. Industrial capitalism and a free press had developed on both sides of the border. It would have been more surprising had the Canadian trade not adopted similar outlooks and techniques. Canadian agents could comfortably consort with their American counterparts in the Associated Clubs movement and adopt the practices they pioneered because they fundamentally shared the same outlook towards the trade in which they were engaged.[4] Seen as business practices, things such as the commission system, applied psychology, and market research appeared to be culturally neutral. It seemed perfectly reasonable for a Canadian agency to incorporate these elements into its business plan, while decrying the presence of American agencies in the Canadian market.

The key difference that distinguished Canadian from American agencies, in the minds of Canadian adworkers, was their 'natural' identifications. In the 1890s McKim Limited could set itself apart from

the likes of Ayer, Rowell, and Thompson through its better understanding of the Canadian periodicals market. The agency took great
pride in the sheer number of periodicals it listed in its directory. The
fact that it named more than the Americans was proof positive that the
Americans were poor judges of the Canadian scene. Then, with the
advent of copywriting and illustration, it was argued that a Canadian
agency would be more familiar with the vernacular of Canadian life
than would an American agency. Few things could have better demonstrated the adworkers' feelings than their self-conscious use of Scottish
regalia at the conventions of the Associated Clubs. Good publicity it
may have been, but their very choice of costume emphasized materi-
ally their separate identity as Canadians. They were even indignant
when 'a band of imitation kilties' from St Petersburg, Florida, arrived
at the 1925 convention.[5] Extending this logic, it was similarly pragmatic to hire a woman copywriter for campaigns targeting female consumers, and a French Canadian for campaigns in Quebec. One could
not expect a man to fully understand the intricacies of the female
thought processes, any more than one could expect an anglophone
Protestant to understand la belle province. To return to the original
point, however: Americans were both mentors and rivals for Canadian
adworkers, separated by a border easily crossed, but only partially
defended by ideas.

The changes that occurred after 1890 brought conflict, discussion,
and organization. It was the publishers, already organized through the
Canadian Press Association, who initiated reforms through cooperative measures. Once the agencies felt that their problems could also be
met through cooperation, they too organized. Both groups of adworkers then joined their peers in corporate advertising departments
through the Associated Clubs movement. While this latter group
addressed the broad interests of the trade, it could not act to improve
the trade without compromising its cooperative structure. Recognizing
this, the Press Association and Canadian Association of Advertising
Agencies continued to play an important role after 1911 because they
continued to represent the economic interests of their members. By
1916 the Toronto Ad Club had dissolved; in 1916 the Association of
Canadian Advertisers took definite shape as the representative trade
association for corporate advertising managers.

Through the associations and the discussions they fostered came an
articulate sense of this new field of expertise. Both through the Truth in
Advertising movement and the campaign to Advertise Advertising,

adworkers rationalized the contribution that their jobs made to their industry and to society at large. At a time when public esteem for their trade was exceptionally low, Truth in Advertising allowed adworkers to stand the common notion of advertising on its head. In their eyes, advertising became the transparent shop window of mass salesmanship in which all goods were held up to the test of public scrutiny. By contrast, it was the non-advertising business that was to be questioned. The Advertising Advertising campaign then broadcast this newly crafted image of the trade to the rest of Canada.

Hand in hand with this attempt to renovate their image in the public eye was their attempt to reform the commercial basis of their trade. As economic actors with competing interests, adworkers used their associations to hammer out internal and intersectoral agreements that set standards of conduct for practitioners. The discussions surrounding rate cards, commissions, rebating, cost accounting, and circulation audits exposed the problems that had made the trade disreputable in the eyes of its own workers. Whether or not the agreements that concluded these discussions brought these questionable practices to an end is debatable. Certainly, there were representatives in each sector who claimed that rebating, secret commissions, and price-cutting continued to be problems into the 1920s. That said, real gains were made. Three stand out. First, even a modest reduction in the number of questionable practices was interpreted as a victory among adworkers. The crusading publisher Hal Donly, who believed that cooperative effort was the only way to place the weeklies on a rational business foundation, never stopped emphasizing this point. Second, the agency agreement of 1907, and the recognition committee that administered its terms, provided a stable environment within which the full-service, independent agencies established their dominance over the field in advertising service. Until they were assured that they would not be undercut by fly-by-night operators, freelancers, or corporate in-house agencies, agents such as McKim, Norris-Patterson, and McConnell and Fergusson did not invest in the personnel and plant necessary to run a full-service agency. Third, the adoption of the Audit Bureau of Circulations placed advertising appropriations on a rational foundation. Advertisers might not know how effective their publicity was, but they would know the approximate number of readers they reached. The bureau set a benchmark in market research by providing a lasting model of statistical expertise employed in the service of advertisers.

The question of the effectiveness of advertising was better addressed by the development of applied psychology and market research. Neither introduced totally new concepts to the field of commerce during this period, but they did offer means to consolidate and standardize existing practices. What had once been left to intuition or chance could now be purposefully planned. Both provided adworkers with the vocabularies and tools necessary to understand and explain their work in the terms of a modern social science. Once these vocabularies and tools were integrated into the trade, it became possible to formulate clearer principles regarding it, and even to teach these principles as aspects of a nascent discipline. Just as the business reforms placed the structure of the trade on a secure economic foundation, the integration of applied psychology and market research placed the content of the trade on a secure social and intellectual foundation. Each gave the adworkers – but especially agents – a clearer sense of their role within the publishing industry. It was a sense that those outside of the trade began to share, as increasing numbers of industrialists and politicians consulted agents for advice before approaching the public. As T. Johnson Stewart put it, the trade was 'emerging from cloudland' in the 1910s. It was no longer dealing with a totally imagined audience and its intuited thought processes, but rather with statistically verifiable constructs that followed scientifically documented consumption patterns. At least, this was the theory.

With the integration of market research into the repertoire of agency services, the chief characteristic that set the Canadian agencies apart from their American competitors began to erode. With the new social science techniques at their disposal, the Americans should have appeared as well equipped to handle the particularities of the Canadian market as they were the handling of various regions of the United States. Further, they hired much of their Canadian-based staff away from Canadian firms. Until 1929, however, none of the American agencies in Toronto had actively cultivated Canadian accounts. Rather, they placed business in Canada for American clients of the head office, or they placed business in Canada for Canadian branch plants of those American clients. J. Walter Thompson signalled the end of those practices. With the most celebrated market research department of any agency in the United States, it entered Canada after having studied the Ontario periodical market in great detail, and staffed its Montreal office with adworkers from McKim and Norris-Patterson. Within the year it had landed a handful of plum Canadian accounts.

The modern trade in advertising was the product not of any one group or event, but of the convergence of interests of four groups: publishers, advertisers, agents, and readers.[6] Each of them had reasons to encourage the massive development of advertising that occurred between 1900 and 1930. Publishers, competing for greater numbers of readers with greater numbers of editions, required greater cash flow to cover the increasing capital costs tied up in new technologies and raw materials. Manufacturers, blessed with new transportation and communications media that allowed them to integrate vast territories into their marketing strategies for the first time, required a means to get news out about their products. Adworkers, but especially agents, recognized the financially lucrative possibilities of joining the publishers and advertisers in a mutually beneficial relationship. And readers – particularly the new, urban, white-collar readers so intensively cultivated by editors and adworkers alike – benefited from advertising's system and its magic. First, so long as they read periodicals blessed by high circulation and the patronage of advertisers, their favourite newspapers and magazines came to them at far below the cost of production. Second, at a time when everything about their lives appeared to be in transition, the ads offered a reassuring message: that order and meaning were only as far away as the nearest corner store.

Out of this mix of interests, modern advertising was born. The scale of the population to be reached and the costs of production determined the costs involved. The costs involved, and the common desire to protect the capital invested in the industry, drove the search for an increasingly sophisticated understanding of how advertising worked. Such a search was in the adworkers' own best interests. Had they been unable to explain their craft to their clients, it is unlikely they would have won the contracts they did.

This knowledge in turn wrought a transformation in the character of the periodicals. The size of the periodicals changed with the amount of new advertising matter published. Beyond this, there was a decided shift away from the previously dominant concerns of politics and religion, and towards more fiction, illustrations, sports, domestic affairs, and cartoons. Periodicals were no longer considered to be purely the means through which good burghers participated in the public sphere. They were no longer solely the vehicles of partisan opinions and theological debates. Now, periodicals were viewed in a much lighter vein, as reading matter, a medium of leisure-time activity in themselves. Where the trade and agricultural papers might still have hewn to a traditional set of generic formulas, the most popular dailies and the con-

sumer magazines had made the transition to the delivery of entertainment as well as news.

The news that was reported was decidedly less partisan and acrimo-
nious in its outlook than ever before. Again, where publishers were
seeking the largest audiences possible, it no longer paid to marginalize
the interests of any sizeable, affluent group within the mainstream of
society. Controversy could be profitably aimed at groups outside of the
middle-class mainstream to generate sales, but controversy was
counter-productive if it stirred animosity among majority members of
the same community. Hence, muckraking journalism that exposed the
foibles of a widely derided capitalist class could be effective for a popular paper such as the *Telegram* or the *Star*; championing the Orange
Lodge against Roman Catholics might have been less so. At the same
time, advertisers became attuned to the fact that consumers responded
to advertising in accordance with the character of the papers in which it
appeared. This had originally been noted with religious periodicals, but
it was an idea that could be generally applied. An even-tempered and
fair-minded journal of record would likely provide a valuable placement for the publicity of a company seeking a respectable readership.

Publishers made themselves most useful to advertisers with the
array of new services they developed after 1900. Technically, there
were several innovations that improved the look of advertising over
the previous century: half-tones, better papers, better inks, and colour
printing were the most obvious advances here. There was also the provision of more conscientious composition and layout in the preparation of ads, not to mention a ready supply of illustrations if such were
required. In a broader sense, however, nothing could have better demonstrated the publishers' new pursuit of advertising than the magazines' decision to integrate their ad content with editorial content, and
to tail reading matter in their back pages. Over time, publishers
learned not simply to place advertising alongside complementary
reading matter, but to create such material from scratch to generate
interest for key advertisers. Within a newspaper or general magazine,
it could be as simple as establishing a domestic column to advertise
foods and household products. Most notable were the ubiquitous
radio departments in urban dailies of the mid-1920s as manufacturers
began to market the first ready-built sets for listeners and stations
began to diversify the entertainments available on regular schedules.[7]

It was only a short step from a department in a daily newspaper or a
general magazine to the creation of a new periodical. At one point in

the mid-1920s there were five radio magazines serving Canada, filled with ads for electrical components, batteries, antennae, ready-made sets, stations, broadcast schedules, and listeners' clubs. Other magazines were aimed at boaters, automobile owners, travellers, photographers – any number of pastimes that required a serious financial outlay before participation was possible. Each of them carried helpful advice and stories of interest to those who engaged in the featured pastime, but more importantly they carried advertising for any product integral to participation. They also carried advertising for products that were not integral but thought to be of interest to people who enjoyed the lifestyle choices associated with the magazines' key subject of interest.

By reconstructing their publications around lifestyle choices centred on consumption, the publishers were responding to the demands of advertisers and agents who sought these kinds of pages to enhance the appeal of their ads, but the publishers were also making their own businesses more lucrative. At the same time, the content of these changes – the actual periodicals and ads that emerged – participated in the wider cultural project of middle-class formation. Evangelical religion, voluntary associations, and progressive political movements helped to articulate a new set of values for the emerging industrial capitalist society, and in the process they allowed their middle-class participants to articulate a sense of themselves and their relationships with one another, the state, and civil society.[8] Advertising performed a similar set of functions, but in a different realm. Rather than prescribing ethical codes and political relations, it prescribed codes of material possession and social relations. Through their selective use of psychological motivations, lifestyle vignettes, and reason-why argumentation, copywriters could graft onto any product or service a particular set of meanings that would allow consumers to integrate that product or service seamlessly into their lives.[9]

The practice of inscribing everyday objects or actions with culturally specific meanings was not new in itself, as Jackson Lears has made abundantly clear in his examination of advertising.[10] Rather, it was the commercial intent behind the deployment of this practice that was new. Adworkers were in the business of grafting meaning onto products purely for the commercial gain that could be realized. Where the goods and services of previous generations may have found their meaning through socially mediated processes and the vagaries of the marketplace, it was the conscious intent of adworkers to short-circuit that process by supplying the meaning for products ready-made – in a way that Walter Dill Scott likened to hypnotism. Their success in maintaining that meaning beyond the point of purchase may be debated, but this was never their intellectual function.

Bertram Brooker believed that adworkers had progressed a great distance in the twenty years leading up to 1924. To his mind, there was still one thing left to accomplish, though this too would soon be in hand. 'We are slowly acquiring,' he wrote, 'the last and most difficult lesson in the curriculum of art, the method of concealing art. The advance in naturalness, in human appeal, in selling force, when this lesson is learned, will be incalculable.'[11] Brooker, like any good magician, knew that half the trick was making it look as if there were no trick at all. Learning that lesson would fall to the next generation of Canadian adworkers.

Appendix

Selected Advertising Agencies in Toronto Handling National Accounts, 1890–1930

Agency	Opened in Toronto	Closed in Toronto	Head Office	Founder and CEO, or First Manager of Toronto Branch	Remained Manager in 1930?	LP = Last Place of Employ of Founder or Manager CA = Comments on Agency Composition or Business FA = Foreign Affiliation
Ackerley-Langley Ltd.	1927		Toronto	A. Ackerley	yes	LP = R.C. Smith and Son
Advertising Service Co. Ltd.	1915	1928	Montreal	C. Truscott Solomon	–	LP = Gagnier Advertising Service CA = combined with National Publicity to form Cockfield, Brown and Co., 1928 FA = handled Canadian business of H.K. McCann Co., Detroit, after 1923
Baker Advertising Agency	1911		Toronto	Robert A. Baker	died	LP = Toronto Star
Bowman-Hoge Ltd.	1924	1931	New York	J. Morland Bowman	yes	LP = J.J. Gibbons Ltd. CA = absorbed by Ronalds Advertising, 1931 FA = Canadian branch of Huber Hoge Inc., New York
Brotherton Co. of Canada Ltd.	1924	1925	New York	A. Ross Malton	–	LP = McConnell and Fergusson Ltd. CA = bought by Smith, Denne, and Moore Ltd., 1925
Campbell-Ewald Advertising	1922	1935	Detroit	Milton D. Bergey	yes	LP = McKim Ltd., Toronto CA = became MacLaren Advertising, 1935
Canadian Advertising Agency	1893	1900	Toronto	John I. Sutcliffe H.E. Stephenson	–	LP = both: McKim Ltd., Montreal
Canadian Advertising Agency	1928		Montreal	Noel R. Barbour	yes	LP = Gagnier Trade Publications
Central Press Agency	1897	1918	Toronto	Fred W. Thompson	–	LP = Holtby Myers and Co. CA = agency owned by Diver Electrotype, and produced ready-prints

Agency	Founded		City	Principal	Living	Notes
Cockfield, Brown and Co. Ltd.	1928		Montreal	T.L. Anderson	yes	LP = Advertising Service Co. CA = formed by merger of National Publicity and Advertising Service Co. FA = handled Canadian business of H.K. McCann Co., Detroit
Crawford-Harris Advertising Service	1930	1931	Vancouver	Bruce Campbell	yes	LP = Winnipeg *Free Press* CA = bought by J.J. Gibbons Ltd., 1931
E. Sterling Dean Advertising Agency	1912	1932	Toronto	E. Sterling Dean	yes	LP = Toronto *Telegram* CA = merged into F.H. Hayhurst Advertising, 1932
A.J. Denne and Co., Ltd.	1921		Toronto	A.J. Denne	yes	LP = Smith, Denne, and Moore Ltd.
Desbarats Advertising Agency	1922		Montreal	Ernest O. Manchee	no	LP = P.C. Larkin and Co. (Salada Tea)
Dominion Advertising Agency	1908		Toronto	Frank Rowe	–	LP = Frank Presbrey Co., New York CA = agency owned by Toronto Type Foundry, and produced ready-prints
Federal Advertising Agency	1926		London	A.L. Robertson	–	CA = bought by McConnell and Fergusson Ltd., 1929
Financial Advertising Co. of Canada Ltd.	1923		Montreal	Roy V. Rittenhouse	yes	LP = Montreal *Financial Times* CA = agency owned by Montreal *Financial Times*
William Findlay Co. Ltd.	1927	1929	Toronto	W.A.H. Findlay	yes	LP = McKim Ltd., Toronto FA = became Canadian branch of Lord and Thomas, Chicago, 1929
James Fisher Co. Ltd.	1919		Toronto	James Fisher	yes	LP = McConnell and Fergusson Ltd.
Gagnier Advertising Service	1907		Toronto	Harold Gagnier	died	LP = Gagnier Trade Publications CA = changed name to Consolidated Advertising Service, 1917
J.J. Gibbons Ltd.	1899		Toronto	John J. Gibbons	yes	LP = Toronto *News*
The F.H. Hayhurst Co. Ltd.	1927		Toronto	Frederick H. Hayhurst	yes	LP = Baker Advertising Agency

APPENDIX—(Continued)
Selected Advertising Agencies in Toronto Handling National Accounts, 1890–1930

Agency	Opened in Toronto	Closed in Toronto	Head Office	Founder and CEO, or First Manager of Toronto Branch	Remained Manager in 1930?	LP = Last Place of Employ of Founder or Manager; CA = Comments on Agency Composition or Business; FA = Foreign Affiliation
F.W. Hunt Advertising Service	1923		Toronto	F.W. Hunt	yes	LP = Massey-Harris Ltd.
Letter and Copy Shop	1908	1909	Toronto	T.J. Tobin / T. Johnson Stewart	–	LP = Tobin: MacLean Publishing Co. / CA = bought by Norris-Patterson Ltd., 1909
Clarke E. Locke Ltd.	1924		Toronto	Clarke E. Locke	yes	LP = Robert Simpson Co. Ltd. / FA = handled Canadian business of Walter Judd Ltd., London (UK), 1924 only
Harold C. Lowrey Organization	1929		Toronto	Harold C. Lowrey	yes	LP = Southam Press
George H. MacDonald Ltd.	1923	1937	Toronto	George H. MacDonald	yes	LP = Norris-Patterson Ltd. / CA = merged into Consolidated Advertising Service, 1937
Theodore F. MacManus Co.	1929	1929	Detroit	R.C. Blackwell	–	LP = Theodore F. MacManus Inc., Detroit
Mail Advertising Agency	1882	1897	Toronto	James T. Wetherald	–	LP = Toronto Mail
H.K. McCann Co., Advertising	1914	1923	Detroit	L.J. Cunniff	–	CA = Canadian operations handled by Advertising Service Co. after 1923
McConnell and Fergusson Ltd.	1906		London	Malcolm M. Fergusson	died	LP = accountant / CA = changed name to McConnell, Eastman Ltd., 1930
McKim Ltd.	1903		Montreal	W.B. Somerset	no	LP = Toronto Mail
McKinney, Marsh, and McMillan Ltd.	1925	1927	Detroit	David McMillan	–	FA = Canadian branch of McKinney, Marsh, and Cushing Advertising, Detroit

Agency	Founded	Closed	City	Principals	Prior experience	Notes
Mitford Advertising Ltd.	1918		Toronto	George Mitford	yes	LP = Famous Players Canadian Corp.
R. Sykes Muller Co. Ltd.	1922		Montreal	R. Sykes Muller	yes	LP = Canadian Advertising Agency, Montreal
Holtby Myers and Co.	1894	1902?	Toronto	Holtby Myers	–	CA = bought by McKim Ltd., 1902?
Norris-Patterson Ltd.	1904		Toronto	J.H. Woods / C.C. Norris / John P. Patterson	no / died / yes	LP = Woods and Norris: Toronto *Mail*; Patterson: *Canadian Courier* / CA = agency named Woods-Norris Ltd., 1904–13
Margaret Pennell Advertising	1928		Toronto	Margaret Pennell	yes	LP = J.J. Gibbons Ltd.
Press Agency Bureau Ltd.	1910		Toronto	J.B. O'Higgins	yes	LP = Woodstock *Sentinel-Review*
Thornton Purkis, Advertising	1919	.	Toronto	Thornton Purkis	yes	LP = J.J. Gibbons Ltd.
Edward W. Reynold and Co.	1926		Toronto	Edward W. Reynolds	yes	LP = Norris-Patterson Ltd.
J.S. Robertson, Advertising	1899	1917?	Toronto	J.S. Robertson	–	LP = independent bookseller and publisher
Ronalds Advertising Agency Ltd.	1929		Montreal	G. Walter Brown	yes	LP = Ford Co. of Canada Ltd.
F. Albany Rowlatt, Advertising	1911	1925	Toronto	F. Albany Rowlatt	–	LP = Norris-Patterson Ltd. / CA = merged into Thornton Purkis, Advertising, 1925
Claude Sanagan Ltd.	1923		Toronto	Claude Sanagan	yes	LP = Willys-Overland Mfg. Co.
George E. Scroggie	1930		Toronto	George E. Scroggie	yes	LP = J.J. Gibbons Ltd.
R.C. Smith and Son Ltd.	1913		Toronto	Robert C. Smith / Adam F. Smith	yes / yes	LP = father: Toronto *Globe*; son: J.J. Gibbons Ltd. / CA = agency named Advertisements Ltd., 1913–16 / FA = handled Canadian business of W.H. Rankin Co., New York, after 1924
Smith, Denne, and Moore Ltd.	1916	1927	Toronto	Frank G. Smith / Harold A. Moore / A.J. Denne	–	LP = all three: J. Walter Thompson / CA = bought by J.J. Gibbons Ltd., 1927

APPENDIX—(Concluded)
Selected Advertising Agencies in Toronto Handling National Accounts, 1890–1930

Agency	Opened in Toronto	Closed in Toronto	Head Office	Founder and CEO, or First Manager of Toronto Branch	Remained Manager in 1930?	LP = Last Place of Employ of Founder or Manager / CA = Comments on Agency Composition or Business / FA = Foreign Affiliation
Tandy Advertising Agency, Ltd.	1927		Toronto	Harry M. Tandy	yes	LP = Smith, Denne, and Moore Ltd. FA = handled Canadian business of Williams and Cunnyngham Inc., Chicago, after 1930
J. Walter Thompson – 1st entry	1911	1916	New York	John C. Kirkwood	–	LP = London *Daily Mail* (UK) CA = bought by its local staff and became Smith, Denne, and Moore Ltd., 1916
– 2nd entry	1930		New York	W.C. Eadie	yes	LP = McKim Ltd.
Larry Webster Advertising	1929		Toronto	Larry Webster	yes	LP = Riley Engraving and Supply
Williams and Cunnyngham Ltd.	1927	1930	New York	Fred W. McLaughlin	yes	LP = Toronto *Globe* FA = Canadian business handled by Tandy Advertising Agency after 1930
Frank Wilson	1895	1897	Toronto	S. Frank Wilson	yes	LP = independent job printer and publisher CA = became a ready-print shop, 1897

Data taken from:
Printer and Publisher, vols. 1–33 (1892–1928).
Canadian Advertising Data, vols. 1–5 (1928–32).
Economic Advertising/Marketing, vols. 1–31 (1908–30).
The Toronto City Directory (Toronto: [publisher varies], 1880–1930).
H.E. Stephenson and C. McNaught, *The Story of Advertising in Canada* (Toronto: Ryerson, 1940).

Notes

Introduction

1 Thomas C. Haliburton, *The Clockmaker* (1836; reprint, Toronto: McClelland & Stewart, 1958), 152–3.
2 Ibid., 153.
3 Ibid., 153.
4 Fred Cogswell, 'Haliburton,' in *Literary History of Canada: Canadian Literature in English*, ed. C.F. Klinck et al. (Toronto: University of Toronto Press, 1965), 97.
5 Haliburton, *Clockmaker*, 1.
6 Albert D. Lasker, *The Lasker Story, As He Told It*, ed. S.R. Bernstein (Lincolnwood, IL: NTC Business Books, 1987), 13–15.
7 Ibid., 19.
8 E.E. Calkins and R. Holden, *Modern Advertising* (New York: Appleton, 1905), 4.
9 On Calkins, see Michele H. Bogart, *Advertising, Artists, and the Borders of Art* (Chicago: University of Chicago Press, 1995).
10 Walter Dill Scott, *The Theory of Advertising* (Boston: Small, Maynard, 1904), chs. 3–4.
11 Henry Foster Adams, *Advertising and Its Mental Laws* (New York: Macmillan, 1920), 4.
12 Keith J. Tuckwell, *Canadian Advertising in Action* (Scarborough: Prentice-Hall, 1988), 3.
13 Richard Ohmann, *Selling Culture: Magazines, Markets, and Class at the Turn of the Century* (New York: Verso, 1996), 31–47; Dallas W. Smythe, *Dependency Road: Communications, Capitalism, Consciousness, and Canada* (Norwood, NJ: Ablex, 1981).

14 Raymond Williams, 'Advertising: The Magic System,' *Problems in Material-ism and Culture* (London: Verso, 1980), 327–35; see also William Leiss, Stephen Kline, and Sut Jhally, *Social Communication in Advertising: Persons, Products, and Images of Well-Being* (Toronto: Methuen, 1986), 270–80.

15 Stuart Chase and F.J. Schlink, *Your Money's Worth* (New York: Macmillan, 1927); on the same theme, see also Stuart Chase, *The Tragedy of Waste* (New York: Macmillan, 1931), and F.J. Schlink and A. Kallett, *100,000,000 Guinea Pigs* (New York: Grosset & Dunlap, 1933).

16 A.S.J. Baster, *Advertising Reconsidered* (London: King & Son, 1935); John Kenneth Galbraith, *The Affluent Society* (Boston: Houghton Mifflin, 1958).

17 Jackson Lears, *Fables of Abundance: A Cultural History of Advertising in Amer-ica* (New York: Basic, 1994), 53.

18 Harold Innis, 'The Newspaper in Economic Development,' *Journal of Economic History*, 2:Suppl. (1942), 1–33; Jürgen Habermas, *The Structural Transformation of the Public Sphere*, trans. T. Berger (Cambridge, MA: MIT Press, 1991). Recent scholars have continued this tradition: see Armand Mattelart, *Advertising International: The Privatisation of Public Space*, trans. M. Chanin (London: Comedia/Routledge, 1989); Herbert I. Schiller, *Culture, Inc.: The Corporate Takeover of Public Expression* (New York: Oxford University Press, 1989).

19 Judith Williamson, *Decoding Advertisements* (London: Marion Boyars, 1978); E.J. Hart, *The Selling of Canada: The CPR and the Beginnings of Canadian Tour-ism* (Banff, AB: Altitude, 1983); M. Susan Bland, 'Henrietta the Homemaker and Rosie the Riveter: Images of Women in Advertising in *Maclean's Maga-zine*, 1939–1950,' in *Canadian Working Class History*, ed. L.S. MacDowell and I. Radforth (Toronto: Canadian Scholars' Press, 1992), 595–622; Leiss et al., *Social Communication in Advertising*, 169–74.

20 Daniel Pope, *The Making of Modern Advertising* (New York: Basic, 1983); Stephen Fox, *The Mirror Makers* (New York: Morrow, 1984); Roland March-and, *Advertising the American Dream: Making Way for Modernity, 1920–1940* (Berkeley, CA: University of California Press, 1986); Jennifer Scanlon, *Inarticulate Longings: The Ladies' Home Journal, Gender, and the Promises of Consumer Culture* (New York: Routledge, 1995); Ellen Gruber Garvey, *The Adman in the Parlor: Magazines and the Gendering of Consumer Culture, 1880s to 1910s* (New York: Oxford University Press, 1996).

21 Olaf P. Rechnitzer, 'Is the Advertiser a Good Judge of His Own Copy?' *Mar-keting* 24:2 (23 January 1926), 42, 50; Richard Surrey [B. Brooker], 'Getting Your Sales Ideas across to the Artist,' *Marketing* 23:7 (3 October 1925), 195; Angela E. Davis, *A Social History of Labour in the Canadian Graphic Arts*

Industry to the 1940s (Montreal: McGill-Queen's University Press, 1995); Bogart, *Advertising, Artists, and the Borders of Art*, 125–70.

22 By practioners: H.E. Stephenson and C. McNaught, *The Story of Advertising in Canada* (Toronto: Ryerson, 1940); Jerry Goodis, *Have I Ever Lied to You Before?* (Toronto: McClelland & Stewart, 1972); John S. Straiton, *Of Women and Advertising* (Toronto: McClelland & Stewart, 1984). By academics: O.J. Firestone, *Broadcast Advertising in Canada: Past and Future Growth* (Ottawa: University of Ottawa Press, 1966); Frederick Elkin, *Rebels and Colleagues: Advertising and Social Change in French Canada* (Montreal: McGill-Queen's University Press, 1973); Paul Rutherford, *The New Icons? The Art of Television Advertising* (Toronto: University of Toronto Press, 1994).

23 J.R. Bone et al., *A History of Canadian Journalism* (Toronto: Canadian Press Association, 1908); W.A. Craick, *A History of Canadian Journalism II: Last Years of the Canadian Press Association, 1908–1919* (Toronto: Ontario Publishing, 1959); W.H. Kesteron, *A History of Journalism in Canada* (Toronto: McClelland & Stewart, 1967); Paul Rutherford, *A Victorian Authority: The Daily Press in Late Nineteenth-Century Canada* (Toronto: University of Toronto Press, 1982), ch. 3; Jean de Bonville, *La Presse Québécoise de 1884 à 1914: Genèse d'un média de masse* (Quebec: Presses de l'Université Laval, 1988); Minko Sotiron, *From Politics to Profits: The Commercialization of Canadian Daily Newspapers, 1890–1920* (Montreal: McGill-Queen's University Press, 1997); Noel Barbour, *Those Amazing People! The Story of the Canadian Magazine Industry, 1778–1967* (Toronto: Crucible, 1982); Fraser Sutherland, *The Monthly Epic: A History of Canadian Magazines, 1789–1989* (Markham, ON: Fitzhenry & Whiteside, 1989); Ken Norris, *The Little Magazine in Canada, 1925–80* (Toronto: ECW, 1984); David MacKenzie, *Arthur Irwin: A Biography* (Toronto: University of Toronto Press, 1993).

24 Hart, *The Selling of Canada*; Leiss et al., *Social Communication in Advertising*.

25 Margali Sarfatti Larson, *The Rise of Professionalism: A Sociological Analysis* (Berkeley, CA: University of California Press, 1977); Harold Perkin, *The Rise of Professional Society: England since 1880* (London: Routledge, 1989).

26 Perkin, *Professional Society*, 2–9.

27 Stuart Blumin, *The Emergence of the Middle Class: Social Experience in the American City, 1760–1900* (New York: Cambridge University Press, 1989).

1: Newspapers, Advertising, and the Rise of the Agency

1 *Printer & Publisher* 2:3 (March 1893), 10.

2 William Meikle, *The Canadian Newspaper Directory* (Toronto: Blackburn's, 1858), 26.

3 A. McKim & Company, *Canadian Newspaper Directory*, 1st ed. (Montreal: McKim, 1892), 59; Meikle, *Canadian Newspaper Directory*, Appendix A. See also Paul Rutherford, *A Victorian Authority: The Daily Press in Late Nineteenth-Century Canada* (Toronto: University of Toronto Press, 1982), 37.

4 A rather acid appraisal of this outlook appears in Mack [Joseph Clark], 'The Country Editor,' *Saturday Night* 6:13 (18 February 1893), 9.

5 George L. Parker, *The Beginnings of the Book Trade in Canada* (Toronto: University of Toronto Press, 1985), ch. 4.

6 *Canadian Newspaper Directory*, 1st ed. (1892), 13–14.

7 'Increasing the Value of the Advertising Columns,' *Printer & Publisher* 19:5 (May 1910), 24–5; J.I. Little, 'Popular Voices in Print: The Local Newspaper Correspondents of an Extended Scots-Canadian Community, 1894,' *Journal of Canadian Studies* 30:3 (Fall 1995), 134–55.

8 *Canadian Newspaper Directory*, 1st ed. (1892), 59.

9 *Saturday Night* 21:22 (14 March 1908), 1; Stewart Lyon, 'Shall the Editor or the Business Manager Reign?' *Printer & Publisher* 25:7 (July 1916), 17–20; Sally F. Zerker, *The Rise and Fall of the Toronto Typographical Union, 1832–1972* (Toronto: University of Toronto Press, 1972); Rutherford, *Victorian Authority*, 96; Jean de Bonville, *La Presse Québécoise de 1884 à 1914: Genèse d'un média de masse* (Quebec: Presses de l'Université Laval, 1988), 88–155; Minko Sotiron, *From Politics to Profits: The Commercialization of Canadian Daily Newspapers, 1890–1920* (Montreal: McGill-Queen's University Press, 1997), 23–38.

10 *Canadian Newspaper Directory*, 2d ed. (1899), 238; *Canadian Newspaper Directory*, 4th ed. (1905), 252; 'The Newspapers of Fort William,' *Printer & Publisher* 23:4 (April 1914), 69; E. Pane and R. Bahr, *Machine Bites Dog: A Study of Technology and Work in the Ontario Newspaper Industry* (Toronto: Southern Ontario Newspaper Group, 1994), 24.

11 A.R. Fawcett, 'The Country Editor,' *Printer & Publisher* 2:10 (October 1893), 6–7; *Printer & Publisher* 18:4 (April 1909), 22; E.E. Calkins and R. Holden, *Modern Advertising* (1905; reprint, New York: Garland, 1985), 82–3; Rutherford, *Victorian Authority*, 66.

12 A.H.U. Colquhoun, *Press, Politics, and People: The Life and Letters of Sir John Willison* (Toronto: Macmillan, 1935), 11–12; Rutherford, *Victorian Authority*, 53–4, 59–60.

13 'Independent Press,' *Printer & Publisher* 14:2 (February 1905), 21.

14 Sir John Willison, *Reminiscences Political and Personal* (Toronto: McClelland & Stewart, 1919), 131–2; Sotiron, *Politics to Profits*, 23–38; Michael Nolan, *Walter J. Blackburn: A Man for All Media* (Toronto: Macmillan, 1989), 2–10.

15 Ramsay Cook, *The Politics of John W. Dafoe and the* Free Press (Toronto:

University of Toronto Press, 1963), 16–18; Ross Harkness, *J.E. Atkinson of the Star* (Toronto: University of Toronto Press, 1963), 18–22.

16 Hector Charlesworth, *More Candid Chronicles* (Toronto: Macmillan, 1928), 175.

17 See, for example, National Archives of Canada (NAC), MG26 E1, Mackenzie Bowell papers, v. 9, f. PPS4313, A. Burrows to A.W. Ross, 22 April 1891; Canada, House of Commons, *Debates* (1903), vol. 3, 5267–74.

18 J.S. Brierly, 'Advertising Rates, Local and Foreign,' in NAC, MG28 I6, CPA records, v. 1, Minute Book 1882–1910, 14 February 1890.

19 'Talk on Foreign Advertising,' *Printer & Publisher* 2:3 (March 1893), 8; *Printer & Publisher* 13:11 (November 1904), 8; Anson McKim, 'Advertising Agencies – Whose Agents Are They?' *Printer & Publisher* 24:11 (November 1915), 17–19.

20 'The Advertising Arena – Patent Medicines,' *Printer & Publisher* 8:7 (July 1899), 4–5; Bonville, *La Presse Québécoise*, 314–16; H.E. Stephenson and C. McNaught, *The Story of Advertising in Canada: A Chronicle of Fifty Years* (Toronto: Ryerson, 1940), 14–16, 134–240.

21 Thomas Kelley, Jr, *The Fabulous Kelley: Canada's King of the Medicine Men* (Don Mills, ON: General, 1974), 1–11; Brooks McNamara, *Step Right Up: An Illustrated History of the American Medicine Show* (Garden City, NY: Doubleday, 1976), 45–64; Daniel Pope, *The Making of Modern Advertising* (New York: Basic, 1983); James D. Norris, *Advertising and the Transformation of American Society, 1865–1920* (New York: Greenwood, 1990); Jackson Lears, *Fables of Abundance: A Cultural History of Advertising in America* (New York: Basic, 1994).

22 Augustus Bridle, 'Senator Fulford – Advertising King,' *Busyman's* 11:2 (November 1905), 7–14; Paul A. Bator, 'George Taylor Fulford,' *Dictionary of Canadian Biography*, vol. 13 (Toronto: University of Toronto Press, 1992), 363–5; Kelley, *Fabulous Kelley*, 137–8.

23 *Printer & Publisher* 2:5 (May 1893), 2; *Printer & Publisher* 6:5 (May 1897), 8. On the prevalence of patent medicine advertising, see E. Desbarats, 'The Building Up of a Mutual Service,' *Printer & Publisher* 27:8 (August 1918), 19–20; Bridle, 'Senator Fulford,' 11; Pope, *Making of Modern Advertising*, 45–6; Stephenson and McNaught, *Story of Advertising*, 234–5.

24 Stephenson and McNaught, *Story of Advertising*, 49–91; Duncan M. McDougall, 'Canadian Manufactured Commodity Output, 1870–1915,' *Canadian Journal of Economics* 4:1 (February 1971), 21–36.

25 NAC, MG24 K9, James Poole papers, v. 2, f. 1861, W. Virgin to J. Poole, 12 September 1861.

26 Richard Ohmann discusses this notion of shared codes in the context of

copywriters and readers; see *Selling Culture: Magazines, Markets, and Class at the Turn of the Century* (London: Verso, 1996), 175.

27 Poole papers, v. 1, f. January–February 1858, R. Watson to J. Poole, n.d.; v. 1, f. January–May 1856, Provincial Insurance Co. to J. Poole, n.d.

28 Canada, Department of Trade and Commerce, *The Canadian Industrial Field*, 2d ed. (Ottawa: King's Printer, 1933), 9; Kenneth Buckley, *Capital Formation in Canada* (Toronto: McClelland & Stewart, 1974), 10–11; T.W. Acheson, 'The National Policy and the Industrialization of the Maritimes, 1880–1910,' *Acadiensis* 1:2 (1972), 3–28.

29 HSC, 2d ed., A68–A69; Department of Trade and Commerce, *Canadian Industrial Field*, 2d ed., 9; O.J. Firestone, *Canada's Economic Development, 1867–1953* (London: Bowes & Bowes, 1958), 76–97.

30 See J.J. Gibbons, 'The Weekly Section,' *Printer & Publisher* 18:4 (April 1909), 21; Bertram Brooker, 'Forty Years of Canadian Advertising [Pt. 4],' *Marketing* 21:5 (6 September 1924), 134–6; Stephenson and McNaught, *Story of Advertising*, 75.

31 Thomas Walkom, 'The Daily Newspaper Industry in Ontario's Developing Capitalistic Economy: Toronto and Ottawa, 1871–1911' (unpublished PhD dissertation, University of Toronto, 1983), 344–404.

32 *Canadian Newspaper Directory*, 1st ed. (1892); *Canadian Newspaper Directory*, 4th ed. (1905); W.J. Taylor, 'Advertising the Real Backbone of the Business,' *Printer & Publisher* 27:6 (June 1918), 22. Two recent studies have come to the same conclusion; see Bonville, *La Presse Québécoise*, 326–9, and Sotiron, *Politics to Profits*, 10–22.

33 *Canadian Advertiser* 1:1 (June 1893); *Economic Advertising* 1:1 (September 1908), 3–4. On the growth of business, see 'The Advertising Men,' *Printer & Publisher* 11:6 (June 1902), 6; W.A. C[raick], 'Brief Interviews,' *Printer & Publisher* 11:7 (July 1902), 17; C.G.H., 'American Advertising,' *Printer & Publisher* 11:10 (October 1902), 17; 'Advertising Arena,' *Printer & Publisher* 12:1 (January 1903), 15; 'Advertising in Montreal,' *Printer & Publisher* 12:5 (May 1903), 16; Brooker, 'Forty Years [Pt. 5],' *Marketing* 21:10 (15 November 1924), 274. The three papers were *Ad World* (1902), *Points of the Star* (1902), and *Publicité-Publicity* (1905).

34 Fawcett, 'Country Editor,' 6–7; 'Co-operation among Local Publishers,' *Printer & Publisher* 4:4 (April 1895), 4–5; 'The Circular on Foreign Advertising,' *Printer & Publisher* 13:12 (December 1904), 12–13; S.D. Scott, 'The Newspaper of 1950,' *Printer & Publisher* 10:3 (March 1901), 17; J.H. Cranston, *Ink on My Fingers* (Toronto: Ryerson, 1953), vii–viii; Rutherford, *Victorian Authority*, 190–227; Michael Bliss, *A Living Profit: Studies in the Social History of Canadian Business, 1883–1911* (Toronto: McClelland &

Stewart, 1974), 33–54; Tom Traves, *The State and Enterprise: Canadian Manufacturers and the State, 1917–1931* (Toronto: University of Toronto Press, 1979), 30–3.

35 J.M.S. Careless, *Brown of the Globe*, vol. 1 (Toronto: Macmillan, 1959), 100; M.E. Nichols, *(CP) The Story of the Canadian Press* (Toronto: Ryerson, 1948). For a different view, see Peter G. Goheen, 'The Changing Bias of Inter-Urban Communications in Nineteenth-Century Canada,' *Journal of Historical Geography* 16:2 (1990), 177–96.

36 Poole papers, v. 2, f. January 1864, W. Riddell to J. Poole, December 1864.

37 Brooker, 'Forty Years [Pt. 1],' *Marketing* 20:9 (3 May 1924), 281.

38 Calkins and Holden, *Modern Advertising*, 13–26; Pope, *Making of Modern Advertising*, 113–14.

39 NAC, MG29 E18, John Lowe papers, v. 40, British American Advertising (BAA) Letterbook, R. Moore to F. Buteau, 28 April 1860.

40 The CPA thought it best to deny any such practice; CPA records, v. 2, Committee on Recognition of Advertising Agencies, 'Minute Book 1910–1919,' 19 April 1918.

41 Ron Poulton, *The Paper Tyrant* (Toronto: Clarke, Irwin, 1971), 22; Public Archives of Ontario (PAO), F138, Maclean-Hunter (M-H) records, b. 54, f. HC MacLean, H.C. MacLean to J.B. Maclean, 3 January 1945.

42 BAA Letterbook, R. Moore to the Montreal *Herald*, 18 February 1860.

43 Ibid., R. Moore to Mr Thomson, 23 February 1860.

44 Ibid., R. Moore to R. Boyle, 10 May 1860.

45 Ibid., R. Moore to G.J. Barthe, 23 February 1860.

46 Ibid., R. Moore to J. Styles, 14 February 1860; R. Moore to S.M. Pettingill, 14 February 1860.

47 Ibid., R. Moore to J. Styles, 22 February 1860.

48 George P. Rowell, *Forty Years an Advertising Agent, 1865–1905* (New York: Franklin, 1926); James W. Young, *Advertising Agency Compensation* (Chicago: University of Illinois Press, 1933), 23–5.

49 Young, *Agency Compensation*, 25–8; Ralph M. Hower, *The History of an Advertising Agency: N.W. Ayer & Son at Work* (Cambridge, MA: Harvard University Press, 1939); James Playsted Wood, *The Story of Advertising* (New York: Ronalds, 1958), 242–5.

50 Stephenson and McNaught, *Story of Advertising*, 49–75; David Monod, *Store Wars: Shopkeepers and the Culture of Mass Marketing, 1890–1939* (Toronto: University of Toronto Press, 1996), 99–148, especially 140–1.

51 Carman Cumming, *Secret Craft: The Journalism of Edward Farrer* (Toronto: University of Toronto Press, 1992); *Canadian Newspaper Directory*, 1st ed. (1892), 222–3; see also Hector Charlesworth, *Candid Chronicles* (Toronto:

Macmillan, 1925), 75; Donald Creighton, *John A. Macdonald: The Old Chieftain* (Toronto: Macmillan, 1955), 115–20.

52 McKim, 'Advertising Agencies,' 17–19; Brooker, 'Forty Years [Pt. 1],' 281–2; Stephenson and McNaught, *Story of Advertising*, 18–35.

53 Brooker, 'Forty Years [Pt. 1],' 282; 'Started in Canada,' *Printer & Publisher* 15:5 (May 1906), 20; George French, *20th Century Advertising* (New York: Van Nostrand, 1926), 224–5.

54 'A Tribute to Anson McKim,' *Printer & Publisher* 16:9 (September 1907), 37.

55 *Montreal Directory* (Lovell: Montreal, [1870–90]); *Toronto City Directory* (various publishers: Toronto, [1871–90]).

56 'The Business of the Modern Newspaper Advertising Agency,' *Canadian Newspaper Directory*, 2d ed. (1899), 26; see also 'The System and Equipment of the Modern Newspaper Advertising Agency,' *Canadian Newspaper Directory*, 3d ed. (1901), 25–6.

57 J.J. Gibbons, 'The Agent's Standpoint,' *Printer & Publisher* 14:4 (April 1905), 20–1; see also W.A. C[raick], 'Brief Interviews,' *Printer & Publisher* 11:9 (September 1902), 18–19.

58 A.R. Coffin, 'The Advertising Agency,' *Printer & Publisher* 15:3 (March 1906), 13.

59 'The Business,' *Canadian Newspaper Directory*, 2d ed. (1899), 26.

60 J.J. Gibbons in *Printer & Publisher* 13:12 (December 1904), 12–13.

61 'The Business,' *Canadian Newspaper Directory*, 2d ed. (1899), 26; *Toronto City Directory* (Toronto: Might, 1890), 1363; *Toronto City Directory* (1900), 990.

62 Sun Life Corporate Archives (SLA), Acc. 00480, b. 84, f. 'Early Advertising Ideas,' Lawrence G. Cluxton, 23 February 1911; Desbarats Advertising Agency, 23 February 1911.

63 Thomas Bengough, 'Improvements in Advertising,' *Biz* 1:2 (January 1894), 2. On artists, see *Canadian Newspaper Directory*, 2d ed. (1899), 29; W.A. C[raick], 'Brief Interviews with Advertising Men,' *Printer & Publisher* 11:9 (September 1902), 18–19; Joan Murray, 'The World of Tom Thomson,' *Journal of Canadian Studies* 26:3 (Fall 1991), 5–51; on copywriters, see Stephenson and McNaught, *Story of Advertising*, 102–5.

64 NAC, MG30 D279, Wilson MacDonald papers, v. 10, f. 10–1, 'Notes on W.M.'s Life'; Cheryl MacDonald, 'A Shakespeare for Canada,' *Beaver* 67:2 (1987), 4–8.

65 *Canadian Newspaper Directory*, 3d ed. (1901), 23–4; Angela E. Davis, 'Art and Work: Frederick Brigden and the History of the Canadian Illustrated Press,' *Journal of Canadian Studies* 21:2 (Summer 1992), 22–36; Angela E. Davis, *Art and Work: A Social History of Labour in the Canadian Graphic Arts Industry to the 1940s* (Montreal: McGill-Queen's University Press, 1995).

66 *Printer & Publisher* 8:11 (November 1899), 4; *Printer & Publisher* 12:5 (May 1903), 16; *Economic Advertising* 3:8 (August 1910), 18; CPA records, v. 2, Recognition Committee, 'Minute Book 1910–19,' 21 June 1910; Brooker, 'Forty Years [Pt. 3],' *Marketing* 21:3 (9 August 1924), 68, 95; Walkom, 'Daily Newspaper Industry,' 39–40.

67 'The Value of Expert Aid,' *Printer & Publisher* 9:1 (January 1900), 16–17; 'Advertising Arena,' *Printer & Publisher* 11:6 (June 1902), 13; 'Advertising Arena,' *Printer & Publisher* 11:11 (November 1902), 18; 'People Who Do Things,' *Saturday Night* 51:10 (11 January 1936), 16.

68 W.A. C[raick], 'Brief Interviews,' *Printer & Publisher* 11:9 (September 1902), 18; 'Advertising Arena,' *Printer & Publisher* 12:11 (November 1903), 12; Brooker, 'Forty Years [Pt. 5],' 272–4.

69 NAC, MG27 II D7, George E. Foster papers, v. 17, f. 1570, J.J. Gibbons to E.O. Osler, 4 August 1915; *Lydiatt's Book*, 9th ed. (1922), 227–43; Brooker, 'Forty Years [Pt. 5],' 272–4, 278.

70 Desbarats Advertising Agency, *The Desbarats Newspaper Directory*, 2d ed. (Montreal: Desbarats, 1912), 4. The two Toronto agencies were run by J.E. McConnell and J.H. Woods; C[raick], 'Brief Interviews,' *Printer & Publisher* 11:9 (September 1902), 18; *Toronto City Directory* (1905), 975.

71 'An Agency Incorporated,' *Printer & Publisher* 10:4 (April 1901), 20; *Canadian Newspaper Directory*, 3d ed. (1901), 23; McKim, 'Advertising Agencies,' 17–19; 'Advertising in Montreal,' *Printer & Publisher* 12:5 (May 1903), 16; 'The System and Equipment of a Modern Newspaper Advertising Agency,' *Canadian Newspaper Directory*, 3d ed. (1901), 21–6; *Printer & Publisher* 16:10 (October 1907), 35; *Printer & Publisher* 16:6 (June 1907), 30; Stephenson and McNaught, *Story of Advertising*, 99–109; French, *20th Century Advertising*, 226–8.

72 R.G. Dun & Company, *The Mercantile Agency Reference Book* (Toronto: Dun, 1904), 265, 423; R.G. Dun & Company, *The Mercantile Agency Reference Book* (Toronto: Dun, 1919), 311, 507, 512, 526. Dun's manuscript credit records for Canada cover the period 1840 to 1880, but no agencies appear in these records. See Harvard University School of Business Administration, Baker Library, R.G. Dun & Company collection; copies held by National Archives of Canada.

73 J.J. Gibbons, 'The Arrangement between the Agents and Publishers,' *Printer & Publisher* 17:2 (February 1908), 32f–g; *Canadian Newspaper Directory*, 3d ed. (1901), 21–2.

74 Canada, Dominion Bureau of Statistics, *Paper-Using Industries in Canada, 1926–1927* (Ottawa: King's Printer, 1930), 17; Buckley, *Capital Formation*, 10–11; W.T. Easterbrook and H.G.J. Aitken, *Canadian Economic History* (Toronto: Macmillan, 1958), 515–57.

75 Canada, Office of Census and Statistics, *Census 1901: Bulletin XI – Occupations of the People* (Ottawa: King's Printer, 1910), Table 2.
76 Canada, Dominion Bureau of Statistics, *Seventh Census of Canada, 1931*, vol. 7: *Occupations and Industries* (Ottawa: King's Printer, 1936), T40, T56.
77 *Lydiatt's Book*, 17th ed. (1931), 310–35; see also Appendix in this text.
78 Canada, Dominion Bureau of Statistics, *Sixth Census of Canada*, vol. 4: *Occupations* (Ottawa: King's Printer, 1929), T2, T3; *Census 1931*, vol. 7, T57.
79 Bonville, *La Presse Québécoise*, 26–7; W.L. Marr and D.G. Paterson, *Canada: An Economic History* (Toronto: Gage, 1980), 108–16, 355–62; H.V. Nelles, *The Politics of Development: Forests, Mines, and Hydro-Electric Power in Ontario, 1849–1941* (Toronto: Macmillan, 1974), 48–107.
80 Donald H. Thain, 'Advertising Agencies in Canada,' in *Marketing in Canada*, ed. E.J. Fox and D.S.R. Leighton (Homewood, IL: Irwin, 1958), 171–91.
81 *Montreal Classified Business Directory* (Montreal: Lovell, 1900), 73; Frederick Elkin, *Rebels and Colleagues: Advertising and Social Change in French Canada* (Montreal: McGill-Queen's University Press, 1973), 17–33. Gerald Tulchinsky has noted the same phenomenon among Montreal's commercial agents in the mid-1800s; see *The River Barons* (Montreal: McGill-Queen's University Press, 1977), 15–16.
82 'Georges Edward Desbarats,' *Montreal: from 1535 to 1914* (Montreal: Clarke, 1914), 469–73; *Canadian Newspaper Directory*, 2d ed. (1899), 36–7; SLA, Sun Life of Canada, 'Advertising Register 1901–1911,' 15; Brooker, 'Forty Years [Pt. 3],' 67; 'Who's Who in Advertising,' *Canadian Advertising Data* 4:6 (June 1931), 22.
83 Maurice Watier, *La Publicité* (Montreal: Pauline, 1985), 65. In Fontaine's opinion, Desbarats was the first; see F.-É. Fontaine, 'Les Débuts des Canadiens Français dans la Publicité,' *La Clé d'Or* 1:9 (November 1926), 242.
84 Fontaine, 'Les Débuts,' 242; on *Le Monde*, see Rutherford, *Victorian Authority*, 64–5.
85 'Advertising Arena,' *Printer & Publisher* 18:1 (January 1909), 25; Canadian Advertising Agency, *French Newspapers and Periodicals of Canada and the United States* (Montreal: Canadian Advertising, 1913), 3–11; Watier, *La Publicité*, 65; Bonville, *La Presse Québécoise*, 330.
86 Coffin, 'The Advertising Agency,' 13; 'Advertising Agency and Publisher,' *Printer & Publisher* 18:8 (August 1909), 13; John C. Kirkwood, 'Is National Advertising Going Where It Ought To Go?' *Printer & Publisher* 23:4 (April 1914), 66.
87 Raoul Renault, 'En quoi l'Esprit Français s'oppose à la Publicité,' *La Clé d'Or* 1:9 (November 1926), 245–8. A later sociological study came to the same conclusion; see Elkin, *Rebels and Colleagues*, 37–43.

88 *Marketing* 31:10 (9 November 1929), 281; Vancouver *Province*, 18 June 1960;
   Vancouver *Province*, 9 January 1950; *Henderson's City of Vancouver and North
   Vancouver Directory* (Vancouver: Henderson [1900–16]); *Wrigley's British
   Columbia Directory* (Vancouver: Wrigley's [1917–20]). On Vancouver's
   growth, see R.A.J. McDonald, *Making Vancouver* (Vancouver: UBC Press,
   1996), ch. 3.
89 *Toronto City Directory* ([1890–1910]).

2: Toronto Adworkers

1 *Printer's Ink*, quoted in *Printer & Publisher* 16:9 (September 1907), 37.
2 F. Albany Rowlatt, 'The Advertising Agency,' *Economic Advertising* 1:12
   (August 1909), 9.
3 M-H records, b. 53, f. JC-Kirkwood, clipping, Owen Sound *Sun-Times*,
   21 October 1942; b. 54, f. HC-MacLean/1, J.C. Kirkwood to J.B. Maclean,
   26 September 1940.
4 NAC, MG27 III E3, Kenneth P. Kirkwood papers, v. 7, John C. Kirkwood
   notebook, 28 September 1902, 51–2; see also 18 July 1903, 111.
5 Ibid., 19 July 1903, 112.
6 Ibid., 19 July 1903, 123.
7 Robert H. Wiebe, *The Search for Order, 1877–1920* (New York: Hill & Wang,
   1967), 111–32.
8 For the United States, see Mary Ryan, *Cradle of the Middle Class: The Family
   in Oneida County, New York, 1790–1865* (Cambridge: Cambridge University
   Press, 1981); Stuart Blumin, *The Emergence of the Middle Class: Social Experience in the American City, 1760–1900* (Cambridge: Cambridge University
   Press, 1989); for Canada, see Michael Katz, *The People of Hamilton, Canada
   West: Family and Class in a Mid-Nineteenth-Century City* (Cambridge, MA:
   Harvard University Press, 1975), 176–208; Colin Howell, 'Reform and the
   Monopolistic Impulse: The Professionalization of Medicine in the Mari-
   times,' *Acadiensis* 2:1 (Autumn 1981), 3–22; Mariana Valverde, *The Age of
   Light, Soap, and Water: Moral Reform in English Canada, 1885–1925* (Toronto:
   McClelland & Stewart, 1991), 44–76; Alan J. Richardson, 'Educational
   Policy and Professional Status: A Case History of the Ontario Accountancy
   Profession,' *Journal of Canadian Studies* 27:1 (Spring 1992), 44–57; Ken
   Rasmussen, 'Administrative Reform and the Quest for Bureaucratic Auton-
   omy, 1867–1919,' *Journal of Canadian Studies* 29:3 (Autumn 1994), 45–62;
   R.D. Gidney and W.P.J. Millar, *Professional Gentlemen: The Professions in
   Nineteenth-Century Ontario* (Toronto: University of Toronto Press, 1994),
   ch. 14.

9 Kenneth Buckley, *Capital Formation in Canada, 1896–1930* (Toronto: McClelland & Stewart, 1974), 214; Paul Axelrod, *Making a Middle Class: Student Life in English Canada during the Thirties* (Montreal: McGill-Queen's University Press, 1990), 7.

10 Roland Marchand, *Advertising the American Dream: Making Way for Modernity, 1920–1940* (Berkeley, CA: University of California Press, 1986), 44–8; see also Rasmussen, 'Administrative Reform,' 45–62.

11 *Census 1921*, vol. 4, T5; *Census 1931*, vol. 7, T53.

12 *Census 1931*, vol. 7, T53, T55.

13 The books: Noel Barbour, *Those Amazing People! The Story of the Canadian Magazine Industry, 1778–1967* (Toronto: Crucible, 1982); W.G. Colgate, *Canadian Art: Its Origin and Development* (Toronto: Ryerson, 1943); W.G. Colgate, *C.W. Jeffreys* (Toronto: Ryerson, 1945); H.E. Stephenson and C. McNaught, *The Story of Advertising in Canada: A Chronicle of Fifty Years* (Toronto: Ryerson, 1940).

14 Marchand, *American Dream*, 2–4.

15 *Census 1931*, vol. 7, T29, T34.

16 'Men and Media,' *Economic Advertising* 6:11 (November 1913), 45; 'Teaching Advertising,' *Economic Advertising* 6:5 (May 1913), 3; see also 'Schools of Advertising,' *Publicité-Publicity* 1:1 (June 1905), 26; 'Advertising in the Universities,' *Economic Advertising* 10:10 (October 1917), 16; George French, *20th Century Advertising* (New York: Van Nostrand, 1926), 308.

17 Truman deWeese, 'The Advertising Manager,' *Economic Advertising* 3:8 (August 1910), 19–31; Harry M. Tedman, 'The Advertising Manager's Job,' *Marketing* 26:6 (19 March 1927), 182–5; PAO, F229, T. Eaton Co. records, Ser. 162, b. 1, f. 0–26, K.M[cPhedran], 'Background Material on Development of City Advertising Department,' 29 January 1959. E.J. Hart's study of CPR publicity implicitly reveals this pattern at Canada's largest company; see *The Selling of Canada: The CPR and the Beginnings of Canadian Tourism* (Banff, AB: Altitude, 1983).

18 J.S. Robertson, 'Another Paper on the Subject,' *Printer & Publisher* 9:2 (February 1900), 20–1; H.R. Cockfield, 'Trends in Advertising Agency Practice,' *Canadian Advertising Data* 3:10 (November 1930), 11, 24.

19 *Canadian Advertising Data* 3:7 (August 1930), 5; see also Appendix in this text.

20 *Canadian Advertising Data*, vols. 3–5 ([1930–2]). Marchand has noted golf's popularity among American adworkers; see *American Dream*, 38.

21 'About Men and Media,' *Economic Advertising* 4:4 (April 1911), 43; 'Toronto Advertising Men Plan Golf Tournament,' *Marketing* 18:8 (21 April 1923), 278; 'Toronto Adcraft Club Formed,' *Marketing* 28:13 (23 June 1928), 473.

22 T.W. Acheson, 'The Social Origins of the Canadian Industrial Elite, 1880–1885,' in *Canadian Business History,* ed. D.S. Macmillan (Toronto: McClelland & Stewart, 1972), 144–74. Again, there are parallels in the United States; see Marchand, *American Dream,* 25–52; Daniel Pope, *The Making of Modern Advertising* (New York: Basic, 1983), 177–80.

23 The Dworkin agency was part of a popular news agency and book room; Stephen A. Speisman, *The Jews of Toronto: A History to 1937* (Toronto: McClelland & Stewart, 1979), 88, 235; *Toronto City Directory* ([1910–17]).

24 Richard Ohmann, *Selling Culture: Magazines, Markets, and Class at the Turn of the Century* (London: Verso, 1996), 118–74; Rasmussen, 'Administrative Reform,' 45–62.

25 T.R. Nevett, *Advertising in Britain: A History* (London: Heinemann, 1982), 61–6; Nevett, 'American Influence on British Advertising before 1920,' in *Historical Perspectives in Marketing,* ed. T. Nevett and R.A. Fullerton (Lexington, MA: Heath, 1988), 223–40.

26 E.E. Calkins and R. Holden, *Modern Advertising* (1905; reprint, New York: Garland, 1985), 16–20; Frank Presbrey, *The History and Development of Advertising* (Garden City, NY: Doubleday, Doran, 1929), 265.

27 *Printer & Publisher* 22:8 (August 1913), 64; *Printer & Publisher* 22:12 (December 1913), 40; J.C. Kirkwood, 'Canadian Advertising Developments,' *Marketing* 12:6 (August 1918), 22–6; Stephen Nicholas, 'The Overseas Marketing Performance of British Industry, 1870–1914,' *Economic History Review* Ser. 2:37 (1984), 489–506. An early Canadian reference to *Printer's Ink* can be found in *Biz* 1:2 (1 January 1894), 5.

28 George F. Hobart, 'Neighbour Canada,' *Printer's Ink* 103:5 (2 May 1918), 100–4.

29 *Printer & Publisher* 7:3 (March 1898), 28; *Economic Advertising* 1:9 (May 1909), 5; *Marketing* 31:5 (31 August 1929), 109; 'Notre Programme,' *Clé d'Or* 1:1 (March 1926), 1; Henri Vathelet, *La Publicité dans le Journalisme* (Paris: Albin Michel, 1911), 68, 212–17; Charles W. Stokes, 'Diary of a Montreal Delegate,' *Marketing* 25:1 (10 July 1926), 6; Nevett, 'American Influence,' 223–40.

30 'Copy That Sells,' *Economic Advertising* 1:1 (September 1908), 22–6; *Economic Advertising* 1:9 (May 1909), 5; Don Tuck, 'An International Convention,' *Economic Advertising* 6:12 (December 1913), 1–3; Mark E. Ting [B. Brooker], 'Hoist the Sales,' *Marketing* 23:7 (3 October 1925), 202.

31 'Agency Items,' *Printer & Publisher* 25:5 (May 1916), 31.

32 *Economic Advertising* 4:11 (November 1911), 46–7; *Economic Advertising* 8:5 (May 1915), 15–17; *Marketing* 15:9 (1 May 1921), 312; L.J. Cunniff, 'International Phases of Advertising,' *Marketing* 16:12 (15 June 1922), 506–8, 516.

33 C. Truscott Solomon, 'The Weaknesses of Long Distance Advertising
    Counsel,' *Marketing* 16:5 (1 March 1922), 208, 236–41.
34 'How Canada Is Treated,' *Printer & Publisher* 22:4 (April 1913), 47.
35 *Economic Advertising* 1:10 (June 1909), 9; *Marketing* 22:1 (15 January 1925),
    cover; Solomon, 'Long Distance Counsel,' 240.
36 W. Campbell et al., *At the Mermaid Inn*, ed. B. Davies (Toronto: University of
    Toronto Press, 1979).
37 Rous & Mann Limited, 'The Artist and the Businessman,' Toronto *Star*,
    24 November 1913; Carleton F. Dyer, 'Why We Buy Canadian Art,' *Market-
    ing* 26:1 (8 January 1927), 10–11; see also Donald Marvin, 'Teaming of
    Science, Art and Industry,' *Marketing* 27:11 (26 November 1927), 396–8.
38 Arthur Lismer, 'A Distinctive Canadian Character,' *Marketing* 15:18
    (15 September 1921), 605–7; F.B. Housser, *A Canadian Art Movement*
    (Toronto: Macmillan, 1926); Dennis Reid, *The Group of Seven* (Ottawa:
    National Gallery of Canada, 1970), 18; Charles C. Hill, *The Group of Seven:
    Art for a Nation* (Toronto: McClelland & Stewart, 1995), 123–7, 176–9;
    R. Stacey with H. Bishop, *J.E.H. MacDonald: Designer* (Ottawa: Carleton
    University Press, 1996).
39 'Our New Cover,' *Marketing* 22:1 (15 January 1925), 3; *Marketing* 24:7 (3
    April 1926), 246; 'Ye Yuletide Appeal,' *Marketing* 25:13 (25 December 1926),
    413; Dyer, 'Why We Buy Canadian,' 10–11; Mark E. Ting [B. Brooker], 'Hoist
    the Sales,' *Marketing* 26:8 (16 April 1927), 332; J.L. Love, 'CNR Employs
    Canadian Artists,' *Marketing* 26:12 (11 June 1927), 468–9; Philip E. Spane
    [B. Brooker], 'The Modern Bug,' *Marketing* 28:8 (14 April 1928), 285–7, 307;
    E.J. Hart, *The Selling of Canada: The CPR and the Beginnings of Canadian Tour-
    ism* (Banff, AB: Altitude, 1983); G.B. Kines, 'Chief Man-of-Many-Sides: J.M.
    Gibbon and His Contributions to the Development of Tourism and the Arts
    in Canada' (unpublished MA thesis, Carleton University, 1988), 134–56.
40 'American Agencies Enter Canada,' *Printer & Publisher* 20:10 (October
    1911), 46.
41 In Toronto: J. Walter Thompson, 1911–16; H.K. McCann, 1914; Brotherton,
    1924; Huber Hoge, 1924; W.H. Rankin, 1924; McKinney, Marsh & Cushing,
    1926; Williams & Cunnyngham, 1927; Lord & Thomas and Logan, 1929; T.F.
    MacManus, 1929. In Montreal: Winsten & Sullivan, 1924. In both: Camp-
    bell-Ewald, 1922; J. Walter Thompson, 1929.
42 'Advertising Agencies Merge,' *Printer & Publisher* 32:6 (June 1923), 41;
    Marketing 26:5 (5 March 1927), 174; Thornton Purkis, 'Lost – *my first
    customer!*' *Marketing* 25:10 (13 November 1926), 305; 'William Findlay
    Company,' *Marketing* 30:6 (16 March 1926), 176; see also *Printer & Publisher*
    19:1 (January 1910), 37.

43 *Census 1931*, vol. 7, T44. Clarke E. Locke Limited handled the Canadian business of Walter Judd Limited, UK.

44 L.J. Cunniff, 'International Phases of Advertising,' *Marketing* 16:12 (15 June 1922), 508.

45 Campbell-Ewald Limited, 'A Canadian Agency,' *Marketing* 25:7 (2 October 1926), 209.

46 In 1916 Smith and two partners acquired JWT's offices in Toronto and London, England, and renamed the whole Smith, Denne, & Moore Limited. 'New Advertising Agency,' *Printer & Publisher* 20:11 (November 1911), 42; *Printer & Publisher* 25:5 (May 1916), 31; 'Who's Who in Advertising,' *Canadian Advertising Data* 3:8 (September 1930), 9; Duke University, JWT Archives, Series: Staff Meetings, b. 1, f. 3, 20 December 1927; *Canadian Advertising Data* 3:6 (July 1930), 40–1; Stephen Fox, *The Mirror Makers: A History of American Advertising and Its Creators* (New York: Morrow, 1984), 78–117.

47 Albert D. Lasker, *The Lasker Story, As He Told It*, ed. S.R. Bernstein (Lincolnwood, IL: NTC Business Books, 1987), 19, 24; Fox, *The Mirror Makers*, 49–51.

48 *Winnipeg Alphabetical Directory* (Winnipeg: Henderson's, [1892–5]); Brooker, 'Forty Years [Pt. 3],' 69; *Marketing* 28:2 (21 January 1928), 68; Fox, *Mirror Makers*, 48–50; Stephenson and McNaught, *Story of Advertising*, 82–90; Lasker, *Lasker Story,* 24.

49 *Economic Advertising* 3:6 (June 1910), 25–30; 'Why Advertising Is Not Guaranteed,' *Economic Advertising* 3:10 (October 1910), 5–11; *Economic Advertising* 3:11 (November 1910), 10–11; Quentin J. Schultze, '"An Honourable Place": The Quest for Professional Advertising Education, 1900–17,' *Business History Review* 56:1 (Spring 1982), 16–32; Fox, *Mirror Makers*, 49–50.

50 Floyd S. Chalmers, *A Gentleman of the Press* (Toronto: Doubleday, 1969), 72–3.

51 'The Advertising Department,' *Printer & Publisher* 7:8 (August 1898), 2; J.[P.] McConnell, 'Advertisers' Rights,' *Printer & Publisher* 8:6 (June 1899), 4–5; W.A. C[raick], 'Brief Interviews,' *Printer & Publisher* 11:9 (September 1902), 18; 'Advertising Arena,' *Printer & Publisher* 12:11 (November 1903), 12; T.J. Tobin, 'Our Biggest General Advertiser,' *Economic Advertising* 1:5 (January 1909), 30–2; Brooker, 'Forty Years [Pt. 5],' 274.

52 *Marketing* 10:11 (November 1917), 38; *Lydiatt's Book*, 9th ed. (1922); 'Malcolm M. Fergusson,' *Marketing* 21:5 (6 September 1924), 153; R.G. Dun & Company, *The Mercantile Agency Reference Book* (Toronto: Dun, 1919), 311.

53 NAC, Franklin Carmichael papers, MG30 D293, v. 1, f. McConnell-&-Fergusson; *Lydiatt's Book*, 9th ed. (1922), 227–43; *Printer & Publisher* 19:11

(November 1910), 45; 'James Fisher Company,' *Marketing* 13:11 (November 1919), 484.

54 'A New Agency,' *Printer & Publisher* 9:5 (May 1900), 18–19; 'The Tillson Campaign,' *Printer & Publisher* 11:12 (December 1902), 14; Brooker, 'Forty Years [Pt. 5],' 278; 'Death of John Pollack McConnell,' *Marketing* 25:2 (24 July 1926), 48.

55 'The Advertising Department,' *Printer & Publisher* 7:8 (August 1898), 2; J.[P.] McConnell, 'Advertisers' Rights,' *Printer & Publisher* 8:6 (June 1899), 4–5; W.A. C[raick], 'Brief Interviews,' *Printer & Publisher* 11:9 (September 1902), 18; 'Advertising Arena,' *Printer & Publisher* 12:11 (November 1903), 12.

56 Michael Nolan, *Walter J. Blackburn: A Man for All Media* (Toronto: Macmillan, 1989), 19–20.

57 M-H records, b. 36, f. 75th-Anniversary, *Newsweekly* 52:39 (16 September 1962), 13–16; Barbour, *Amazing People!* ch. 22; Fraser Sutherland, *The Monthly Epic* (Markham, ON: Fitzhenry & Whiteside, 1989), 129–49; Chalmers, *Gentleman*, 1–17.

58 'Report of the Committee on Resolutions,' *Printer & Publisher* 2:3 (March 1893), 11; M-H records, b. 3, MacLean Publishing Company, Board of Directors and Shareholders, *Minutes*, vol. 3, 10 May 1929; R. Neil Matheson, 'Thomas Winning Dyas,' *Dictionary of Canadian Biography*, vol. 12 (Toronto: University of Toronto Press, 1990), 285–7; Chalmers, *Gentleman*, 20–1.

59 'Sphinx Club Hailed,' *Printer's Ink* 97:3 (19 October 1916), 76, 81; M-H records, b. 54, f. SS-McClure, several letters; b. 54, f. Mail-&-Empire, F. Munsey to J.B. Maclean, 7 May 1906; b. 50, f. R-Borden, J.B. Maclean to R. Borden, 7 July 1917; J.B. Maclean, 'Sketch of Frank A. Munsey,' *Printer & Publisher* 7:2 (February 1898), 4–5; *Printer & Publisher* 7:3 (March 1898), 19–25; 'The Agency Question,' *Printer & Publisher* 7:11 (November 1898), 6–7; *Printer & Publisher* 17:1 (January 1908), 30–1; 'Northcliffe and Munsey,' *Printer & Publisher* 18:2 (February 1909), 26–8.

60 M-H records, b. 52, f. HT-Hunter/1904–12, H.T. Hunter to J.B. Maclean, 3 March 1904; 'Annual Conference MacLean Publishing Co.,' *Printer & Publisher* 18:1 (January 1909), 26.

61 *Boy's Own Philatelist* 1:1 (December 1897); J.C. Kirkwood, 'Who is Lydiatt?' *Economic Advertising* 11:2 (February 1918), 4–5; 'W.A. Lydiatt,' *Printer & Publisher* 27:2 (February 1918), 23–4; *Marketing* 46:44 (1 November 1941), 1.

62 'W.A. Lydiatt,' 24.

63 W.A. Lydiatt, quoted in 'W.A. Lydiatt,' 23.

64 JCK notebook, 4 April 1903, 75–6; 20 June 1903, 83; 17 January 1904, 146–7; 2 March 1904, 157–9; M-H records, b. 53, f. HC-MacLean/1, J.C. Kirkwood to J.B. Maclean, 26 September 1940.

65 M-H records, b. 53, f. JC-Kirkwood, J.C. Kirkwood, 'My Goods Friends,' enclosed in letter to J.B. Maclean, 31 January 1938; see also ibid., clipping: 'John Kirkwood Honoured,' *MacLean's Weekly* (22 January 1938); JCK notebook, 29 August 1905, 187.
66 See for example JCK notebook, 23 April 1905, 177; 1 January 1911, 290–9; Kirkwood papers, v. 24, f. 24–3, J.C. Kirkwood to K.P. Kirkwood, 15 March 1918; J.C. Kirkwood to K.P. Kirkwood, 9 May 1919; v. 24, f. 24–7, J.C. Kirkwood to K.P. Kirkwood, 24 May 1925; J.C. Kirkwood to K.P. Kirkwood [1932].
67 JCK notebook, 23 August 1905, 192.
68 Kirkwood papers, v. 24, f. 24–3, J.C. Kirkwood to K.P. Kirkwood, 9 August 1916.
69 University of Manitoba Archives, MSS16, Bertram Brooker papers, b. 10, f. 17, draft notes for a speech, 1 October 1927.
70 Bertram Brooker, *Think of the Earth* (Toronto: Nelson, 1936). On his artistic work, see *Provincial Essays* 7 (1989); Carole F. Luff, 'Progress Passing through the Spirit: The Modernist Vision of Bertram Brooker and Lionel LeMoine Fitzgerald as Redemptive Art' (unpublished MA thesis, Carleton University, 1991); Ann Davis, *The Logic of Ecstasy: Canadian Mystical Painting* (Toronto: University of Toronto Press, 1992).
71 Brooker papers, b. 10, f. 18, V. Brooker to D. Reid, 11 October 1972. For an example of his duelling pseudonyms, see The End Man, 'The Copy End,' *Marketing* 23:13 (26 December 1925), 392; Mark E. Ting, 'Hoist the Sales,' *Marketing* 30:4 (16 February 1929), 110.
72 Brooker papers, b. 1, f. 7, E. [J. Somers] to B. Brooker, 25 July 1925; b. 1, f. 16, Brooker diary, 10 March 1920; b. 1, f. 17, Account Book, 1927–30; *Canadian Advertising Data* 3:11 (December 1930), 14–17; Kirkwood papers, v. 24, f. 24–11, 14 February 1930; Surrey, *Copy Technique in Advertising* (New York: McGraw-Hill, 1929); Surrey, *Layout Technique in Advertising* (New York: McGraw Hill, 1930); Dennis Reid, *Bertram Brooker* (Ottawa: National Gallery of Canada, 1979), 7–8.
73 G.D. Taylor and P.A. Baskerville, *A Concise History of Business in Canada* (Toronto: Oxford University Press, 1994), 338.
74 *Census 1931*, vol. 7, T29; see also Elsinore MacPherson, 'Careers of Canadian University Women' (unpublished MA thesis, University of Toronto, 1920), 46; Graham S. Lowe, 'Women, Work, and the Office: The Feminization of Clerical Occupations in Canada, 1901–31,' in *Rethinking Canada*, 2d ed., ed. V. Strong-Boag and A.C. Fellman (Toronto: Copp Clark Pitman, 1991), 269–85.
75 *Census 1931*, vol. 7, T29, T34, T53, T56, T58; Mary Vipond, 'The Image of

Women in Mass Circulation Magazines in the 1920s,' in *The Neglected Majority,* ed. S.M. Trofimenkoff and A. Prentice (Toronto: McClelland & Stewart, 1977), 116–24.

76 Roland Marchand and Jennifer Scanlon have examined the role of women in the American trade by focusing on copywriting, but as Marchand points out, women were far more likely to occupy positions among the clerical and research staff than among the creative and executive staff; Marchand, *American Dream,* 33–5; Scanlon, *Inarticulate Longings: The Ladies' Home Journal, Gender, and the Promises of Consumer Culture* (New York: Routledge, 1995), 169–96.

77 Brooker, 'Forty Years [Pt. 5],' 274; *Marketing* 26:3 (5 February 1927), 97; Roxanne Labrie, 'Whither Goest Thou,' *Marketing* 88:39 (26 September 1983), 27; Tim Falconer, 'A Club of Their Own,' *Marketing* 98:46 (15 November 1993), 48. For Pennell's writing, see for example, 'The Circulation of Canadian Daily Newspapers,' *Printer & Publisher* 29:4 (April 1920), 19; 'Securing National Advertising,' *Marketing* 31:6 (June 1922), 29–31; *Marketing* 25:6 (18 September 1926), 158.

78 *Marketing* 28:11 (26 May 1928), 416; *Lydiatt's Book,* 15th ed. (1927), 312–32.

79 Paul Johnson, 'The Letters of a Young Man to His Dad,' *Economic Advertising* 1:6 (February 1909), 11; Charles C. Nixon, 'Are Women's Magazines Justified?' *Economic Advertising* 7:6 (June 1914), 53–4; Margaret Brown, 'Women Join Movement to Boost Canadian Made Products,' *Marketing* 24:12 (12 June 1926), 416; see also Marchand, *American Dream,* 33–5; Scanlon, *Inarticulate Longings,* 169–96.

80 William Thompson, 'Human Advertising,' *Economic Advertising* 3:2 (February 1910), 14.

81 'The Woman's Viewpoint,' *Economic Advertising* 6:12 (December 1913), 3–5.

82 Eaton records, Ser. 6, b. 1, f. POC-Employment, A.B. Merrill to Eaton Ltd., 26 January 1900; H.[?] to Mr Moreland, 30 January 1900; Merrill to Moreland, 5 February 1900; Ser. 162, b. 1, f. 0–26, clipping: 'Miss Edith Macdonald,' 25 January 1971; 'Mary Etta MacPherson,' *Business Woman* 3:1 (January 1928), 7; Joy L. Santink, *Timothy Eaton and the Rise of His Department Store* (Toronto: University of Toronto Press, 1990), 189–91; Sarah Smith Malino, 'From across the Counter: A Social History of Female Department Store Employees, 1870–1920' (PhD dissertation, Columbia University, 1982); Susan Porter Benson, *Counter Cultures: Saleswomen, Managers, and Customers in American Department Stores, 1890–1940* (Urbana, IL: University of Illinois Press, 1988), 124–76.

83 'Can Men Advertise to Women?' *Marketing* 16:8 (15 April 1922), 316.

84 NAC, MG31 K27, Miriam Sheridan papers, v. 3, f. 3–31, C.W. Sheridan to

M. Marshall, 23 October [1920]; v. 5, f. 5–4, M. Marshall to C.W. Sheridan [20 September 1923]; 'Laree R. Spray,' *Business Woman* 3:9 (September 1928), 6; *Business Woman* 2:1 (January 1927), 10; *Marketing* 27:9 (29 October 1927), 351.

85 Falconer, 'A Club of Their Own,' 48.

86 Labrie, 'Whither Goest Thou,' 27.

87 *Census 1931*, vol. 7, T40, T50; Estella M. Place, 'Woman's Day in Advertising Is Just Dawning,' *Business Woman* 4:5 (May 1929), 8; Mabel Stoakley, 'Advertising Agency Has a Place for Women,' *Canadian Advertising Data* 2:7 (August 1929), 57; *Marketing* 27:13 (24 December 1927), 506; see also Minna Hall Simmons, 'Women in Advertising,' in French, *20th Century Advertising*, 189–200; 'Jane Solicits,' *Business Woman* 2:8 (September 1927), 16.

88 *Census 1931*, vol. 7, T56, T58; Labrie, 'Whither Goest Thou,' 27; John S. Straiton, *Of Women and Advertising* (Toronto: McClelland & Stewart, 1984), 9–18; J. Goodis with G. O'Keefe, *Goodis: Shaking the Canadian Advertising Tree* (Markham, ON: Fitzhenry & Whiteside, 1991), 1.

89 Lears, *Fables of Abundance*, 97–8.

90 'Canadians Win Prizes,' *Economic Advertising* 8:9 (September 1915), 7–11; *Marketing* 26:8 (16 April 1927), 336; 'Harvard Advertising Award,' *Marketing* 28:4 (18 February 1928), 107; Langton Fife, 'Corset Campaign Brings Mailbag Trophy,' *Marketing* 27:11 (26 November 1927), 399.

91 See, for example, the cover of *Economic Advertising* 7:6 (June 1914); Carl Berger, *The Sense of Power: Studies in the Ideas of Canadian Imperialism, 1867–1914* (Toronto: University of Toronto Press, 1970); Wallace Clement, *The Canadian Corporate Elite: An Analysis of Economic Power* (Ottawa: Carleton University Press, 1986), 297–8.

92 Kirkwood papers, v. 24, f. 24–6, J.C. Kirkwood to K.P. Kirkwood, 24 June 1921.

3: A Professional Ideal

1 F.H. Dobbin, 'A Plea for the Advertising Agent,' *Printer & Publisher* 4:10 (October 1895), 10.

2 *Marketing* 21:4 (23 August 1924), 127.

3 'Unique Carnival and Circus Held,' Toronto *World*, 23 April 1915.

4 Richard Surrey [B. Brooker], 'The Copy Outlook for 1924,' *Marketing* 20:1 (12 January 1924), 10–12.

5 Frank Presbrey, *The History and Development of Advertising* (Garden City, NY: Doubleday, Doran, 1929), 211–26; on Barnum generally, see A.H. Saxon, *P.T. Barnum: The Legend and the Man* (New York: Columbia University Press,

1989); Raymond Fitzsimmons, *Barnum in England* (London: Godfrey Bles, 1969).

6   P.T. Barnum, *Struggles and Triumphs: or, Forty Years' Recollections* (New York: American News, 1871); published in Canada as *The Life of Barnum* (Paris, ON: J.S. Brown, [1890?]); 'Advertising as a Fine Art,' *Saturday Night* 1:1 (3 December 1887), 7; Elbert Hubbard, 'The Vice of Being Too Virtuous,' *Economic Advertising* 8:5 (May 1915), 13; UTA, B91–0029, Harold Innis papers, b. 8, f. 1, bibliography on advertising; Innis, 'The Newspaper in Economic Development,' *Journal of Economic History* 2:Suppl. (December 1942), 1–33; Innis, 'A Note on the Advertising Problem,' *Commerce Journal* NS:3 (April 1943), 65–6; Innis, 'Technology and Public Opinion in the United States,' *The Bias of Communication* (Toronto: University of Toronto Press, 1991), 172; see also Jackson Lears, *Fables of Abundance: A Cultural History of Advertising in America* (New York: Basic, 1994), 265–7.

7   'Too Proud to Advertise,' *Marketing* 16:10 (15 May 1922), 432; Richard Surrey [B. Brooker], 'The Copy Outlook for 1924,' *Marketing* 20:1 (12 January 1924), 10–12; C.T. Solomon, 'Advertising Needs Men of Business,' *Canadian Magazine* 17:4 (April 1927), 17; A.J. Denne, 'This Thing Called Advertising,' *Canadian Magazine* 67:5 (June 1932); Karl Bernhardt, 'A Critique of Marketing Techniques,' *Marketing Organization and Technique* (Toronto: University of Toronto Press, 1940), 83–97; see also Roland Marchand, *Advertising the American Dream: Making Way for Modernity, 1920–1940* (Berkeley, CA: University of California Press, 1986), 7–9; Lears, *Fables of Abundance*, 213–15.

8   James H. Young, *Toadstool Millionaires: A Social History of Patent Medicines in America before Federal Regulation* (Princeton, NJ: Princeton University Press, 1961), 212–44; James P. Wood, *The Story of Advertising* (New York: Ronald, 1952), 327–34; Denis Goulet, *Le Commerce des Maladies: La publicité des remèdes au début du siècle* (Quebec: Institut québécois de recherche, 1987), 27–8; Canada, House of Commons, *Debates* (21 February 1907), 3464–5; (15 June 1908), 10551–3; (10 July 1908), 12622–8; Proprietary Medicines Act, 7–8 Edward VII (1908), ch. 56.

9   CPA records, v. 1, Minute Book 1882–1910, 14 February 1890; *Printer & Publisher* 2:5 (May 1893), 2; *Printer & Publisher* 19:4 (April 1910), 47.

10 B.H. Bramble, 'A Space Buyer on Objectionable Advertising,' *Printer & Publisher* 25:9 (September 1916), 17–20; E.H. Macklin, 'Patent Medicine Advertising,' *Printer & Publisher* 22:5 (May 1913), 51.

11 'Toronto Ad Club,' *Economic Advertising* 4:6 (June 1911), 31; 'Missionary Work,' *Economic Advertising* 4:12 (December 1911), 9–11; Toronto *World*, 8 April 1912.

12 'Toronto Ad Club,' *Economic Advertising* 4:6 (June 1911), 32–3.

13 'Ad Clubs and Their Usefulness,' *Economic Advertising* 4:5 (May 1911), 13.

14 'Toronto Ad Club,' *Economic Advertising* 4:6 (June 1911), 31; 'Toronto Ad Club,' *Economic Advertising* 4:10 (October 1911), 42–3; 'Toronto Ad Club,' *Economic Advertising* 4:11 (November 1911), 42–3; 'Missionary Work,' *Economic Advertising* 4:12 (December 1911), 9–11; on Brazil, see A.L. McCredie, 'The Story of the AACA Convention in Dallas,' *Printer & Publisher* 21:6 (June 1912), 1.

15 S.C. Dobbs, 'What the Advertising Clubs Can Do,' *Printer's Ink*, reprinted in *Economic Advertising* 3:4 (April 1910), 12–13; see also 'New Advertising Association,' *Printer & Publisher* 13:10 (October 1904), 10.

16 George French, *20th Century Advertising* (New York: Van Nostrand, 1926), ch. 10.

17 O.C. Pease, 'The Usefulness of Conventions,' *Economic Advertising* 5:5 (May 1912), 19, 21.

18 'The Boston Convention,' *Economic Advertising* 4:8 (August 1911), 39–45; French, *20th Century Advertising*, 122–5.

19 Ronald Fullerton, 'Karl Knies's Theory of Advertising,' 8th Conference on Historical Research in Marketing and Marketing Thought, Kingston, Ontario, May 1997.

20 Jackson Lears talks of this tendency in terms of a 'plain speech' tradition within American advertising; *Fables of Abundance*, 53–63.

21 W.A. Olsen, 'The Death Knell of Untruthful Advertising,' *Economic Advertising* 7:10 (January 1914), 38–40.

22 'Eliminating the Fraud and Fake,' *Economic Advertising* 6:3 (March 1913), 3; see also 'An Advertising Censor Wanted,' *Economic Advertising* 3:11 (November 1910), 4–5; 'The False Advertising Bill,' *Economic Advertising* 7:6 (June 1914), 5; 'New Law,' *Printer & Publisher* 23:6 (June 1914), 53; Canada, House of Commons, *Debates* (8 May 1914), 3466–9. This episode fits with Bennett's other legislative interests during this time; see James Gray, *R.B. Bennett: The Calgary Years* (Toronto: University of Toronto Press, 1991), 113–49.

23 Canada, Senate, *Debates* (15 May 1914), 464.

24 'The False Advertising Bill,' *Economic Advertising* 7:6 (June 1914), 5. The bill became s. 406a of the Revised Statutes of Canada, 1906. Canada, House of Commons, *Debates* (7 May 1914), 3397–8; (8 May 1914), 3466–73, 3480–1; 4–5 George V (1914), ch. 24, s.1.

25 'What's Doing in the Clubs,' *Economic Advertising* 7:1 (January 1914), 28; 'What's Doing in the Clubs,' *Economic Advertising* 8:1 (January 1915), 23; *Marketing* 20:4 (23 February 1924), 127; *Marketing* 26:9 (30 April 1927), 386; Alexander Wilson, 'Advertising and the Law,' *Marketing* 30:9 (27 April

1929), 285–7, 306; 'How Better Business Bureaus Protect Legitimate Enterprise,' *Marketing* 28:2 (21 January 1928), 66–7; *Marketing* 29:3 (4 August 1928), 84.

26 Vancouver City Archives (VCA), Add. Mss. 300, Vancouver Board of Trade, v. 55, Advertising Bureau, Minutes 1920–5, 18 March 1921; 20 March 1922; 21 January 1924; *Marketing* 20:4 (23 February 1924), 127.

27 *Economic Advertising* 4:10 (October 1911), 43; Toronto *World*, 8 April 1912; 'Conventionotes,' *Economic Advertising* 6:7 (July 1913), 37; McCredie, 'AACA Convention,' 1.

28 'The Toronto Convention,' *Economic Advertising* 7:7 (July 1914), 1. The guidelines can be found in George French, *Advertising: The Social and Economic Problem* (New York: Ronald, 1915), 244–58.

29 CPA records, v. 2, Minute Book 1910–9, 6 October 1911; William Findlay, 'Advertising Our Advertising,' *Printer & Publisher* 20:12 (December 1911), 37–8.

30 'Advertising Advertising throughout Canada,' *Printer & Publisher* 21:4 (April 1912), 37–9.

31 Findlay, 'Advertising Advertising,' 39; '95 Daily Newspapers,' *Printer & Publisher* 22:11 (November 1913), 62–3.

32 'Let the Buyer Beware,' Toronto *World*, 13 August 1912.

33 'My Business Is Unique,' Toronto *World*, 12 April 1912.

34 'Be Suspicious,' Toronto *World*, 29 March 1912; see also 'Keep Out!' Toronto *World*, 19 April 1912; 'Count Your Blessings,' Toronto *World*, 24 April 1912.

35 'Keep Out!' Toronto *World*, 19 April 1912; see also Upton Sinclair, *The Jungle* (1906; reprint, New York: New American, 1961); Young, *Toadstool Millionaires*, 239.

36 'Keep Out!' Toronto *World*, 19 April 1912; see also 'Let the Buyer Beware,' Toronto *World*, 13 August 1912; 'A Modern Force in Business,' Toronto *World*, 26 March 1912; 'When the People Refuse to Pay,' Toronto *World*, 30 April 1912.

37 'Your Best Shopping Guide,' Toronto *World*, 16 April 1912; see also 'A Hermit for Five Years,' Toronto *World*, 26 April 1912.

38 'Count Your Blessings,' Toronto *World*, 24 April 1912.

39 'You Can Thank Advertising,' Toronto *World*, 15 March 1912.

40 'Count Your Blessings,' Toronto *World*, 24 April 1912.

41 'Better than Ringing Door-bells,' Toronto *World*, 10 May 1912; 'Lowering the Cost,' Toronto *World*, 7 May 1912; see also Bertram Brooker, 'Crazy Consumers ...!' *Marketing* 27:8 (15 October 1927), 279–80, 300; A.J. Denne, 'This Thing Called Advertising,' *Canadian Magazine* 67:5 (June 1932), 16, 49–50.

42 'You Are on the Bench,' Toronto *World*, 2 April 1912; Daniel Pope and Roland Marchand have found the same ambivalence among American adworkers; Daniel Pope, *The Making of Modern Advertising* (New York: Basic, 1983), 250–1; Marchand, *American Dream*, 52–87.

43 'A Modern Force in Business,' Toronto *World*, 26 March 1912; 'Keep Out!' Toronto *World*, 19 April 1912.

44 'A Modern Force in Business,' Toronto *World*, 26 March 1912; 'My Business Is Unique,' Toronto *World*, 12 April 1912; 'Better than Ringing Door-bells,' Toronto *World*, 10 May 1912; 'When a Man Marries,' Toronto *World*, 23 July 1912.

45 'Advertising Advertising throughout Canada,' *Printer & Publisher* 21:4 (April 1912), 37–9; 'Men and Media,' *Economic Advertising* 5:4 (May 1912), 48.

46 'Report of the Recognition Committee,' *Printer & Publisher* 21:7 (July 1912), 36–7; CPA records, v. 1, 'Minute Book 1882–1910,' 5 June 1913; *Printer & Publisher* 22:7 (July 1913), 54; 'Cashing In,' *Printer & Publisher* 22:9 (September 1913), 62–3; 'An Advertising Advertising Campaign,' *Printer & Publisher* 23:3 (March 1914), 57; 'Report of the Advertising Committee,' *Printer & Publisher* 23:8 (August 1914), 40–1; 'CPA Gives Facts,' *Printer & Publisher* 23:10 (October 1914), 46–7.

47 'CPA Adopted Objectionable Ad Standard,' *Printer & Publisher* 23:8 (August 1914), 72–4; 'Canadian General Advertisers Organizing,' *Printer & Publisher* 23:10 (October 1914), 54; Frank H. Rowe, 'The Status of the Toronto Ad Club,' *Printer's Ink* 97:11 (14 December 1916), 28.

48 See, for instance, Foster papers, v. 17, f. 1570, J.J. Gibbons to E.B. Osler, 4 August 1915.

49 Anson McKim, 'Bank Advertising,' *Printer & Publisher* 17:3 (March 1908), 60–1; 'Financial Advertising,' *Economic Advertising* 1:11 (July 1909), 1; 'Churches Must Advertise More,' *Economic Advertising* 1:6 (February 1909), 20–1; 'Churches Should Advertise,' *Printer & Publisher* 20:3 (March 1911), 52–3; *Printer & Publisher* 7:4 (April 1914), 23; 'Church Must Advertise,' *Economic Advertising* 9:7 (August 1916), 14.

50 'New Era in Advertising,' *Printer & Publisher* 23:11 (November 1914), 28; 'Commission on Government Advertising,' *Printer & Publisher* 23:12 (December 1914), 45.

51 'New Era in Advertising,' *Printer & Publisher* 23:11 (November 1914), 28; 'Continued Success of the Apple Campaign,' *Printer & Publisher* 23:12 (December 1914), 45; Harold C. Lowrey, 'Advertising Campaigns of the Canadian Government,' *Printer's Ink* 97:4 (26 October 1916), 89–99; John C. Kirkwood, 'Canadian Advertising Developments of War-time,' *Economic Advertising* 12:6 (August 1918), 22–6; W.A. Craick, *A History of Canadian*

Journalism II: Last Years of the Canadian Press Association, 1908–1919 (Toronto: Ontario Publishing, 1959), 105–6.

52 CPA records, v. 1, Minute Book 1910–19, 5 December 1910; 'Dominion Government Advertising Campaign,' *Printer & Publisher* 25:4 (April 1916), 45; John M. Imrie, 'How Governments of Canada Use Advertising,' *Printer & Publisher* 26:5 (May 1917), 17.

53 'Agricultural Advertising,' *Printer & Publisher* 24:3 (March 1915), 40; 'Government Advertising Honest Economy,' *Saturday Night* 32:31 (17 May 1919), 1. On civil service reform, see John English, *The Decline of Politics: The Conservatives and the Party System, 1901–1920* (Toronto: University of Toronto Press, 1977), 72–7, 96–101.

54 John M. Imrie, 'How Governments of Canada Use Advertising,' *Printer & Publisher* 26:5 (May 1917), 17.

55 Kirkwood, 'Canadian Advertising Developments,' 22–6; 'Agricultural Advertising,' 40; Lowrey, 'Advertising Campaigns,' 89–99; French, *20th Century Advertising*, 558–62; H.E. Stevenson and C. McNaught, *The Story of Advertising in Canada: A Chronicle of Fifty Years* (Toronto: Ryerson, 1940), 159–85.

56 Foster papers, v. 17, f. 1570, G.E. Foster to R.B. Borden, 2 February 1916; Hamilton Public Library, Hamilton Recruiting League, Microfilm 544, 'Minutes' 1915–17, 7 July 1915, 14 November 1916; 'Recruiting Advertising,' *Printer & Publisher* 25:10 (October 1916), 39; 'When Advertising Has Done Its Utmost,' *Economic Advertising* 10:3 (March 1917), 9–12; R. Matthew Bray, 'Fighting as an Ally: English-Canadian Patriotic Response to the Great War,' *Canadian Historical Review* 61:2 (1980), 141–68; Paul Maroney, 'The Great Adventure: The Context and Ideology of Recruiting in Ontario, 1914–1917,' *Canadian Historical Review* 77:1 (1996), 62–98.

57 CPA records, v. 2, Minute Book 1910–9, 14 March 1916; Foster papers, v. 24, f. 3512, T. White to G.E. Foster, 25 March 1916; 'Launching Canada's Fourth Domestic War Loan,' *Printer & Publisher* 26:10 (October 1917), 17–18; 'Canada Floats Fourth War Loan,' *Printer's Ink* 110:12 (20 September 1917), 51–2.

58 'Commission on Government Advertising,' *Printer & Publisher* 23:12 (December 1914), 45; Craick, *Canadian Journalism II*, 139–40, 153–4.

59 CPA records, v. 2, Minute Book 1910–9, 14 March 1916.

60 Foster papers, v. 17, f. 1570, J.J. Gibbons to G.E. Foster, 23 July 1915; J.J. Gibbons to G.E. Foster, 27 October 1915; 'Dominion Government Advertising,' *Printer & Publisher* 25:4 (April 1916), 45; 'A Second Government Fiasco,' *Economic Advertising* 9:7 (August 1916), 3–7; 'Canadian Government Advertising Third War Loan,' *Printer & Publisher* 26:4 (April 1917), 41.

61 CPA records, v. 2, Minute Book 1910–9, 22 June 1918, 17 July 1918, 30 July
   1918; Craick, *Canadian Journalism II*, 144–5; 'Canada's Victory Loan,'
   Economic Advertising 10:9 (September 1917), 28; 'Launching Canada's
   Fourth Domestic War Loan,' *Printer & Publisher* 26:10 (October 1917), 17–18;
   Stevenson and McNaught, *Story of Advertising*, 177–80.
62 Don Tuck, 'The Might of Advertising,' *Economic Advertising* 8:4 (April 1915),
   1; 'Launching Canada's Fourth Domestic War Loan,' *Printer & Publisher*
   26:10 (October 1917), 18.
63 Lowrey, 'Advertising Campaigns,' 89–99; J.I. Romer, 'How Can We Overcome the Government's Antagonism?' *Printer's Ink* 98:12 (22 March 1917),
   46–50; 'Canada Plans to Float Fourth War Loan,' *Printer's Ink* 100:12 (20 September 1917), 60; Harold C. Lowrey, 'Paid Advertising,' *Printer's Ink* 101:11
   (13 December 1917), 87–8; 'Again Canada Advertises,' *Printer's Ink* 103:11
   (13 June 1918), 38; French, *20th Century Advertising*, 558–62.
64 Stevenson and McNaught, *Story of Advertising*, 185.
65 'The Dignity of Advertising,' *Economic Advertising* 8:5 (April 1915), 7.

4: The Industry Takes Shape

 1 A.R. Coffin, 'The Advertising Agency,' *Printer & Publisher* 15:3 (March
   1906), 11.
 2 Paul Rutherford, *A Victorian Authority* (Toronto: University of Toronto
   Press, 1986), 111.
 3 Ibid., 190–227.
 4 'Report of the Committee on Resolutions,' *Printer & Publisher* 2:3 (March
   1893), 11; 'Printer & Publisher 25 Years Old This Month,' *Printer & Publisher*
   25:5 (May 1916), 17–22.
 5 Editorial, *Economic Advertising* 1:1 (September 1908), 3–4.
 6 'Why Don't You Run Your Own Business?' *Printer & Publisher* 1:6 (October
   1892), 6–7; J.H. Thompson, 'What Does Your Space Cost You?' *Printer &
   Publisher* 4:6 (June 1895), 3; A. McKim, 'The Advertising Agencies,' *Printer
   & Publisher* 6:2 (February 1897), 14–15; F.J. Gibson, 'The Publishers' Duty to
   Advertisers,' *Printer & Publisher* 7:3 (March 1898), 27–30; 'A Symposium of
   Publishers' Opinions,' *Printer & Publisher* 10:11 (November 1901), 14–17;
   Jean de Bonville, *La Presse Québécoise de 1884 à 1914: Genèse d'un média de
   masse* (Quebec: Presses de l'Université Laval, 1988), 124–6.
 7 F.H. Dobbin, 'A Plea,' *Printer & Publisher* 4:10 (October 1893), 10; McKim,
   'The Advertising Agencies,' 14–15.
 8 'Commission to Agents,' *Printer & Publisher* 15:12 (December 1906), 12.
 9 *Printer & Publisher* 17:2 (February 1908), 30; see also 'Advertising Methods

of Toronto Banking Institutions,' *Printer & Publisher* 11:11 (November 1902), 16–17.

10 A. McKim, 'Bank Advertising,' *Printer & Publisher* 17:3 (March 1908), 60–1.

11 *Canadian Newspaper Directory,* 2d ed. (1899), 30.

12 SLA, Sun Life Advertising Committee, Advertising Register 1904–11, 10–17; b. 84, f. 'Early Advertising Ideas,' Desbarats Advertising, estimate for advertising, 23 February 1911.

13 'Guileless and Innocent,' *Printer & Publisher* 3:5 (May 1894), 4; 'The Policy of Maintaining Rates,' *Printer & Publisher* 5:5 (May 1896), 2; Coffin, 'The Advertising Agency,' 11–15.

14 *Printer & Publisher* 2:3 (March 1893), 8; *Printer & Publisher* 10:11 (November 1901), 15; M.A. Jones, letter to the editor, *Printer & Publisher* 12:10 (October 1903), 11.

15 *Printer & Publisher* 13:12 (December 1904), 12–13; see also 'Why Don't You Run Your Own Business?' *Printer & Publisher* 1:6 (October 1892), 6–7; 'Stick to Your Rates,' *Printer & Publisher* 2:5 (May 1893), 9; A.R. Fawcett, 'The Country Editor and the Advertising Agent,' *Printer & Publisher* 2:10 (October 1893), 6–7; *Printer & Publisher* 14:2 (February 1905), 20; W.J. Taylor, 'Newspaper Advertising,' *Printer & Publisher* 14:12 (December 1905), 22–3.

16 *Printer & Publisher* 15:3 (March 1906), 1; see also 'An Absurd Proposition,' *Printer & Publisher* 7:11 (November 1898), 6; 'Advertising Agencies,' *Printer & Publisher* 8:11 (November 1899), 4.

17 P.D. Ross, 'Co-operation among Local Publishers,' *Printer & Publisher* 4:4 (April 1895), 4; 'Policy of Maintaining Rates,' *Printer & Publisher* 5:5 (May 1896), 2; 'A Symposium of Publishers' Opinions,' *Printer & Publisher* 10:11 (November 1901), 14–17; Fawcett, 'The Country Editor,' 6–7; F.J. Gibson, 'The Publishers' Duty to Advertisers,' *Printer & Publisher* 7:3 (March 1898), 27–30; Mr Wood, in *Printer & Publisher* 14:2 (February 1905), 19.

18 Coffin, 'The Advertising Agency,' 14.

19 'Cheap Advertising,' *Printer & Publisher* 4:1 (January 1895), 14; 'The Advertising Agencies,' *Printer & Publisher* 6:2 (February 1897), 14–15; *Printer & Publisher* 11:3 (March 1902), 4; 'Payments for Space in Stock,' *Printer & Publisher* 10:4 (April 1901), 18; Hector Charlesworth, *Candid Chronicles* (Toronto: Macmillan, 1925), 296.

20 Anonymous, in Coffin, 'The Advertising Agency,' 12; see also 'Report of the Committee on Resolutions,' *Printer & Publisher* 2:3 (March 1893), 11; 'Advertising Agencies,' *Printer & Publisher* 8:11 (November 1899), 4; 'Does Foreign Advertising Pay?' *Printer & Publisher* 10:4 (April 1901), 18.

21 H.J. Pettypiece, 'Deadhead Advertising,' *Printer & Publisher* 12:2 (February

1903), 15–16. The practice of price-cutting was common among all branches of commerce at this time. See P.D. Ross, *Retrospects of a Newspaper Person* (Toronto: Oxford University Press, 1931), 32; Michael Bliss, *A Living Profit: Studies in the Social History of Canadian Business, 1883–1911* (Toronto: McClelland & Stewart, 1974), 33–54; David Monod, *Store Wars: Shopkeepers and the Culture of Mass Marketing, 1890–1939* (Toronto: University of Toronto Press, 1996), 230–85.

22 McKim, 'The Advertising Agencies,' 14–15.

23 E. Desbarats, 'The Building Up of a Mutual Service,' *Printer & Publisher* 27:8 (August 1918), 19–20. McKim's client list appears in *Canadian Newspaper Directory*, 2d ed. (1899), 30–3.

24 *Printer & Publisher* 13:2 (February 1904), 9; *Printer & Publisher* 16:2 (February 1907), 8.

25 'The Business of the Modern Newspaper Advertising Agency,' *Canadian Newspaper Directory*, 2d ed. (1899), 33–4.

26 HSC, 2d ed., K38.

27 *Printer & Publisher* 13:2 (February 1904), 9.

28 Ibid., 8–9.

29 CPA records, v. 1, Minute Book 1882–1910, 22 February 1889; CPA, 'Foreign Advertising Rates, 1891,' *Printer & Publisher* 13:11 (November 1904), 8; 'New Schedule of Advertising Rates,' *Printer & Publisher* 13:11 (November 1904), 8–9; 'The Circular on Foreign Advertising,' *Printer & Publisher* 13:12 (December 1904), 12–13; see also Bonville, *La Presse Québécoise*, 124.

30 George Scroggie, 'Some Phases of Advertising,' *Printer & Publisher* 9:2 (February 1900), 16–20; 'A Symposium of Publishers' Opinions,' *Printer & Publisher* 10:11 (November 1901), 14–17; *Printer & Publisher* 17:3 (March 1908), 35; John M. Imrie, 'Fair Play,' *Printer & Publisher* 20:6 (June 1911), 39; Rutherford, *Victorian Authority*, 190–227. On combines, see Bliss, *Living Profit*, 33–54, 139–42; Tom Traves, *The State and Enterprise: Canadian Manufacturers and the Federal Government, 1917–1931* (Toronto: University of Toronto Press, 1979), 73–100.

31 'Advertising Rates,' *Printer & Publisher* 14:2 (February 1905), 13.

32 'The Circular on Foreign Advertising,' *Printer & Publisher* 13:12 (December 1904), 12–13.

33 Ibid., 12–13; 'Advertising Rates,' *Printer & Publisher* 14:2 (February 1905), 13.

34 Pense in *Printer & Publisher* 15:2 (February 1906), 25.

35 Ibid., 20, 25; see also 'Advertising Arena,' *Printer & Publisher* 14:1 (January 1905), 12.

36 *Printer & Publisher* 14:2 (February 1905), 13.

37 Ibid., 22.
38 'The Agency Question,' *Printer & Publisher* 7:11 (November 1898), 6–7; James W. Young, *Advertising Agency Compensation, In Relation to the Total Cost of Advertising* (Chicago: University of Illinois Press, 1933), 38–9; George Britt, *Forty Years – Forty Millions: The Career of Frank A. Munsey* (New York: Farrar & Rinehart, 1935), 101–2; Harold S. Wilson, *McClure's Magazine and the Muckrakers* (Princeton, NJ: Princeton University Press, 1970), 60–5.
39 'Opinions of Canadian Advertising Managers,' *Printer & Publisher* 7:11 (November 1898), 7.
40 Julian Street, 'Agents and Their Fees,' *Profitable Advertising*, reprinted in *Printer & Publisher* 13:11 (November 1904), 9; Daniel Pope, *The Making of Modern Advertising* (New York: Basic, 1983), 154–6.
41 Young, *Agency Compensation*, 32–5; Pope, *Making of Modern Advertising*, 156–7.
42 CPA records, v. 1, Minute Book 1882–1910, 2 February 1905; 'Commission to Advertising Agents,' *Printer & Publisher* 14:2 (February 1905), 20.
43 J.J. Gibbons, 'The Agents Respond,' *Printer & Publisher* 14:4 (April 1905), 20–1.
44 Coffin, 'The Advertising Agency,' 13; see also 'Weekly Section,' *Printer & Publisher* 16:2 (February 1907), 17.
45 Young, *Agency Compensation*, 37–8.
46 'Commission to Advertising Agents,' *Printer & Publisher* 14:2 (February 1905), 22.
47 'Advertising Rates,' *Printer & Publisher* 14:2 (February 1905), 13; see also 'Weekly Section,' *Printer & Publisher* 16:2 (February 1907), 10.
48 'Advertising Rates,' *Printer & Publisher* 14:2 (February 1905), 13.
49 M-H records, b. 52, f. HT-Hunter/1904–12, H.T. Hunter to J.B. Maclean, 3 March 1904; *Printer & Publisher* 16:2 (February 1907), 10; *Printer & Publisher* 26:4 (April 1917), 24.
50 'A New Association,' *Printer & Publisher* 14:6 (June 1905), 14; 'Weekly Section,' *Printer & Publisher* 16:2 (February 1907), 10.
51 'A Queer Agency,' *Printer & Publisher* 1:6 (October 1892), 8; 'Fake Advertising Agencies,' *Printer & Publisher* 2:10 (October 1893), 5; *Printer & Publisher* 15:2 (February 1906), 20; 'Define the Agencies,' *Printer & Publisher* 15:11 (November 1909), 17; CPA records, v. 2, Recognition Committee, Minute Book 1910–9, 25 February 1913; 'Newspapers Sue Agency for Non-Payment,' *Economic Advertising* 10:2 (February 1917), 24.
52 'Commission to Advertising Agents,' *Printer & Publisher* 14:2 (February 1905), 20; 'The Manufacturers and the Press,' *Printer & Publisher* 15:1 (January 1906), 25.

53 J.J. Gibbons, 'The Arrangement between the Agents and the Publishers,'
    Printer & Publisher 17:2 (February 1908), 32f–g; F.A. Rowlatt, 'The Advertising
    Agency,' *Economic Advertising* 1:2 (August 1909), 10; see also CPA records,
    v. 2, Recognition Committee, Minute Book 1910–9, 16 November 1916.
54 *Printer & Publisher* 14:6 (June 1905), 14.
55 See, for instance, 'Atlantic Pulp Directors,' *Printer & Publisher* 11:10
    (October 1902), 17; Desbarats, 'Mutual Service,' 19–20.
56 J.F. MacKay, 'The Recognition Committee,' *Printer & Publisher* 20:11
    (November 1911), 33–6. On the influence of the *Star*, see A.H.U. Colquhoun,
    'The Man Who Made the Montreal Star,' *Printer & Publisher* 4:4 (April 1895),
    6–7; 'Advertising Agencies Agreement,' *Printer & Publisher* 19:6 (June 1910),
    37; Bonville, *La Presse Québécoise*, 220–2.
57 W.W. Butcher, *Canadian Newspaper Directory* (London: Speaker, 1886), [2];
    'Annual Meeting of the CPA,' *Printer & Publisher* 19:6 (June 1910), 25;
    MacKay, 'The Recognition Committee,' *Printer & Publisher* 20:11 (November
    1911), 33–6.
58 *Printer & Publisher* 2:10 (October 1893), 1; *Printer & Publisher* 2:3 (March
    1893), 11.
59 *Printer & Publisher* 16:3 (March 1907), 23.
60 Gibbons, 'The Arrangement,' 32f–g; Rowlatt, 'The Advertising Agency,' 10.
61 John M. Imrie, 'Fair Play,' *Printer & Publisher* 20:6 (June 1911), 37–9.
62 *Printer & Publisher* 16:4 (April 1907), 13.
63 Imrie, 'Fair Play,' 37–9.
64 JCK notebook, 8 January 1905. On Gibbons and McClary, see 'The Advertis-
    ing Arena,' *Printer & Publisher* 12:11 (November 1903), 12; Bertram Brooker,
    'Forty Years of Canadian Advertising [Pt. 5],' *Marketing* 21:10 (15 November
    1924), 274, 278.
65 'Annual Report,' *Printer & Publisher* 18:5 (May 1905), 9; Gibbons, 'The
    Arrangement,' 32f–g.
66 'Agreement between the Canadian Press Association and the Canadian
    Association of Advertising Agencies,' s. 13, *Printer & Publisher* 16:4 (April
    1907), 12–13.
67 Ibid., s. 13.
68 C.A. Abraham, 'Advertising in Smaller Provincial Dailies,' *Printer & Pub-
    lisher* 6:12 (December 1897), 4; 'Departmental Store Ads,' *Printer & Publisher*
    11:4 (April 1902), 4; W.G. Colgate, 'The Problem of the Local Advertiser,'
    Printer & Publisher 17:12 (December 1908), 24–5; *Economic Advertising* 7:4
    (April 1914), 9; Bliss, *Living Profit*, 38–40; Monod, *Store Wars*, 195–229; Joy L.
    Santink, *Timothy Eaton and the Rise of His Department Store* (Toronto: Univer-
    sity of Toronto Press, 1990), 203–22.

69 'Daily Section Report,' *Printer & Publisher* 17:3 (March 1908), 34–5; Imrie, 'Fair Play,' 37–9.

70 'Define the Agencies,' *Printer & Publisher* 15:11 (November 1906), 17; *Printer & Publisher* 20:11 (November 1911), 34.

71 W.B. O'Beirne, 'Daily Section Report,' *Printer & Publisher* 17:3 (March 1908), 34–5; 'Advertising Regulations,' *Printer & Publisher* 17:10 (October 1908), 26–7; 'Our Relations with the Advertising Agencies,' *Printer & Publisher* 21:7 (July 1912), 40.

72 *Printer & Publisher* 19:6 (June 1910), 31, 37; 'Small City Dailies,' *Printer & Publisher* 23:5 (May 1914), 84; W.A. Craick, *A History of Canadian Journalism II: Last Years of the Canadian Press Association, 1908–1919* (Toronto: Ontario Publishing, 1959), 35–6, 169–70.

73 Gibbons, 'The Arrangement,' 32f–g.

74 Ibid., 32f–g; 'Daily Section Report,' *Printer & Publisher* 17:3 (March 1908), 34–5; Imrie, 'Fair Play,' 37–9.

75 *Printer & Publisher* 16:2 (February 1907), 7–8, 18; 'Circulation Statements: Falsifiers and Verifiers,' *Printer & Publisher* 23:1 (January 1914), 64–6.

76 'The Weekly Section,' *Printer & Publisher* 18:4 (April 1909), 18–24; 'Annual Report,' *Printer & Publisher* 18:5 (May 1909), 9; CPA records, v. 1, Minute Book 1910–9, 2 September 1910; Imrie, 'Fair Play,' 37–9; MacKay, 'The Recognition Committee,' 33–6.

77 Stephenson and McNaught, Bonville, and Sotiron make no reference to this agreement; it was drafted outside the time period covered by Rutherford's *A Victorian Authority.*

78 *Toronto City Directory* (Toronto: Might, 1905), 1271–2; CPA records, v. 2, Recognition Committee, Minute Book 1910–9, 21 June 1910.

79 'Advertising Rates,' *Printer & Publisher* 14:2 (February 1905), 13; 'Men and Media,' *Economic Advertising* 6:8 (August 1913), 35; 'Men and Media,' *Economic Advertising* 6:10 (October 1913), 39; 'CPA to Have Permanent Assistant Manager,' *Economic Advertising* 9:6 (June 1916), 13–15; Craick, *Canadian Journalism II*, 27–8, 50, 60–1.

80 *Printer & Publisher* 23:10 (October 1914), 54; Tom Blakely, 'Industry's Marquis of Queensberry,' *Marketing* 88:39 (26 September 1983), 23–4; S.D. Clark, *The Canadian Manufacturers' Association: A Study in Collective Bargaining and Political Pressure* (Toronto: University of Toronto Press, 1939).

81 W.A. Lydiatt, *Lydiatt's Book*, 7th ed. (1920), 272–3.

82 A.J. Denne, 'How an Agency Buys Space,' *Economic Advertising* 24:7 (July 1915), 25–6.

83 Hal Donly, in *Printer & Publisher* 24:11 (November 1915), 25.

84 'The Circulation Question,' *Printer & Publisher* 5:5 (May 1896), 10.
85 'Views on the Auditing of Canadian Circulations,' *Printer & Publisher* 24:8 (August 1915), 22–6; 'High Explosives in the Battle for Advertising,' *Printer & Publisher* 24:8 (August 1915), 37; 'The Association of Canadian Advertisers,' *Printer & Publisher* 25:5 (May 1916), 24.
86 CPA records, v. 1, Minutes 1910–9, 28 May 1915; 'Views on the Auditing of Canadian Circulation,' *Printer & Publisher* 24:8 (August 1915), 22; 'Finding Out What We Get for Our Money,' *Economic Advertising* 9:10 (October 1916), 32.
87 'Views on the Auditing of Canadian Circulation,' *Printer & Publisher* 24:8 (August 1915), 22; Charles O. Bennett, *Facts without Opinion: Fifty Years of the Audit Bureau of Circulations* (Chicago: ABC, 1965), 39–70.
88 'Finding Out What We Get for Our Money,' *Economic Advertising* 9:10 (October 1916), 23, 32; 'Canadian Advisory Board for ABC,' *Printer & Publisher* 25:4 (April 1916), 45; Bennett, *Facts without Opinion*, 62–3.
89 'Finding Out What We Get for Our Money,' *Economic Advertising* 9:10 (October 1916), 32; 'ABC in Canada,' *Printer & Publisher* 26:7 (July 1917), 32; *Marketing* 20:12 (14 June 1924), 378–9; Craick, *Canadian Journalism II*, 107.
90 'Views on the Auditing of Canadian Circulations,' *Printer & Publisher* 24:8 (August 1915), 23; 'ACA to Combine Reports with ABC,' *Economic Advertising* 9:2 (February 1916), 32–4; Craick, *Canadian Journalism II*, 121.
91 'Finding Out What We Get for Our Money,' *Economic Advertising* 9:10 (October 1916), 31.
92 *Printer & Publisher* 25:5 (May 1916), 24.
93 Ibid., 32; see also 'Association of Canadian Advertisers Hold Third Annual Meeting,' *Economic Advertising* 9:10 (October 1916), 7, 9.
94 *Printer & Publisher* 16:2 (February 1907), 15; George French, *20th Century Advertising* (New York: Van Nostrand, 1926), 141–52.
95 Desbarats Advertising Agency, *The Desbarats Newspaper Directory*, 2d ed. (Montreal: Desbarats, 1912), 4; Don Tuck, 'Agency Commission,' *Economic Advertising* 5:3 (March 1912), 7–11.
96 'Two Agencies Inaugurate Service Charge,' *Printer & Publisher* 20:6 (June 1911), 51; 'Announcement,' *Economic Advertising* 6:11 (November 1913), 24; 'Agents for Advertisers,' *Printer & Publisher* 24:7 (July 1915), 34.
97 *Printer & Publisher* 21:7 (July 1912), 39.
98 'Publisher Should Not Pay,' *Marketing* 15:8 (15 April 1921), 254–8.
99 CPA records, v. 1, Minute Book 1910–9, 19 April 1918; 'The Manufacturers and the Press,' *Printer & Publisher* 15:1 (January 1906), 25; 'Agency Commission,' *Economic Advertising* 5:3 (March 1912), 7–11.

100 'Agents for the Advertisers,' *Printer & Publisher* 24:7 (July 1915), 34.

101 'Salada Sticks to Same Style Copy,' *Marketing* 28:4 (18 February 1928), 110.

102 'Agency Commission,' *Printer & Publisher* 24:7 (July 1915), 44; *Printer & Publisher* 22:1 (January 1913), 64; 'Association of Canadian Advertisers Severs Relations,' *Printer's Ink* 99:7 (17 May 1917), 90–2. During this debate the organization of the CP wire service was stalled because the same group refused to divide costs equally with their colleagues in western Canada; M.E. Nichols, *(CP) The Story of the Canadian Press* (Toronto: Ryerson, 1948), 74–9, 124–30.

103 'Split Developing in Canadian Press Association,' *Printer & Publisher* 25:7 (July 1916), 31.

104 'The Fight between Toronto Dailies and ACA,' *Printer & Publisher* 26:4 (April 1917), 23–6; 'ACA after Toronto Publishers,' *Printer & Publisher* 25:11 (November 1916), 28.

105 'The Fight between Toronto Dailies and the ACA,' *Printer & Publisher* 26:4 (April 1917), 25; 'A Dangerous Situation,' *Economic Advertising* 10:3 (March 1917), 3; 'Trouble in Toronto Terminated,' *Economic Advertising* 12:10 (December 1918), 21; 'Toronto Dailies to Pay Agency Commissions,' *Printer's Ink* 105:11 (12 December 1918), 84.

106 'Split Developing in the Canadian Press Association,' *Printer & Publisher* 25:7 (July 1916), 31; Craick, *Canadian Journalism II*, 117–18, 134–7, 165–9.

107 'Move to Clean Up Agency Situation,' *Marketing* 15:7 (1 April 1921), 213.

108 Ibid., 214; CPA records, v. 2, Recognition Committee, Minute Book 1910–9, 19 April 1918; Interim, 'Les Journaux qui disparaissent,' *La Clé d'Or* 1:10 (December 1926), 273–4.

109 'The Agents' Toll,' *Marketing* 15:6 (15 March 1921), 194.

110 Ibid., 194; 'Move to Clean Up Agency Situation,' *Marketing* 15:7 (1 April 1921), 213.

111 *Who's Who in Canadian Advertising*, 2d ed. (Toronto: Lydiatt, 1915), 34–70.

112 'Move to Clean Up Agency Situation,' *Marketing* 15:7 (1 April 1921), 213; see also 'Payment of Agencies,' *Marketing* 14:15 (1 November 1920), 649.

113 'Move to Clean Up Agency Situation,' *Marketing* 15:7 (1 April 1921), 213–14, 236–7.

114 Ibid., 214.

115 'Why Not Better Agency Relations?' *Marketing* 15:9 (1 May 1921), 300–3; 'Daily Newspaper Publishers Reaffirm Confidence in Agency System,' *Marketing* 16:12 (15 June 1922), 492.

116 'Recognition of Agencies,' *Printer & Publisher* 29:5 (May 1920), 49; 'Decidedly Opposed to Rebating,' *Printer & Publisher* 31:5 (May 1922), 52–4; 'Meeting at Vancouver,' *Printer & Publisher* 33:6 (June 1924), 42–3; 'First

Annual Convention of CNNPA,' *Printer & Publisher* 31:5 (May 1922), 52–4; Craick, *Canadian Journalism II*, 186–8, 201–4.

117 Ron Verzuh, *Radical Rag: The Pioneer Labour Press in Canada* (Ottawa: Steel Rail 1988).

118 *Canadian Magazine* 8:5 (March 1897), 466.

119 CPA records, v. 2, Recognition Committee, Minute Book 1910–9, 4 July 1913; 'Relations with Agencies,' *Printer & Publisher* 23:7 (July 1914), 50.

120 The thesis is implicit throughout their book, *Story of Advertising*, but see especially pages 18–35 and 337–53. See also Rowlatt, 'The Advertising Agency,' 9.

121 Bonville, *La Presse Québécoise*, 360–1.

5: Copywriting, Psychology, and the Science of Advertising

1 'Trailblazing,' *Economic Advertising* 4:10 (October 1911), 5.

2 E. Desbarats, 'The Building Up of Mutual Service,' *Printer & Publisher* 27:8 (August 1918), 19–20; Bertram Brooker, 'Forty Years of Canadian Advertising,' *Marketing* 20:9 (3 May 1924), 281–4; Brooker, 'Forty Years of Canadian Advertising,' *Marketing* 20:13 (28 June 1924), 447–8; Frank Presbrey, *The History and Development of Advertising* (Garden City, NY: Doubleday, Doran, 1929), 244–52; William Leiss et al., *Social Communication in Advertising: Persons, Products, and Images of Well-Being* (Toronto: Methuen, 1986) 123–4.

3 Jackson Lears, *Fables of Abundance: A Cultural History of Advertising in America* (New York: Basic, 1994), 53.

4 P.T. Barnum, *Struggles and Triumphs: or, Forty Years' Recollections* (New York: American News Company, 1871), 76.

5 Ibid., 125–6; Neil Harris, *Humbug: The Art of P.T. Barnum* (Boston: Little, Brown, 1973), 53–5; Thomas P. Kelley, Jr, *The Fabulous Kelley: Canada's King of the Medicine Men* (Don Mills, ON: General, 1974); Brooks McNamara, *Step Right Up! An Illustrated History of the American Medicine Show* (Garden City, NY: Doubleday, 1976), 1–18.

6 Barnum, *Struggles and Triumphs*, 130; see also Harris, *Humbug*, 62–7.

7 Barnum, *Struggles and Triumphs*, 125.

8 John E. Powers cited in J.K. Fraser, 'Wanted – A Plainer Advertising Diet,' *Marketing* 29:12 (8 December 1928), 378; Presbrey, *History*, 302–9; Daniel Pope, *The Making of Modern Advertising* (New York: Basic, 1983), 133–5, 237–42; Stephen Fox, *The Mirror Makers: A History of American Advertising and Its Creators* (New York: Morrow, 1984), 25–7.

9 Merle Curti, 'The Changing Concept of Human Nature in the Literature of American Advertising,' *Business History Review* 41 (1967), 335–57.

10 William Leach, *Land of Desire: Merchants, Power, and the Rise of a New American Culture* (New York: Pantheon, 1993), 153–90; Laurence Levine, *Highbrow/Lowbrow: The Emergence of Cultural Hierarchy in America* (Cambridge, MA: Harvard University Press, 1988), 85–168.

11 On Canadian evangelicalism, see Michael Gauvreau, 'Protestantism Transformed,' in *The Canadian Protestant Experience, 1760–1990*, ed. G. Rawlyk (Burlington, ON: Welch, 1990), 48–97; David Marshall, *Secularizing the Faith: Canadian Protestant Clergy and the Crisis of Belief, 1850–1940* (Toronto: University of Toronto Press, 1992), 26–30. On the religious inclinations of Toronto businessmen, see Phyllis D. Airhart, *Serving the Present Age: Revivalism, Progressivism, and the Methodist Tradition in Canada* (Montreal: McGill-Queen's University Press, 1992), 123–41; Gale Wills, *A Marriage of Convenience: Business and Social Work in Toronto, 1918–1957* (Toronto: University of Toronto Press, 1995), 33–55; C. Armstrong and H.V. Nelles, *The Revenge of the Methodist Bicycle Company: Sunday Streetcars and Municipal Reform in Toronto, 1888–1897* (Toronto: Peter Martin, 1977), 4–7; Angela E. Davis, 'Art and Work,' *Journal of Canadian Studies* 27:2 (1992), 22–36.

12 John MacDonald, quoted in Hugh Johnston, *A Merchant Prince: Life of Hon. Senator John MacDonald* (Toronto: Briggs, 1893), 107–8, 118–24.

13 Eaton records, Ser. 162, b. 1, f. O-38, T. Eaton to unknown, c. 1890. On Eaton's, see Joy L. Santink, *Timothy Eaton and the Rise of His Department Store* (Toronto: University of Toronto Press, 1990), especially 119–21; Mary Etta Macpherson, *Shopkeepers to a Nation: The Eatons* (Toronto: McClelland & Stewart, 1963).

14 Airhart, *Serving the Present Age*, 122–41; see also N. Christie and M. Gauvreau, *A Full Orbed Christianity: The Protestant Churches and Social Welfare in Canada, 1900–1940* (Toronto: University of Toronto Press, 1996), 2–36, 44–6.

15 'The New Code of Advertising Morals,' *Economic Advertising* 6:7 (July 1913), 38; see also Pope, *Making of Modern Advertising*, 177–80, 195–9.

16 Association of Canadian Advertisers, 'Standard of Advertising,' *Economic Advertising* 9:10 (October 1916), 2.

17 'The Toronto Convention,' *Economic Advertising* 7:7 (July 1914), 1.

18 Presbrey, *History*, 320–1.

19 J.S. Robertson, 'Ad Display,' *Printer & Publisher* 10:3 (March 1901), 27.

20 Montreal *Star*, 10 January 1869.

21 James H. Imrie, 'Putting the Brakes on American Competition,' *Economic Advertising* 7:6 (June 1916), 11; S. Roland Hall, *The Advertising Handbook*, 2d ed. (New York: McGraw-Hill, 1930), 268; Paul Rutherford, *A Victorian Authority: The Daily Press in Late Nineteenth-Century Canada* (Toronto:

University of Toronto Press, 1982), 51–7, 64–5; Jean de Bonville, *La Presse Québécoise de 1884 à 1914: Genèse d'un média de masse* (Quebec: Presses de l'Université Laval, 1988), 88–155.

22 'Advertising as a Fine Art,' *Saturday Night* 1:1 (3 December 1887), 7. See also *Saturday Night* 1:1–8 (December 1887–January 1888); Morris Wolfe, *A Saturday Night Scrapbook* (Toronto: New Press, 1973), 1.

23 'Advertising as a Fine Art,' *Saturday Night* 1:3 (17 December 1887), 3; *Saturday Night* 1:5 (31 December 1887), 6.

24 *Toronto City Directory 1893* (Toronto: Might, 1893), 1403.

25 'The ABC of Advertising,' *Canadian Advertiser* 1:1 (June 1893), 4.

26 Barnum, *Struggles and Triumphs*, 121.

27 'The ABC of Advertising,' *Canadian Advertiser* 1:1 (June 1893), 4.

28 Ibid., 4–5.

29 Ibid., 4–5.

30 Ibid., 5.

31 Harold Innis, 'Foreword,' in *Marketing Organization and Technique*, ed. J. McKee (Toronto: University of Toronto Press, 1940), xv; Lears, *Fables of Abundance*, 79–81.

32 'The ABC of Advertising,' *Canadian Advertiser* 1:1 (June 1893), 5.

33 Albert D. Lasker, *The Lasker Story: As He Told It*, ed. S.R. Bernstein (Lincolnwood, IL: NTC Business Books, 1987), 19–22; Fox, *Mirror Makers*, 50–2.

34 Fox, *Mirror Makers*, 50–2.

35 This contrast was noted by Fox, *Mirror Makers*, 42–9.

36 NAC, MG30 D111, J.E.H. MacDonald papers, b. 3, f. 3–7, lecture notes, 15 December 1922; Mark E. Ting [B. Brooker], 'Hoist the Sales!' *Marketing* 31:10 (9 November 1929), 276.

37 E.E. Calkins and R. Holden, *Modern Advertising* (New York: Appleton, 1905); for a more detailed discussion of Calkins, see Michele H. Bogart, *Advertising, Artists, and the Borders of Art* (Chicago: University of Chicago Press, 1995), 209–12; Fox, *Mirror Makers*, 40–8.

38 The earliest use of the word 'psychology' I have noticed appeared in 1904; J.J. Gibbons, 'Mr Post Answered,' *Printer & Publisher* 13:9 (September 1904), 13.

39 On Wundt and his contributions, see Edwin G. Boring, *A History of Experimental Psychology* (New York: Century, 1929), 310–44; George Humphrey, 'Wilhelm Wundt: The Great Master,' in *Historical Roots of Contemporary Psychology*, ed. B.B. Wolman (New York: Harper & Row, 1968), 275–97; G.A.Kimble and K. Schlesinger, *Topics in the History of Psychology*, vol. 1 (Hillsdale, NJ: Erblaum, 1985), 11–12.

40 Quentin J. Schultze, '"An Honourable Place": The Quest for Professional

Advertising Education, 1900–1917,' *Business History Review* 56:1 (Spring 1982), 17–20; Thomas M. Nelson, 'Psychology at Alberta,' in *History of Academic Psychology in Canada*, ed. M.J. Wright and C.R. Myers (Toronto: C.J. Hogrefe, 1982), 195. On eugenics in Canada, see Angus McLaren, *Our Own Master Race* (Toronto: McClelland & Stewart, 1990).

41 Harlow Gale, *Psychological Studies* #1 (Minneapolis: the author, 1900), 39–69.

42 Gale, *Studies*, 59–67; E.K. Strong, Jr, 'Application of the "Order of Merit Method" to Advertising,' *Journal of Philosophy, Psychology, and Scientific Methods* 8:21 (October 1911), 600–11; Henry F. Adams, 'The Relative Memory Value of Duplication and Variation in Advertising,' *Journal of Philosophy, Psychology, and Scientific Methods* 13:6 (March 1916), 141–52.

43 Gale, *Studies*, 59.

44 Walter Dill Scott, *The Theory of Advertising* (Boston: Small, Maynard, 1904); Peggy Kreshel, 'Advertising Research in the Pre-Depression Years,' *Journal of Current Issues and Research in Advertising* 15:1 (Spring 1993), 59–64.

45 Scott, *Theory*, 39–40.

46 Ibid., 47–60, 208–28; David P. Kuna, 'The Concept of Suggestion in the Early History of Advertising Psychology,' *Journal of the History of the Behavioural Sciences* 12 (1976), 347–53.

47 Scott, *Theory*, 68; see also 74–5.

48 Ibid., 52; see also Kuna, 'Concept of Suggestion,' 348–50.

49 Scott, *Theory*, 1–2.

50 Ibid., 204.

51 John B. Watson, *Behaviorism* (Chicago: University of Chicago Press, 1924), 3–5; David Cohen, *J.B. Watson: The Founder of Behaviourism* (London: Routledge & Kegan Paul, 1979), 82–112; John M. O'Donnell, *The Origins of Behaviorism: American Psychology, 1870–1920* (New York: New York University Press, 1985), 179–208.

52 On copy appeals, see Hollingsworth, 'Judgments of Persuasiveness,' *Psychological Review* 18:4 (July 1911), 234–56. Each of the psychologists named eventually collected his articles in books: Hollingsworth, *Advertising and Selling* (New York: Appleton, 1913); Hollingsworth et al., *Advertising: Its Principles and Practice* (New York: Ronald, 1915); Starch, *Advertising* (Chicago: Scott, Foresman, 1914); Adams, *Advertising and Its Mental Laws* (New York: Macmillan, 1920); Starch, *Principles of Advertising* (Chicago: Shaw, 1923); Strong, *Psychology of Selling and Advertising* (New York: McGraw-Hill 1925).

53 Bruce Bliven, 'Can Your Goods Sell to the "Subconscious" Mind?' *Printer's Ink* 102:13 (28 May 1918), 3–8, 92–6.

54 Hollingsworth, 'Judgments of Persuasiveness,' 234–56; Adams, *Advertising*, 317–8.

55 E.F. Scott, 'Some Doubts about Psychology,' *Canadian Journal of Religious Thought* 1 (1924), 10. On psychology in Canada, see M.J. Wright and C.R. Myers, eds., *History of Academic Psychology in Canada* (Toronto: C.J. Hogrefe, 1982); Donald O. Hebb, 'Chancellor Hebb Describes Psychological Research at McGill,' in *The McGill You Knew*, ed. E.A. Collard (Don Mills, ON: Longman, 1975), 166–8; E.D. MacPhee, *Footsteps* (Vancouver: Versatile, 1978), 50–62; Stanley B. Frost, *McGill University: For the Advancement of Learning: Volume II, 1895–1971* (Montreal: McGill-Queen's University Press, 1984), 147–8; Michael Gauvreau, 'Philosophy, Psychology, and History: George Sidney Brett and the Quest for a Social Science at the University of Toronto, 1910–1940,' Canadian Historical Association *Historical Papers* (1988), 209–36; A.B. McKillop, *Matters of Mind: The University in Ontario, 1791–1951* (Toronto: University of Toronto Press, 1994), 486–94.

56 Fox, *Mirror Makers*, 63–5.

57 Ibid., 63–5, 70; Curti, 'Human Nature,' 334–57.

58 Scott, *Theory*, 211; Scott, *The Psychology of Advertising* (Boston: Small, Maynard, 1908), 186–7. On the piano trade, see H.E. Stephenson and C. McNaught, *The Story of Advertising in Canada* (Toronto: Ryerson, 1940), 186–8; Frances Roback, 'Advertising Canadian Pianos and Organs, 1850–1914,' *Material History Bulletin* 20 (Fall 1984), 31–43.

59 'Strategy in Advertising,' *Economic Advertising* 4:11 (November 1911), 1.

60 'Straight Talks: What's In a Name?' *Economic Advertising* 1:1 (September 1908), 3–4.

61 T.J. Stewart, 'Sentiment or Logic,' *Economic Advertising* 2:5 (January 1910), 8.

62 'The Fundamental Essential,' *Economic Advertising* 3:2 (February 1910), 6–7.

63 'The Advertising Value of Sentiment,' *Economic Advertising* 2:5 (January 1910), 22.

64 William Leiss et al. argue that these ideas became implicit in actual ads after 1890; *Social Communication in Advertising*, 270–80.

65 T.J. Tobin, 'Advertised Goods Preferred,' *Economic Advertising* 1:1 (September 1908), 27–9.

66 'Increasing the Value of the Advertising Columns,' *Printer & Publisher* 19:5 (May 1910), 24–5.

67 Presbrey, *History*, 544; George French, *20th Century Advertising* (New York: Van Nostrand, 1926); *Marketing* 30:6 (16 March 1929), 166.

68 George French, quoted in T.J. Stewart, 'The Science of Advertising,' *Economic Advertising* 1:2 (October 1908), 38–9.

69 Rous & Mann Limited, 'The Artist and the Businessman,' Toronto *Star*, 24 November 1913.

70 Stewart, 'Science of Advertising,' 38–9.

71 Ibid., 39.

72 Michael Bliss, *A Living Profit: Studies in the Social History of Canadian Business, 1883–1911* (Toronto: McClelland & Stewart, 1974), 116–19.

73 S. Roland Hall, *The Advertising Handbook*, 2d ed. (New York: McGraw-Hill, 1930), 231–2; Carl Richard Greer, *Advertising and Its Mechanical Reproduction* (New York: Tudor, 1931), v–vii; Daniel Starch, *Advertising* (Chicago: Scott, Foresman, 1920), 106–16; Adams, *Advertising and Its Mental Laws*, 63–4, 88–90, 120–1, 221–4.

74 Gale, *Studies*, 51–5; 'Annual Report of the Canadian Press Association,' *Printer & Publisher* 18:5 (May 1909), 16.

75 Charles S. Ricker, 'Oracle on the Future Copywriter,' *Economic Advertising* 4:2 (February 1911), 37.

76 *Lydiatt's Book*, 5th ed. (1918), 261.

77 *Canadian Newspaper Directory*, 7th ed. (1911), xvi.

78 *Economic Advertising* 5:7 (July 1912), 34.

79 Herbert N. Casson, 'Scientific Management in the Sales Department,' *Economic Advertising* 4:12 (December 1911), 13–15; 'Why Advertising Is Not Guaranteed,' *Economic Advertising* 3:10 (October 1910), 7.

80 Deborah J. Coon, '"Not a Creature of Reason:" The Alleged Impact of Watsonian Behaviorism on Advertising in the 1920s,' in *Modern Perspectives on John B. Watson and Classical Behaviorism*, ed. J.T. Todd and E.K. Morris (Westport, CT: Greenwood, 1994), 37–63; see also Curti, 'Human Nature,' 349; Kuna, 'Concept of Suggestion,' 353.

81 For Brett, see *Printer & Publisher* 33:6 (June 1924), 39; Brett, 'Some Beliefs about Psychology,' *Canadian Journal of Religious Thought* 1:6 (1924), 473–80. For Bridges, see 'Valuable Instruction,' *Printer & Publisher* 32:9 (September 1923), 48–50; *Marketing* 19:9 (3 November 1923), 270; *Printer & Publisher* 32:11 (November 1923), 58, 61; Bridges, *Psychology Normal and Abnormal* (New York: Appleton, 1930); Bridges, *Personality, Many in One: An Essay in Individual Psychology* (Boston: Stratford, 1932). For MacPhee, see Association of Canadian Advertisers, *Proceedings* (Toronto: ACA, 1928); MacPhee, *Footsteps*, 50–62.

82 H.J. Dalzell, letter to the editor, *Marketing* 18:2 (27 January 1923), 78; T.D. Rimmer, 'When You've Run through All Your Brain Waves,' *Marketing* 31:6 (14 September 1929), 145.

83 Curti, 'Human Nature,' 334–57.

84 W.A. Dutton, letter to the editor, *Marketing* 22:8 (18 April 1925), 248.

85 French, *20th Century Advertising*, 59–60.
86 Brooker papers, b. 7, f. 1, Richard Surrey [B. Brooker], 'Mrs Legion's Affections,' undated typescript copy. Apparently the story was never published; see b. 1, f. 12, A.R.M., 'Reader's Report: Mrs Legion's Affections,' n.d.
87 Richard Surrey [B. Brooker], 'Shunning Shakespeare,' *Printer's Ink* (November 1925), 17–20; see also Surrey, 'What Should Copy Writers Read?' *Printer's Ink* (15 March 1923).
88 Philip E. Spane [B. Brooker], 'Make Advertising Believable,' *Marketing* 28:3 (4 February 1928), 75.
89 Ibid., 76.
90 Ibid., 75.
91 Richard Surrey [B. Brooker], *Copy Technique in Advertising* (New York: McGraw-Hill, 1930), 18.
92 Ibid., 26.
93 Brooker papers, b. 1, f. 9, B. Brooker to L. Fitzgerald, 17 [October 1930]; Toronto *Globe*, 24 November 1930; Dennis Reid, *Bertram Brooker* (Ottawa: National Gallery of Canada, 1979).
94 George French, 'An Ad. Man's Qualifications,' *Economic Advertising* 5:7 (July 1912), 41–3.

6: Market Research and the Management of Risk

1 'Advertising – "The Common Language of Trade,"' *Canadian Advertising Data* 1:1 (July 1928), 76.
2 Eaton records, Ser. 6, b. 1, f. POC-Tetley's, [T. Eaton] to P.K. Read, 23 December 1889; see also Joy L. Santink, *Timothy Eaton and the Rise of His Department Store* (Toronto: University of Toronto Press, 1990), 168–9.
3 Eaton records, Ser. 6, b. 1, f. POC-Tetley's, T. Eaton to J. Tetley & Co., 26 December 1889.
4 Ibid., Eaton to Read, 23 December 1889; Eaton to Tetley & Co., 26 December 1889.
5 American Marketing Association, Definitions Committee, 'Report,' *Journal of Marketing* 13:2 (October 1948), 202–17.
6 C.L. Burton, *A Sense of Urgency: Memoirs of a Canadian Merchant* (Toronto: Clarke, Irwin, 1952), 41.
7 Alfred D. Chandler, Jr, *The Visible Hand: The Managerial Revolution in American Business* (Cambridge, MA: Harvard University Press, 1977), 215–24, 285–314; Vincent P. Norris, 'Advertising History – According to the Textbooks,' *Journal of Advertising* 9:3 (1980), 3–11; R.A. Fullerton, 'How Modern Is Modern Marketing? Marketing's Evolution and the Myth of the "Produc-

tion Era,"' *Journal of Marketing* 52 (1988), 108–25; David Monod, *Store Wars: Shopkeepers and the Culture of Mass Marketing, 1890–1939* (Toronto: University of Toronto Press, 1996), 99–148; G.D. Taylor and P.A. Baskerville, *A Concise History of Business in Canada* (Toronto: Oxford University Press, 1994), 313–16.

8 'The Christie Girl,' *Economic Advertising* 1:11 (July 1909), 36–8; see also W.A. C[raick], 'Brief Interviews,' *Printer & Publisher* 11:9 (September 1902), 18; Norris, 'Advertising History,' 3–11.

9 *Canadian Newspaper Directory,* 7th ed. (1911), xvi; J.F. MacKay, 'Why These Imports?' *Economic Advertising* 1:10 (June 1909), 12; see also E.E. Calkins and R. Holden, *Modern Advertising* (1905; reprint, New York: Garland, 1985), 47; 'What about Your Trademark?' *Economic Advertising* 2:5 (January 1910), 15–16; 'You Are on the Bench,' Toronto *World*, 2 April 1912; 'Who Is Your Customer?' Toronto *World*, 14 May 1912; C.M. Pasmore, 'Naming the New Product,' *Marketing* 28:10 (12 May 1928), 358.

10 On the parcel post, see Santink, *Timothy Eaton*, 122–4; B. Osborne and R. Pike, 'Lowering the Walls of Oblivion: The Revolution in Postal Communications in Central Canada, 1851–1911,' *Canadian Papers in Rural History* 4 (Gananoque, ON: Langdale, 1984), 200–25; Robert M. Campbell, *The Politics of the Post: Canada's Postal System from Public Service to Privatization* (Peterborough: Broadview, 1994), 25–36. On trade papers, see F.A. Rowlatt, 'The Advertising Agency,' *Economic Advertising* 1:12 (August 1909), 9; *Canadian Newspaper Directory,* 20th ed. (1920); *Lydiatt's Book,* 7th ed. (1920).

11 For the international context, see Michel Foucault, 'Governmentality,' in *The Foucault Effect: Studies in Governmentality,* ed. G. Burchell et al. (Chicago: University of Chicago Press, 1991), 87–104; P. Corrigan and D. Sayer, *The Great Arch: English State Formation as Cultural Revolution* (Oxford: Blackwell, 1991), 134–5; Donald A. MacKenzie, *Statistics in Britain, 1865–1930: The Social Construction of Scientific Knowledge* (Edinburgh: University of Edinburgh Press, 1981), 1–50; Theodore M. Porter, *The Rise of Statistical Thinking, 1820–1900* (Princeton, NJ: Princeton University Press, 1986), 16–39; Jean M. Converse, *Survey Research in the United States: Roots and Emergence, 1890–1960* (Berkeley: University of California Press, 1987), 11–53; Martin Bulmer et al., eds., *The Social Survey in Historical Perspective* (Cambridge: Cambridge University Press, 1991). For Canada, see Paul Craven, *An Impartial Umpire: Industrial Relations and the Canadian State, 1900–1911* (Toronto: University of Toronto Press, 1980), 208–40; Marlene Shore, *The Science of Social Redemption: McGill, the Chicago School, and the Origins of Social Research in Canada* (Toronto: University of Toronto Press, 1987), 24–67; George Emery, *The Facts of*

Life: The Social Construction of Vital Statistics, Ontario, 1869–1952 (Montreal: McGill-Queen's University Press, 1993), 17–30; N. Christie and M. Gauvreau, *A Full-Orbed Christianity: The Protestant Churches and Social Welfare in Canada, 1900–1940* (Montreal: McGill-Queen's University Press, 1996), 3–36.

12 For the international context, see Converse, *Survey Research in the United States*, 54–86; Alain Desrosières, 'The Part in Relation to the Whole: How to Generalize? The Prehistory of Representative Sampling,' in *The Social Survey in Historical Perspective*, 217–44. For Canada, see *History of Academic Psychology in Canada* (Toronto: Hogrefe, 1982), 36–45, 68–99, 192–219; T. Copp and B. McAndrew, *Battle Exhaustion: Soldiers and Psychiatrists in the Canadian Army, 1925–1945* (Montreal: McGill-Queen's University Press, 1990); Allan D. English, *The Cream of the Crop: Canadian Aircrew, 1939–1945* (Montreal: McGill-Queen's University Press, 1996).

13 Melvin T. Copeland, *And Mark an Era: The Story of the Harvard Business School* (Boston: Little, Brown, 1958), 209–16; Robert Bartels, *The Development of Marketing Thought* (Homewood, IL: Irwin, 1962), 47–9; D.G. Brian Jones, 'Origins of Marketing Thought' (unpublished PhD dissertation, Queen's University, 1987), 70–115, 116–52.

14 Cherington, *Advertising as a Business Force* ([Garden City, NY]: Doubleday, Page, 1913), especially 3–28, 500–2; Cherington, *The Advertising Book 1916* ([Garden City, NY]: Doubleday, Page, 1916), especially 311–65. See also Copeland, *And Mark an Era*, 209–16; George French, *Advertising: The Social and Economic Problem* (New York: Ronald, 1915), 164–6; Chandler, *Visible Hand*, 466–8.

15 Canada, Dominion Bureau of Statistics, *Report 1922, Sessional Papers* #10 (Ottawa: King's Printer, 1923), 5–7.

16 R.H. Coats, in ibid., 7.

17 R.H. Coats, in ibid., 9. See also Doug Owram, *The Government Generation: Canadian Intellectuals and the State, 1900–45* (Toronto: University of Toronto Press, 1986), 131–2.

18 'How the Census Can Help Us Sell,' *Marketing* 15:22 (15 November 1922), 781.

19 H.R. Cockfield, 'Trend in Advertising Agency Service (Pt. II),' *Canadian Advertising Data* 4:1 (January 1931), 49.

20 A few did, a fact made evident in Cherington, *The Advertising Book*, 311–12.

21 See, for example, the ad for the Montreal *Star*, in *Canadian Newspaper Directory*, 2d ed. (1899), 261.

22 For the *Star*, see *Canadian Newspaper Directory*, 2d ed. (1899), 261; for the *Sun*, see *Marketing* 15:8 (15 April 1921), 257.

23 'The Gamble of Space Buying,' *Economic Advertising* 4:10 (October 1911), 19–21; F.A. Rowlatt, 'The Advertising Agency,' *Economic Advertising* 1:12 (August 1909), 10. See also Jean de Bonville, *La Presse Québécoise de 1884 à 1914: Genèse d'un média de masse* (Quebec: Presses de l'Université Laval, 1988), 326–9.

24 *Marketing* 30:7 (30 March 1929), 246.

25 'Cover Canada ... Do Not Overlook French Canada,' *Canadian Newspaper Directory* 14th ed. (1920), 164–5.

26 See, for example, ads for the *Jewish Daily Eagle* in *Marketing* 30:7 (30 March 1929), 246, and the *Progresso Italo-Canadese* and *Danish Review* in *Canadian Advertising Data* 4:1 (January 1931), 49. See also O.K. Thomassen, 'The Foreign Language Press,' *Marketing* 26:7 (2 April 1927), 302; Watson Kirkconnell, 'The European-Canadians in Their Press,' in Canadian Historical Association, *Report* (Toronto: University of Toronto Press, 1940), 85–92; Victor Turek, *The Polish-Language Press in Canada* (Toronto: Polish Alliance, 1962), 17–39; Paul Rutherford, *A Victorian Authority: The Daily Press in Late Nineteenth-Century Canada* (Toronto: University of Toronto Press, 1982), 41–2.

27 A.J. Denne, 'How an Agency Plans,' *Printer & Publisher* 24:7 (July 1915), 25–6.

28 On the domestic magazines, see Ann Douglas, *The Feminization of American Culture* (New York: Anchor/Doubleday, 1977); Jennifer Scanlon, *Inarticulate Longings: The Ladies' Home Journal, Gender, and the Promises of Consumer Culture* (New York: Routledge, 1995), 11–47; Ellen Gruber Garvey, *The Adman in the Parlor: Magazines and the Gendering of Consumer Culture* (New York: Oxford University Press, 1996), 137–65; on the advent of women's pages, see Ted Ferguson, *Kit Coleman, Queen of Hearts* (Toronto: Doubleday, 1978), frontispiece, 1–10; Barbara M. Freeman, *Kit's Kingdom: The Journalism of Kathleen Blake Coleman* (Ottawa: Carleton University Press, 1989), 49–79; Kay Rex, *No Daughter of Mine: The Women and History of the Canadian Women's Press Club, 1904–71* (Toronto: Cedar Cave, 1995), 3–21. Children's pages were also developed; see N.L. Lewis, ed., *'I Want to Join Your Club': Letters from Rural Children, 1900–20* (Waterloo: Wilfrid Laurier University Press, 1996), 1–12.

29 Scanlon, *Inarticulate Longings*, 15–16.

30 See, for example, the ad for *Alberta Farmer* in *Marketing* 14:4 (April 1920), 213.

31 'High Explosives,' *Printer & Publisher* 24:8 (August 1915), 37; Cecil Riopel, 'Scientific Space Buying,' *Marketing* 15:7 (1 April 1921), 226; Dallas W. Smythe, *Dependency Road: Communications, Capitalism, Consciousness, and*

Canada (Norwood, NJ: Ablex, 1981), 22–51; Richard Germain, 'The Adoption of Statistical Methods in Market Research: The Early Twentieth Century,' *Research in Marketing*, suppl. 6: *Explorations in the History of Marketing*, ed. J.N. Sheth and R.A. Fullerton (Greenwich, CT: JAI, 1994), 87–101.

32 Cherington, *The Advertising Book*, 314; Converse, *Survey Research*, 87–127; Bartels, *Development of Marketing Thought*, 108–9; Stephen Fox, *The Mirror Makers: A History of American Advertising and Its Creators* (New York: Morrow, 1984), 83–6.

33 F.S. Jawfs, in 'Value of Quality and Locality,' *Printer & Publisher* 23:3 (March 1914), 68.

34 *Canadian Newspaper Directory*, 7th ed. (1911), xv; Margaret Pennell, in 'High Explosives,' *Printer & Publisher* 24:8 (August 1915), 37; Toronto *Mail & Empire*, 'The Increasing Responsibility,' *Canadian Newspaper Directory*, 14th ed. (1920), 14–15; 'Value of Quality and Locality,' *Printer & Publisher* 23:3 (March 1914), 68; see also A.J. Denne, 'How an Agency Plans,' *Printer & Publisher* 24:7 (July 1915), 25–6; Cecil Riopel, 'Scientific Space Buying,' *Marketing* 15:7 (1 April 1921), 226.

35 Fox, *Mirror Makers*, 30–2, 78–82; Scanlon, *Inarticulate Longings*, 169–96; Frank Presbrey, *The History and Development of Advertising* (Garden City, NY: Doubleday, Doran, 1929), 272.

36 Fox, *Mirror Makers*, 30–2, 78–86; Peggy Kreshel, 'Advertising Research in the Pre-Depression Years,' *Journal of Current Issues and Research in Advertising* 15:1 (1993), 59–75.

37 The coefficient of correlation between the three groups was $r = .62, .60$, and .61; the average coefficient for individual subjects with the group was .68. See Hollingsworth, 'Judgments of Persuasiveness,' *Psychological Review* 18 (1911), 245–6; see also Hollingsworth, 'Judgment of the Comic,' *Psychological Review* 18 (1911), 132–56.

38 Walter Dill Scott, *The Psychology of Advertising* (Boston: Small, Maynard, 1921), 205–6.

39 Fox, *Mirror Makers*, 30–2, 78–86; J. Walter Thompson Company, *Population and Its Distribution*, 6th ed. (New York: Harper, 1941), iii–iv, ix; J.L. Mahin, *Advertising Data Book* (New York: Mahin, 1914); see also J.L. Mahin, *Advertising: Selling the Consumer* ([Garden City, NY]: Doubleday, Page, 1914). JWT's first published study on Canada was *The Canadian Market* (New York: McGraw-Hill, 1958).

40 On Cherington, see Cherington, *The Consumer Looks at Advertising* (New York: Harper, 1928), 34–53. Descriptions of 'typical' research departments appeared in Norman Lewis, *How to Become an Advertising Man* (New York:

Ronald, 1927), 76–89; Roland S. Vaile, *Economics of Advertising* (New York: Ronald, 1927), 19–36; Lloyd D. Herrold, *Advertising Copy: Principles and Practice* (Chicago: Shaw, 1927), 64–91.

41 Cherington, *Advertising as a Business Force*, 493–536; James W. Young, *Advertising Agency Compensation, In Relation to the Total Cost of Advertising* (Chicago: University of Illinois Press, 1933), 36–8. Kreshel suggests that the agencies' adoption of market research during this time lacked any practical purpose, yet she oddly overlooks its relevance to media-buying; see Kreshel, 'Advertising Research,' 64–70.

42 *Lydiatt's Book*, 1st ed. (1914), 6; John C. Kirkwood, 'Who Is Lydiatt?' *Economic Advertising* 11:2 (February 1918), 4–6; 'W.A. Lydiatt,' *Printer & Publisher* 27:2 (February 1918), 23–4; see also 'Men and Media,' *Economic Advertising* 4:7 (July 1911), 47.

43 W.A. Lydiatt, introduction, *Lydiatt's Book*, 6th ed. (1919), 5; see also *Lydiatt's Book*, 1st ed. (1914), 15–70. The same year that he started the newspaper directory, Lydiatt also started an advertisers directory entitled *Who's Who in Canadian Advertising*, 1st ed. (Toronto: W.A. Lydiatt, 1914).

44 Duke University, Special Collections Library, J. Walter Thompson Archives (JWTA), Series: Staff Meetings, b. 6, f. 1, Representatives Meeting (13 March 1928), 1–8; 'Advertising,' *The Encyclopaedia of Canada*, vol. 1, ed. W.S. Wallace (Toronto: University Associates, 1936), 14–15.

45 W.A. Lydiatt, quoted in 'W.A. Lydiatt,' *Printer & Publisher* 27:2 (February 1918), 24.

46 *Marketing* 12:1 (March 1918).

47 'W.A. Lydiatt,' *Printer & Publisher* 27:2 (February 1918), 23–4; 'Editorial Personnel for 1925,' *Marketing* 21:10 (15 November 1924), 279.

48 'How the Census Can Help Us Sell,' *Marketing* 15:22 (15 November 1921), 781–5. A census of distribution was approved by the government for 1931; M.J. Patton, 'Government Sources of Information,' *Printer & Publisher* 31:12 (December 1922), 48; 'The Reasons for Taking Census of Merchandising in Canada,' *Canadian Advertising Data* 4:7 (July 1931), 8; Canada, Dominion Bureau of Statistics, *Seventh Census of Canada*, vol. 10: *Merchandising and Service Establishments* (Ottawa: King's Printer, 1934).

49 Bertram Brooker, 'Census of Merchandising in Canada Approaches Reality,' *Marketing* 22:5 (7 March 1925), 117; Canada, Dominion Bureau of Statistics, *Annual Report 1924*, *Annual Departmental Reports* #10 (Ottawa: King's Printer, 1925), 5.

50 Bertram Brooker, 'A Statistical Picture of the Average Canadian Consumer,' *Marketing* 20:12 (14 June 1924), 394, 396, 438.

51 Ibid., 438; see also Brooker, 'How the Census Can Help Us Sell,' 781–5.

52 Bertram Brooker, 'Millions of Dollars to Unearth,' *Marketing* 21:12 (13 December 1924), 318–9, 328; see also Garvey, *Adman in the Parlor*, 51–79.
53 Bertram Brooker, 'Markets Are People!' *Marketing* 22:1 (15 January 1925), 6–7, 22. Brooker cites J.A. Hobson, *Work and Wealth: A Human Valuation* (New York: Macmillan, 1914). See also The End Man [B. Brooker], 'Knowing WHY the Public Buys,' *Marketing* 27:11 (26 November 1927), 401–2; Bertram Brooker, 'The Best Isn't Good Enough,' *Marketing* 27:3 (6 August 1927), 79; Langton Fife, 'Corset Campaign Brings Mailbag Trophy,' *Marketing* 27:11 (26 November 1927), 399–400; C.M. Pasmore, 'Must Discover Consumer's Needs,' *Marketing* 28:13 (23 June 1928), 455, 468.
54 Quotation from *Marketing* 15:4 (15 February 1921), 131. On Love, see *Marketing* 22:12 (13 June 1925), 358.
55 *Lydiatt's Book*, 12th ed. (1925), 275–93; *Marketing* 24:3 (6 February 1926), 76; *Marketing* 59:35 (28 August 1954), 1.
56 Bruce Bliven, 'What British Advertisers Have Learned,' *Printer's Ink* 104:6 (8 August 1918), 3; 'Editorial Personnel for 1925,' *Marketing* 21:10 (15 November 1924), 279; V. Fisher, letter to the editor, *Marketing* 29:13 (22 December 1928), 425; A.B. Blankenship et al., *A History of Marketing Research in Canada* (Toronto: Professional Marketing Research Society, 1985), 20–1. One sample of Fisher's work is *St Catharines, Ontario, and the Welland Ship Canal* (Toronto: Canadian Business Research Bureau, 1933).
57 *Canadian Advertising Data* 3:11 (December 1930), 14, 17.
58 *Prominent People of the Province of Ontario* (Ottawa: Canadian Biographies, 1925), 71; 'Advertising World,' *Canadian Advertising Data* 5:6 (August 1926), 22.
59 'William Findlay,' *Marketing* 25:6 (18 September 1926), 200.
60 'The New Alignment,' *Marketing* 25:11 (27 November 1926), 355.
61 'The Golden Key,' *Marketing* 24:7 (3 April 1926), 180–1.
62 'The New Alignment,' 355.
63 Ibid., 355.
64 Ibid., 355.
65 'Advertising in the Prairie Zone,' *Marketing* 26:8 (16 April 1927), inside front cover; this ad ran again in *Marketing* 27:3 (6 August 1927), inside front cover.
66 All four articles had the same title, 'Do Alberta and British Columbia Form a New Marketing Zone?' Pt. 1, *Marketing* 25:12 (11 December 1926), 398; Pt. 2, *Marketing* 25:13 (25 December 1926), 417–18; Pt. 3, *Marketing* 26:2 (22 January 1927), 56–7; Pt. 4, *Marketing* 26:3 (5 February 1927), 94.
67 W. McCurdy, letter to the editor, in Pt. 3, *Marketing* 26:2 (22 January 1927), 56–7.

68 R.W. Brown, letter to the editor, in Pt. 4, *Marketing* 26:3 (5 February 1927), 94.
69 'The Coverage Problem of Western Canada,' *Marketing* 26:7 (2 April 1927), 291.
70 'Advertising in the Prairie Zone,' *Marketing* 26:8 (16 April 1927), inside front cover.
71 T.A. Torgeson, letter to the editor, in Pt. 2, *Marketing* 25:13 (25 December 1926), 418.
72 G.M. Bell, letter to the editor, in Pt. 2, *Marketing* 25:13 (25 December 1926), 418.
73 *Marketing* 24:7 (3 April 1926), 249.
74 'Advertising Agency Association,' *Marketing* 27:8 (15 October 1927), 307; see also H.R. Cockfield, 'Trend in Advertising Agency Practice (Pt. II),' *Canadian Advertising Data* 4:1 (January 1931), 19.
75 H.E. Stephenson and C. McNaught, *The Story of Advertising in Canada* (Toronto: Ryerson, 1940), 345.
76 W.H. Mahatoo, 'Marketing,' *Executive* (April 1968), 34–9. In 1957 a veteran practitioner similarly confirmed that there were 'very few' in Canada before 1940; see W.H. Poole, 'Marketing Research in Canada,' *Commerce Journal* (February 1957), 22.
77 On agricultural marketing, see for example Hugh J.E. Abbott, 'The Marketing of Livestock in Canada' (unpublished PhD dissertation, University of Toronto, 1923); Theodore Herbert Harris, *The Economic Prospects of the Crowsnest Pass Rates Agreement*, McGill University Economic Studies No. 13 (Toronto: Macmillan, 1930). For industrial marketing, see Hubert R. Kemp, *Canadian Marketing Problems: Ten Essays* (Toronto: University of Toronto Press, 1939); Jane McKee, ed., *Marketing Organization and Technique* (Toronto: University of Toronto Press, 1940); McGill School of Commerce, *Selling Tomorrow's Production* (Montreal: McGill University, School of Commerce, 1945). On economics in Canada, see Robin Neill, *A History of Canadian Economic Thought* (London: Routledge, 1991), 109–28; Barry Ferguson, *Remaking Liberalism: The Intellectual Legacy of Adam Shortt, O.D. Skelton, W.C. Clark, and W.A. Mackintosh, 1890–1925* (Montreal: McGill-Queen's University Press, 1993); Michael Gauvreau, 'Philosophy, Psychology, and History: George Sidney Brett and the Quest for a Social Science at the University of Toronto, 1910–1940,' Canadian Historical Association *Historical Papers* (1988), 209–36; A.B. McKillop, *Matters of Mind: The University in Ontario, 1791–1951* (Toronto: University of Toronto Press, 1994); A. Moritz and T. Moritz, *Leacock: A Biography* (Toronto: Stoddart, 1985), 86–90; Vincent Bladen, *Bladen on Bladen: Memoirs of a Political Economist* (Toronto: University of Toronto Press, 1978), 19–24.

78 Michell should not be confused with H.E. Mihell, president of the ACA
    in the 1920s. Neill, *History of Canadian Economic Thought*, 124; Charles M.
    Johnston, *McMaster University*, vol. 1: *The Toronto Years* (Toronto: University
    of Toronto Press, 1976), 162, 206. For Michell's work, see *The Problem of
    Agricultural Credit in Canada* (Kingston: Jackson, 1914); *The Grange in Canada*
    (Kingston: Jackson, 1914); *The Co-operative Store in Canada* (Kingston: Jack-
    son, 1916); 'Statistics of Prices,' *Statistical Contributions to Canadian Economic
    History*, vol. 2. (Toronto: Macmillan, 1931).
79 JWTA, Staff Meetings, b. 1, f. 4., 13 March 1928; b. 1, f. 7, 13 March 1929; b. 2,
    f. 3, 14 May 1930; b. 4, f. 9, 9 February 1932.
80 JWTA, Staff Meetings, b. 1, f. 5, 8 August 1928.
81 JWTA, Newsletters, b. 1, f. 1923, *News Bulletin* (April 1923), 10; *News Bulletin*
    (August 1923), 16–17; JWTA, Staff Meetings, b. 1, f. 3, 20 December 1927, 2;
    b. 1, f. 5, 18 July 1928, 5–6; b. 1, f. 7, 13 March 1929, 2–4; *Lydiatt's Book*, 14th
    ed. (1927), 312–33.
82 JWTA, Staff Meetings, b. 1, f. 3, 20 December 1927, 3; b. 1, f. 7, 4 January
    1929, 7; 27 February 1929, 3; JWTA, Newsletters, oversize box, *JWT News*
    (June 1930), 3; *Canadian Advertising Data* 3:6 (July 1930), 40–1; 'Who's Who
    in Advertising,' *Canadian Advertising Data* 3:8 (September 1930), 9.
83 *Canadian Advertising Data* 3:10 (November 1930), 19.
84 'The Announcement of Cockfield, Brown,' *Marketing* 29:12 (8 December
    1928), 379; W.H. Poole, 'Marketing Research in Canada,' *Commerce Journal*
    (February 1957), 21–2.
85 'Begin Campaign to Swell Macaroni Sales,' *Marketing* 21:7 (4 October 1924),
    189; 'Why We Employ a Canadian Agency,' *Marketing* 23:7 (3 October 1925),
    194; 'Corset Campaign Brings Mailbag Trophy,' *Marketing* 27:11 (26 Novem-
    ber 1927), 399–400; H.R. Cockfield, 'Trend in Advertising Agency Practice,'
    Canadian Advertising Data 3:10 (November 1930), 24.
86 'Advertising Agency Association,' *Marketing* 27:8 (15 October 1927), 307;
    H.R. Cockfield, 'Trend in Advertising Agency Practice (Pt. II),' *Canadian
    Advertising Data* 4:1 (January 1931), 19.
87 UTA, A65–0005, Department of Political Economy records, b. 6, f. 4, W.W.
    Goforth to G.E. Jackson, 26 February 1930; Goforth to Jackson, 3 March
    1930; Henry King, 'The Beginning of Market Research in Canada,' *The
    Marketer* 2:1 (Spring/Summer 1966), 4–5; reprinted in *Marketing Research in
    Canada*, ed. W.H. Mahatoo (Toronto: Nelson, 1968), 20–2; Daniel Robinson,
    'Tapping the Consumer Mind: The Rise of Market Research Surveys in
    Interwar Canada,' paper presented to the Eighth Conference on Historical
    Research in Marketing and Marketing Thought (Kingston: June 1997), 7–8.
88 NAC, MG32 G9, H.E. Kidd papers, v. 25, f. 14, 'Advertising Reports and

Statistics, 1935–1944'; King, 'Beginning of Market Research,' 21–2; Cock-field, Brown & Co., *Summary Report on the Marketing of Canadian Fish and Fish Products* (Ottawa: King's Printer, 1932).

89 H.R. Cockfield, 'Trend in Advertising Agency Practice,' *Canadian Advertising Data* 3:10 (November 1930), 24.

90 King, 'Beginning of Market Research,' 21–2; Blankenship et al., *History of Marketing Research*, 18–20; Robinson, 'Tapping the Consumer Mind,' 7–8.

91 J.D. Neill, 'Tea Cup Lore Used to Introduce New Lipton Line,' *Marketing* 21:8 (18 October 1924), 213.

92 Alec Waugh, *The Lipton Story: A Centennial Biography* (London: Non-Fiction Book Club, [1950]), 50–9.

93 Neill, 'Tea Cup Lore,' 213–14.

94 Ibid., 213–14.

95 Chandler, *Visible Hand*, 287–314.

96 Daniel J. Robinson, *The Measure of Democracy: Polling, Market Research, and Public Life, 1930–1945* (Toronto: University of Toronto Press, 1999), 126–57.

7: The Canadian Market, Magazines, and the New Logic of Advertising

1 W.J. Healy, 'The Position of the Daily Paper,' *Economic Advertising* 1:3 (November 1908), 21–2.

2 A.J. Denne, 'How an Agency Plans a Campaign,' *Printer & Publisher* 24:7 (July 1915), 25–6.

3 *Lydiatt's Book*, 5th ed. (1917), 90. There was a 5 per cent duty on 'Books, printed, and periodicals, pamphlets, etc.,' but this was intended only for bound items with pre-printed content, such as children's puzzle books or annual directories; An Act Imposing Duties of Customs, 31 Victoria (1870) ch. 44, schedule B.

4 Balancing the higher number of 5 to 10¢ magazines against the higher prices of the less popular magazines, 15¢ might be taken as an arbitrary figure for the average price of all of these periodicals. This is probably conservative.

5 Mary Vipond, 'Canadian Nationalism and the Plight of Canadian Magazines in the 1920s,' *Canadian Historical Review* 58:1 (March 1977), 43–63.

6 Stephen Fox, *The Mirror Makers: A History of American Advertising and Its Creators* (New York: Morrow, 1984), 29–34.

7 Ellery Sedgwick, *The Atlantic Monthly, 1857–1909: Yankee Humanism at High Tide and Ebb* (Amherst: University of Massachusetts Press, 1994).

8 Harold S. Wilson, *McClure's Magazine and the Muckrakers* (Princeton, NJ: Princeton University Press, 1970), 60–101; Jan Cohn, *Creating America:*

George Horace Lorimer and the Saturday Evening Post (Pittsburgh: University of Pittsburgh Press, 1989), 21–46.

9 Wilson, *McClure's Magazine*, 104–40; Cohn, *Creating America*, 21–46; Jennifer Scanlon, *Inarticulate Longings: The* Ladies' Home Journal, *Gender, and the Promises of Consumer Culture* (New York: Routledge, 1995), 11–48.

10 It was the eighth magazine to use that name; A.H.U. Colquhoun, 'A Century of Canadian Magazines,' *Canadian Magazine* 17:2 (May 1901), 141–9.

11 *Canadian Newspaper Directory*, 3d ed. (1901), 78.

12 Fraser Sutherland, *The Monthly Epic: A History of Canadian Magazines* (Toronto: Fitzhenry & Whiteside, 1989), 113.

13 *Canadian Courier*, vol. 1 (1906–7).

14 Ellen Gruber Garvey, *The Adman in the Parlor: Magazines and the Gendering of Consumer Culture, 1880s to 1910s* (New York: Oxford University Press, 1996), 80–105.

15 Sutherland argues in his history of Canadian magazines that *Canadian* best represented the transition from the traditional literary journal to the modern mass magazine, but the *Courier* stands as a far better candidate. See Sutherland, *Monthly Epic*, 96–111.

16 *Canadian Newspaper Directory*, 9th ed. (1915), 43.

17 Ibid., 37.

18 'The National Directory of Standard Products,' *Canadian Courier* 21:25 (19 May 1917), 26–7.

19 *Canadian Newspaper Directory*, 9th ed. (1915); *Canadian Newspaper Directory*, 14th ed. (1920).

20 *Canadian Newspaper Directory*, 5th ed. (1907), 116.

21 Sutherland, *Monthly Epic*, 156.

22 'Men and Media,' *Economic Advertising* 7:8 (August 1914), 34; 'Men and Media,' *Economic Advertising* 7:11 (November 1914), 34; *Printer & Publisher* 23:12 (December 1914), 45.

23 Sutherland, *Monthly Epic*, 122; J.L. Granatstein, *Forum: Canadian Life and Letters, 1920–1970* (Toronto: University of Toronto Press, 1970).

24 Frank Luther Mott, *A History of American Magazines*, vol. 3 (Cambridge, MA: Harvard University Press, 1967), 453–79.

25 See, for example, A.D. DesCelles, 'Les Fêtes de Québec,' *Canadian Collier's* 61:19 (1 August 1908), 32.

26 'Wanted: A National Anthem,' *Canadian Collier's* 63:2 (17 April 1909), 7; 'Canadian Magazines,' *Economic Advertising* 1:10 (June 1909), 30–1; 'Sing "O Canada,"' *The Maple Leaf* 1:7/8 (September/October 1922), 18–19, 52; Noel R. Barbour, *Those Amazing People! The Story of the Canadian Magazine Industry, 1778–1967* (Toronto: Crucible, 1982), 85–6.

27 *Canadian Collier's*, vols. 61–4 (1908–10); *Economic Advertising* 6:4 (April 1913), 41; Sutherland, *Monthly Epic*, 93; Mott, *American Magazines*, vol. 3, 465. The American edition of *Collier's* retained some thirty thousand Canadian readers into the 1930s; see *Lydiatt's Book* from 1916 on.

28 'What's Doing in the Clubs,' *Economic Advertising* 8:2 (February 1915), 29; Mott, *American Magazines*, vol. 4, 72–87.

29 Murray Simonski, 'Power of a National Press,' *Everywoman's* 13:1 (July 1920), 1; see also Charles C. Nixon, 'Twixt Us & You,' *Everywoman's* 1:1 (February 1914), 38; 'The Nation-Wide Appeal,' *Marketing* 15:21 (1 November 1921), 759; Vipond, 'Canadian Nationalism and the Plight of Canadian Magazines,' 43–63.

30 'The Nation-Wide Appeal,' *Marketing* 15:21 (1 November 1921), 759.

31 Charles C. Nixon, 'Are Women's Magazines Justified?' *Economic Advertising* 7:6 (June 1914), 53–4. Jackson Lears suggests that statistics on women shoppers were nothing more than mythical representations of commonly held beliefs since writers rarely mentioned the source of their data; *Fables of Abundance: A Cultural History of Advertising in America* (New York: Basic, 1994), 209.

32 K.S. Fenwick, 'The Magazine and Farm Paper Situation in Canada,' *Economic Advertising* 8:6 (June 1915), 25; *Lydiatt's Book*, 4th ed. (1917), 14.

33 *Economic Advertising* 8:9–12 (1915); *Economic Advertising* 9:1–4 (1916); *Economic Advertising* 10:12 (December 1917), 1.

34 Charles C. Nixon, 'Twixt Us & You,' *Everywoman's* 1:2 (February 1914), 38.

35 'Romance of Modern Business, No. 1: The Story of a Fountain Pen,' *Everywoman's* 1:2 (February 1914), 20.

36 Garvey, *Adman in the Parlor*, 80–105; Scanlon, *Inarticulate Longings*, 69–70.

37 'A New Canadian Magazine,' *Economic Advertising* 6:9 (September 1913), 37.

38 *Printer & Publisher* 4:10 (October 1895), 11; Bertram Brooker, 'Forty Years of Canadian Advertising,' *Marketing* 21:3 (9 August 1924), 69.

39 *Lydiatt's Book*, 5th ed. (1918), 102; see also *Business* 11:1 (October 1905), 6; 'Canadian Magazines,' *Economic Advertising* 1:12 (August 1909), 30–2. On the *Saturday Evening Post*, see Cohn, *Creating America* 21–46; Christopher P. Wilson, 'The Rhetoric of Consumption: Mass Market Magazines and the Demise of the Gentle Reader, 1880–1920,' *The Culture of Consumption* (New York: Random House, 1983), 39–64.

40 'Inside with the Publishers,' *Business* 11:1 (October 1905), 6.

41 *Business* 11:2 (November 1905), 3.

42 *Busyman's* 21:4 (February 1911); Sutherland, *Monthly Epic*, 141–2.

43 M-H records, b. 55, f. AT-Vance, A.T. Vance to J.B. Maclean, 23 September 1905; *Canadian Newspaper Directory*, 3d ed. (1901), 108.

44 M-H records, b. 50, f. TB-Costain, H.T. Hunter to J.B. Maclean, 16 October 1947; T.B. Costain, 'Magazine Publishers' Efforts,' *Economic Advertising* 9:8 (August 1916), 20–2.

45 M-H records, b. 50, f. TB-Costain, J.B. Maclean to T. Costain, 21 April 1917; T. Costain to J.B. Maclean, 19 February 1920.

46 M-H records, b. 50, f. TB-Costain, J.B. Maclean to T.B. Costain, 21 April 1917.

47 M-H records, b. 50, f. TB-Costain, T.B. Costain, 'Report on Western Trip,' 11 September 1919; see also David MacKenzie, *Arthur Irwin: A Biography* (Toronto: University of Toronto Press, 1993), 86–7.

48 'MacLean's Magazine,' *Printer's Ink* 105:12 (19 December 1918), 106; 'The Logical Advertising Campaign,' *Canadian Newspaper Directory*, 14th ed. (1920), 161.

49 'The Purchasing Power in Canada,' *Marketing* 20:12 (14 June 1924), 375.

50 'Covering the National Market,' *Canadian Advertising Data* 2:12 (December 1929), 54; 'Cater to Classes,' *Marketing* 15:22 (15 November 1921), inside front cover.

51 'Cater to Classes,' *Marketing* 15:22 (15 November 1921), inside front cover.

52 NAC, MG31 E97, W. Arthur Irwin papers, v. 18, f. 25, *MacLean's 1928* (Toronto: MacLean, 1928), 46; see also pages 25, 37, 44.

53 *Lydiatt's Book*, 9th ed. (1922), 14; *Lydiatt's Book*, 18th ed. (1931), 14; see also MacKenzie, *Arthur Irwin*, 63–76, 79–87; Mott, *American Magazines*, vol. 4, 708.

54 Desbarats Advertising, *The Desbarats Newspaper Directory 1912* (Montreal: Desbarats, 1912), 4.

55 Thomas L. Walkom, 'The Daily Newspaper Industry in Ontario's Developing Capitalistic Economy: Toronto and Ottawa, 1871–1911' (unpublished PhD dissertation, University of Toronto, 1983), 37–8.

56 Fred Landon, 'The Agricultural Journals of Upper Canada (Ontario),' *Agricultural Journal* 9 (1935), 167–75; *Canadian Newspaper Directory*, 9th ed. (1915); J.M.S. Careless, *Brown of the Globe*, vol. 2, *Statesman of Confederation, 1860–1889* (Toronto: Macmillan, 1963), 113, 269.

57 *Canadian Newspaper Directory*, 1st ed. (1892), 243–4; *Lydiatt's Book*, 14th ed. (1927), 14; Sutherland, *Monthly Epic*, 118–19; Jean de Bonville, *La Presse Québécoise de 1884 à 1914: Genèse d'un média de masse* (Quebec: Presses de l'Université Laval, 1988), 240–2.

58 Walkom, 'Daily Newspaper Industry,' 21–72, especially 39–40; Hector Charlesworth, *Candid Chronicles* (Toronto: Macmillan, 1925), 131–2; Hector Charlesworth, *More Candid Chronicles* (Toronto: Macmillan, 1928), 169.

59 Walkom, 'Daily Newspaper Industry,' 120–89; Ross Harkness, *J.E. Atkinson*

of the Star (Toronto: University of Toronto Press, 1963), 18–23, 72–3; J.H. Cranston, *Ink on My Fingers* (Toronto: Ryerson 1953), 74–77, 86–88.

60 Cranston, *Ink on My Fingers*, 161; M-H records, Ser. B-1-2-A, b. 54, f. AE-Nash, H.V. Tyrrell to J.B. Maclean, 9 February 1939.

61 'Cater to Classes,' *Marketing* 15:22 (15 November 1921), inside front cover.

62 *Canadian Newspaper Directory*, 14th ed. (1920).

63 *Lydiatt's Book*, 6th ed. (1919), 92.

64 *Lydiatt's Book*, 8th ed. (1921), 14.

65 *Marketing* 16:1 (1 January 1922), 38.

66 *Canadian Magazine* vols. 63–5 (1924–6); Sutherland, *Monthly Epic*, 102–11.

67 M-H records, Ser. B-1-2-A, b. 54, f. AE-Nash, H.V. Tyrrell to J.B. Maclean, 2 February 1939; H.V. Tyrrell to J.B. Maclean, 9 February 1939; *Lydiatt's Book*, 18th ed. (1931), 14; Sutherland, *Monthly Epic*, 104–7.

68 Stanley Brice Frost, *McGill University, For the Advancement of Learning*, vol. 2: *1895–1971* (Montreal: McGill-Queen's University Press, 1984), 51–5; Frederick W. Gibson, *Queen's University*, vol. 2: *To Serve and Yet to Be Free* (Montreal: McGill-Queen's University Press, 1983), 6, 117.

69 Sir John Willison, *Reminiscences Political and Personal* (Toronto: McClelland & Stewart, 1919); *Canadian Newspaper Directory*, 19–22 eds. (1926–9); A.H.U. Colquhoun, *Press, Politics, and People: The Life and Letters of Sir John Willison* (Toronto: Macmillan, 1935), 276–7; Michael Bliss, *A Canadian Millionaire: The Life and Business Times of Sir Joseph Flavelle, Bart., 1858–1939* (Toronto: Macmillan, 1978), 146–51, 172–3, 182–3.

70 Mott, *American Magazines*, vol. 5, 3–26; M.K. Singleton, *H.L. Mencken and the American Mercury Adventure* (Durham, NC: Duke University Press, 1962), 11–54.

71 Ken Norris, *The Little Magazine in Canada, 1925–80* (Toronto: ECW, 1984), 16–20.

72 Doug Owram, *The Government Generation: Canadian Intellectuals and the State, 1900–1945* (Toronto: University of Toronto Press, 1986); Barry Ferguson, *Remaking Liberalism: The Intellectual Legacy of Adam Shortt, O.D. Skelton, W.C. Clark, and W.A. Mackintosh, 1890–1925* (Montreal: McGill-Queen's University Press, 1993).

73 McNaught also co-authored *The Story of Advertising in Canada* (Toronto: Ryerson, 1940). Michiel Horn, *The League for Social Reconstruction: Intellectual Origins of the Democratic Left in Canada, 1930–1942* (Toronto: University of Toronto Press, 1980), 129–33; Ioan Davies, 'Theory and Creativity in English Canada: Magazines, the State and Cultural Movement,' *Journal of Canadian Studies* 30:1 (Spring 1995), 5–19.

74 *Lydiatt's Book*, 6th ed. (1919), 116.

75 United Church of Canada Archives (UCA), LC79.170c, Westminster Company, b. 1, f. 3, ad proof.

76 Westminster Company, b. 1, Directors, Minutes 1897–1916, 20 March 1912; *Marketing* 15:5 (1 March 1921), 149; SLA, Sun Life Advertising Committee, Minutes 1925–31, 29 January 1927; VCA, Vancouver Board of Trade, v. 55, Advertising and Publicity Bureau, Minute Book 1919–25, 15 December 1921.

77 UCA, LC83.061c, UCC Board of Publications records, b. 12, f. 2, 'The Methodist Book and Publishing House ... What It Is and What It Does' [1925].

78 *Canadian Newspaper Directory,* 14th ed. (1920), 160; *Lydiatt's Book,* 7–12 eds. ([1920–5]).

79 *New Outlook* 1:2 (17 June 1925), 1; *Canadian Newspaper Directory,* 24th ed. (1930), 573; *Lydiatt's Book,* 17th ed. (1930), 14. The title might have been inspired by an American religious paper, *The Outlook*; Mott, *American Magazines,* vol. 4, 59.

80 John Webster Grant, *A Profusion of Spires: Religion in Nineteenth Century Ontario* (Toronto: University of Toronto Press, 1988).

81 E.J. Hart, *The Selling of Canada: The CPR and the Beginnings of Canadian Tourism* (Banff, AB: Altitude, 1983), 97–110.

82 UCA, LC 82.026c, UCC Commission on Church Publications, f. 1, H.S.T. Piper to L. Eedy, 4 April 1938.

83 UCC Board of Publications, b. 30, f. 19, profit and loss statement, 1931–2.

84 UCC Commission on Church Publications, f. 1, Minutes, 8 October 1937; 22 November 1937; H.S.T. Piper to L. Eedy, 4 April 1938.

85 Brief discussions of the trade press appear in Keith Walden, 'Speaking Modern: Language, Culture and Hegemony in Grocery Store Window Displays, 1887–1920,' *Canadian Historical Review* 70 (1989), 285–310; Michael Bliss, *A Living Profit: Studies in the Social History of Canadian Business, 1883–1911* (Toronto: McClelland & Stewart, 1974); David Monod, *Store Wars: Shopkeepers and the Culture of Mass Marketing, 1890–1939* (Toronto: University of Toronto Press, 1996). For a list of Toronto trade press publishers, see any volume of *Lydiatt's Book* or the *Canadian Newspaper Directory* for the 1920s.

86 Norah L. Lewis, 'Goose Grease and Turpentine: Mother Treats the Family Illnesses,' in *Rethinking Canada: The Promise of Women's History,* 2d ed., ed. V. Strong-Boag and A.C. Fellman (Toronto: Copp Clark Pitman, 1991), 234–48.

87 Sutherland, *Monthly Epic,* 9.

88 *Journal of Agriculture* 16:8 (February 1913), front cover; *Lydiatt's Book,* 1st ed. (1914), 14.

89 *Journal of Agriculture* 16:8 (February 1913).

90 'A New Departure,' *Economic Advertising* 6:5 (May 1913), 9.

91 'The Journal's New Dress,' *Journal of Agriculture* 17:7 (January 1914), 129.

92 *Journal of Agriculture* 28 (1920).

93 *Lydiatt's Book*, 18th ed. (1931), 14.

94 Angela E. Davis, 'Country Homemakers: The Daily Lives of Prairie Women as Seen through the Women's Page of the Grain Growers' Guide,' *Canadian Papers in Rural History* 8 (Gananoque, ON: Langdale, 1992), 163–74.

95 *Lydiatt's Book*, 1st ed. (1914); *Lydiatt's Book*, 8th ed. (1920).

96 See, for instance, 'The Farmer as a Factor in Local Advertising,' *Printer & Publisher* 24:3 (March 1915), 31–2; 'American Magazines No Menace,' *Marketing* 13:11 (November 1919), 496; T.J. Tobin, 'Do Farm Folks Buy Your Brands?' *Marketing* 19:11 (1 December 1923), 338; G.A. Gamsby, 'What Kind of Advertising Will the Farmer Read?' *Marketing* 22:13 (27 June 1925), 373, 385; C.M. Pasmore, 'Farm Consciousness Less Obvious in Farm Paper Advertising,' *Marketing* 28:11 (26 May 1928), 390.

97 G.B. Sharpe, 'Advertising from the Dealer's Standpoint,' *Economic Advertising* 4:12 (December 1911), 36–7.

98 *Economic Advertising* 9:1 (January 1916), 16.

99 *Economic Advertising* 10:4 (April 1917), 1–2.

100 *Marketing* 14:5 (May 1920), 254–5.

101 *Marketing* 29:10 (10 November 1928), 337.

102 *Marketing* 16:3 (1 February 1922), 101; see also *Printer & Publisher* 31:2 (February 1922), 50.

103 Vipond, 'Canadian Nationalism,' 43–63; J.H. Thompson with A. Seager, *Canada 1922–1939: Decades of Discord* (Toronto: McClelland & Stewart, 1985), 158–92; Paul Audley, *Canada's Cultural Industries: Broadcasting, Publishing, Records, and Film* (Toronto: Lorimer, 1983), 54–84.

Conclusion

1 *Canadian Newspaper Directory*, 17th ed. (1923), vi.

2 Mark E. Ting [B. Brooker], 'Hoist the Sales!' *Marketing* 22:6 (21 March 1925), 168.

3 H.E. Stephenson and C. McNaught, *The Story of Advertising in Canada: A Chronicle of Fifty Years* (Toronto: Ryerson, 1940), 18–35, 337–53.

4 This point has been made about Canadian business more broadly by Kenneth Dewar, 'Toryism and Public Ownership in Canada: A Comment,' *Canadian Historical Review* 64:3 (September 1983), 404–19. For views of American advertising from outside English Canada, see Henri Vathelet,

La Publicité dans le Journalisme (Paris: Albin Michel, 1911), 7; Mark E. Ting [B. Brooker], 'Hoist the Sales,' *Marketing* 23:7 (3 October 1925), 202; Raoul Renault, 'Notre Program,' *La Clé d'Or* 1:1 (March 1926), 1.

5 Charles W. Stokes, 'What a Canadian Saw,' *Marketing* 22:11 (30 May 1925), 317.

6 Richard Ohmann has carried this thesis for the United States; see his *Selling Culture: Magazines, Markets, and Class at the Turn of the Century* (London: Verso, 1996).

7 'Taking Radio Tide at the Flood,' *Marketing* 20:5 (8 March 1924), 131–2.

8 Paul Johnson, *A Shopkeeper's Millennium: Society and Revivals in Rochester, New York, 1815–1837* (New York: Hill & Wang, 1978); Stuart Blumin, *The Emergence of the Middle Class* (Cambridge: Cambridge University Press, 1989); Mariana Valverde, *The Age of Light, Soap, and Water* (Toronto: McClelland & Stewart, 1991), 15–33; Lawrence W. Levine, *Highbrow/Lowbrow: The Emergence of Cultural Hierarchy in America* (Cambridge, MA: Harvard University Press, 1988); John F. Kasson, *Rudeness and Civility: Manners in Nineteenth-Century Urban America* (New York: Hill & Wang, 1990).

9 Ohmann, *Selling Culture*, 81–117, especially 91–4; Jackson Lears, 'From Salvation to Self-Realization: Advertising and the Therapeutic Roots of the Consumer Culture, 1880–1930,' in *The Culture of Consumption*, ed. R.W. Fox and J. Lears (New York: Pantheon, 1983), 1–38.

10 Jackson Lears, *Fables of Abundance: A Cultural History of Advertising in America* (New York: Basic, 1994).

11 Richard Surrey [B. Brooker], 'The Copy Outlook for 1924,' *Marketing* 20:1 (12 January 1924), 11.

Selected Bibliography

Archival Materials

Duke University Special Collections Library, Durham, North Carolina
J. Walter Thompson Company Archives

Hamilton Public Library Special Collections, Hamilton, Ontario
Hamilton Recruiting League Records

National Archives of Canada, Ottawa, Ontario
Canadian Press Association Records
George E. Foster Papers
Arthur Irwin Papers
H.E. Kidd Papers
Kenneth Kirkwood Papers
John Lowe Papers
J.E.H. MacDonald Papers
James Poole Papers
Wilson Pugsley MacDonald Papers
Miriam Sheridan Papers

Public Archives of Ontario, Toronto, Ontario
T. Eaton Company Records
Maclean-Hunter Company Records

Sun Life Assurance of Canada Corporate Archives, Scarborough, Ontario
Advertising Committee Records

Thomas Fisher Rare Book Library, Toronto, Ontario
Gilbert Jackson Papers

United Church of Canada Archives, Toronto, Ontario
Methodist Book and Publishing House/Ryerson Press Records

University of Manitoba Archives and Special Collections, Winnipeg, Manitoba
Bertram Brooker Papers

University of Toronto Archives, Toronto, Ontario
Department of Political Economy Records
Harold Innis Papers

Vancouver City Archives, Vancouver, British Columbia
Vancouver Board of Trade Records

Theses

Jones, D.G. Brian. 'Origins of Marketing Thought.' Unpublished PhD disserta-
    tion, Queen's University, 1987.
MacPherson, Elsinore. 'Careers of Canadian University Women.' Unpublished
    MA thesis, University of Toronto, 1920.
Walkom, Thomas L. 'The Daily Newspaper Industry in Ontario's Developing
    Capitalistic Economy: Toronto and Ottawa, 1871–1911.' Unpublished PhD
    dissertation, University of Toronto, 1983.

Periodicals

Business Woman [1926–9].
Canadian Advertiser 1893.
Canadian Advertising Data 1928–32.
Canadian Newspaper Directory 1892–1930.
La Clé d'Or 1926–8.
Commerce Journal [1939–50].
Economic Advertising 1908–18.
Lydiatt's Book: What's What in Canadian Advertising 1914–20.
Lydiatt's Book: Canadian Market and Advertising Data 1921–31.
Marketing (and Business Management) 1918–30.
Montreal City Directory and Classified Business Directory [1863–1930].
Printer & Publisher 1892–1928.

Publicité-Publicity [1905–20].
Toronto City Directory [1859–1930].
Who's Who in Canadian Advertising 1915, 1916.

Canadian Government Publications

Department of Agriculture. *Dominion Year Book*. Ottawa: Queen's/King's
Printer, 1898–1931.
Department of Customs. *Tables of the Trade and Navigation of Canada*. Ottawa:
Queen's/King's Printer, 1881–1932.
Department of Trade & Commerce. *The Canadian Industrial Field*. 2d ed. Ottawa:
King's Printer, 1933.
Dominion Bureau of Statistics. *Dominion Bureau of Statistics: Its Origin, Constitu-
tion, and Organization*. Ottawa: King's Printer, 1935.
– *Paper-Using Industries in Canada, 1926–27*. Ottawa: King's Printer, 1930.
– *Report 1922, Sessional Papers* #10. Ottawa: King's Printer, 1923.
– *Seventh Census of Canada, 1931* Vol. 7: *Occupations and Industries*. Ottawa:
King's Printer, 1936.
– *Seventh Census of Canada, 1931* Vol. 10: *Merchandising and Service Establish-
ments*. Ottawa: King's Printer, 1934.
– *Sixth Census of Canada, 1921* Vol. 4: *Occupations*. Ottawa: King's Printer, 1929.
Office of Census and Statistics. *Census 1901: Bulletin XI – Occupations of the
People*. Ottawa: King's Printer, 1910.

Secondary Sources

Adams, Henry Foster. *Advertising and Its Mental Laws*. New York: Macmillan,
1920.
– 'The Relative Memory Value of Duplication and Variation in Advertising.'
Journal of Philosophy, Psychology, and Scientific Methods 13:6 (March 1916),
141–52.
Aitken, Margaret, with Byrne Hope Sanders. *Hey Ma! I Did It*. Toronto: Clarke,
Irwin, 1953.
Barbour, Noel Robert. *Those Amazing People! The Story of the Canadian Magazine
Industry, 1778–1967*. Toronto: Crucible, 1982.
Barnum, P.T. *Struggles and Triumphs: or, Forty Years' Recollections*. New York:
American News Company, 1871.
Bartels, Robert. *The Development of Marketing Thought*. Homewood, IL: Irwin,
1962.
– *Marketing Theory and Metatheory*. Homewood, IL: Irwin, 1970.

Blankenship, A.B., et al. *A History of Marketing Research in Canada*. Toronto: Professional Marketing Research Society, 1985.

Bliss, Michael. *A Living Profit: Studies in the Social History of Canadian Business, 1883–1911*. Toronto: McClelland & Stewart, 1974.

Bogart, Michele H. *Advertising, Artists, and the Borders of Art*. Chicago: University of Chicago Press, 1995.

Bone, John R., et al., eds. *A History of Canadian Journalism*. Toronto: Canadian Press Association, 1908.

Bonville, Jean de. *La Presse Québécoise de 1884 à 1914: Genèse d'un média de masse*. Quebec: Presses de l'Université Laval, 1988.

Brooker, Bertram. *Think of the Earth*. Toronto: Nelson, 1936.

– [as Richard Surrey]. *Copy Technique in Advertising*. New York: McGraw-Hill, 1930.

– [as Richard Surrey]. *Layout Technique in Advertising*. New York: McGraw-Hill, 1931.

Bulmer, M., et al., eds. *The Social Survey in Historical Perspective*. Cambridge: Cambridge University Press, 1991.

Burton, C.L. *A Sense of Urgency: Memoirs of a Canadian Merchant*. Toronto: Clarke, Irwin, 1952.

Butler, Ralph Starr. *Marketing Methods*. New York: Alexander Hamilton Institute, 1917.

Calkins, E.E., and R. Holden. *Modern Advertising*. 1905. Reprint, New York: Garland, 1985.

Canadian Advertising Agency. *French Newspapers and Periodicals of Canada and the United States*. Montreal: Canadian Advertising, 1913.

Chalmers, Floyd S. *A Gentleman of the Press*. Toronto: Doubleday Canada, 1969.

Chandler, Alfred D., Jr. *The Visible Hand: The Managerial Revolution in American Business*. Cambridge, MA: Harvard University Press, 1977.

Cherington, Paul T. *Advertising as a Business Force*. [Garden City, NY]: Doubleday, Page, 1913.

– *The Advertising Book 1916*. [Garden City, NY]: Doubleday, Page, 1916.

– *The Consumer Looks at Advertising*. New York: Harper, 1928.

Cohen, David. *J.B. Watson: The Founder of Behaviourism*. London: Routledge & Kegan Paul, 1979.

Cohn, Jan. *Creating America: George Horace Lorimer and the Saturday Evening Post*. Pittsburgh: University of Pittsburgh Press, 1989.

Colquhoun, A.H.U. *Press, Politics, and People: The Life and Letters of Sir John Willison*. Toronto: Macmillan, 1935.

Converse, Jean M. *Survey Research in the United States: Roots and Emergence, 1890–1960*. Berkeley, CA: University of California Press, 1987.

Coon, Deborah J. '"Not a Creature of Reason:" The Alleged Impact of Watsonian Behaviorism on Advertising in the 1920s.' In *Modern Perspectives on John B. Watson and Classical Behaviorism*, ed. J.T. Todd and E.K. Morris, 37–63. Westport, CT: Greenwood, 1994.

Cranston, J.H. *Ink on My Fingers*. Toronto: Ryerson, 1953.

Cumming, Carman. *Secret Craft: The Journalism of Edward Farrer*. Toronto: University of Toronto Press, 1992.

Curti, Merle. 'The Changing Concept of "Human Nature" in the Literature of American Advertising.' *Business History Review* 61:4 (Winter 1967), 334–57.

Davenport-Hines, R.P.T., ed. *Markets and Bagmen: Studies in the History of Marketing and British Industrial Performance, 1830–1939*. Aldershot, UK: Gower, 1986.

Davis, Angela E. 'Art and Work: Frederick Brigden and the History of the Canadian Illustrated Press.' *Journal of Canadian Studies* 21:2 (Summer 1992), 22–36.

– *Art and Work: A Social History of Labour in the Canadian Graphic Arts Industry to the 1940s*. Montreal: McGill-Queen's University Press, 1995.

– 'Country Homemakers: The Daily Lives of Prairie Women as Seen through the Woman's Page of the Grain Growers' Guide, 1908–1928.' In *Canadian Papers in Rural History*. Vol. 8. Gananoque, ON: Langdale, 1992.

Eaman, Ross A. *Channels of Influence: CBC Audience Research and the Canadian Public*. Toronto: University of Toronto Press, 1994.

Elkin, Frederick. *Rebels and Colleagues: Advertising and Social Change in French Canada*. Montreal: McGill-Queen's University Press, 1973.

Ferguson, Ted. *Kit Coleman, Queen of Hearts*. Toronto: Doubleday, 1978.

Fetherling, Douglas. *The Rise of the Canadian Newspaper*. Toronto: Oxford University Press, 1990.

Fox, E.J., and D.S.R. Leighton, eds. *Marketing in Canada*. Homewood, IL: Irwin, 1958.

Fox, Stephen. *The Mirror Makers: A History of American Advertising and Its Creators*. New York: Morrow, 1984.

French, George. *Advertising: The Social and Economic Problem*. New York: Ronald, 1915.

– *20th Century Advertising*. New York: Van Nostrand, 1926.

Fullerton, Ronald A. 'How Modern is Modern Marketing? Marketing's Evolution and the Myth of the "Production Era."' *Journal of Marketing* 52 (January 1988), 108–25.

– 'A Prophet of Modern Advertising: Germany's Karl Knies.' Paper presented at the 8th Conference on Historical Research in Marketing and Marketing Thought. Kingston. June 1997.

Gale, Harlow. *Psychological Studies #1*. Minneapolis, MN: the author, 1900.

Garvey, Ellen Gruber. *The Adman in the Parlor: Magazines and the Gendering of Consumer Culture, 1880s to 1910s*. New York: Oxford University Press, 1996.

Gauvreau, Michael. 'Philosophy, Psychology, and History: George Sidney Brett and the Quest for a Social Science at the University of Toronto, 1910–1940.' In *Historical Papers 1988*. Ottawa: Canadian Historical Association, 1988.

Germain, Richard. 'The Adoption of Statistical Methods in Market Research: The Early Twentieth Century.' In *Explorations in the History of Marketing*. Vol. 6, *Research in Marketing*, ed. J.N. Sheth and R. Fullerton, 87–101. Greenwich, CT: JAI, 1994.

Greer, Carl Richard. *Advertising and Its Mechanical Reproduction*. New York: Tudor, 1931.

Hall, S. Roland. *Advertising Handbook*. 2d ed. New York: McGraw-Hill, 1930.

Ham, George H. *Reminiscences of a Raconteur*. Toronto: Musson, 1921.

Harker, Douglas E. *The Woodwards: The Story of a Distinguished British Columbia Family, 1850–1975*. Vancouver: Mitchell, 1976.

Harkness, Ross. *J.E. Atkinson of the Star*. Toronto: University of Toronto Press, 1963.

Hart, E.J. *The Selling of Canada: The CPR and the Beginnings of Canadian Tourism*. Banff, AL: Altitude, 1983.

Hedland, E.W. *Newspaper Cost Accounting*. New York: National Association of Cost Accountants, 1926.

Herrold, Lloyd D. *Advertising Copy: Principles and Practice*. Chicago: Shaw, 1927.

Hollingsworth, H.L. *Advertising and Selling*. New York: Appleton, 1913.

– 'Judgments of Persuasiveness.' *Psychological Review* 18:4 (July 1911), 234–56.

– Review of *Influencing Men in Business* (1911), by W.D. Scott. *Journal of Philosophy, Psychology, and Scientific Methods* 9:4 (February 1912), 110–11.

Hollingsworth, H.L., et al. *Advertising: Its Principles and Practice*. New York: Ronald, 1915.

Hower, Ralph M. *The History of an Advertising Agency: N.W. Ayer & Son at Work*. Cambridge, MA: Harvard University Press, 1939.

Innis, Harold A. *The Bias of Communication*. Toronto: University of Toronto Press, 1951.

– 'The Newspaper in Economic Development.' *Journal of Economic History* 2: Supplement (December 1942), 1–33.

J. Walter Thompson Company. *Population and Its Distribution*. 6th ed. New York: Harper, 1958.

Johnston, Hugh. *A Merchant Prince: Life of Hon. Senator John MacDonald*. Toronto: Briggs, 1873.

Kemp, Hubert R. *Canadian Marketing Problems: Ten Essays*. Toronto: University of Toronto Press, 1939.

Kinnear, Mary. *In Subordination: Professional Women, 1870–1970*. Montreal: McGill-Queen's University Press, 1995.

Kirkconnell, Watson. 'The European-Canadians in Their Press.' *Canadian Historical Association Annual Report*, ed. R.G. Riddell. Toronto: University of Toronto Press, 1940.

Kuna, David P. 'The Concept of Suggestion in the Early History of Advertising Psychology.' *Journal of the History of the Behavioral Sciences* 12 (1976), 347–53.

Landon, Fred. 'The Agricultural Journals of Upper Canada (Ontario).' *Agricultural Journal* 9 (1935), 167–75.

Larned, W. Livingston. *Illustration in Advertising*. New York: McGraw-Hill, 1925.

Lasker, Albert D. *The Lasker Story: As He Told It*. Ed. S.R. Bernstein. Lincolnwood, IL: NTC, 1987.

Leach, William. *Land of Desire: Merchants, Power, and the Rise of a New American Culture*. New York: Pantheon, 1993.

Lears, Jackson. *Fables of Abundance: A Cultural History of Advertising in America*. New York: Basic Books, 1994.

– 'From Salvation to Self-Realization: Advertising and the Therapeutic Roots of the Consumer Culture, 1880–1930.' *The Culture of Consumption*. Ed. R.W. Fox and J. Lears. New York: Pantheon, 1983.

Leiss, William, Stephen Kline, and Sut Jhally. *Social Communication in Advertising: Persons, Products, and Images of Well-Being*. Toronto: Methuen, 1986.

Lewis, Norman. *How to Become an Advertising Man*. New York: Ronald, 1927.

MacKenzie, David. *Arthur Irwin: A Biography*. Toronto: University of Toronto Press, 1993.

MacKenzie, Donald A. *Statistics in Britain, 1865–1930: The Social Construction of Scientific Knowledge*. Edinburgh: Edinburgh University Press, 1981.

Mahatoo, Winston H. 'Marketing.' *Executive* 10:4 (April 1968), 34–9.

– *Marketing Research in Canada: Principles, Readings, and Cases*. Toronto: Thomas Nelson, 1968.

Mahin, J.L. *Advertising: Selling the Consumer*. [Garden City, NY]: Doubleday, Page, 1914.

McGill School of Commerce. *Selling Tomorrow's Production*. Montreal: McGill University, School of Commerce, 1945.

McKay, Ian. *The Quest of the Folk: Anti-Modernism and Cultural Selection in Twentieth Century Nova Scotia*. Montreal: McGill-Queen's University Press, 1994.

McKee, Jane, ed. *Marketing Organization and Technique*. Toronto: University of Toronto Press, 1940.

Meikle, William. *The Canadian Newspaper Directory.* Toronto: Blackburn's, 1858.

Monod, David. *Store Wars: Shopkeepers and the Culture of Mass Marketing, 1890–1939.* Toronto: University of Toronto Press, 1996.

Moriarty, W.D. *The Economics of Marketing and Advertising.* New York: Harper, 1923.

Mott, Frank Luther. *A History of American Magazines.* 5 vols. Cambridge, MA: Harvard University Press, 1930–68.

Neill, Robin. *A History of Canadian Economic Thought.* London: Routledge, 1991.

Nevett, T.R. *Advertising in Britain: A History.* London: Heinemann, 1982.

Nevett, T.R., and R.A. Fullerton. *Historical Perspectives in Marketing.* Lexington, MA: Heath, 1988.

Nichols, M.E. *(CP) The Story of the Canadian Press.* Toronto: Ryerson, 1948.

Norris, Ken. *The Little Magazine in Canada, 1925–80.* Toronto: ECW, 1984.

Norris, Vincent P. 'Advertising History – According to the Textbooks.' *Journal of Advertising* 9:3 (1980), 3–11.

Ohmann, Richard. *Selling Culture: Magazines, Markets, and Class at the Turn of the Century.* London: Verso, 1996.

Osborne, Brian S. 'Trading on a Frontier: The Function of Pedlars, Markets, and Fairs in Nineteenth-Century Ontario.' In *Canadian Papers in Rural History.* Vol. 2. Gananoque, ON: Langdale, 1980.

Pane, E., and R. Bahr. *Machine Bites Dog: A Study of Technology and Work in the Ontario Newspaper Industry.* Toronto: Southern Ontario Newspaper Group, 1994.

Parker, George L. *The Beginnings of the Book Trade in Canada.* Toronto: University of Toronto Press, 1985.

Pollay, Richard W. 'Thank the Editors for the Buy-ological Urge!' In *Explorations in the History of Marketing.* Suppl. 6, *Research in Marketing,* ed. J.N. Sheth and R.A. Fullerton, 221–35. Greenwich, CT: JAI, 1994.

Pope, Daniel. *The Making of Modern Advertising.* New York: Basic, 1983.

Porter, Theodore M. *The Rise of Statistical Thinking, 1820–1900.* Princeton, NJ: Princeton University Press, 1986.

Poulton, Ron. *The Paper Tyrant: John Ross Robertson of the Toronto Telegram.* Toronto: Clarke, Irwin, 1971.

Presbrey, Frank. *The History and Development of Advertising.* Garden City, NY: Doubleday, Doran, 1929.

Russell, Gilbert. *Nuntius: Advertising and Its Future.* London: Kegan Paul, Trench, Trubner, 1926.

Rutherford, Paul. *The Making of the Canadian Media.* Toronto: McGraw-Hill Ryerson, 1978.

– *A Victorian Authority: The Daily Press in Late Nineteenth-Century Canada.* Toronto: University of Toronto Press, 1982.

Santink, Joy L. *Timothy Eaton and the Rise of His Department Store.* Toronto: University of Toronto Press, 1990.

Saxon, A.H. *P.T. Barnum: The Legend and the Man.* New York: Columbia University Press, 1989.

Scanlon, Jennifer. *Inarticulate Longings: The* Ladies' Home Journal, *Gender, and the Promise of Consumer Culture.* New York: Routledge, 1995.

Schultze, Quentin J. '"An Honourable Place": The Quest for Professional Advertising Education, 1900–1917.' *Business History Review* 56:1 (Spring 1982), 16–32.

Scott, Walter Dill. *The Theory of Advertising.* Boston: Small, Maynard, 1904.

– *The Psychology of Advertising.* Boston: Small, Maynard, 1908.

Smythe, Dallas W. *Dependency Road: Communications, Capitalism, Consciousness, and Canada.* Norwood, NJ: Ablex, 1981.

Sotiron, Minko. *From Politics to Profits: The Commercialization of Canadian Daily Newspapers, 1890–1920.* Montreal: McGill-Queen's University Press, 1997.

Starch, Daniel. *Advertising.* Chicago: Scott, Foresman, 1914.

– *Principles of Advertising.* Chicago: Shaw, 1923.

Strong, E.K., Jr. 'Application of the "Order of Merit Method" to Advertising.' *Journal of Philosophy, Psychology, and Scientific Methods* 8:21 (October 1911), 600–11.

– 'The Effect of Size of Advertisements and Frequency of Their Presentation.' *Psychological Review* 21:2 (March 1914), 136–52.

– *Psychology of Selling and Advertising.* New York: McGraw-Hill, 1925.

Sutherland, Fraser. *The Monthly Epic: A History of Canadian Magazines, 1789–1989.* Markham, ON: Fitzhenry & Whiteside, 1989.

Taylor, Graham D., and Peter A. Baskerville. *A Concise History of Business in Canada.* Toronto: Oxford University Press, 1994.

Tipper, Harry, et al. *Advertising: Its Principles and Practice.* New York: Ronald, 1915.

Vaile, Roland S. *Economics of Advertising.* New York: Ronald, 1927.

Vathelet, Henri. *La Publicité dans le Journalisme.* Paris: Albin Michel, 1911.

Verzuh, Ron. *Radical Rag: The Pioneer Labour Press in Canada.* Ottawa: Steel Rail, 1988.

Vipond, Mary. 'The Canadian Authors' Association in the 1920s: A Case Study in Cultural Nationalism.' *Journal of Canadian Studies* 15 (Spring 1980), 68–79.

– 'Canadian Nationalism and the Plight of Canadian Magazines in the 1920s.' *Canadian Historical Review* 58:1 (March 1977), 43–63.

– 'The Image of Women in Mass Circulation Magazines in the 1920s.' *The*

Neglected Majority. Ed. S.M. Trofimenkoff and A. Prentice. Toronto: McClelland & Stewart, 1977.

- *The Mass Media in Canada.* Toronto: Lorimer, 1989.

Walden, Keith. 'Speaking Modern: Language, Culture, and Hegemony in Grocery Window Displays, 1887–1920.' *Canadian Historical Review* 70:3 (1989), 285–310.

Watier, Maurice. *La Publicité.* Montreal: Pauline, 1985.

Watson, John B. *Behaviorism.* Chicago: University of Chicago Press, 1924.

Weill, Georges. *Le Journal: Origines, évolution, et rôle de la presse périodique.* Paris: Albin Michel, 1934.

Willison, Sir John. *Reminiscences Political and Personal.* Toronto: McClelland & Stewart, 1919.

Wilson, Christopher P. 'The Rhetoric of Consumption: Mass Market Magazines and the Demise of the Gentle Reader, 1880–1920.' *The Culture of Consumption.* New York: Random House, 1983.

Wood, James Playsted. *The Story of Advertising.* New York: Ronald, 1958.

Wright, Mary J., and C. Roger Myers, eds. *History of Academic Psychology in Canada.* Toronto: C.J. Hogrefe, 1982.

Young, James H. *Toadstool Millionaires: A Social History of Patent Medicines in America before Federal Regulation.* Princeton: Princeton University Press, 1961.

Young, James W. *Advertising Agency Compensation, in Relation to the Total Cost of Advertising.* Chicago: University of Illinois Press, 1933.

Index